SEXUAL ABUSE RECALLED

Treating Trauma in the Era of the Recovered Memory Debate

Edited by
Judith L. Alpert, Ph.D.

JASON ARONSON INC.
Northvale, New Jersey
London

The editor gratefully acknowledges permisssion to reprint material from the following sources:

From "On the Pulse of Morning," by Maya Angelou. Copyright © 1993 by Maya Angelou. Reprinted by permission of Random House, Inc.

"The Body Keeps the Score: The Evolving Psychobiology of Post Traumatic Stress," here titled "The Body, Memory, and the Psychobiology of Trama," by Bessel van der Kolk, in *Harvard Review of Psychology,* © 1994, vol. 1, pp. 253–265, with permission from Mosby-Year Book, Inc.

This book is set in 10 point Baskerville by TechType of Upper Saddle River, New Jersey, and printed and bound by Book-mart Press of North Bergen, New Jersey

Library of Congress Cataloging-in-Publication Data

Alpert, Judith L.
    Sexual abuse recalled : treating trauma in the era of the recovered memory debate / edited by
Judith L. Alpert
        p.   cm.
    Includes bibliographical references and index.
    ISBN 1-56821-363-8 (alk, paper)
    1. Adult child sexual abuse victims. 2. Recovered memory.
RC569.A.A28A44   1995
616.85'8369 — dc20   95-4702

Manufactured in the United States of America. Jason Aronson Inc. offers books and cassettes. For information and catalog write to Jason Aronson Inc., 230 Livingston Street, Northvale, New Jersey 07647.

Contents

PART V   CONCLUSIONS

Foreword

I wholeheartedly welcome the publication of this important volume as a response to the recent critiques of therapy put forth by false memory proponents. It is a much-needed resource, a compass of sorts by researchers and clinicians regarding many of the issues that arise when a client remembers or suspects previous childhood sexual abuse during the course of therapy. The chapters in this volume address the complexity of the issues, including what really happens in professional therapeutic relationships, in stark contrast to many of the simplistic and overgeneralized assumptions about therapy made by some of its critics.

Since Freud's time, the reporting of past sexual abuse by patients has been a vexing problem for therapists. Freud opened and then closed exploration of the possibility of real sexual abuse with his shift from the seduction to the oedipal theory. With this theoretical reversal, therapists discounted, disbelieved, and/or prematurely foreclosed discussion of sexual abuse when a patient disclosed or speculated about it. In the past decade, under the influence of the study of war trauma, disaster trauma, sexual assault, child abuse, and other forms of domestic violence, and with the inclusion of the diagnosis of Post-traumatic Stress Disorder in the *DSM-III* (American Psychiatric Association 1980), another shift has taken place. Therapists began to consider more seriously the possibility of past sexual abuse in the personal history of their patients. Furthermore, they began to identify it as a traumatic stressor with strong potential for marked negative consequences, both initially and across the life span.

Some background is necessary in which to contextualize and understand the current controversy. In recent years, therapeutic recognition has occurred as the topic of incest has gained an unprecedented measure of public exposure and acknowledgment. This first occurred at the grass-roots level at consciousness-raising groups and speak-outs organized by feminists to break the silence around rape, wife battering, and other forms of family violence. Women began to speak publicly (and quite hesitantly at first) about the most private and shameful of violations—incest, sexual abuse perpetrated not only by a stranger but by a family member, usually in the home. Simultaneously, a number of first-person accounts of incest and sexual abuse and the first wave of professional and self-help books on these and related topics were published. In turn, these attracted the attention of TV, radio, and print media, which further publicized them. The story then widened to include simultaneous attention to other previously unacknowledged family problems, especially parental alcoholism, the dysfunctions within such a family system, and the co-occurrence of alcoholism and many forms of abuse within dysfunctional families.

The early media coverage accorded to victims was quite sensitive and scrupulous. However, by the early '90s, this situation changed dramatically. Talk shows proliferated and dominated the airwaves, causing rating wars that directed both the choice of topic and the reporting style. Tabloid-style formats became the norm and the most extreme and bizarre stories were featured. Incest and other forms of sexual abuse were given saturation coverage, often with the most aberrant and excessive occurrences presented as the norm. The net result was that within less than a decade, incest went from the most taboo and shameful of personal and family secrets to one that permeated the media, was highly sensationalized, and was ultimately overexposed and trivialized.

These events were cataclysmic in their impact. At no other time in human history has the topic of incest been so publicly exposed. There was no mass media (or Oprah!) during Freud's time so his seduction theory was not widely disseminated before it was withdrawn. As a consequence, dormant (i.e., repressed/suppressed/sublimated/denied/undisclosed/dissociated) memories went undisturbed and symptoms of past abuse, if they were displayed at all, were usually manifested in the coded somatosensory symptoms of the hysteric. The contemporary rediscovery and exposure of incest are quite different matters. The media saturation has served to create an ongoing trigger or cue for the disruption of these dormant or undisclosed memories for a large number of former victims. This greater exposure has led more and more adults to remember and report abuse in their past or to question whether, in fact, it could have happened and would account for some of their contemporary personal and family difficulties.

Many of these individuals then sought help with their symptoms and recollections through reading the newly available self-help literature and viewing widely disseminated media presentations (such as the Bradshaw series on shame and family dysfunction broadcast repeatedly on PBS), through participation in self-help groups and 12-step meetings, and through participation in a wide range of therapeutic activities. Many sought formal psychotherapy with mainstream licensed practitioners. However, many others engaged in alternative therapies provided by a wide range of practitioners, many of whom had little or no mental-health training or certification, yet who held themselves up as skilled in the treatment of incest and post-abuse conditions.

As these changes were occurring and as more and more patients sought therapy for help with abuse-related memories and issues, changes occurred in the clinical setting as well. Most therapists had had no training in the identification or treatment of post-traumatic conditions or sexual abuse in either graduate school or in their clinical placements. Consequently, they were hard pressed to know how to respond to the influx of self-defined adult survivors seeking their assistance. Many therapists ended up receiving their training in treating adult survivors "on the job and in the trenches," and through continuing education workshops, peer consultation, and the newly available clinical writing on the treatment of incest and sexual abuse. These resources all emphasized the variety of aftereffects associated with a history of sexual abuse and how constellations of aftereffects might be indicative of an abuse history.

The treatment literature also discussed the difficulty many adults had with disclosing past abuse, and advised therapists to incorporate questions about family abuse and sexual contact into their standard intake and assessment protocols. They were further advised that disclosure might not be forthcoming for those individuals with a positive history due to a number of factors, among them, the dynamics of secrecy and divided loyalty that surround family abuse, the lack of conscious recall of abuse experiences, and/or the inability or unwillingness to identify these experiences as abuse. As the treatment literature developed, supplemented by clinical research studies, dissociation, amnesia, and the delayed onset of memory were increasingly presented as normal post-traumatic variants in a subset of abused individuals.

As these changes were occurring in the therapy context, other societal changes were taking place, particularly in the legal setting. Virtually all states changed their statutes of limitations and delayed discovery requirements to allow adult survivors to bring delayed civil actions against alleged perpetrators. Clinicians were often called as experts for plaintiffs to explain both their patients' sustained damages as the result of abuse and, more important to the emergence of this controversy, the process by which memories emerged after a period of being repressed or delayed. Defense attorneys began to hire memory experts, cognitive psychologists who challenged the concept of repressed memory as inconsistent with the available literature on the workings of human memory. The defense experts further criticized as naive and in error therapists who believed their patients' delayed memory productions as the veridical representation of historical truth rather than as narrative reconstruction replete with error and inaccuracy.

These critiques reached the public domain in the spring of 1992 with the coining of the term *false memory syndrome* and establishment of the False Memory Syndrome Foundation to research and publicize its occurrence and damaging consequences to both primary and secondary victims and to prevent new cases. False Memory Syndrome is defined as

> a condition in which a person's identity and interpersonal relationships are centered around a memory of traumatic experience which is objectively false but in which the person strongly believes. Note that the syndrome is not characterized by false memories as such. . . . Rather, the syndrome may be diagnosed when the memory is so deeply engrained that it orients the individual's entire personality and lifestyle, in turn disrupting all sorts of other adaptive behaviors.

[Definition attributed to Dr. John F. Kihlstrom, False Memory Foundation brochure, 1993]

False Memory Syndrome is believed by its proponents to be the result of a disastrous therapeutic program of memory enhancement techniques or Recovered Memory Therapy through which therapists suggest or implant memories of past abuse in their patients as the sole explanation for their symptoms and as a means of making them dependent on therapy for the therapist's financial gain. Furthermore, many patients use these false memories as the basis for false allegations of abuse against other family members thus creating a set of secondary victims of the syndrome.

The False Memory Syndrome Foundation gathered a scientific and professional advisory board of prominent researchers and clinicians who have been very active in challenging the delayed and repressed memory concepts and whose academic credentials have lent great credibility to the critique. Once again, the media picked up on the story, this time, however, providing extensive coverage to the Foundation and its message of an epidemic of false memories of abuse, the implantation of forms of more and more bizarre abuse (e.g., satanic ritual abuse and a highly organized worldwide conspiracy of child abuse), and the role of therapists in creating the problem. The critique has been strident and was covered verbatim and without substantial challenge or investigation by the media. False memory took over where delayed memory reports left off and, again, the media sensationalized the issue.

Over the past three years, the pendulum has swung away from the reality of abuse reports and the damage done by real abuse to the problem of "false" or "illusory" memories for abuse that never occurred, abuse suggested by therapists. With the direct support of the false memory proponents, the critique has moved beyond the media into the courtroom and state legislatures. Third-party suits have been mounted against therapists by the aggrieved who say they are falsely accused (the most well-known example being the Ramona case in California in which a counselor and a psychiatrist were found guilty of malpractice in using sodium amytal and in what they told their patient about memory processes to help her with memory retrieval) and as "false memory syndrome" has been used routinely by the defense in cases involving allegations of past abuse.

(This strategy is even being used when the abuse is in the present or the immediate past, when repressed or delayed memory is not an issue. It has nevertheless been a potent tool for the defense.) In addition to litigation, the aggrieved have been encouraged to bring ethics charges and licensing challenges against treating therapists. On the legislative front, a bill titled "The Mental Health Consumer Protection Act" (sponsored by five state chapters of Friends of FMS) has been introduced into several state legislatures with the aim of protecting consumers from harmful and fraudulent therapy practices (of which repressed memory therapy is a prime example) by regulating the practice of psychotherapy.

The controversy, including its rapid escalation, its high visibility, its inclusiveness in criticizing all therapists who treat adults who report abuse (ascribing poor practice to all regardless of degree status, training, legitimacy, caution, etc.), and its ferocity and vehemence in suggesting redress via lawsuit and regulatory challenge has caught many therapists by surprise. Some have reacted by refusing to treat anyone seeking therapy for suspicion of abuse and others by practicing overly defensive "lawsuit therapy." Others have been less surprised by the controversy but are confused as to whether it constitutes a needed corrective to excesses in the field and to therapists using techniques that outstrip their knowledge base and/or are based on erroneous assumptions or whether it constitutes a backlash against new discoveries about abuse and new ways of working with abuse-related syndromes and memories, including those that are delayed.

It is in response to this controversy that this book was commissioned. Its stated goal is to assist working therapists by providing a discussion of clinical issues, practice guidelines, and knowledge from state-of-the-art research. It brings clinical issues back to the domain of the clinician and, as such, is a much-needed resource to guide and reassure the practicing therapist. A peculiar and rather novel part of the current controversy is that researchers in the cognitive sciences are challenging practice without having been trained in providing therapy and their opinions are holding sway in a way that suggests that clinicians have no specialized training or expertise. Thus, this book, in addition to its stated purpose as educative, reclaims therapeutic authority over the ground being overtaken by the critics, most of whom are not therapists by training.

The book also serves to articulate what therapists do and how they work and provides data to challenge some of the most oft repeated of the therapy critiques. For example, no research is currently available to support the claim of either a therapist's ability to implant a detailed memory of abuse or a set of complicated post-traumatic reactions. Preliminary data suggest that rather than being cued by therapists' inquiries and suggestions, the primary triggers to the return of absent memory in a high percentage of clients are reports in the media. The role of hypnosis and related techniques in creating pseudomemories (or pseudomemory reports) is quite overstated based upon the available empirical data, and, more important, is not what appears to be the most significant variable in their creation. Therapeutic observation of perpetrators and their dynamics has resulted in knowledge about their defensive operations, namely false memories or denial about the occurrence of real abuse and a propensity to attack those who challenge their prerogatives and the secrecy surrounding their behavior. The current emphasis on false memories only as it applies to victims is asymmetrical and tells only one side of the abuse story. False memories are, on average, more likely in real perpetrators than they are in real victims. These are but a few of the salient issues of which the practicing clinician must be informed.

The authors of this book also make major contributions to correcting the oversimplification that has characterized the debate by articulating the complexities of the issues in both the research and practice domains. In terms of practice they stress, both individually and collectively, that therapy ought to be the place to explore an individual's subjective experience and history safely and that it is the logical and expectable place for the forbidden or split-off to emerge. They argue that the therapist or patient may never know for sure if real abuse occurred but that they should err neither on the side of over-belief nor of under-belief in the reality of historical abuse. Most importantly, the ultimate authority over memories, personal history, and narrative belongs to the patient, not the therapist. The therapist's job is to create and maintain an environment conducive to exploration, an atmosphere that is neutral in position yet supportive in stance. It is not just the technique that is used but how it is used that may contribute to the potential for memory distortion.

Finally, all authors indicate that in order not to return to the

denial of incest post-Freud nor to overreach the available information on human memory processes, it is necessary to achieve some
middle ground by collaborating on rather than polarizing the issues.
Clinicians and academics who study memory must become informed
about each others' fields and must take great pains to communicate
with each other. Currently, a trauma-focused clinical paradigm that
does not attend to the reconstructive nature of memory is incomplete,
as is a memory research paradigm that does not attend to the possible
impact of personally experienced trauma on memory.

Therapists are currently under a great deal of scrutiny for both
conduct and technique. This book shows how some of the authorities
in the field of trauma and its treatment have taken the challenge and
used it productively. They have taken their own advice and merged
information about reconstruction and recontextualization of memory
with information about trauma and its impact on memory. They
have produced a set of chapters that provide guidance to their
colleagues about their ongoing practices of psychotherapy. They also
provide a foundation upon which to continue to build and evolve
clinical practice of individuals with delayed recall of sexual abuse.

Christine A. Courtois

Contributors

Judith L. Alpert, Ph.D., is a practicing psychoanalyst in New York City, Professor of Applied Psychology at New York University, and a faculty member of the Postdoctoral Program in Psychotherapy and Psychoanalysis at New York University. She serves as co-chair of the American Psychological Association's Working Group on Investigation of Memories of Childhood Abuse. She had edited four books and has published more than eighty articles in refereed journals.

Dan Brown, Ph.D., a psychologist who has written extensively on hypnosis, is currently co-authoring (with A. Scheflin and D. Corydon Hammond) *Memory, Therapy, and the Law*.

Laura Brown, Ph.D., is in the private practice of clinical and forensic psychology in Seattle, Washington and Clinical Professor of Psychology at the University of Washington. She has served as an expert evaluator in nearly 100 legal cases brought by adults alleging childhood sexual abuse, and serves as a consultant to therapists working with that population. She serves on the American Psychological Association's Working Group on Investigation of Memories of Childhood Abuse.

Christine A. Courtois, Ph.D., Director of Clinical Training at The Center: Post-traumatic and Dissociative Disorders Program, The Psychiatric Institute of Washington, Washington, DC, is the author of *Healing the Incest Wound: Adult Survivors in Therapy.* She is in private practice in Washington, DC and has written extensively on the treatment of sexual abuse survivors. She serves on the American Psychological Association's Working Group on Investigation of Memories of Childhood Abuse.

Sue Grand, Ph.D., a psychoanalyst, is Adjunct Assistant Clinical Professor at Teachers College, Columbia University, and faculty and supervisor at The Greenwich Institute for Psychoanalysis. Her writings have focused on psychoanalytic treatment and delayed memories.

D. Corydon Hammond, Ph.D., is a Professor, University of Utah School of Medicine and first president of the American Society of Clinical Hypnosis. He has published more than 100 journal articles, chapters, reviews, or sections in books, and five books, including the recent *Handbook of Hypnotic Suggestions and Metaphors.* He is currently co-authoring (with A. Scheflin and D. Brown) *Memory, Therapy, and the Law.*

Elizabeth Hegeman, Ph.D., a psychoanalyst, is a member of the faculty of the William Alanson White Institute, the Institute for Contemporary Psychotherapy, and the John Jay College of Criminal Justice, CUNY, Department of Anthropology. She is the co-author of *Valuing Emotions,* with Michael Stocker, and has been writing, speaking, and teaching about dissociative disorders, traumatic transference, and the treatment of sexual abuse. She is in private practice in New York City and supervises therapists who are struggling with vicarious traumatization.

Helene Kafka, Ph.D., a psychoanalyst, is on the faculties of the William Alanson White Institute and the National Institutes for the Psychotherapies in New York City. She has written extensively on developmental and clinical issues of aloneness and loneliness, the character disorders, sexual abuse, and techniques for facilitating healing. She is in private practice in New York City, working with individuals, couples, and groups.

Michelle Price, CSW, a psychoanalyst, is Director, Treatment Center for Incest and Abuse at the Karen Horney Clinic in New

York. She is a faculty member and supervisor at the Karen Horney Psychoanalytic Institute and Center and the Mt. Sinai School of Medicine. Her writings and presentations have focused on identity and transference–countertransference configurations and enactments emerging in the treatment of sexual abuse survivors, as well as the areas of gender and postmodernism.

Evelyn Pye, Ph.D., is a psychologist in private practice in Northampton, Massachusetts. Her work is in the areas of imagination, memory, mourning, and the psychology of becoming a subject.

Bruce E. Reis, Ph.D., a matriculant in the New York University Postdoctoral Program in Psychoanalysis and Psychotherapy, is a psychologist in private practice in New York City.

Sue Shapiro, Ph.D., a psychoanalyst and faculty member at the New York University Postdoctoral Program in Psychoanalysis and Psychotherapy, is Director of the Center for the Study of Abuse and Incest, Manhattan Institute of Psychoanalysis.

Bessel van der Kolk, M.D., a psychiatrist at the Massachusetts General Hospital, Trauma Clinic, Harvard Medical School, is well known for his ground-breaking writing on trauma.

Introduction

JUDITH L. ALPERT

The controversy over the validity and impact of adult memories of childhood abuse has been oversimplified by the media and has resulted in a division. One side of the controversy acknowledges that memories for childhood abuse may be delayed and recalled decades after the abuse. The other side believes that recovered memories of childhood trauma are more likely the result of suggestion from misinformed therapists, self-help books, or other forms of influence. This dialogue, which has been played out in the media, has been harmful to the mental health professions, practitioners, and the people served by them.

In addition to confusing the public, the dialogue has baffled and alarmed some mental health professionals. Most clinicians have received little education or training on the evaluation of adult memories of childhood abuse and are confused about how to work with such memories. As of this writing, there are no books that focus on delayed memories and clinical practice. While existing articles focus on some aspect of the delayed memory issue, there are scant compilations that pull together several of the issues surrounding the controversy and derive implications for clinical practice. Most of the professional articles appear in journals that are not routinely read by clinicians. In addition, clinical implications are seldom advanced. The purpose of this book is to further therapeutic treatment of adults who may have been abused as children by providing clinical issues, relevant practice guidelines, and knowledge from state-of-the-art research. Mental health professionals should find this psychodynamically oriented book helpful when confronted with a dilemma, question, or concern related to adults who may have been abused as children.

The book contains fourteen chapters organized into five sections (Overview, Psychological Science, Professional Practice and Selected Issues, Professional Practice and Selected Situations, and Conclusions). The first introductory section includes a consideration of some of the clinical issues and historical and contemporary perspectives inherent in the delayed memory controversy. Here I summarize issues concerning the recovered memory debate. I place the debate in historical context and indicate that investigations of traumas have been influenced by the political, intellectual, and social surround and have flourished in association with political movements. Then I tell the contemporary story by considering the roles of memory scientists and the media and by giving voice to the mental health professionals. It is argued that memory scientists and clinicians need to engage in joint inquiry and work to develop research on real traumatic memory that has ecological validity and helps us to identify those conditions under which individuals would be more suggestive, and research on real traumatic memory that would help us to understand the processes ongoing in the forgetting and retrieving of trauma.

The second section includes three chapters that address research relevant to memory, suggestibility, and hypnosis. Bessel van der Kolk reports in Chapter 2 that trauma is stored in somatic memory and expressed as changes in the biological stress response. He points out that intense emotions at the time of the trauma initiate the long-term conditional responses to reminders of the trauma, and are responsible for the amnesias and hyperamnesias characteristic of posttraumatic stress disorder (PTSD). He, thus, explains amnesia by means of psychobiology.

In Chapter 3, Daniel Brown criticizes the false memory argument, and points out that it is overstated, oversimplified, and only weakly supported by existing data derived from research on memory suggestibility. He delineates four areas of research that have been used in the context of delayed memories and explains which literature is relevant to the delayed memory controversy. He points out that the false memory argument is being used prematurely as the basis of legal arguments in the courts in defense of alleged perpetrators of abuse and in malpractice cases against therapists who are alleged to have been unduly suggestive. It is his position that false reports about the past, and sometimes illusory memories about abuse, can occur in psychotherapy under specific conditions.

In Chapter 4, D. Corydon Hammond reviews relevant research on hypnosis and memory. He acknowledges that hypnotized individuals can distort and produce false information, particularly when hypnosis is misused, and that startling and accurate information has sometimes been retrieved through the use of hypnosis. He emphasizes that hypnosis is not innately distorting. Rather, it is the manner in which hypnosis is sometimes used in eliciting recall of memories and the nature of the individual being hypnotized that contribute to distortion.

The third section (Professional Practice: Selected Issues) includes five chapters that focus on different aspects of delayed memory and issues relevant to clinical practice.

In Chapter 5, Helene Kafka points out that traumatic memories, whether true or false, are not the data analysts seek. Rather, they are symptomatic of a more pervasive memory dysfunction resulting from adult betrayal and penetration of the child's self. She holds that we can more readily learn about the probability of abuse from the ways in which dysfunctional memory has impact on the disorganization of the survivor's personality, from attending to memories that plague rather than soothe, and from listening to the unconscious messages that manifest themselves in behaviors, dreams, and feelings. Kafka maintains that analysis of the damaged self must be integrated with attention to the multiple ways memory is disordered.

Evelyn Pye, in Chapter 6, reports that one of the problems with the debate about delayed versus false memory is that it sets up an opposition between memory and imagination. Rather than thinking in terms of whether images are memory or imagination, she points out that the *form* of both can be analyzed. From this perspective, she holds that one can differentiate between structures of mind (including memory, imagination, thought, emotion and bodily experience) that are persecutory and structures of mind that are agentic in which the individual can reflect on her memories and fantasies. The focus of the chapter is on some aspects of the therapeutic work that underlie achievement of the agentic.

In Chapter 7, Elizabeth Hegeman reports that the concept of dissociation can now provide a bridge between relational psychoanalytic theory and conflict-based models. She explores how dissociation fragments the incested person's experience of self, of people, and reality, and how through dissociation the person's inner organization becomes adapted to blocking out the betrayal trauma. She discusses how the central meanings of the impact of trauma in the treatment may be communicated at first through enactments rather than verbal or symbolic language, most likely due to the patient's diminished capacity for verbal processing and symbolization of the traumatic experience. To make sense to the patient, transference interpretations must include reference to the retraumatization the patient fears, rather than being based on an inaccurate assumption of the patient's capacity for object ambivalence. Hegeman holds that only through a transference interpretation that brings enacted despair and self-defeating gestures into the relationship can the patient be helped toward developing a relational capacity for self-observation.

In Chapter 8, Bruce Reis suggests that trauma represents a rupture in the individual's experience of continuous time. Traumatic memory is then "relived" as a backflow in the stream of time where the past coexists with the present, and memory and perception become indistinct. Dissociative segmenting of experience allows what is known to exist in parallel fashion with what is not known. This is represented in physiologic states, interpersonal interactions, fragmented self systems, and a variety of traumatic memory phenomena. Case material illustrates how this disturbance influences the transference and countertransference as a lived experience (e.g., event) in the treatment setting and how it disturbs the ontological base of the subject.

In Chapter 9, Sue Grand considers the nature of the object tie between perpetrator and survivor. Grand writes that during incest, the parental subject coerces recognition from the objectified child, simultaneously annihilating and defining the child's secret self and authentic subjectivity. Intrinsic to this process is the perpetrator's obfuscation of history. The survivor continually retains a fantasy of the perpetrator as a potential strong parental subject to whom she can return in the hope for recognition, the restoration of subjectivity and the reclamation of history. This intersubjective exchange precludes the possibility of the mutual, simultaneous, symbolically encoded memory of incestuous history. The attainment of parental recognition is critical to the survivor's recovery of memory; this must occur within the analysis. The patient must locate the perpetrator-in-the-analyst and receive recognition for historical process within the analysis.

In the fourth section (Professional Practice: Selected Situations) there are four chapters focusing on different situations that occur in therapeutic work around delayed memory. In Chapter 10, Sue Grand focuses on the rare situations involving confabulated memory occurring in context of therapeutic persuasion. She considers two factors that are relevant to those cases of confabulated incest memory. First, the patient may readily resonate with incest imagery because the patient was raised in a context of physical/emotional abuse and/or emotional incest. She points out that this may give rise to a well-founded but dissociated hatred of the parents and wish for revenge. The second factor involves the personal epistemological positions of the therapist–patient dyad and the methods through which the "truth" about incest is investigated. Grand offers some clinical recommendations.

In Chapter 11, Michelle Price discusses situations where individuals claim to "know" that they have been sexually abused but have no concrete memories in the way that we commonly identify memories. Contained in this are many different aspects and dilemmas regarding our understanding of memory, dissociation, knowledge, and epistemology. Price considers such issues as the postmodernist concept of multiplicity and multiple selves, which paves the way for understanding and considering dissociation as an individual's inability to access particular self and discourse, language, and signification. She also considers the possibility that a person's state of knowing without memories in fact does not represent a history of abuse. She highlights various transference/countertransference configurations including the therapist experiencing herself as shifting between states of knowing and not knowing within the relational context.

Sue Shapiro, in Chapter 12, discusses situations involving the confirmation of long-held memories. She points out that patients' decisions to seek confirmation of memories represent an important treatment issue, and that the decision to seek external validation from family members is potentially explosive and needs to be fully explored. She considers some of the possible complex consequences of confirmation of memories. Increasingly, survivors of childhood sexual abuse who recover memories during the course of treatment, or who begin to make the connections between never-forgotten abuse and their lifelong emotional difficulties, bring legal actions against their alleged perpetrators. This places the psychotherapy process into the forensic arena of litigation.

In Chapter 13, Laura Brown addresses the special problems that can arise when a therapist's client becomes the plaintiff in litigation against an alleged perpetrator of childhood sexual abuse. Because this is an unusual situation in the professional life of most psychotherapists, the chapter begins with a review of terms and norms within the civil court system, describing the process of discovery and the procedures that can be expected to ensue in a litigation process. Next the question of assessing client readiness to participate in a lawsuit is explored. Special attention is given to examination of those factors that might help or hinder a client, and to the question of for whose benefit a lawsuit is being initiated. Other issues relevant to the litigation experience are considered as well.

In Chapter 14, I present some preliminary criteria that should assist in determining whether a patient has been sexually abused and in understanding the genuine experience of the patient and what aspects of the experience have been damaging. While the chapter does not focus on psychological science, it is informed by such understanding. The chapter repeats many of the themes that have emerged throughout the book.

PART I

Overview

Professional Practice, Psychological Science, and the Delayed Memory Debate[1]

JUDITH L. ALPERT

There are two literatures that have relevance to our understanding of delayed memories of childhood abuse. One is based on the scientific memory research, and the other on the scholarly literature on trauma and child sexual abuse. The literatures have been developed by professionals who were trained differently and who work differently. In general, those engaged in scientific memory research are cognitive psychologists who have no clinical training or experience, while those engaged in the scholarly literature on trauma and child sexual abuse are practitioners or scientist-practitioners who treat victims of trauma and may also be engaged in the scientific study and research of traumatology. Until recently the experimental writings have been published in journals and books that are not oriented to clinicians. Similarly, the more clinical writings have been published in journals and books that are not oriented to scientists. Consequently, there has been little consolidation. What has been incorporated from one

[1]This chapter is based on a paper that was presented at the conference entitled "Childhood Sexual Abuse and Memories: Current Controversies," at the University of Kansas Medical Center, Kansas City, Kansas, March 31, 1995.

literature to the other has often been misinformation. While this schism does not do justice to the existence of some heterogeneity, it is telling.

I am a scientist-practitioner *and* a practicing psychoanalyst. My orienting frame is that both clinicians and researchers should be informed about each other's many contributions to the issue of recalled memories of child sexual abuse. Parallel work by memory and trauma experts does not contribute to science, practice, or the people we serve. What is needed is a trauma-focused clinical paradigm that attends to the reconstructive nature of memory as well as a memory research paradigm that tends to traumatic events and their possible impact on memory as Alpert and colleagues (unpublished manuscript) indicate. It is my hope that such cross-fertilization of scholarship will facilitate research, theory, and practice and that, ultimately, all of psychology will advance.

THE STORY

I will tell a story. It is the notable story that Judith Herman (1992) detailed in *Trauma and Recovery*. She considers the history of the ways in which mental health professionals and others have misunderstood, denounced, and only sometimes understood victims of posttraumatic disorders. She notes the similarity among responses to various traumas such as wife battering and combat experiences. She points out that victims have been responded to differently in different historical times. She illustrates how the standard responses to psychological trauma (denial, repression, and dissociation) also exist on the social level.

As Herman elucidates, throughout the history of the field there has been disagreement about whether individuals with posttraumatic stress disorder, victims of combat, incest, wife battering, and other disasters, are entitled to care and concern or deserving of contempt and ridicule, whether they have truly agonized or not, whether their life stories are reliable, credible, and real, or imagined, fabricated, and false. Throughout history those who have been victims of posttraumatic stress disorder, such as victims of childhood sexual abuse, have been misunderstood and doubted by the general populace and provided with inadequate and improper care by the mental health profession. Further, this story of abuse of trauma victims has its beginnings in the inception of mental health treatment. Thus, it is a tale of villains, disbelievers, accusers, victims, scapegoats, charges, and blame. The doctor-characters consist of Charcot, Janet, Freud, Breuer, military psychiatrists, and other mental health professionals. The doctor-characters do or do not make unwarranted inferences, do or do not implant atrocious scenes into the memory of patients, and do or do not impose an elaborate form of mind management.

The tale also consists of hysterical women, war veterans, rape victims, battered women, sexually abused children, and adults who were sexually abused as children. These characters play conflicting roles in different historical times and even within any one historical time, depending on who is telling the story. They are cast, on the one hand, as crazy, defective, liars, constitutionally inferior, malingerers, cowards, moral invalids, suggestible, irrational, or vengeful, and, on the other hand, as human or noble. They are regarded with contempt and disdain or with dignity and respect, and are attended to with shame, threats, punishment, court martial, electric shock, rap groups, and consciousness-raising groups, or with humane treatment based on psychodynamic principles.

Unfortunately the complex issues raised about the nature of human beings and our society are not conveyed by these groupings. These dichotomies ignore the following issues: the enormous learning from human behavior that can be used as a touchstone to consider the destructive impulses and forces of negativity existing in human beings; the matter of social and antisocial behavior; the assertion that he to whom evil is done may do evil in return, and he to whom good is done may do good in return, the understanding of the nature of the traumatized individual which is that some of the traumatized traumatize others; and the need for socialization by humane, good treatment and a just and protective society.

Dr. Herman's tale recounts that (1) there is a history of polemics as to how to regard and treat patients with posttraumatic conditions; (2) there is a long-standing controversy as to whether the stories of these patients are authentic, credible, and real, or erroneous and the products of imagination, vicious fabrication, or construction; (3) there is a history of contention as to whether mental health professionals construct something new or participate in reconstructing something old; and (4) the investigations of trauma have been influenced by the political, intellectual, and social surround and have flourished in association with political movements.

THE CONTEMPORARY STORY

In this chapter I will further develop the story. I will tell the contemporary story. Contemporary characters in this tale include academic researchers who, for the most part, study memory for normal events in experimental laboratories with volunteer subjects. They play disbelieving and, in some cases, accusatory roles. As I tell this story I will consider some of the work of memory scientists. At least some memory scientists fervently promulgate the view that the abuser is now the therapist who pursues buried memories and that patients develop false memories of abuse as a direct result of this search and the utilization of such techniques as direct suggestion, guided visualization, hypnotic age regression, sexualized dream interpretation, sodium amytal, and body memory analysis. Although there are no laboratory studies of memory suggestibility in psychotherapy, this is nevertheless believed. These memory scientists seem to imply that the victims are no longer the ones who are molested but rather the ones who are falsely accused.

Following a consideration of the work of some memory scientists who are critical of mental health professionals, I will further develop the contemporary story. I will consider the role the media has played. Then, I will give voice to the mental health professionals. I will address the writings of clinicians that are relevant to work with patients who enter treatment with no or partial memories of child sexual abuse and who develop a fuller abuse story as treatment progresses. I do so because there seems to be bewilderment about the nature of thinking among clinicians.

I will conclude with some comments for both scientists and practitioners. My remarks have implications for forensic activity, clinical practice, and research.

MEMORY SCIENTISTS

Memory and trauma experts seem to agree on a number of points. I mention some here. Based on the interim report of members of the

American Psychological Association's Working Group on Investigation of Memories of Childhood Abuse (1994) some points of agreement are that child sexual abuse is a complex and pervasive problem in America that has historically gone unacknowledged; most people who were sexually abused as children remember all or part of what happened to them; it is possible for memories of abuse that have been forgotten for a long time to be remembered and similarly it is possible to construct pseudomemories for events that never occurred; and mechanisms for either of these occurrences are not well understood. Further, memory and trauma experts agree that memories for events and the actual events may not be isomorphic. Memories of trauma can correspond to the central events of traumatic experiences. Memories can also reproduce the traumatic experience in homomorphic terms. In addition, they agree that some people, especially young children, are suggestible, and that certain events may be more difficult to change, such as those that are personally salient (e.g., disturbing), central, and experienced and that certain events may be easier to believe, such as those that are positive and plausible. While common, sexual abuse is not a plausible event to many people. Also, memory and trauma scientists and scholars seem to agree that both psychotherapy and research vary enormously and that both can be poorly conducted. These are some areas of agreement.

There are also some significant points of disagreement. A contemporary story that is being promulgated by some of the more vocal memory scientists is that psychotherapists pursue buried memories and that patients develop false memories of abuse as a direct result of this search, with the concomitant utilization of techniques. This search for buried memories is not promoted by professional programs in psychology or mainstream professional literature on treatment of adult survivors (e.g, Briere 1989, Courtois 1988, Herman 1992, Jehu 1988, Kluft 1990). There is no training program or mainstream literature that presents memory retrieval to the exclusion of other therapeutic tasks as the treatment goal or that promulgates the utilization of techniques that are suggestive. Nor is there support for this position from laboratory studies of memory suggestibility in psychotherapy. While suggestibility effects could theoretically occur in therapy, it does not follow that they indeed do.

In general, some memory scientists hold that a considerable

number of therapists, believing that it is customary for people to have repressed sexual abuse memories, delve for such memories in patients who enter treatment without abuse recollections. From a reading of the study by Poole and colleagues (1995), one cannot assert that a significant number of therapists are misapplying therapeutic strategies. Although some therapists report that they are using hypnosis, for example, use and abuse cannot be equated. It is not that hypnosis is intrinsically misleading. The important issue concerns how one uses hypnotic techniques. Those therapists who follow the recommendations put forward by the American Society of Clinical Hypnosis for the use of hypnosis with memory would be maintaining the highest standards of therapeutic work, as Hammond indicates in Chapter 4 in this volume. As another example, dream interpretation is a well-established component of psychodynamic psychotherapy. The detailing of the injurious story and the integrating of the traumatic memories with their associated affects is not the same as pursuing buried memories. However, we need to remember that dreams serve many functions (Alpert 1995a). Sometimes they serve to tell exactly what happened. Sometimes, for the dreamer, they exist to obscure exactly what happened. Dreams can replicate the central events of traumatic experiences. Dreams can also reproduce the traumatic experiences in metamorphic terms. Dreams can be isomorphic. Sometimes they are homomorphic. Usually we do not know which occurs when. Transformations do scramble, reverse, omit, and add. Interpretations of dreams is a very complex business.

Further, there are studies (e.g., Poole et al. 1995, Waltz 1994, Yapko 1994) that support the finding that, in those therapy cases where abuse is reported or suspected, most therapists do not have as their main focus the retrieval of memories. Yapko found that some therapists held inaccurate beliefs about the nature of memory, memory retrieval, and hypnosis, and he held that these beliefs could lead to suggestive practices in therapy. However, there is a difference between what is plausible and what actually occurs.

Memories sometimes return in treatment, and this finding is consistent with Bower's (1981) theory of state-dependent memory. This theory posits a connection between affect and content and indicates that memory recall is strengthened by mood congruity. Therapy can induce a state that is similar to that which took place during the traumatic event, and this induced state, in turn, can result in recall. The return of memories in treatment can thus be explained. However, what has been found (Elliott 1994) is that therapy is the least likely trigger for the return of memory, while the media is the most commonly reported stimulus for memory retrieval. What is the basis, then, for this contemporary story of therapists pursuing buried memories and misapplying therapeutic techniques or utilizing questionable ones?

Results from laboratory studies on suggestibility with traumatized children or adults are applied to psychotherapy. The studies on children and suggestibility are designed with the intent to mislead children. Children are repeatedly asked questions by interviewers who presuppose the truth of the suggested material. Children, in turn, are required to elaborate on them. The results of these studies cannot be generalized to all children who report sexual abuse or to adults who remember abuse experiences from childhood.

Much of the data in the laboratory studies with adults concern word lists, pictures, or stories that do not parallel the real-life traumatic experience of sexual abuse. As indicated elsewhere (Alpert et al. unpublished manuscript), recalling such items as nonexistent broken glass and tape recorders, a clean-shaven man as having a moustache, straight hair as curly, or stop signs as yield signs, is different from remembering fictional, recurrent scenes of father-daughter incest and developing associated posttraumatic symptomatology. As I indicate later, memory for trauma and memory for normal events may perform differently. In contrast to memory for normal events, emotional memories have been described as detailed, accurate, and not prone to error (Christianson 1992). It is unfortunate that few memory scientists have studied trauma. Further, it is unfortunate that when it has been studied, it has been defined in a way that could be conceptualized as nontrauma or less significant trauma. Witnessing other people's disasters, for example, is less traumatic than personally experiencing them. Seeing and hearing the space shuttle Challenger explode on television and talking about the event is very different from experiencing violation to one's body by one's caregiver and being silenced about it.

It is important that research focus on the truly traumatic. As Christianson (1992) indicates in his review, emotional events are remembered differently from neutral or ordinary events. It appears that memory for trauma may be different from memory for normal events, as I indicate elsewhere and explicate briefly below (Alpert 1995). The limited research discussed here exemplifies a large body of findings that point to significant difference. For example, one interpretation of some memory literature is that encoding is influenced by the possession of prior knowledge to understand and to interpret the experience. From this it follows that a child would not have the foundation to remember if there was not understanding of the event. However, this reasoning does not attend to the fact that prior knowledge is also composed of affect and sensory experiences, and that children clearly have these. In fact, recent research supports that there can be accurate verbal and cognition retrieval for experiences enacted prior to the onset of speech (Hewitt 1994, Terr 1988, 1989). Memory of abuse may be encoded without language to articulate it or a full understanding of the significance of the event. Memory for nontraumatic events may encode differently than memory for traumatic events and may be experienced in sensorimotor or somatosensory ways (Fisler et al. 1994, Saporta and van der Kolk 1992, van der Kolk 1988, van der Kolk and van der Hart 1991). It may occur nonverbally by means of startle responses, flashbacks, obsessions, compulsions, reenactments, and dreams. Noncognitive expressions of abuse memory are relevant for an understanding of memory for the nontraumatic. It appears that at least some vocal memory scientists discount the noncognitive and focus almost exclusively on the cognitive.

A second example involves amount of exposure to an event. The research on normal memory suggests that the amount of exposure to a particular event and, specifically, the length of exposure and the number of repetitions, would have the potential to strengthen traces in memory and therefore, potentially be more readily retrieved (Crowder 1976). When the focus is on traumatic memory, research findings seem to differ. In the trauma literature it is consistently reported that repeated abuse may be less likely to be retrieved. Terr (1991), for example, conceptualizes two types of childhood trauma. Type I trauma involves single-blow traumas, such as a disaster, and is associated with full, detailed memories, "omens," and misperceptions. Type II trauma involves variable, multiple, or long-standing traumas, common in incest, and associated with denial and numbing, self-hypnosis and dissociation, and rage. These two types of trauma correspond to what is referred to within the psychoanalytic literature as discrete shock trauma and prolonged strain or cumulative trauma, respectively. The finding that children who experience single-blow traumas tend to present with full, detailed, etched-in memories while those who experience long-standing or repeated trauma do not, contrasts with the research on normal memory cited before.

A third example involves memory over time. According to the memory research, passage of time is associated with increased difficulty in recall. In contrast, according to the trauma literature, unavailable, traumatic, repeated abuse memories may vacillate, may return over time, or may always be constant (Herman 1992, van der Kolk 1984, 1987). The return of these memories may differ from the return of memories for normal events. Flashbacks and extreme responses to stimuli that would not elicit such responses from most individuals are often associated with the return of memories (Horowitz 1986, van der Kolk 1987). These flashbacks and extreme responses are presently perceived as the result of dissociated affect and trauma information (Spiegel and Cardena 1991). This brief comparison of a few general findings from the two literatures illustrates that memory for trauma may be different from normal memory. Another possibility, however, is that they may be similar in, as yet, unexplicated ways.

Earlier I mentioned that the schism into two camps (the practitioners or scientist-practioners who treat victims of trauma on the one hand and the memory scientists on the other), does not do justice to the existence of some heterogeneity. For example, there is a large body of research that points to the relative accuracy of memory (e.g., Christianson 1984, Heuer and Reisberg 1990, Reisberg et al. 1988, Yuille and Cutshall 1986). Also, there are some memory scientists whose work indicates that children seldom or never make up false stories of abuse, even when questioned in a way that pulls for false reports. These studies support the notion that children are not highly suggestible in cases involving trauma and that they have better memory when there is interpersonal support at or around the time of the traumatic event.

Studies that most approximate the trauma of sexual abuse are those by Goodman and her associates (e.g., Goodman and Aman 1990, Goodman and Reed 1986, Goodman et al. 1990, 1991, 1994,

Rudy et al. 1991, Saywitz et al. 1991). In one study (Goodman et al. 1994) involving urinary tract catheterization, children were involved in a painful and embarrassing procedure involving genital penetration and public urination. The study points to the *forgetting* of trauma. A few children out of the sample of forty-six denied that they experienced the medical test. Also such factors as embarrassment, lack of discussion of the procedure with parents, and posttraumatic stress disorder (PTSD) symptoms were predictive of poor memory performance in their study. These three factors are associated with sexual abuse.

In yet another study (Saywitz et al. 1991) seventy-two 5- and 7-year-old girls underwent a standardized medical checkup. For half the children, the check-up included a vaginal and anal examination (genital condition). For the other half, there was a scoliosis examination (nongenital condition). Children's memories were evaluated by means of free recall, anatomically detailed dolls, prop demonstration, and direct and misleading questions. It was found that the majority of children in the genital condition revealed vaginal and anal contact only when asked directly about it. Errors regarding vaginal and anal touch in response to direct questions were predominantly due to omissions. That is, some children in the genital condition, when asked directly, denied vaginal and anal contact. Children in the nongenital condition never falsely reported genital touch in free recall or doll demonstration. Further, with direct questioning, the false report rate was rare. Thus, they found that young children only tell their "true genital touching" story when specifically asked and that those who were not touched were able to say so.

A document developed by a group of memory scientists and practitioners of the British Psychological Society (1995) is, in general, consistent with many of the points I develop here. Some of the points included in the report are (1) memories may be recovered within or independent of therapy, (2) memory recovery is reported by highly experienced and well-qualified therapists who are well aware of the dangers of inappropriate suggestion and interpretation, (3) there is no reliable evidence that the creation of false memories by therapists is a widespread phenomenon, and (4) there is evidence for incorrect memories but much less evidence for the creation of false memories. Thus, not all memory scientists see things the same way and not all laboratory studies on memory indicate the inaccuracy of memory. Memory can be strong and functionally accurate. Memory can also be quite malleable. We need to learn more about those conditions that make it more likely to be open to error and those that keep it secure. We need to learn more about whether factors related to the vulnerability of memory parallel those existing within the traumatic experience of child sexual abuse.

I have discussed the contemporary story promulgated by some vocal memory scientists. Another and quite different story could have been written. *Abusers* cause their *victims* to develop *false memories* of *nonabuse*. They do so as a direct result of the utilization of such techniques as direct suggestion, guided visualization, interpretation, and threats. An example would be the perpetrator-father telling the child he was abusing to go back to sleep and that it was all a dream. He thus created a false memory. The child-victim would develop this false memory of nonabuse and would believe that it was all a dream. Later, she might develop posttraumatic symptomatology. She would be confused by these symptoms. She might present with other symptoms and diagnoses. The flashbacks, nightmares, and intrusive images would be bewildering. She might suspect sexual abuse but be quick to deny. The media might serve to implant the false memory of nonabuse as well.

There is another story I heard recently. It is the story of a woman whose adult sister alleged father–daughter incest following recovery of abuse memories. The woman went with her father to a "therapist" of his choosing. The therapist utilized the session to inform her that her sister had "false memory syndrome" and that she should not allow her sister to press charges. The woman later learned that this "therapist" had also been accused of father–daughter incest. Further, her sister's abuse was later validated by a brother. What is interesting about these two stories is that they could utilize the same terms, such as *false memory, creating, implanting,* and the same results from the same suggestibility studies in order to support the story.

There are problems with applying the literature on memory suggestibility to the case of sexual abuse, as I have indicated. The literature offers little support for either these stories of *false memory of nonabuse* or the earlier story of *false memory of abuse*. However, if the memory literature is used to support one of the positions, it could be applied to the other as well. If the literature is used to support one story rather than the other, the issue of bias, interpretation and selective application must be raised. Elsewhere the term *False Issue Syndrome* (FIS) was placed into currency (Alpert et al. in press). FIS is a condition in which one believes that numerous therapists are planting memories of sexual abuse in their patients, memories that never took place. Further, FIS victims hold that there is little objective scientific evidence to support the forgetting and recall of traumatic events. We developed the term to counteract the term "False Memory Syndrome."

In sum, the literature on memory suggestibility offers little support for the story that is being circulated, the story that patients develop false memories of abuse as a direct result of therapists' dredging, implanting, and creating. The story holds a great deal more complexity. There is inadequate support for the statement that an individual's memory may have changed; it is possible, for example, that individuals who tell a different story in response to suggestion may be giving a compliant report in response to social factors. Their reporting of an event may have changed while their memory may have remained constant. There is no research that indicates that most mental health professionals working with adults who assert child sexual abuse do treatment that is suggestive and almost exclusively focused on memory retrieval, with little attention to other therapeutic aims. As of this writing, there are no laboratory studies of memory suggestibiliy in psychotherapy by memory scientists. Unfortunately, this undeveloped body of research is being used prematurely in the courtroom for purposes of defending alleged abuse perpetrators and prosecuting therapists alleged to have used suggestion.

It is not surprising that there are problems with ecological validity. Memory science has only become an applied science over the last twenty years, and until recently the focus has been on eyewitness report of crimes. The application of laboratory research to the issue of delayed memory of childhood trauma is a new development. It is more likely to thrive if there is cross-fertilization of scholarship.

MEDIA

The media seem to have played a role in developing the contemporary story. The focus of the current media story is on those traumatized people who have total memory loss and delayed recall. However, this situation, that of total amnesia for a lengthy time and the ensuing recalled and detailed recollection, represents the minority of sexual abuse stories. Data indicate that most of those who have been traumatized retain total, partial, or oscillating mcmory, whether they fully understood it or disclosed it (Briere and Conte 1993, Gold and Hughes unpublished manuscript, Herman and Schatzow 1987, Loftus et al. 1994, Williams 1994). I am not suggesting that the story of those who have total memory loss and delayed recall should not be told. I am simply pointing out that there are other stories and that the media have focused mainly on one minority account.

The media seem to have identified the modern victims as those who have been alleged to abuse. The position that seems to be taken by much of the media is that the only error to avoid is the false allegation of abuse. Further, mental health professionals are often seen as well-intentioned villains in the contemporary story.

A powerful example of media attention is provided by Ofra Bikel's "Divided Memories," a four-hour, two-part program for PBS's "Frontline." Mental health professionals served as commentators. They were interspersed with alleged victims and nonmainstream therapists. Examples of techniques by these nonmainstream therapists consisted of such nontraditional practices as regression into past lives. In some of these "treatment" victims were encouraged to rant, rave, and punch pillows and mattresses, which represented the alleged parent-abusers. As these techniques were scattered throughout the program, it appeared that the respected mental health professionals were supporting these "therapies." Regression into past lives or recovering memories from alien abductions or Fallopian tubes is not mainstream therapeutic practice. The selection of examples and the placement of them as well as the commentators did not point to objective, open-minded reporting. The effort was sensational story and a misrepresentation of mainstream treatment.

Another powerful example of media attention is provided by Herman (1994). She considers the case of Paul Ingram, a sheriff's deputy in Olympia, Washington, who confessed to sexually abusing his two daughters. Ingam was intensively and repeatedly questioned by police. Questionable methods were used. He then declared that he remembered having committed more crimes than he actually had, crimes involving bizarre satanic cult rituals and group sex. Initially he had been sentenced to prison. However, after pleading guilty to the original charge of incest, he disclaimed all that he had confessed and indicated that he had been pressured and coerced. The point is we really do not know what happened. While the daughters' original memories of abuse may have been more or less true, police coercion seems to have intensified charges and affirmations. As Herman indicates, the author of the story, which appeared in the *New Yorker* (Wright 1988), while acknowledging more than one conceivable interpretation to the facts in this case, seemed to have reasoned that one erroneous accusation pointed to all false accusations in this as well as other cases. Herman indicates that some of these stories are aroused by the False Memory Syndrome Foundation (FMSF) advocacy. FMSF is composed mainly of parents, many of whom have been accused of child sexual abuse. According to Butler (1995a), this group has been associated with the Truth and Responsibility in Mental Health Practices Act, which is presently being introduced in state legislatures. It has already been presented to the New Hampshire legislature. Some of the stipulations of this act would require therapists to certify to private and public health insurance programs that their therapy is "safe and effective" and to provide citations from scientific journals as proof. In those cases in which these standards were not met, therapy might be ineligible for reimbursement. Butler raises this question: "Why are a relatively small group of accused parents so close to setting the clinical agenda for millions of genuine abuse survivors and eclipsing public awareness of the more than 130,000 children who are newly sexually victimized each year?" (p. 32).

While some, or even many, of these stories may have been aroused by FMSF advocacy, it is reporters in the media who have elected to present them. It is unfortunate that these media reports have oversimplified the story and confused the public. It appears that they have damaged victims, served abusers, and been harmful to the mental health professions and practitioners.

THE PSYCHOANALYTIC CLINICIAN AND RECONSTRUCTION

I turn now to another character in this contemporary story: the clinician. Up to now, the story I have told focuses on the roles of memory scientists and, to a lesser extent, the media. They have been telling us what the clinician does. However, we cannot learn about what clinicians do from the writings of memory scientists. While they will not tell the full story, the writings of clinicians need to be considered. Some mainstream literature that points to how clinicians work with sexual abuse victims is that by Briere (1989, 1992), Courtois (1988), Herman (1992), Kluft (1990), McCann and Pearlman (1990), and Wilson and Raphael (1993). In general this literature indicates that therapists must use their training in neutrality, observation, and analysis in working with patients who report delayed memory, and that therapists should not suggest abuse to explain symptoms nor fail to explore abuse when warranted.

Another clinical literature that has received relatively little attention within the general memory discourse is that on psychoanalysis. Psychoanalysts continue to grapple with the question: How does the analyst know? The discussion that is ongoing within psychoanalysis speaks to the intricacy of the issues and the acknowledgment of uncertainty surrounding the nature of mind and memory and the topic of therapeutic action. This wrestling with the integrity of the clinical process is ongoing among mental health professionals of varying theoretical orientations. I tell the psychoanalytic story because it has not received much attention in the broader discourse on delayed memory. It is also a story in which I am presently most immersed.

Let me be clear and state my position at the outset. I am not implying that the work of all psychoanalysts or all mental health professionals is privileged, justified, and above condemnation. Rather, what I am saying is that it is highly unlikely that most are engaged in therapeutic action that could be considered capricious, careless, or coercive. There are bad and poorly trained therapists. Similarly, there are bad and poorly trained researchers.

The word *reconstruction* should have its place in this story. While it is seldom mentioned in this debate, it is central to the discourse. The technique of reconstruction is a foundation of clinical psychoanalysis. In reconstruction, fragments from the patient's past are joined into a cohesive life story that makes sense in the present. Freud held that an analyst should place before the patient, in a timely fashion, an event that the patient does not remember but the analyst presumes to have occurred. He held that an inaccurate reconstruction was harmless since the patient would reject it. His reconstructions were quite specific and included such details as what took place, when, where, and with whom. Freud's task was complex. Believing that later events may retrogressively influence the significance of earlier events, he had the difficult task of determining the patient's relative age at the time of the event. For example, while it did not hold psychic significance until it was reactivated in a dream four years later, when he was experiencing the oedipal conflict, Freud (1919) inferred that the Wolf Man observed the primal scene at 18 months. It seems as if some memory scientists are assuming that Freud's paradigmatic reconstructions are still operative today.

The word *reconstruction* took on new meaning as time progressed. While Freud believed that reconstructions of what actually happened was possible, the ego psychologists viewed the recovery of actual memories and reconstructions of discrete events as outdated aspirations. The ego psychologists were interested in the present experience of the past rather than in reconstructing what actually happened. Instead of focusing on the event itself, they focused on the immediate and subsequent thought processes and feelings that were elaborations of the event. Thus, they focused on that which did not exist at the time of the event.

Since Freud wrote about reconstruction, there has been substantial reconceptualization and a steady shift away from the belief that a veridical account of the past can be reconstructed. Many different theoretical, sociocultural developments have converged to result in a deemphasis of the actual historical reality of past events. This is the time of radical deconstruction.

At present contemporary psychoanalysts are struggling with the question, How does the analyst know? Consider the following, written by Sue Grand, in Chapter 9 in this book:

> On this particular day, I have read yet another media exposé on the false-memory controversy. I realize that this outspoken, serious and assertive woman would confront her stepfather if thoroughly convinced that he incested her; this litigious volatile man would lie and very possibly sue me for "implanting" an incest memory. Her stepfather suddenly appears to be powerful, vindictive, and relentless in his retaliation; I am helpless, vulnerable, small. . . . Financially ruined, professionally humiliated, I am a little girl, terrorized, with a shameful secret. Even as she weeps, she does not yet know, but she has lost

me. . . . I am inauthentic, subtly coercive and secretly ashamed. It is one of my worst moments as an analyst. [p. 249]

Freud's epistemology was derived from realism. His philosophy of science was based on positivism. Contemporary thinking within psychoanalysis is challenging the traditional objectivist approach. The field seems to have moved from a positivist model for understanding theory and practice to a constructivist model. The contemporary movement no longer regards psychoanalysis as a science. Rather, it regards psychoanalysis as some form of hermeneutics in which there is recognition that facts do not exist apart from interpretation.

Rather than scientific objectivism, one contemporary hermeneutic trend emphasizes the role of narrative. The ego psychological approach to reconstruction leads naturally to the subjectivist, relativist positions of Spence (1982, 1993) and Schafer (1991), which point to the inaccessibility and irrelevance of historical truth. Clinical material is regarded as dependent on the observer, and reconstructed stories that are epistemologically consistent and clinically useful are considered not necessarily veridical. Reality is constructed by means of a theoretical perspective. A story that is told is but one of many versions that could be told and is only one version of the truth. In yet another hermeneutic trend (Hoffman 1991), the analyst's personal involvement is included within the constructivist position. The term *social constructivism* incorporates both the role of the immediate analytic interaction, involving participation and reciprocal, interpersonal influence in the historical reconstruction as well as the construction of a clouded reality. Within social constructivism there is recognition that neither the analyst nor the patient has access to reality and that their individual and collective understanding is in process. Thus, current analytic thinking that takes into account constructivism, perspectivism, or narration acknowledges visions or versions of reality and the impossibility of knowing historical truth.

Even contemporary classical theorists (e.g., Blum 1994) indicate that reconstructions are only approximations, as are all interpretive interventions. Contemporary classical proponents of reconstruction attempt to reconstruct the actual experience, the psychic trauma, the developmental-phase disturbance, the sequence, and the sequelae. They view reconstruction as a process that is continually revised as analysis deepens.

When we move to a relational analytic paradigm within a constructivist model, there is a repudiation of historical truth in preference for intersubjective truth. Within this paradigm, there is a belief that reconstruction is impossible and the work is more appropriately called construction. Some relational psychoanalysts (e.g., Davies and Frawley 1994) focus on the reenactment in the transference-countertransference work. Their sense of reconstruction, a word which is generally not used, is that whatever happens now, as evidenced within the transference, probably happened then. Memory is played out in transference phenomena. Relational analysts work collaboratively with the patient to encounter anew feelings from the past and to resolve these feelings. They are not concerned with the absolute truth of the life story, and seem to hold that one should not assume truth. The focus is less on the recovery of memories and more on the reintegration of those repudiated memories into a modified life story. The reliving and resolving, however, are different from the recovery of repressed memories. There is no assumption that the revised stories represent a true reality. The concepts of ambiguity, interaction, construction, and co-construction are given recognition.

The challenge for some analysts (e.g., Slavin 1993; see Grand, Chapters 9 and 10 in this volume) becomes how to rescue reconstruction within the relational paradigm. Grand would like to retain the egalitarian treatment model of social constructivism without negating the significance and accessibility of historical truth. Implicit here are the beliefs that reality is not entirely mutually constructed, that truth is not merely narrative, and that confusion and uncertainty can coexist with knowing something. There are times when we think we do know; there are times when the evidence is simply that substantial and convincing. The challenge for contemporary psychoanalysts who work within this theoretical frame of relational co-constructed reality in the analytic dyad is to find a way to acknowledge that there are some things that we do know and that not all historical accounts are equally valid, coherent, telling, or plausible.

The story that I have related contrasts sharply with the

simplistic story of the impulsive, thoughtless therapist who pursues buried memories. As Harris (1995) writes,

> To counter the caricaturing of all therapists as destructive agents with primitive tools to divide and destroy families and persons, it is always important to assert the modest but terrifying goal of psychoanalytic work: the relief of suffering the development of the courage not to act but to bear loss that is irredeemable. In the treatment of abused patients, the losses can be particularly terrible: lost time, lost opportunities, above all lost innocence. [p. 15]

Thus, contemporary psychoanalysts, across orientations, are incorporating a therapeutic action paradigm in which there is recognition that experience is constructed and, at least within some of these paradigms, that the analyst is inescapably and intricately involved in a manner that influences the structure of understanding by means of narratives and the patient's self experiences. The belief that we know would bring welcome serenity to all the doubt and confusion that takes place within the analytic context. While occasionally the evidence is substantial and convincing, in those cases in which there is no memory it is difficult to know.

CONCLUSION

We need to keep in mind that victimizers have something to gain by distorting, disavowing, and misrepresenting. It is difficult to distinguish perpetrators from normal men and regular fathers. Our impulse may be to believe the victimizers. We do not want to believe that human beings could do such terrible things to children. We do not want to believe that debauchery survives. Also, victimizers can be very convincing. They may even have convinced themselves. It may be that they have disowned and dissociated from their abusing selves, and that they truly believe that they have not committed acts of abuse. We need to keep all this in mind. At the same time we also must keep in mind that the alleged victimizers may, in fact, be nonvictimizers. It is a difficult tightrope that we walk.

There are numerous themes in this story. One theme is that

memory is very complex and that a memory's accuracy may be affected by a number of factors. Another theme is that there is no reliable evidence that a plethora of therapists engage in the creation of false memories of child sexual abuse with their adult patients. Another theme is that the conviction that mental health professionals know would be a welcome comfort given all the doubt that takes place within the analytic context.

In addition to these, there are themes of bias and politics. The standard research situation is packed with occasion for bias. The occasion starts when a researcher decides what to study and opens more broadly when making decisions about how to study it. The opportunity for bias is opened even wider when the researcher attempts to interpret. As I illustrated, the same data could be applied to support either false memory of nonabuse or false memory of abuse. The occasion for bias is wider still when the researcher decides when and where and for what purpose to present the research. Unfortunately the undeveloped body of memory research is being used prematurely in the courtroom in defending alleged abuse perpetrators and in prosecuting therapists alleged to have used suggestion.

The story of reckless and suggestive therapists is diverting us from the real victims of child sexual abuse. What can we do to put the focus back on the child who has been victimized and the adult who remembers in whatever way he or she does? Memory scientists and clinicians need to engage in joint inquiry and work to develop (1) research on real traumatic memory that has ecological validity and helps us to identify those conditions under which individuals would be more suggestive, and (2) research on real traumatic memory that would help us to understand the processes ongoing in the forgetting and retrieving of trauma. Memory scientists and clinicians need to place some developed scientific material on the topics of trauma and memory processes into the standard curriculum of all students in psychology. Therapists need to be knowledgeable about the risks of improper suggestion and interpretation. Memory researchers need to be knowledgeable about human traumatization; it must not be minimized. Forensic psychologists need to specify limitations with respect to ecological validity and generalizability. Sometimes research is so far afield that it is best left off-field. Lastly, the scapegoating of therapists should cease. It is poor judgment to think that delayed incest memories can be explained away by pointing to bad therapy. Rather than focus our revulsion on therapy, we need to face the overshadowed issue, which is that many children in this society are abused.

REFERENCES

Alpert, J. L. (1995a). Dreams, trauma, and clinical observation: comments on C. Brooks Brenneis's article. *Psychoanalytic Psychology,* 12(2): 325–328.

———— (1995b). Trauma, dissociation, and clinical study as a responsible beginning. *Cognition and Consciousness,* 4:1–5.

Alpert, J. L., Brown, L. S., and Courtois, C. A. *Symptomatic clients and memories of childhood abuse: what the trauma and child sexual abuse literature tells us.* Unpublished manuscript.

———— (in press). False Issue Syndrome: sexual abuse recalled and the implantation of an issue. *Journal of Child Sexual Abuse.*

American Psychological Association (1994). Interim Report of the APA Working Group on Investigation of Memories of Childhood Abuse.

Blum, H. P. (1994). *Reconstruction in Psychoanalysis: Childhood Revisited and Recreated.* Madison, CT: International Universities Press.

Bower, G. H. (1981). Mood and memory. *American Psychologist* 36:129–148.

Briere, J. (1989). *Therapy for Adults Molested as Children.* New York: Springer.

———— (1992). *Child Abuse Trauma: Theory and Treatment of the Lasting Effects.* Newbury Park, CA: Sage.

Briere, J., and Conte, J. (1993). Self-reported amnesia for abuse in adults molested as children. *Journal of Traumatic Stress,* 6(1):21–31.

British Psychological Society. (1995). *Recovered memories: the report of the working party of the British Psychological Society.* Unpubished manuscript.

Butler, K. (1995a). Caught in the crossfire. *Family Therapy Networker.* March/April: 1–34, 8–79.

———— (1995b). Like herding cats. *Family Therapy Networker.* March/April, 35–39, 80.

Christianson, S-A. (1984). The relationship between induced emotional arousal and amnesia. *Scandinavian Journal of Psychology* 25:147–160.

———— (1992). Emotional stress and eyewitness memory. *Psychological Bulletin,* 112(2):284–309.

Courtois, C. A. (1988). *Healing the Incest Wound: Adult Survivors in Therapy.* New York: Norton.

Crowder, R. G. (1976). *Principles of Learning and Memory.* Hillsdale, NJ: Lawrence Erlbaum.

Davies, J. M., and Frawley, M. G. (1994). *Treating the Adult Survivor of*

Childhood Sexual Abuse: A Psychoanalytic Perspective. New York: Basic Books.

Elliott, D. M. (1994). Trauma and dissociated memory: prevalence across events. In *Delayed Trauma Memories: Victim Experiences and Clinical Practice,* L. Berliner, Chair. Paper presented at the annual meeting of the International Society of Traumatic Stress Studies, Chicago, IL, November.

Fisler, R. E., Vardi, D. J., and van der Kolk, B. A. (1994). Nontraumatic autobiographical memories in trauma survivors: a preliminary study. Paper presented at the Harvard Medical School, Cambridge, MA.

Freud, S. (1919). From the history of an infantile neurosis. *Standard Edition* 17:7–12.

Gold, S. N., and Hughes, D. M. *Degrees of memory of childhood sexual abuse among female survivors in therapy.* Unpublished manuscript.

Goodman, G., and Aman, C. 1990. Children's use of anatomically detailed dolls to recount an event. *Child Development* 61:1859–1871.

Goodman, G. S., Hirschman J. E., Hepps, D., and Rudy, L. (1991). Children's memory for stressful events. *Merrill-Palmer Quarterly* 37:109–158.

Goodman, G. S., Quas, J., Batterman-Fance, J. M., et al. (1994). Predictors of accurate and inaccurate memories of traumatic events experienced in childhood. *Consciousness and Cognition* 3(3):269–294.

Goodman, G. S., and Reed, R. S. (1986). Age differences in eyewitness testimony. *Law and Human Behavior* 19:317–332.

Goodman, G. S., Rudy, L., Bottoms, B. L., and Aman, C. (1990). Children's concerns and memory: issues of ecological validity in the study of children's eyewitness testimony. In *Knowing and Remembering in Young Children,* ed. R. Fivush and J. Hudson, pp. 249–284. New York: Cambridge University Press.

Harris, A. (1995). False memory; false memory syndrome; "false memory syndrome"; the so-called false memory syndrome? Paper presented at the White Institute Conference on Delayed Memories, New York City.

Herman, J. L. (1992). *Trauma and Recovery.* New York: Basic Books.

—— (1994). Presuming to know the truth. *Moving Forward* 3(1):1, 12–13.

Herman, J. L., and Schatzow, E. (1987). Recovery and verification of memories of childhood sexual trauma. *Psychoanalytic Psychology* 4:1–14.

Heuer, F., and Raisberg, D. (1992). Emotion, arousal, and memory for detail. In *The Handbook of Emotion and Memory,* ed. S. A. Christianson, pp. 151–506. Hillsdale, NJ: Lawrence Erlbaum.

Hewitt, S. A. (1994). Preverbal sexual abuse: what two children report in later years. *Child Abuse and Neglect* 18(10):821–826.

Hoffman, I. Z. (1991). Discussion: toward a social-constructivist view of the psychoanalytic situation, *Psychoanalytic Dialogues: A Journal of Relational Perspectives* 1(1):74–105.

Horowitz, M. (1986). *Stress Response Syndromes*. New York: Jason Aronson.

Jehu, D. (1988). *Beyond Sexual Abuse: Therapy with Women Who Were Childhood Victims*. New York: Wiley.

Kluft, R. P. (1990). Incest and subsequent revictimization. In *Incest-related Syndromes of Adult Psychopathology* pp. 263–288. Washington, DC.: American Psychiatric Press.

Loftus, E. F., Polonsky, S., and Fullilove, M. T. (1994). Memories of childhood sexual abuse: remembering and repressing. *Psychology of Women Quarterly* 18:67–84.

McCann, I. L., and Pearlman, L. A. (1990). *Psychological Trauma and the Adult Survivor*. New York: Brunner/Mazel.

Poole, D. A., Lindsay, D. S., Memon, A., and Bull, R. (1995). Psychotherapy and the recovery of memories of childhood sexual abuse: U.S. and British practitioners' opinions, practices, and experiences. *Journal of Consulting and Clinical Psychology* 63(3)426–437.

Raisberg, D., Heuer, F., McLean, J., and O'Shaugnessy, M. (1988). The quantity, not quality, of affect predicts memory vividness. *Bulletin of the Psychonomic Society* 26:100–103.

Rudy, L., Goodman, G. S., Nicholas, E., and Moan, S. (1991). Effects of participation on children's reports: implications for children's testimony. *Developmental Psychology* 27:1–26.

Saporta, J. A., and van der Kolk, B. A. (1992). Psychobiological consequences of severe trauma. In *Torture and Its Consequences,* ed M. Basogh, pp. 151–181. New York: Cambridge University Press.

Saywitz, K. J., Goodman, G. S., Nichols, E., and Moan, S. F. (1991). Children's memories of a physical examination involving genital touch: implications for reports of child sexual abuse. *Journal of Consulting and Clinical Psychology* 59(5):682–691.

Schafer, R. (1992). *Retelling a Life: Narration and Dialogue in Psychoanalysis*. New York: Basic Books.

Slavin, J. (1993). The poisoning of desire: memory, fantasy, dissociation, and agency in sexual abuse. Discussion presented at the annual meeting of the American Psychological Association, Toronto, August.

Spence, D. (1982). *Narrative Truth and Historical Truth: Meaning and Interpretation in Psychoanalysis. New York: Norton.*

———— (1993). The hermeneutic trun: soft science or loyal opposition? *Psychoanalytic Dialogues* 3(1):1–11.

Spiegel, D., and Cardena, E. (1991). Disintegrated experience: the dissociative disorders revisited. *Journal of Abnormal Psychology* 100(3)366–378.

Terr, L. (1988). What happens to the early memories of trauma? A study of twenty children under age five at the time of documented traumatic events. *American Journal of Child and Adolescent Psychiatry* 27:96–104.

———— (1989). Treating psychic trauma in children: a preliminary discussion. *Journal of Tramatic Stress* 2(1):3–20.

———— (1991). Childhood traumas: an outline and overview. *American Journal of Psychiatry* 148(1):10–20.

van der kolk, B. A. (1984). *Post-traumatic Stress Disorder: Psychological and Biological Sequelae*. Washington, DC: American Psychiatric Press.

———— (1987). *Psychological Trauma*. Washington, DC: American Psychiatric Press.

———— (1988). The trauma spectrum: the interaction of biological and social events in the genesis of the trauma response. *Journal of Traumatic Stress* 1:273–290.

van der Kolk, B. A., and van der Hart, O. (1991). The intrusive past: the flexibility of memory and the engraving of trauma. *American Image* 48:425–454.

Waltz, J. (1994). Treatment and memory recall. *Delayed trauma memories: victim experiences and clinical practice*. Symposium conducted at the annual meeting of the International Society for Traumatic Stress Studies, L. Berliner, ed. Chicago, IL, November.

Williams, L. M. (1994). Recall of childhood trauma: a prospective study of women's memories of child sexual abuse. *Journal of Consulting and Clinical Psychology* 62(6):1167–1176.

Wilson, J. P., and Raphael, B., eds. (1993). *International Handbook of Traumatic Stress Syndromes*. New York: Plenum.

Wright, L. (1993). Remembering Satan. Parts I and II. *The New Yorker,* May 17 and May 24.

Yapko, M. D. (1994) Suggestibility and repressed memories of abuse: a survey of psychotherapists' beliefs. *American Journal of Clinical Hypnosis* 36(3):163–171.

Yuille, J. C., and Cutshall, J. L. (1986). A case study of eyewitness memory of a crime. *Journal of Applid Psychology* 71(2):291–301.

PART II
Psychological Science

2

The Body, Memory, and the Psychobiology of Trauma

BESSEL A. VAN DER KOLK

For more than a century, ever since people's responses to overwhelming experiences were first systematically explored, researchers have noted that the psychological effects of trauma are stored in somatic memory and expressed as changes in the biological stress response. In 1889 Pierre Janet postulated that intense emotional reactions make events traumatic by interfering with the integration of the experience into existing memory schemes. Intense emotions, Janet thought, cause memories of particular events to be dissociated from consciousness and to be stored, instead, as visceral sensations (anxiety and panic) or visual images (nightmares and flashbacks). Janet also observed that traumatized patients seemed to react to reminders of the trauma with emergency responses that had been relevant to the original threat but had no bearing on current experience. He noted that, unable to put the trauma behind them, victims had trouble learning from experience; their energy was funneled toward keeping their emotions under control, at the expense of paying attention to current exigencies. They became fixated on the past, in some cases by being obsessed with the trauma, but more often by behaving and feeling as if they were traumatized over and over again without being able to locate the origins of these feelings (van der Kolk and van der Hart 1989, 1991).

Freud (1919) also considered the tendency to remain fixated on the trauma to be biologically based: "After severe shock . . . the dream life continually takes the patient back to the situation of his disaster from which he awakens with renewed terror. . . . The patient has undergone a physical fixation to the trauma." Pavlov's (1926) investigations continued the tradition of explaining the effects of trauma as the result of lasting physiological alterations. He, and others using his paradigm, coined the term *defensive reaction* for a cluster of innate reflexive responses to environmental threat. Many studies have shown how the response to potent environmental stimuli (unconditional stimuli) becomes a conditioned reaction. After repeated aversive stimulation, intrinsically nonthreatening cues associated with the trauma (conditional stimuli) can elicit the defensive reaction by themselves (conditional response). A rape victim may respond to conditioned stimuli, such as the approach of an unknown man, as if she were about to be raped again — and experience panic. Pavlov also pointed out that individual differences in temperament accounted for the diversity of long-term adaptations to trauma.

Abraham Kardiner (1941), who first systematically defined posttraumatic stress for American audiences, noted that sufferers of "traumatic neuroses" develop an enduring vigilance for and sensitivity to environmental threat. He stated:

> The nucleus of the neurosis is a physioneurosis. This is present on the battlefield and during the entire process of organization; it outlives every intermediary accommodative device, and persists in the chronic forms. The traumatic syndrome is ever present and unchanged.

In *Men Under Stress,* Grinker and Spiegel (1945) catalogued the physical symptoms of soldiers in acute posttraumatic states: flexor changes in posture, hyperkinesis, "violently propulsive gait," tremor at rest, masklike facies, cogwheel rigidity, gastric distress, urinary incontinence, mutism, and a violent startle reflex. They noted the similarity between many of these symptoms and those of diseases of the extrapyramidal motor system. Today we understand them to result from stimulation of biological systems, particularly of ascending amine projections. Contemporary research on the biology of posttraumatic stress disorder (PTSD), generally uninformed by this earlier research, confirms that there are persistent and profound alterations in stress hormone secretion and memory processing in subjects with PTSD.

SYMPTOMATOLOGY

Starting with Kardiner (1941) and closely followed by Lindemann (1944), a vast literature on combat trauma, crimes, rape, kidnapping, natural disasters, accidents, and imprisonment (American Psychiatric Association 1987, 1994, Horowitz 1978, van der Kolk 1987b) has shown that the trauma response is bimodal: hypermnesia, hyperreactivity to stimuli, and traumatic reexperiencing coexist with psychic numbing, avoidance, amnesia, and anhedonia. These responses to extreme experiences are so consistent across the different forms of traumatic stimuli that this bimodal reaction appears to be the normative response to any overwhelming and uncontrollable experience. In many persons who have undergone severe stress, the posttraumatic response fades over time, whereas in others it persists. Much work remains to be done to spell out issues of resilience and vulnerability, but magnitude of exposure, previous trauma, and social support appear to be the three most significant predictors for development of chronic PTSD (Kulka et al. 1990, McFarlane 1988).

In an apparent attempt to compensate for chronic hyperarousal, traumatized people seem to shut down — on a behavioral level by avoiding stimuli reminiscent of the trauma, and on a psychobiological level by emotional numbing, which extends to both trauma-related and everyday experience (Litz and Keane 1989). Thus subjects with chronic PTSD tend to suffer from a numbed responsiveness to the environment, punctuated by intermittent hyperarousal in reaction to conditional traumatic stimuli. However, as Pitman and colleagues (1990, 1993) have pointed out, in PTSD the stimuli that precipitate emergency responses may not be conditional enough; many triggers not directly related to the traumatic experience may precipitate extreme reactions. Subjects with PTSD suffer both from generalized hyperarousal and from physiological emergency reactions to specific reminders (American Psychiatry Association 1987, 1994).

The loss of affective modulation that is so central in PTSD may help to explain the observation that traumatized persons lose the capacity to use affect states as signals (Krystal 1978). In subjects with PTSD, feelings are not used as cues to attend to incoming information and arousal is likely to precipitate flight-or-fight reactions (Strian and Klicpera 1978). Thus they often go immediately from stimulus to response without psychologically assessing the meaning of an event. This makes them prone to freeze or, alternatively, to overreact and intimidate others in response to minor provocations (van der Kolk 1987b, van der Kolk and Ducey 1989).

PSYCHOPHYSIOLOGY

Abnormal psychophysiological responses in PTSD have been observed at two different levels: (1) in response to specific reminders of the trauma, and (2) in response to intense but neutral stimuli, such as unexpected noises. The first paradigm implies heightened physiological arousal to sounds, images, and thoughts related to specific traumatic incidents. Many studies (Blanchard et al. 1986, Dobbs and Wilson 1960, Kolb and Multipassi 1982, Malloy et al. 1983, Pitman et al. 1987, van der Kolk and Ducey 1989) have confirmed that traumatized individuals respond to such stimuli with significant conditioned autonomic reactions — for example, increases in heart rate, skin conductance, and blood pressure. The highly elevated physiological responses accompanying the recall of traumatic experiences that happened years, and sometimes decades, before illustrate the intensity and timelessness with which traumatic memories continue to affect current experience (Pitman et al. 1993, van der Kolk and van der Hart 1991). This phenomenon has been understood in the light of Lang's (1979) work, which shows that emotionally laden imagery correlates with measurable autonomic responses. Lang has proposed that emotional memories are stored as "associative networks" that are activated when a person is confronted with situations that stimulate a sufficient number of elements within such networks. One significant measure of treatment outcome that has become widely accepted in recent years is a decrease in physiological arousal in response to imagery related to the trauma (Keane and Kaloupek 1982). However, Shalev and coworkers (1992) have shown that desensitization to specific trauma-related mental images does not necessarily generalize to recollections of other traumatic events as well.

Kolb (1987) was the first to propose that excessive stimulation of the central nervous system (CNS) at the time of the trauma may result in permanent neuronal changes that have a negative effect on learning, habituation, and stimulus discrimination. These neuronal changes would not depend on actual exposure to reminders of the trauma for expression. The abnormal startle response characteristic of PTSD (American Psychiatric Association 1994) exemplifies such neuronal changes.

Although abnormal acoustic startle response (ASR) has been seen as a cardinal feature of the trauma response for more than half a century, systematic explorations of the ASR in PTSD have just begun. The ASR is a characteristic sequence of muscular and autonomic responses elicited by sudden and intense stimuli (Davis 1984, Shalev and Rogel-Fuchs, in press). The neuronal pathways involved consist of only a small number of mediating synapses between the receptor and effector and a large projection to brain areas responsible for CNS activation and stimulus evaluation (Davis 1984). The ASR is mediated by excitatory amino acids such as glutamate and aspartate and is modulated by a variety of neurotransmitters and second messengers at both the spinal and the supraspinal levels (Davis 1986). Habituation to the ASR in normal human subjects occurs after three to five presentations (Shalev and Rogel-Fuchs, in press).

Several studies (Butler et al. 1990, Ornitz and Pynoos 1989, Ross et al. 1989, Shalev et al. 1993) found a failure to habituate to both CNS- and autonomic nervous system–mediated responses to ASR in 93 percent of subjects in the PTSD group, compared with 22 percent of the control subjects. Interestingly, persons who previously met criteria for PTSD but no longer do so continue to show failure of habituation to the ASR (van der Kolk et al., unpublished data, 1991–1992; Pitman et al., unpublished data, 1991–1992), which raises the question of whether abnormal habituation to acoustic startle may be a marker or a vulnerability factor for development of PTSD.

The failure to habituate to acoustic startle suggests that traumatized people have difficulty evaluating sensory stimuli and mobilizing appropriate levels of physiological arousal (Shalev and Rogel-

Fuchs, in press). Thus the inability of people with PTSD properly to integrate memories of the trauma and the tendency they have to get mired in a continuous reliving of the past are mirrored physiologically by the misinterpretation of innocuous stimuli, such as unexpected noises, as potential threats.

HORMONAL STRESS RESPONSE AND PSYCHOBIOLOGY

PTSD develops after exposure to events that are intensely distressing. Extreme stress is accompanied by the release of endogenous neurohormones, such as cortisol, epinephrine and norepinephrine, vasopressin, oxytocin, and endogenous opioids. These hormones help the organism to mobilize the energy required to deal with the stress; they induce reactions ranging from increased glucose release to enhanced immune function. In a well-functioning organism, stress produces rapid and pronounced hormonal responses. However, chronic and persistent stress inhibits the effectiveness of the stress response and induces desensitization (Axelrod and Reisine 1984).

Much still remains to be learned about the specific roles of the different neurohormones in the stress response. Norepinephrine is secreted by the locus ceruleus and distributed through much of the CNS, particularly the neocortex and the limbic system, where it plays a role in memory consolidation and helps to initiate fight-or-flight behaviors. Corticotropin is released from the anterior pituitary and activates a cascade of reactions, eventuating in release of glucocorticoids from the adrenal glands. The precise interrelation between hypothalamic-pituitary-adrenal (HPA) axis hormones and the catecholamines in the stress response is not entirely clear, but it is known that stressors that activate norepinephrine neurons also increase the concentration of corticotropin-releasing factor in the locus ceruleus (Dunn and Berridge 1987), and intracerebral ventricular infusion of corticotropin-releasing factor increases norepinephrine in the forebrain (Valentino and Foote 1988). Glucocorticoids and catecholamines may modulate each other's effects; in acute stress, cortisol helps to regulate the release of stress hormones via a negative feedback loop to the hippocampus, hypothalamus, and pituitary (Munck et al. 1984), and there is evidence that corticosteroids normalize catecholamine-induced arousal in limbic midbrain structures in response to stress (Bohus and DeWied 1978). Thus the simultaneous activation of corticosteroids and catecholamines could stimulate active coping behaviors, whereas increased arousal in the presence of low glucocorticoid levels may promote undifferentiated fight-or-flight reactions (Yehuda et al. 1990).

Although acute stress mobilizes the HPA axis and increases glucocorticoid levels, organisms adapt to chronic stress by activating a negative feedback loop that results in (1) decreased resting glucocorticoid levels (Meaney et al. 1989), (2) decreased glucocorticoid secretion in response to subsequent stress (Yehuda et al. 1990), and (3) increased concentration of glucocorticoid receptors in the hippocampus (Sapolsky et al. 1984). Yehuda, Giller, et al. (1991) suggested that increased concentration of glucocorticoid receptors could facilitate a stronger negative glucocorticoid feedback, resulting in a more sensitive HPA axis and a faster recovery from acute stress.

Chronic exposure to stress affects both acute and chronic adaptation: it permanently alters how an organism deals with its environment on a day-to-day basis and interferes with how it copes with subsequent acute stress (Yehuda, Giller, et al. 1991).

NEUROENDOCRINE ABNORMALITIES

Because there is an extensive literature on the effects of inescapable stress on the biological stress response of animal species such as monkeys and rats, much of the biological research on people with PTSD has focused on testing the applicability of those research findings to human subjects with PTSD (Krystal et al. 1989, van der Kolk et al. 1985). Subjects with PTSD, like chronically and inescapably shocked animals, seem to have a persistent activation of the biological stress response after exposure to stimuli reminiscent of the trauma (Table 2–1).

Catecholamines

Neuroendocrine studies of Vietnam veterans with PTSD have found good evidence for chronically increased sympathetic nervous system activity in PTSD. One investigation (Kosten et al. 1987) discovered elevated twenty-four-hour urinary excretion of norepinephrine and

TABLE 2-1

Biological Abnormalities in Posttraumatic Stress Disorder

A. Psychophysiological
   1. Extreme autonomic responses to stimuli reminiscent of the trauma
   2. Nonhabituation to startle stimuli
B. Neurotransmitter
   1. Noradrenergic
      a. Elevated urinary catecholamines
      b. Increased MHPG to yohimbine challenge
      c. Reduced platelet MAO activity
      d. Down-regulation of adrenergic receptors
   2. Serotonergic
      a. Decreased serotonin activity in traumatized animals
      b. Best pharmacological responses to serotonin uptake inhibitors
   3. Endogenous opioids: increased opioid response to stimuli reminiscent of trauma
C. Hypothalamic-pituitary-adrenal
   1. Decreased resting glucocorticoid levels
   2. Decreased glucocorticoid response to stress
   3. Down-regulation of glucocorticoid receptors
   4. Hyperresponsiveness to low-dose dexamethasone
D. Memory
   1. Amnesias and hypermnesias
   2. Traumatic memories precipitated by noradrenergic stimulation, physiological arousal
   3. Memories generally sensorimotor rather than semantic
E. Miscellaneous
   1. Traumatic nightmares often not oneiric but exact replicas of visual elements of trauma; may occur in stage II or III sleep
   2. Decreased hippocampal volume (?)
   3. Impaired psychoimmunologic functioning (?)

MAO, monoamine oxidase; MHPG, 3-methoxy-4-hydroxyphenylglycol.

epinephrine in PTSD combat veterans compared with patients who had other psychiatric diagnoses. Although Pitman and Orr (1990a) did not replicate these findings in twenty veterans and fifteen combat control subjects, the mean urinary excretion of norepinephrine in their combat control subjects (58.0 μg/day) was substantially higher than values previously reported in normal populations. The expected compensatory down-regulation of adrenergic receptors in response to increased levels of norepinephrine was confirmed by a study (Perry et al. 1987) that found decreased platelet α_2-adrenergic receptors in combat veterans with PTSD compared with normal control subjects. Another study (Lerer et al. 1987) also found an abnormally low α_2-adrenergic receptor–mediated adenylate cyclase signal transduction. Recently Southwick and colleagues (1993) used yohimbine injections (0.4 mg/kg), which activate noradrenergic neurons by blocking the α_2-autoreceptor, to study noradrenergic neuronal dysregulation in Vietnam veterans with PTSD. Yohimbine precipitated panic attacks in 70 percent of subjects and flashbacks in 40 percent. Subjects responded with larger increases in plasma 3-methoxy-4-hydroxyphenylglycol (MHPG) than control subjects. Yohimbine precipitated significant increases in all PTSD symptoms.

Corticosteroids

Two studies (Southwick et al. 1993, Yehuda et al. 1990) have shown that veterans with PTSD have low urinary excretion of cortisol, even when they have comorbid major depressive disorder. Other research (Pitman and Orr 1990a) failed to replicate this finding. In a series of studies, Yehuda and co-workers (1980, Yehuda, Lowy, and Southwick 1991) found increased numbers of lymphocyte glucocorticoid receptors in Vietnam veterans with PTSD. Interestingly, the number of glucocorticoid receptors was proportional to the severity of PTSD symptoms. Yehuda, Lowy, and Southwick (1991) also reported the findings of an unpublished study by Heidi Resnick, in which acute cortisol response to trauma was studied in blood samples from twenty rape victims in the emergency room. Three months later, trauma histories were taken and the subjects were evaluated for the presence of PTSD. Development of PTSD after the rape was significantly more likely in victims with histories of sexual abuse than in victims with no such histories. Cortisol levels shortly after the rape were correlated with histories of previous assaults: the mean initial cortisol levels of individuals with assault histories were 15 μg/dl, compared with 30 μg/dl in the control subjects. These findings can be interpreted to mean that previous exposure to traumatic events results either in a blunted cortisol response to subsequent trauma or in a quicker return of cortisol to baseline after stress. That Yehuda, Giller, and colleagues (1991) also found subjects with PTSD to be hyperresponsive to low doses of dexamethasone argues for an enhanced sensitivity of the HPA feedback in traumatized patients.

Serotonin

Although the role of serotonin in PTSD has not been systematically investigated, the facts that decreased CNS serotonin levels develop in inescapably shocked animals and that serotonin reuptake blockers are effective pharmacological agents in the treatment of PTSD justify a brief consideration of the potential role of this neurotransmitter in PTSD. Decreased serotonin in humans has been correlated repeatedly with impulsivity and aggression (Brown et al. 1979, Cocarro et al. 1989, Mann 1987). The authors of these investigations tend to assume that these relationships are based on genetic traits. However, studies of impulsive, aggressive, and suicidal patients (e.g., Green [1978], van der Kolk et al. [1991], and Lewis [1992]) seem to find at least as robust an association between those behaviors and histories of childhood trauma. Probably both temperament and experience affect relative serotonin levels in the CNS (van der Kolk 1987b).

Low serotonin levels in animals are also related to an inability to modulate arousal, as exemplified by an exaggerated startle response (Gerson et al. 1980, Jenike et al. 1990) and by increased arousal in reaction to novel stimuli, handling, or pain (Dupue and Spoont 1989). The behavioral effects of serotonin depletion in animals include hyperirritability, hyperexcitability, hypersensitivity, and an "exaggerated emotional arousal and or aggressive display to relatively mild stimuli" (Dupue and Spoont 1989). These behaviors bear a striking resemblance of the phenomenology of PTSD in humans. Furthermore, serotonin reuptake inhibitors have been found to be the most effective pharmacological treatment for obsessive thinking in subjects with obsessive-compulsive disorder (Jenike et al. 1990) and for involuntary preoccupation with traumatic memories in subjects with PTSD (van der Kolk et al., in press, van der Kolk and Saporta 1991). Serotonin probably plays a role in the capacity to monitor the environment flexibly and to respond with behaviors that are situation-appropriate, rather than reacting to internal stimuli that are irrelevant to current demands.

Endogenous Opioids

Stress-induced analgesia has been described in experimental animals after a variety of inescapable stressors such as electric shock, fighting, starvation, and cold water swim (Akil et al. 1983). In severely stressed animals opiate withdrawal symptoms can be produced either by termination of the stress or by naloxone injections. Motivated by the findings that fear activates the secretion of endogenous opioid peptides and that stress-induced analgesia can become conditioned to subsequent stressors and to previously neutral events associated with the noxious stimulus, we tested the hypothesis that in subjects with PTSD, reexposure to a stimulus resembling the original trauma will cause an endogenous opioid response that can be indirectly measured as naloxone-reversible analgesia (Pitman et al. 1990, van der Kolk et al. 1989). We found that two decades after the original trauma, opioid-mediated analgesia developed in subjects with PTSD in response to a stimulus resembling the traumatic stressor, which we correlated with a secretion of endogenous opioids equivalent to 8 mg of morphine. Self-reports of emotional responses suggested that endogenous opioids were responsible for a relative blunting of emotional response to the traumatic stimulus.

Endogenous Opioids and Stress-Induced Analgesia: Implications for Affective Function

When young animals are isolated or older ones are attacked, they respond initially with aggression (hyperarousal-fight-protest) and then, if that does not produce the required results, with withdrawal (numbing-fight-despair). Fear-induced attack or protest patterns serve in the young to attract protection and in mature animals to prevent or counteract the predator's activity. During external attacks, pain inhibition is a useful defensive capacity because attention to pain would interfere with effective defense; grooming or licking wounds may attract opponents and stimulate further attack (Siegfried et al. 1990). Thus defensive and pain-motivated behaviors are mutually inhibitory. Stress-induced analgesia protects organisms against feeling pain while engaged in defensive activities. As early as 1946, Beecher, after observing that 75 percent of severely wounded soldiers on the Italian front did not request morphine, speculated that "strong emotions can block pain." Today, we can reasonably assume that this is caused by the release of endogenous opioids (Pitman et al. 1990, van der Kolk et al. 1989).

Endogenous opioids, which inhibit pain and reduce panic, are secreted after prolonged exposure to severe stress. Siegfried and colleagues (1990) have observed that memory is impaired in animals when they can no longer actively influence the outcome of a threatening situation. They showed that both the freeze response and panic interfere with effective memory processing; excessive endogenous opioids and norepinephrine both interfere with the storage of experience in explicit memory. Freeze-numbing responses may serve the function of allowing organisms to not "consciously experience" or to not remember situations of overwhelming stress (thus also preventing their learning from experience). We have proposed that the dissociative reactions of subjects in response to trauma may be analogous to this complex of behaviors that occurs in animals after prolonged exposure to severe uncontrollable stress (van der Kolk et al. 1989).

DEVELOPMENTAL LEVEL AND THE PSYCHOBIOLOGICAL EFFECTS OF TRAUMA

Although most studies on PTSD have been done on adults, particularly war veterans, in recent years a few prospective investigations have documented the differential effects of trauma at various age levels. Anxiety disorders, chronic hyperarousal, and behavioral disturbances have been regularly described in traumatized children (e.g., Bowlby [1969], Cicchetti [1985], and Terr [1991]. In addition to the reactions to discrete, one-time, traumatic incidents documented in these studies, intrafamilial abuse is increasingly recognized to produce complex posttraumatic syndromes (Cole and Putnam 1991) that involve chronic affect dysregulation, destructive behavior against self and others, learning disabilities, dissociative problems, somatization, and distortions in concepts about self and others (Herman 1992, van der Kolk 1988). The field trials for *DSM-IV* showed that this conglomeration of symptoms tended to occur together and that the severity of the syndrome was proportional to the duration of the trauma and the age of the child when it began (van der Kolk et al. 1992).

Although current research on traumatized children is outside the scope of this chapter, it is important to recognize that a range of neurobiological abnormalities are beginning to be identified in this population. Frank Putnam's as-yet-unpublished prospective studies (personal communications, 1991, 1992, and 1993) are showing major neuroendocrine disturbances in sexually abused girls compared with nonabused girls. Research on the psychobiology of childhood trauma can be profitably informed by the vast literature on the psychobiological effects of trauma and deprivation in nonhuman primates (Reite and Fields 1985, van der Kolk 1987b).

TRAUMA AND MEMORY

The Flexibility of Memory and the Engraving of Trauma

A century ago, Janet (1889) suggested that the most fundamental of mental activities are the storage and categorization of incoming sensations into memory and the retrieval of those memories under appropriate circumstances. He, like contemporary memory researchers, understood that what is now called semantic, or declarative, memory is an active and constructive process and that remembering depends on existing mental schemata (Calvin 1990, van der Kolk and van der Hart 1991): once an event or a particular bit of information is integrated into existing mental schemes, it will no longer be accessible as a separate, immutable entity but will be distorted both by previous experience and by the emotional state at the time of recall (van der Kolk and van der Hart 1991). PTSD, by definition, is accompanied by memory disturbances that consist of both hypermnesias and amnesias (APA 1987, 1994). Research into the nature of traumatic memories (van der Kolk and van der Hart 1991) indicates that trauma interferes with declarative memory (i.e., conscious recall of experience) but does not inhibit implicit, or nondeclarative, memory, the memory system that controls conditioned emotional responses, skills and habits, and sensorimotor sensations related to experience (Figure 2–1). There is now enough information available about the biology of memory storage and retrieval to start building coherent hypotheses regarding the underlying psychobiological processes involved in these memory disturbances (Pitman and Orr 1990b, Pitman et al. 1987, 1993, van der Kolk and van der Hart 1991).

Early in this century Janet (1919/1925) noted that "certain

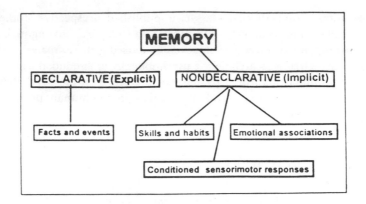

FIGURE 2-1.   Schematic representation of different forms of memory.

happenings . . . leave indelible and distressing memories — memories to which the sufferer continually returns, and by which he is tormented by day and by night." Clinicians and researchers dealing with traumatized patients have repeatedly observed that the sensory experiences and visual images related to the trauma seem not to fade over time and appear to be less subject to distortion than ordinary experiences (Janet 1889, Pitman and Orr 1990a, van der Kolk et al. 1984). When people are traumatized, they are said to experience "speechless terror"; the emotional impact of the event may interfere with the capacity to capture the experience in words or symbols. Piaget (1962) thought that under such circumstances, failure of semantic memory leads to the organization of memory on a somatosensory or iconic level (such as somatic sensations, behavioral enactments, nightmares, and flashbacks). He pointed out:

> It is precisely because there is no immediate accommodation that there is complete dissociation of the inner activity from the external world. As the external world is solely represented by images, it is assimilated without resistance [i.e., unattached to other memories] to the unconscious ego.

The State Dependency of Traumatic Memories

Research has shown that under ordinary conditions many traumatized people, including rape victims (Kilpatrick et al. 1985), battered women (Hilberman and Munson 1978), and abused children (Green 1980) have a fairly good psychosocial adjustment. However, they do not respond to stress in the way that other people do. Under pressure they may feel or act as if they were being traumatized all over again. Thus high states of arousal seem selectively to promote retrieval of traumatic memories, sensory information, or behaviors associated with previous traumatic experiences (APA 1987, 1994). The tendency of traumatized organisms to revert to irrelevant emergency behaviors in response to minor stress has been well documented in animals, as well. Studies at the Wisconsin Primate Laboratory have shown that rhesus monkeys with histories of severe early maternal deprivation display marked withdrawal or aggression in response to emotional or physical stimuli (such as exposure to loud noises or the administration of amphetamines), even after a long period of good social adjustment (Kraemer 1985). In experiments with mice, Mitchell and coworkers (1985) found that the relative degree of arousal interacts with previous exposure to high stress to determine how an animal will react to novel stimuli. In a state of low arousal, animals tend to be curious and seek novelty. During high arousal, they are frightened, avoid novelty, and perseverate in familiar behavior, regardless of the outcome. Under ordinary circumstances, an animal will choose the more pleasant of two alternatives. When hyperaroused, it will seek whatever is familiar, regardless of the intrinsic rewards. Thus animals that have been locked in a box in which they were exposed to electric shocks and then released return to those boxes when they are subsequently stressed. Mitchell and colleagues concluded that this perseveration is nonassociative (i.e., uncoupled from the usual reward systems).

Analogous phenomena have been documented in humans; memories (somatic or symbolic) related to the trauma are elicited by heightened arousal (Solomon et al. 1985). Information acquired in an aroused or otherwise altered state of mind is retrieved more readily when subjects are brought back to that particular state of mind (Phillips and LePiane 1980, Rawlins 1980). State-dependent memory retrieval may also be involved in dissociative phenomena in which traumatized persons may be wholly or partially amnestic for memories or behaviors enacted while in altered states of mind (Putnam 1989, van der Kolk and van der Hart 1989, 1991).

Contemporary biological researchers have shown that medications that stimulate autonomic arousal may precipitate visual images and affect states associated with previous traumatic experiences in people with PTSD but not in control subjects. In patients with PTSD, the injection of drugs such as lactate (Charney et al. 1993) and yohimbine (Southwick et al. 1993) tends to precipitate panic attacks, flashbacks (exact reliving experiences) of earlier trauma, or both. In our own laboratory approximately 20 percent of PTSD subjects responded with a flashback of a traumatic experience when they were presented with acoustic startle stimuli.

Trauma, Neurohormones, and Memory Consolidation

When humans are under severe stress, they secrete endogenous stress hormones that affect the strength of memory consolidation. Based on animal models, researchers have widely assumed that massive secretion of neurohormones at the time of the trauma plays a role in the long-term potentiation (and thus, the overconsolidation) of traumatic memories (Charney et al. 1993, van der Kolk et al. 1985, van der Kolk and van der Hart 1991). Mammals seem to be equipped with memory-storage mechanisms that ordinarily modulate the strength of memory consolidation according to the strength of the accompanying hormonal stimulation (McGaugh 1989; McGaugh et al. 1985). This capacity helps the organism to evaluate the importance of subsequent sensory input according to the relative strength of associated memory traces. The phenomenon appears to be largely mediated by input of norepinephrine to the amygdala (Adamec 1978, LeDoux 1990) (Figure 2-2). In traumatized organisms the capacity to access relevant memories appears to have gone awry; they become overconditioned to access memory traces of the trauma and to "remember" the trauma whenever aroused. Although norepinephrine seems to be the principal hormone involved in producing long-term potentiation, other neurohormones secreted under particular stressful circumstances (endorphins and oxytocin, for example) actually inhibit memory consolidation (Zager and Black 1985).

The role of norepinephrine in consolidating memory has been shown to have an inverted U-shaped function (McGaugh 1989, McGaugh et al. 1985): both very low and very high levels of norepinephrine activity in the CNS interfere with memory storage. The release of excessive norepinephrine, as well as of other neuro-

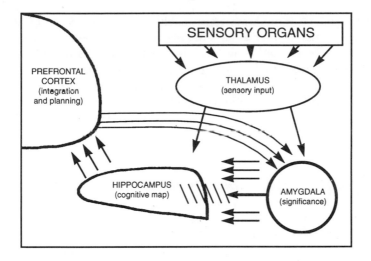

FIGURE 2-2. Schematic representation of the effects of emotional arousal on declarative memory. The thalamus, amygdala, and hippocampus are all involved in the integration and interpretation of incoming sensory information. Moderate to high activation of the amygdala enhances the long-term potentiation of declarative memory that is mediated by the hippocampus, accounting for hypermnesias for stressful experiences. Excessive stimulation of the amygdala interferes with hippocampal functioning, inhibiting cognitive evaluation of experience and semantic representations. Memories are then stored in sensorimotor modalities: somatic sensations and visual images. These emotional memories are thought to be relatively indelible, but their expression can be modified by feedback from the prefrontal cortex (Adamec 1978, LeDoux et al. 1991, McGaugh et al. 1985, Pitman et al. 1993, van der Kolk and van der Hart 1991).

hormones such as endogenous opioids, oxytocin, and vasopressin, at the time of the trauma probably plays a role in creating the hypermnesias and amnesias that are a quintessential part of PTSD (APA 1987, 1994). Interestingly, childbirth, which can be extraordinarily stressful, almost never seems to result in posttraumatic problems (Moleman et al. 1992). Oxytocin may protect against the overconsolidation of memories surrounding childbirth.

Physiological arousal in general can trigger trauma-related memories; conversely, trauma-related memories precipitate generalized physiological arousal. The frequent reliving of a traumatic event in flashbacks or nightmares probably causes a rerelease of stress hormones that further kindles the strength of the memory trace (van der Kolk et al. 1985). Such a positive feedback loop could cause subclinical PTSD to escalate into clinical PTSD (Pitman et al. 1993), in which the strength of the memories appears to be so deeply engraved that Pitman and Orr (1990b) have called it "the black hole" in the mental life of the PTSD patient; it attracts all associations to it and saps current life of its significance.

MEMORY, TRAUMA, AND THE LIMBIC SYSTEM

The limbic system is thought to be the part of the CNS that maintains and guides the emotions and behavior necessary for self-preservation and for survival of the species (MacLean 1985) and is critically involved in the storage and retrieval of memory. During both waking and sleeping states, signals from the sensory organs continuously travel to the thalamus, from which they are distributed to the cortex (setting up a "stream of thought"), the basal ganglia (setting up a "stream of movement"), and the limbic system (setting up a "stream of emotions" (Papez 1937) that determines the emotional significance of the sensory input). Most processing of sensory input occurs outside of conscious awareness, with only novel, significant, or threatening information being selectively passed on to the neocortex for further attention. Because subjects with PTSD appear to overinterpret sensory input as a recurrence of past trauma and because recent studies have suggested limbic-system abnormalities in brain-imaging studies of traumatized patients (Bremner et al. 1992, Saxe et al. 1992), a review of the psychobiology of trauma would be incomplete without considering the role of the limbic system in PTSD (see also Teicher et al., in press). Two particular areas of the limbic system have been implicated in the processing of emotionally charged memories: the amygdala and the hippocampus (Table 2-2).

The Amygdala

Of all areas in the CNS, the amygdala is most clearly implicated in the evaluation of the emotional meaning of incoming stimuli (LeDoux 1986). Several investigators have proposed that the amygdala

TABLE 2-2
Functions of Limbic Structures and Effects of Lesions

Hippocampus	Amygdala
Functions of limbic structures	
Categorization of experience	Conditioning of fear responses
Creation of a spatial map	Attachment of affect to neutral stimuli
Storage of simple memory	Establishment of associations between
	sensory. modalities
Creation of summary sketch/index	
Effects of lesions	
Declarative memory lost	Loss of fear responses
Skill-based memory spared	Meaningful social interaction lost
Immediate memory spared	Declarative memory intact

assigns free-floating feelings of significance to sensory input, which the neocortex then further elaborates and imbues with personal meaning (Adamec 1991, 1986, MacLean 1985, O'Keefe and Bouma 1969). Moreover, it is thought to integrate internal representations of the external world in the form of memory images with emotional experiences associated with those memories (Calvin 1990). After assigning meaning to sensory information, the amygdala guides emotional behavior by projections to the hypothalamus, hippocampus, and basal forebrain (Adamec 1991, LeDoux 1986, Squire and Zola-Morgan 1991).

The Septohippocampal System

The septohippocampal system, which is adjacent to the amygdala, is thought to record in memory the spatial and temporal dimensions of experience and to play an important role in the categorization and storage of incoming stimuli in memory. Proper functioning of the hippocampus is necessary for explicit or declarative memory (Squire and Zola-Morgan 1991). The hippocampus is believed to be involved in the evaluation of spatially and temporally unrelated events, comparing them with previously stored information and determining whether and how they are associated with each other and with reward, punishment, novelty, or nonreward (Adamec 1991, Gray 1982). The hippocampus also plays a role in the inhibition of exploratory behavior and in obsessional thinking. Damage to the hippocampus is associated with hyperresponsiveness to environmental stimuli (Altman et al. 1973, O'Keefe and Nadel 1978).

The slow maturation of the hippocampus, which is not fully myelinated until after the third or fourth year of life, is believed to be the cause of infantile amnesia (Jacobs and Nadel 1985, Schachter and Moscovitch 1984). In contrast, the memory system that encodes the affective quality of experience (roughly speaking, procedural, or "taxon," memory) matures earlier and is less subject to disruption by primarily sensorimotor (motoric action) and perceptual representations (iconic) to symbolic and linguistic organization of mental experiences (Piaget 1962). With maturation, there is an increasing ability to categorize experience and link it with existing mental schemes. However, even as the organism matures, this capacity, and with it the hippocampal localization system, remains vulnerable to disruption (Adamec 1991, Gray 1982, Nadel and Zola-Morgan 1984, Sapolsky et al. 1990, Yehuda, Giller, et al. 1991). Various external and internal stimuli, including stress-induced corticosterone production (Pfaff et al. 1971), decrease hippocampal activity. However, even when stress interferes with hippocampally mediated memory storage and categorization, some mental representation of the experience is probably laid down by means of a system that records affective experience but has no capacity for symbolic processing or placement in space and time (Figure 2).

Decreased hippocampal functioning causes behavioral disinhibition, possibly by causing incoming stimuli to be interpreted in the direction of "emergency" (fight-or-flight) responses. The neurotransmitter serotonin plays a crucial role in the capacity of the septohippocampal system to activate inhibitory pathways that prevent the initiation of emergency responses until it is clear that they will be of use (Gray 1982). This observation made us very interested in a possible role for serotonergic agents in the treatment of PTSD.

"Emotional Memories are Forever"

In animals high-level stimulation of the amygdala interferes with hippocampal functioning (Adamec 1991, Squire and Zola-Morgan 1991). This implies that intense affect may inhibit proper evaluation and categorization of experience. One-time intense stimulation of the amygdala in mature animals will produce lasting changes in neuronal excitability and enduring behavioral changes in the direction of either fight or flight (LeDoux et al. 1991). In kindling experiments with animals, Adamec and colleagues (1988) showed that, after growth in amplitude of amygdaloid and hippocampal seizure activity, permanent alterations in limbic physiology cause lasting changes in defensiveness and predatory aggression. Preexisting "personality" played a significant role in the behavioral effects of stimulation of the amygdala in cats: animals that are temperamentally insensitive to threat and prone to attack tend to become more aggressive, whereas defensive animals show increased behavioral inhibition (Adamec et al. 1980).

In a series of experiments, LeDoux and coworkers (1991) used repeated electrical stimulation of the amygdala to produce conditioned fear responses. They found that cortical lesions prevent their extinction. This led them to conclude that, once formed, the subcortical traces of the conditioned fear response are indelible, and that "emotional memory may be forever." In 1987 Kolb postulated that patients with PTSD suffer from impaired cortical control over the subcortical areas responsible for learning, habituation, and stimulus discrimination. The concept of indelible subcortical emotional responses, held in check to varying degrees by cortical and septohippocampal activity, has led to the speculation that delayed-onset PTSD may be the expression of subcortically mediated emotional responses that escape cortical, and possibly hippocampal, inhibitory control (Charney et al. 1993, Nijenhuis 1991, Pitman et al. 1993, Shalev et al. 1992, van der Kolk and van der Hart 1991).

Decreased inhibitory control may occur under a variety of circumstances: under the influence of drugs and alcohol, during sleep (as in nightmares), with aging, and after exposure to strong reminders of the traumatic past. Conceivably, traumatic memories then could emerge, not in the distorted fashion of ordinary recall but as affect states, somatic sensations, or visual images, for example, nightmares (Janet 1919/1925) or flashbacks (Southwick et al. 1993) that are timeless and unmodified by further experience.

PSYCHOPHARMACOLOGICAL TREATMENT

The goal of treating PTSD is to help people live in the present, without feeling or behaving according to irrelevant demands belonging to the past. Psychologically, this means that traumatic experiences need to be located in time and place and differentiated from current reality. However, hyperarousal, intrusive reliving, numbing, and dissociation get in the way of separating current reality from past trauma. Hence, medications that affect these PTSD symptoms are often essential for patients to begin to achieve a sense of safety and perspective from which to approach their tasks.

Although numerous articles have been written about the drug treatment of PTSD, to date only 134 people with PTSD have been enrolled in published double-blind studies. Most of these have been Vietnam combat veterans. Unfortunately, until recently only medications that seem to be of limited therapeutic usefulness have been subjected to adequate scientific scrutiny. Because the only published double-blind studies of medications for treating PTSD have involved tricyclic antidepressants and monoamine oxidase (MAO) inhibitors (Bleich et al. 1987, Davidson and Nemeroff 1989; Frank et al. 1988), it is sometimes assumed that these agents are the most effective. Three double-blind trials of tricyclic antidepressants have been published (Davidson et al. 1989, Davidson and Nemeroff 1989, Frank et al. 1988, Reist et al. 1989); two showed modest improvement in PTSD symptoms. Although positive results have been claimed for numerous other medications in case reports and open studies, at the present time there are no data about which patient and which PTSD symptom will predictably respond to any of them. Success has been claimed for just about every class of psychoactive medication, including benzodiazepines (van der Kolk, 1987a), tricyclic antidepressants (Falcon et al. 1985, Frank et al. 1988, Reist et al. 1989), MAO inhibitors (Frank et al. 1988, Hogben and Cornfield 1981), lithium carbonate (van der Kolk 1987a), β-adrenergic blockers (Kolb et al. 1984), clonidine (Kolb et al. 1984), carbamazepine (Falcon et al. 1985, Frank et al. 1988; Reist et al. 1989), and antipsychotic agents. The accumulated clinical experience seems to indicate that understanding the basic neurobiology of arousal and appraisal is the most useful guide in selecting medications for people with PTSD (Davidson and Nemeroff 1989, Reist et al. 1989). Autonomic arousal can be reduced at different levels in the CNS: through inhibiting noradrenergic activity in the locus ceruleus with clonidine and the β-adrenergic blockers (Famularo et al. 1988, Kolb et al. 1984), or by increasing the inhibitory effect of the γ-

aminobutyric acid (GABA)-ergic system with GABA-ergic agonists (the benzodiazepines).

During the past two years several case reports and open clinical trials of fluoxetine have been published, followed by our double-blind study of sixty-four PTSD subjects treated with fluoxetine (van der Kolk et al., in press). Unlike the tricyclic antidepressants, which were effective on either the intrusive (imipramine) or numbing (amitriptyline) symptoms of PTSD, fluoxetine proved to be effective for the entire spectrum of PTSD symptoms. It also acted more rapidly than the tricyclics. The fact that fluoxetine has proved to be such an effective treatment for PTSD supports a larger role for the serotonergic system in PTSD (van der Kolk and Saporta 1991). Rorschach tests administered by "blinded" scorers revealed that subjects taking fluoxetine became able to achieve distance from the emotional impact of incoming stimuli and to use cognition in harnessing emotional responses to unstructured visual stimuli (van der Kolk et al., unpublished data, 1991–1992).

Although the subjects improved clinically, their startle habituation worsened (van der Kolk et al., unpublished data, 1991–1992). The 5-HT$_{1A}$ agonist buspirone shows some promise in facilitating habituation (Giral et al. 1988) and thus may play a useful adjunctive role in the pharmacotherapy of PTSD. Even newer research has suggested abnormalities of the N-methyl-D-aspartate receptor and of glutamate in PTSD (Krystal 1993), opening up potential new avenues for the psychopharmacological treatment of this disorder.

ACKNOWLEDGMENT

The author wishes to thank Rita Fisler, EdM, for her editorial assistance.

REFERENCES

Adamec, R. E. (1978). Normal and abnormal limbic system mechanisms of emoting biasing. In *Limbic Mechanisms,* ed. K. E. Livingston and O. Hornykiewicz. New York: Plenum.

———— (1991). Partial kindling of the ventral hippocampus: identification of changes in limbic physiology which accompany changes in feline aggression and defense. *Physiology and Behavior* 49:443-454.

Adamec, R. E., Stark-Adamec, C., and Livingston, K. E. (1980). The development of predatory aggression and defense in the domestic cat. *Neural Biology* 30:389-447.

Akil, H., Watson, S. J., and Young, E. (1983). Endogenous opioids: biology and function. *Annual Review of Neuroscience* 7:223-255.

Altman, J., Brunner, R. L., and Bayer, S. A. (1973). The hippocampus and behavioral maturation. *Behavioral Biology* 8:557-596.

American Psychiatric Association. (1987). *Diagnostic and Statistical Manual of Mental Disorders*, 3rd ed., rev. Washington, DC: APA.

———— (1994). *Diagnostic and Statistical Manual of Mental Disorders*, 4th ed. Washington, DC: APA.

Axelrod, J., and Reisine, T. D. (1984). Stress hormones, their interaction and regulation. *Science* 224:452-459.

Beecher, H. K. (1946). Pain in men wounded in battle. *Annals of Surgery* 123:96-105.

Blanchard, E. B., Kolb, L. C., and Gerardi, R. J. (1986). Cardiac response to relevant stimuli as an adjunctive tool for diagnosing posttraumatic stress disorder in Vietnam veterans. *Behavioral Therapy* 17:592-606.

Bleich, A., Siegel, B., Garb, B., et al. (1987). PTSD following combat exposure: clinical features and pharmacological management. *British Journal of Psychiatry* 149:365-369.

Bohus, B., and DeWied, D. (1978). Pituitary-adrenal system hormones and adaptive behavior. In *General, Comparative, and Clinical Endocrinology of the Adrenal Cortex*, vol. 3, ed. I. Chester-Jones and I. W. Henderson. New York: Academic Press.

Bowlby, J. (1969). *Attachment and Loss*, vol. 1. New York: Basic Books.

Bremner, J. D., Seibyl, J. P., and Scott, T. M. (1992). *Depressed hippocampal volume in posttraumatic stress disorder* (New Research Abstract 155). Proceedings of the 145th Annual Meeting of the American Psychiatric Association, Washington, DC, May.

Brown, G. L., Ballenger, J. C., Minichiello, M. D., and Goodwin, F. K. (1979). Human aggression and its relationship to cerebrospinal fluid 5-hydroxy-indolacetic acid, 3-methoxy-4-hydroxy-phenyl-glycol, and homovannilic acid. In *Psychopharmacology of Aggression*, ed. M. Sandler. New York: Raven.

Butler, R. W., Braff, D. L., Rausch, J. L., et al. (1990). Physiological evidence of exaggerated startle response in a subgroup of Vietnam veterans with combat-related PTSD. *American Journal of Psychiatry* 147:1308-1312.

Calvin, W. H. (1990). *The Cerebral Symphony*. New York: Bantam.

Charney, D. S,. Deutch, A. Y., Krystal, J. H., et al. (1993). Psychobiologic mechanisms of posttraumatic stress disorder. *Archives of General Psychiatry* 50:294–305.

Cicchetti, D. (1985). The emergence of developmental psychopathology. *Child Development* 55:1–7.

Coccaro, E. F., Siever, L. J., Klar, H. M., and Maurer, G. (1989). Serotonergic studies in patients with affective and personality disorders. *Archives of General Psychiatry* 46:587–598.

Cole, P. M., and Putnam, F. W. (1991). Effect of incest on self and social functioning: a developmental psychopathology perspective. *Journal of Consulting and Clinical Psychology* 60:174–184.

Davidson, J., Kudler, H., and Smith, R. (1990). Treatment of posttraumatic stress disorder with amitriptyline and placebo. *Archives of General Psychiatry* 47:259–266.

Davidson, J. R. T., and Nemeroff, C. B. (1989). Pharmacotherapy in PTSD: historical and clinical considerations and future directions. *Psychopharmacology Bulletin* 25:422–425.

Davis, M. (1984). The mammalian startle response. In *Neural Mechanisms of Startle Behavior,* ed. R. C. Eaton. New York: Plenum.

―――― (1986). Pharmacological and anatomical analysis of fear conditioning using the fear-potentiated startle paradigm. *Behavioral Neuroscience* 100:814–824.

Dobbs, D., and Wilson, W. P. (1960). Observations of the persistence of traumatic war neurosis. *Journal of Nervous and Mental Disease* 21:40–46.

Dunn, A. J., and Berridge, C. W. (1987). Corticotropin-releasing factor administration elicits stresslike activation of cerebral catecholamine systems. *Pharmacology, Biochemistry, and Behavior* 27:685–691.

Dupue, R. A., and Spoont, M. R. (1989). Conceptualizing a serotonin trait: a behavioral model of constraint. *Annals of the New York Academy of Sciences* 12:47–62.

Falcon, S., Ryan, C., and Chamberlain, K. (1985). Tricyclics: possible treatment for posttraumatic stress disorder. *Journal of Clinical Psychiatry* 46:385–389.

Famularo, R., Kinscherff, R., and Fenton, T. (1988). Propranolol treatment for childhood posttraumatic stress disorder, acute type: a pilot study. *American Journal of Diseases of Children* 142:1244–1247.

Frank, J. B., Kosten, T. R., Giller, E. L., and Dan, E. (1988). A randomized clinical trial of phenelzine and imipramine in PTSD. *American Journal of Psychiatry* 145:1289–1291.

Freud, S. (1919). Introduction to psychoanalysis and the war neuroses. *Standard Edition* 17:207–210.

Gerson, S. C., and Baldessarini, R. J. (1980). Motor effects of serotonin in the central nervous system. *Life Sciences* 27:1435–1451.

Giral, P., Martin, P., and Soubrie, P. (1988). Reversal of helpless behavior in rats by putative 5-HT$_{1A}$ agonists. *Biological Psychiatry* 23:237–242.

Gray, J. (1982). *The Neuropsychology of Anxiety. An Inquiry into the Functions of the Septo-hippocampal System.* London: Oxford University Press.

Green, A. H. (1978). Self-destructive behavior in battered children. *American Journal of Psychiatry* 135:579–582.

_____ (1980). *Child Maltreatment.* New York: Jason Aronson.

Grinker, R. R., and Spiegel, J. J. (1945). *Men Under Stress.* New York: McGraw-Hill.

Herman, J. L. (1992). Complex PTSD: a syndrome in survivors of prolonged and repeated trauma. *Journal of Trauma and Stress* 5:377–391.

Hilberman, E., and Munson, M. (1978). Sixty battered women. *Victimology* 2:460–461.

Hogben, G. L., and Cornfield, R. B. (1981). Treatment of traumatic war neurosis with phenelzine. *Archives of General Psychiatry* 38:440–445.

Horowitz, M. (1978). *Stress Response Syndromes,* 2nd ed. New York: Jason Aronson.

Jacobs, W. J., and Nadel, L. (1985). Stress-induced recovery of fears and phobias. *Psychological Review* 92:512–531.

Janet, P. (1889). *L'automatisme Psychologique.* Paris: Alcan.

_____ (1919/1925). *Les Medications Psychologiques.* Paris: Alcan.

Janike, M. A., Baer, L., Summergrad, P., et al. (1990). Sertroline in obsessive-compulsive disorder: a double-blind study. *American Journal of Psychiatry* 147:923–928.

Kardiner, A. (1941). *The Traumatic Neuroses of War.* New York: Hoeber.

Keane, T. M., and Kalpoupek, D. G. (1982). Imaginal flooding in the treatment of posttraumatic stress disorder. *Journal of Consulting and Clinical Psychology* 50:138–140.

Kilpatrick, D. G., Veronen, L. J., and Best, C. L. (1985). Factors predicting psychological distress in rape victims. In *Trauma and its Wake,* ed. C. Figley. New York: Brunner/Mazel.

Kolb, L. C., Burris, B. C., and Griffiths, S. (1984). Propranolol and clonidine in the treatment of posttraumatic stress disorder of war. In *Posttraumatic Stress Disorder: Psychological and Biological Sequelae,* ed. B. A. van der Kolk. Washington, DC: American Psychiatric Press.

Kolb, L. C., and Multipassi, L. R. (1982). The conditioned emotional response: a subclass of chronic and delayed posttraumatic stress disorder. *Psychiatric Annual* 12:979–987.

Kosten, T. R., Mason, J. W., Giller, E. L., et al. (1987). Sustained urinary norepinephrine and epinephrine elevation in PTSD. *Psychoneuroendocrinology* 12:13–20.

Kraemer, G. W. (1985). Effects of differences in early social experiences on primate neurobiological-behavioral development. In *The Psychobiology of Attachment and Separation,* ed. M. Reite, and T. Fields. Orlando, FL: Academic Press.

Krystal, H. (1978). Trauma and affects. *Psychoanalytic Study of the Child* 33:81–116. New Haven, CT: Yale University Press.

—— (1993). *Neurobiological mechanisms of dissociation.* Paper presented at the American Psychiatric Association meeting, San Francisco, May.

Krystal, J. H., Kosten, T. R., Southwick, S., et al. (1989). Neurobiological aspects of PTSD: review of clinical and preclinical studies. *Behavioral Therapy* 20:177–198.

Kulka, R. A., Schlenger, W. E., Fairbank, J. A., et al. (1990). *Trauma and the Vietnam War Generation: Report of Findings from the National Vietnam Veterans' Readjustment Study.* New York: Brunner/Mazel.

Lang, P. J. (1979). A bio-informational theory of emotional imagery. *Psychophysiology* 16:495–512.

LeDoux, J. (1986). *Mind and Brain: Dialogues in Cognitive Neuroscience.* New York: Cambridge University Press.

—— (1990). Information flow from sensation to emotion: plasticity of the neural computation of stimulus value. In *Learning Computational Neuroscience: Foundations of Adaptive Networks,* ed. M. Gabriel, and J. Morre. Cambridge, MA: MIT Press.

LeDoux, J. E., Romanski, L., and Xagoraris, A. (1991). Indelibility of subcortical emotional memories. *Journal of Cognitive Neuroscience* 1:238–243.

Lerer, B., Bleich, A., and Kotler, M. (1987). Posttraumatic stress disorder in Israeli combat veterans: effect of phenylzine treatment. *Archives of General Psychiatry* 44:976–981.

Lewis, D. O. (1992). From abuse to violence: psychophysiological consequences of maltreatment. *Journal of the American Academy of Child and Adolescent Psychiatry* 31:383–391.

Lindemann, E. (1944). Symptomatology and management of acute grief. *American Journal of Psychiatry* 101:141–148.

Lipper, S., Davidson, J. R. T., and Grady, T. A., et al. (1986). Preliminary study of carbamazepine in posttraumatic stress disorder. *Psychosomatics* 27:849–854.

Litz, B. T., and Keane, T. M. (1989). Information processing in anxiety disorders: application to the understanding of posttraumatic stress disorder. *Clinical Psychology Review* 9:243–257.

MacLean, P. D. (1985). Brain evolution relating to family, play, and separation call. *Archives of General Psychiatry* 42:405–417.

Malloy, P. F., Fairbank, J. A., and Keane, T. M. (1983). Validation of a multimethod assessment of posttraumatic stress disorders in Vietnam veterans. *Journal of Consulting and Clinical Psychology* 51:4–21.

Mann, J. D. (1987). Psychobiologic predictors of suicide. *Journal of Clinical Psychiatry* 48:39-43.

Mason, J., Giller, E. L., and Kosten, T. R. (1988). Elevated norepinephrine/ cortisol ratio in PTSD. *Journal of Nervous and Mental Disorders* 176:498-502.

McFarlane, A. C. (1988). The longitudinal course of posttraumatic morbidity: the range of outcomes and their predictors. *Journal of Nervous and Mental Diseases* 176:30-39.

McGaugh, J. L. (1989). Involvement of hormonal and neuromodulatory systems in the regulation of memory storage. *Annual Review of Neuroscience* 2:255-287.

McGaugh, J. L., Weinberger, N. M., Lynch, G., and Granger, R. H. (1985). Neural mechanisms of learning and memory: cells, systems, and computations. *Naval Research Review* 37:15-29.

Meaney, M. J., Aitken, D. H., Viau, V., et al. (1989). Neonatal handling alters adrenocortical negative feedback sensitivity and hippocampal type II glucocorticoid binding in the rat. *Neuroendocrinology* 50:597-604.

Mitchell, D., Osborne, E. W., and O'Boyle, M. W. (1985). Habituation under stress: shocked mice show non-associative learning in a T-maze. *Behavioral Neurology and Biology* 43:212-217.

Moleman, N., van der Hart, O., and van der Kolk, B. A. (1992). The partus stress reaction: a neglected etiological factor in postpartum psychiatric disorders. *Journal of Nervous and Mental Diseases* 180:271-272.

Munck, A., Guyre, P. M., and Holbrook, N. J. (1984). Physiological functions of glucocorticoids in stress and their relation to pharmacological actions. *Endocrine Review* 93:9779-9783.

Nadel, L., and Zola-Morgan, S. (1984). Infantile amnesia: a neurobiological perspective. In *Infant Memory,* ed. M. Moscovitch. New York: Plenum.

Nijenhuis, F. (1991). *Multiple personality disorder, hormones, and memory.* Paper presented at the International Conference of Multiple Personality Disorder, Chicago, November 5.

O'Keefe, J., and Bouma, H. (1969). Complex sensory properties of certain amygdala units in the freely moving cat. *Experimental Neurology* 23:384-398.

O'Keefe, J., and Nadel, L. (1978). *The Hippocampus as a Cognitive Map.* Oxford: Clarendon.

Ornitz, E. M., and Pynoos, R. S. (1989). Startle modulation in children with posttraumatic stress disorder. *American Journal of Psychiatry* 146:866-870.

Papez, J. W. (1937). A proposed mechanism of emotion. *Archives of Neurology and Psychiatry* 38:725-743.

Pavlov, I. P. (1926). *Conditioned Reflexes: An Investigation of the Physiological Activity of the Cerebral Cortex,* trans. G. V. Anrep. New York: Dover.

Perry, B. D., Giller, E. L., and Southwick, S. M. (1987). Altered plasma alpha-2 adrenergic receptor affinity states in PTSD. *American Journal of Psychiatry* 144:1511-1512.

Pfaff, D. W., Silva, M. T., and Weiss, J. M. (1971). Telemetered recording of hormone effects on hippocampal neurons. *Science* 172:394-395.

Phillips, A. G., and LePiane, F. G. (1980). Disruption of conditioned taste aversion in the rat by stimulation of amygdala: a conditioning effect, not amnesia. *Journal of Comparative Physiology and Psychology* 94:664-674.

Piaget, J. (1962). *Plays, Dreams, and Imitation in Childhood.* New York: Norton.

Pitman, R. K., and Orr, S. P. (1990a). Twenty-four hour urinary cortisol and catecholamine excretion in combat-related posttraumatic stress disorder. *Biological Psychiatry* 27:245-247.

———— (1990b). The black hole of trauma. *Biological Psychiatry* 26:221-223.

Pitman, R. K., Orr, S. P., Forgue, D. F., et al. (1987). Psychophysiologic assessment of posttraumatic stress disorder imagery in Vietnam combat veterans. *Archives of General Psychiatry* 44:970-975.

Pitman, R. K., Orr, S. P., and Shalev, A. (1993). Once bitten twice shy: beyond the conditioning model of PTSD. *Biological Psychiatry* 33:145-146.

Pitman, R. K., van der Kolk, B. A., Orr, S. P., and Greenberg, M. S. (1990). Naloxone reversible stress induced analgesia in posttraumatic stress disorder. *Archives of General Psychiatry* 47:541-547.

Putnam, F. W. (1989). *Diagnosis and Treatment of Multiple Personality Disorder.* New York: Guilford.

Rainey, J. M., Aleem, A., Ortiz, A., et al. (1987). Laboratory procedure for the inducement of flashbacks. *American Journal of Psychiatry* 144:1317-1319.

Rawlins, J. N. P. (1980). Associative and non-associative mechanisms in the development of tolerance for stress: the problem of state dependent learning. In *Coping and Health,* ed. S. Levine, and H. Ursin. New York: Plenum.

Reist, C., Kauffman, C. D., and Haier, R. J. (1989). A controlled trial of desipramine in 18 men with posttraumatic stress disorder. *American Journal of Psychiatry* 146:513-516.

Reite, M., and Field, T., eds. (1985). The Psychobiology of Attachment and Separation. Orlando, FL: Academic Press.

Ross, R. J., Ball, W. A., and Cohen, M. E. (1989). Habituation of the startle response in posttraumatic stress disorder. *Journal of Neuropsychiatry* 1:305-307.

Sapolsky, R. M., Hideo, U., Rebert, C. S., and Finch, C. E. (1990). Hippocampal damage associated with prolonged glucocorticoid exposure in primates. *Journal of Neuroscience* 10:2897-2902.

Sapolsky, R. M., Krey, L., McEwen, B. S. (1984). Stress down-regulates corticosterone receptors in a site specific manner in the brain. *Endocrinology* 114:287-292.

Saxe, G. N., Vasile, R. G., Hill, T. C., et al. (1992). SPECT imaging and multiple personality disorder. *Journal of Nervous and Mental Diseases* 180:662-663.

Schachter, D. L., and Moscovitch, M. (1984). Infants, amnesics, and dissociable memory systems. In *Infant Memory*, ed. M. Moscovitch. New York: Plenum.

Shalev, A. Y., Orr, S. P., Peri, T., et al. (1992). Physiological responses to loud tones in Israeli patients with posttraumatic stress disorder. *Archives of General Psychiatry* 49:870-875.

Shalev, A. Y., and Rogel-Fuchs, Y. (In press). Psychophysiology of PTSD: from sulfur fumes to behavioral genetics. *Journal of Nervous and Mental Diseases*.

Shalev, A., Rogel-Fuchs, Y., and Pitman, R. (1992). Conditioned fear and psychological trauma. *Biological Psychiatry* 31:863-865.

Siegfried, B., Frischknecht, H. R., Nunez de Souza, R. (1990). An ethnological model for the study of activation and interaction of pain, memory, and defensive systems in the attacked mouse: role of endogenous opioids. *Neuroscience and Biobehavioral Reviews* 14:481-490.

Solomon, Z., Garb, R., Bleich, A., and Grupper, D. (1985). Reactivation of combat-related posttraumatic stress disorder. *American Journal of Psychiatry* 144:51-55.

Southwick, S. M., Krystal, J. H., Morgan, A., et al. (1993). Abnormal noradrenergic function in posttraumatic stress disorder. *Archives of General Psychiatry* 50:266-274.

Squire, L. R., and Zola-Morgan, S. (1991). The medial temporal lobe memory system. *Science* 253:2380-2386.

Strian, F., and Klicpera, C. (1978). Die Bedeutung psychoautonomische Reaktionen im Entstehung und Persistenz von Angstzustanded. *Nervenarzt* 49:576-583.

Teicher, M. H., Glod, C. A., Surrey, J., and Swett, C. (In press). Early childhood abuse and limbic system ratings in adult psychiatric outpatients. *Journal of Neuropsychiatry and Clinical Neuroscience*.

Terr, L. C. (1991). Childhood traumas: an outline and overview. *American Journal of Psychiatry* 148:10-20.

Valentino, R. J., and Foote, S. L. (1988). Corticotropin releasing hormone increases tonic, but not sensory-evoked activity of noradrenergic locus coeruleus in unanesthetized rats. *Journal of Neuroscience* 8:1016-1025.

van der Kolk, B. A. (1987a). Drug treatment of posttraumatic stress disorder. *Journal of Affective Disorders* 13:203-213.

———— (1987b). *Psychological Trauma.* Washington, DC: American Psychiatric Press.

———— (1988). The trauma spectrum: the interaction of biological and social events in the genesis of the trauma response. *Journal of Trauma and Stress* 1:273-290.

van der Kolk, B. A., Blitz, R., Burr, W., and Hartmann, E. (1984). Nightmares and trauma. *American Journal of Psychiatry* 141:187-190.

van der Kolk, B. A., Dreyfuss, D., Michaels, M., et al. (In press). *Fluoxetine in posttraumatic stress disorder. Journal of Clinical Psychiatry.*

van der Kolk, B. A., and Ducey, C. P. (1989). The psychological processing of traumatic experience: Rorschach patterns in PTSD. *Journal of Trauma and Stress* 2:259-274.

van der Kolk, B. A., Greenberg, M. S., Boyd, H., and Krystal, J. H. (1985). Inescapable shock, neurotransmitters and addiction to trauma: towards a psychobiology of posttraumatic stress. *Biological Psychiatry* 20:314-315.

van der Kolk, B. A., Greenberg, M. S., Orr, S., and Pitman, R. K. (1989). Endogenous opioids and stress induced analgesia in posttraumatic stress disorder. *Psychopharmacology Bulletin* 25:108-112.

van der Kolk, B. A., Perry, J. C., and Herman, J. L. (1991). Childhood origins of self-destructive behavior. *American Journal of Psychiatry* 148:1665-1671.

van der Kolk, B. A., Roth, S., and Pelcovitz, D. (1992). *Field Trials for DSM IV, Posttraumatic Stress Disorder II: Disorders of Extreme Stress.* Washington, DC: American Psychiatric Association.

van der Kolk, B. A., and Saporta, J. (1991). The biological response to psychic trauma: mechanisms and treatment of intrusion and numbing. *Anxiety Research* 4:199-212.

van der Kolk, B. A., and van der Hart, O. (1989). Pierre Janet and the breakdown of adaptation in psychological trauma. *American Journal of Psychiatry* 146:1530-1540.

———— (1991). The intrusive past: the flexibility of memory and the engraving of trauma. *American Imago* 48:425-454.

Yehuda, R., Giller, E. L., Southwick, S. M., et al. (1991). Hypothalamic-pituitary-adrenal dysfunction in posttraumatic stress disorder. *Biological Psychiatry* 30:1031-1048.

Yehuda, R., Lowy, M. T., and Southwick, S. M. (1991). Lymphocyte glucocorticoid receptor number in posttraumatic stress disorder. *American Journal of Psychiatry* 148:499-504.

Yehuda, R., Southwick, S. M., Mason, J. W., and Giller, E. L. (1990). Interactions of the hypothalamic-pituitary-adrenal axis and the catecholaminergic system in posttraumatic stress disorder. In *Biological Assessment and Treatment of PTSD,* ed. E. L. Giller. Washington, DC: American Psychiatric Press.

Zager, E. L., and Black, P. M. (1985). Neuropeptides in human memory and learning processes. *Neurosurgery* 17:355–369.

3

Sources of Suggestion and Their Applicability to Psychotherapy

DANIEL BROWN

The false-memory controversy has become an increasingly heated debate among memory scientists and clinicians. On one side of the debate clinicians and researchers argue that a subpopulation of patients remain fully or partially amnestic for childhood traumatic experiences like childhood sexual abuse (CSA), and after a long retention interval, typically in adulthood, recover the memories and affects associated with the CSA, either spontaneously or in the context of psychotherapy (Briere and Conte 1993, Brown and Fromm 1986, Courtois 1992, Herman and Schatzow 1987, Terr 1994). On the other side of the debate advocates of the false-memory position argue that there is very little evidence supporting repression of CSA, and that reports of delayed, recovered memories of CSA occurring in psychotherapy are largely fabrications, typically the result of therapeutic suggestion.

The essential argument of the false-memory position is that therapists are suggesting abuse to patients, specifically suggesting child sexual abuse (and sometimes satanic ritual abuse) to patients that never really occurred, and that as a result patients come to believe these false memories or illusory memories with great conviction (Lindsay and Read 1994, Loftus 1993, Yapko 1994). Based on that conviction, patients cut off relationships with family members or initiate legal action against alleged perpetrators. Accused family members, in turn, are increasingly attempting to take legal action against therapists for allegedly suggesting false memories of abuse. In certain cases harm is caused to all parties involved.

The recent emergence of the false-memory controversy, in a certain respect, is an outgrowth of a transition within the scientific study of memory itself. About twenty years ago memory science underwent a radical transformation, from its nearly ninety-year history of largely laboratory-based investigations of serial learning tasks, like memory for nonsense syllables and word lists, to the study of everyday memory, including autobiographical memory, the development of memory in childhood, and memory for eyewitnessing crimes. Since the landmark conference on practical aspects of memory in 1976 (Gruneberg et al. 1978), memory science has broken with its history and increasingly has become an applied science. The first major area of application was memory for eyewitnessing crimes (Loftus 1979a). The second and quite recent major area of application is memory in psychotherapy. The study of everyday memory is a very young science (Cohen 1989) and nearly all of the literature applying memory research to psychotherapy is less than three years old.

Nevertheless, there is remarkable agreement among the advocates of the false memory position in their essential argument about memory suggestion in psychotherapy (Kihlstrom in press, Lindsay and Read 1994, Loftus 1993, Ofshe and Watters 1993, Yapko 1994). Memory scientists like John Kihlstrom, Steve Lindsay, and Elizabeth Loftus have based their argument on a long tradition of laboratory research on memory suggestibility. They argue that the therapist's beliefs greatly influence a patient's memory in psychotherapy (Yapko 1994). When a therapist has a strong belief that childhood sexual abuse or satanic ritual abuse has occurred, even in the absence of a patient's report of or memory for such abuse, these beliefs exert a "powerful influence" (Yapko 1994, p. 20) on the therapeutic process, and result in the patient also coming to believe that s/he was abused. It is important to note that the exact mechanisms by which therapists's beliefs become translated into a patient's memory for childhood sexual abuse is seldom elaborated.

A second aspect of the false memory argument is that psychotherapists sometimes directly or indirectly suggest plausible but false premises about abuse to the patient (Ceci and Loftus 1994, Loftus 1993, Yapko 1994). Sometimes such suggestion is said to occur when a therapist offers, or suggests, a diagnosis of abuse to a patient whose referring problem is other than abuse (Ofshe and Watters 1993, Yapko 1994). Sometimes the therapist is said to make indirect or direct suggestions to the patient about presumed but fictitious abuse (Yapko 1994). Sometimes the therapist is said to use "more powerful persuasive tactics" such as "interpersonal pressure" and "old fashioned propaganda" (Ofshe and Watters 1993, pp. 7, 15). Whatever the form of suggestion, false-memory advocates assume that suggestions given by therapists play a central role in the development of false memories for abuse in patients with delayed, recovered memories for CSA. The underlying assumption implicit in the false memory argument is that the patient readily internalizes the therapist's allegedly biased suggestions with uncritical acceptance, almost as if patients were "blank canvases on which the therapists paint" (Ofshe and Watters 1993).

A third aspect of the false memory argument is that therapists utilize memory recovery techniques. Frankel (1993) has argued that false memories occur because of "persistent encouragement to recall past events" (p. 954). Others have argued that therapists narrowly use and overuse a range of so-called memory recovery techniques. Memory recovery techniques are said to include guided imagery, dream work, hypnosis, and journal writing. Accordingly, the patient is encouraged to access fantasy as well as memory and to guess or speculate about the past, and in a sense, is given permission to more easily confuse a fantasy with an actual memory (Lindsay and Read 1994, Loftus 1993, Ofshe and Watters 1993, Yapko 1994).

Another assumption is that therapists generally operate with a confirmatory bias, which Loftus (1993) defines as "a tendency to search for evidence that confirms their hunches rather than searching for evidence that disconfirms" (p. 530). There is long tradition in dynamic psychotherapy where clinicians generally assume that the operation of psychological defenses contributes to memory distortion in the form of fragmentation and symbolization of the conscious memory report (Ross 1991, Terr 1994). In contrast to the way trauma clinicians generally think about memory distortion, false-memory advocates simply have assumed that therapists readily accept the patient's often fragmentary and symbolized memory report uncritically, as if it were a statement of absolute historical truth, and as if adopting a critical attitude toward the emerging memory report by both patient and therapist alike were not part of ongoing therapeutic work (Brown 1995).

The position taken is this chapter is that false reports about the past, and sometimes illusory memories about abuse, *can* occur in psychotherapy, at least under very specific conditions. However, my criticism of the false memory argument as it currently stands, is that it is overstated, oversimplified, and only weakly supported by existing data derived from research on memory suggestibility. Insofar as this largely speculative position is currently being used extensively, albeit prematurely, as the basis of legal arguments in the courts in defense of alleged perpetrators of abuse and in malpractice cases against therapists who are alleged to have been unduly suggestive, extreme caution is warranted; what is needed is a program of systematic, carefully designed research on suggestion in psychotherapy prior to publishing speculations about suggestibility in psychotherapy and prior to using these speculations as the basis for public statements to the media or in expert court testimony.

Contemporary memory scientists have not conducted a single laboratory study on memory suggestion in psychotherapy (Brown 1995). The false-memory advocates have rather enthusiastically applied the knowledge from laboratory studies on suggestibility with presumably normal, nontraumatized college students to the domain of psychotherapy with patients having posttraumatic stress symptoms under the assumption that these findings are readily generalizable to a clinical population. It is reasonable that some hypotheses about the effects of suggestion in psychotherapy are generated from laboratory studies on memory. However, the memory scientists who currently advocate the false-memory position have designed very little research to test these hypotheses more directly on the clinical population in question. The argument that ethical constraints prevent memory scientists from studying suggestion in therapy is not credible (Loftus and Coan in press). Creative research strategies drawn from other areas could be brought to bear on the question, experimentally manipulating suggestion variables in laboratory-simulated coun-seling sessions (cf. Corrigan et al. 1980, for a review), or investi-gating the effects of hypnotic interaction on pseudomemory production (e.g., Pettinati 1988). Until the memory scientists design appropriate research to test their hypotheses on the clinical population in question, the evidence used to support the false-memory argument remains entirely "indirect" (Schooler in press).

A second reason for caution is that the sources of evidence used to support the false-memory argument are not drawn from areas of suggestibility best matched to the hypothesis that illusory memories for abuse are being suggested by therapists. In this chapter I will review four different sources of human suggestibility research: (1) misinformation suggestibility, (2) interrogatory suggestibility, (3) coercive persuasion or thought reform, and (4) hypnotic suggestion and pseudomemory production. The essential theme of my argument is that research on interrogatory suggestibility and hypnotic pseudomemory production, under very specific conditions, yields very high base rates for false recollections even about central actions, and that these studies are directly relevant to our understanding of the conditions under which psychotherapy might contribute to the generation of false memories for abuse. Advocates of the false-memory argument, however, seldom cite this literature, and instead cite less-relevant sources of evidence on memory suggestibility. Loftus (1993), for example, builds her argument for false-memory production in therapy almost entirely around her pioneering research on misinformation suggestibility, even though these studies on adults consistently yield a relatively low base rate of memory commission errors, and are for the most part limited to memory errors for relatively minor details in a complex event. Thus, when Loftus draws upon these studies to support her false-memory argument, she necessarily overstates the case from the data sources available to her. Likewise, Richard Ofshe builds his argument on false-memory production in psychotherapy around his previous research on coercive persuasion or thought reform. Drawing primarily upon this source of evidence, Ofshe's argument necessarily comes out too extreme, as if psychotherapy could be likened to a form of brainwashing.

Overall, when we critically evaluate the false memory argument as it currently stands, it is quite lacking, first, in terms of establishing a standard of scientific research to test the hypotheses about memory suggestion in therapy directly on the population in question, and second, in terms of its theoretical soundness, in that the argument does not draw upon the best available sources of evidence to understand how illusory memories for abuse might come about in therapy. Moreover, there is a significant logical fallacy in the false-memory position; the fact that suggestibilty effects *can* occur in psychotherapy does not mean that they *necessarily* occur. The main theme of this chapter is that memory commission errors *might* occur in psychotherapy only when one or both of two conditions are met: (1) the patient is highly suggestible; (2) a particular pattern of systematic interpersonal pressure is applied.

MISINFORMATION SUGGESTIBILITY

The original idea that post-event information can alter the memory for a given event is attributed to Munsterberg (1908). He found that asking eyewitnesses leading and inaccurate questions about a crime sometimes led to significantly distorted memory reports. This phenomenon was rediscovered by contemporary memory scientists like Elizabeth Loftus, who pioneered modern laboratory research on memory suggestibilty of eyewitnesses to crimes (Loftus 1975, 1979a,b, Loftus et al. 1978, Loftus and Palmer 1974, Loftus and Zanni 1975). The original experimental design used to investigate post-event misinformation suggests that effects in the laboratory consist of three phases. In the first phase subjects, typically presumably normal college students, witness a complex, emotionally arousing event in the laboratory. The event may be a brief videotape, slide presentation, or live, staged scenario, the subject of which may be a car accident, bank robbery, mugging, or theft. The complex stimulus event contains a large number of perceivable items, such as the various actions that take place and the descriptive characteristics of each person in the scene and the objects in the environment that are either relevant or irrelevant to the central plot of the event. A few of these items are designated as critical items, in that they are subsequently targeted for possible post-event memory contamination effects. In the experimental condition subjects are shown an emotionally arousing version of the stimulus event, like a pedestrian being injured in a car accident or an innocent bystander being wounded by bank robbers. In the control condition subjects watch essentially the same stimulus event without the emotionally arousing section.

The second phase of the research is the post-event misinformation manipulation. All subjects are asked a series of structured questions about or read a narrative about the original stimulus event shortly after witnessing it. While all of the information given to control subjects is accurate, experimental subjects are exposed to several critical items of inaccurate or misleading post-event information. If, for example, the original slide presentation of the car accident contained a stop sign, the post-event misinformation suggestion would contain a yield sign embedded in a plausible narrative or series of questions. After a designated retention interval, a memory test is given, typically in the form of a forced-choice recognition test. Subjects are presented with slide pairs containing an original stimulus item and an item not contained in the original stimulus event. For the critical experimental items subjects are presented with either the original target item or the post-event misleading item. The magnitude of the misinformation effect is usually calculated in terms of the percentage of experimental subjects choosing the post-event misinformation item relative to the control group (Loftus 1979a, Loftus et al. 1978). The results of such experiments demonstrate that a significant portion of subjects presented with post-event misleading information subsequently report the misinformation as part of their recollection. This phenomenon is known as the *misinformation effect*.

Using essentially the same original research paradigm Loftus and her associates have shown that subtle changes in the language of post-event misinformation significantly change the recollection (Loftus and Zanni 1975). She has also shown that experimental subjects readily incorporate nonexistent items into their recollections. If, for example, the post-event misinformation included a question about a nonexistent barn in the background after the subject witnessed a slide presentation about a car accident, a significant portion of subjects would falsely incorporate the barn into their recollection of the event (Loftus 1975, 1979a). However, subsequent research showed that subjects did not incorporate just any type of post-event misinformation into their recollections. Blatantly false information was not readily incorporated into the subject's memory report; the post-event misinformation had to be "plausible" (Loftus 1979a).

There is little doubt after nearly two decades of research that the misinformation effect is a robust and replicable finding across many studies with adult subjects (cf. Loftus and Hoffman 1989, for a review). However, the evolving studies is this area of memory research do not entirely support Loftus's original and current interpretation of the data. Loftus has made four claims based on these studies: (1) the misinformation effect is easy to create and is an example of the "malleability" of human memory (Loftus 1979b); (2) the magnitude of the misinformation effect is generally quite high (ranging from 4 to 25 percent in her experiments); (3) the misinformation effect is an example of a memory commission error—the memory representation for the original target item is permanently altered or transformed by the post-event misinformation; (4) in generalizing these findings from laboratory misinformation suggestion research to suggestion in psychotherapy, Loftus speaks of the "creation" of false memories (Loftus and Coan in press).

One problem with Loftus's generalizations is that they are overstated. Memory commission errors as a result of post-event misinformation are easy to create, and the magnitude of the misinformation effect appears to be relatively high only when the research design fails to control for the type of post-event misleading information suggested. Some memory researchers have designed experiments that vary the type of post-event misinformation suggested to subjects. If, for example, post-event misinformation is categorized into three broad categories—action themes; descriptions of the physical characteristics of the people involved, such as race, sex, height, weight, hair color; and objects in the environment that are either relevant or irrelevant to the central plot—then the studies consistently show that the greater portion of the variance of the misinformation effect is limited to peripheral details, quite irrelevant to the central action, like the shooting of an innocent bystander or running over a pedestrian (Christiaansen and Ochelak 1983, Dritsas and Hamilton 1977, Reisberg et al. 1993). Furthermore, Loftus's original research design failed to control for whether or not the subjects actually encoded the original stimulus event in their memories. It was simply assumed that the subjects encoded all the items presented in the video or slide show. When subsequent research controlled for memory encoding, not surprisingly, the magnitude of the misinformation effect was found to be much less than in Loftus's original reports (Frischholz 1990, McCloskey and Zaragoza 1985, Wagenaar and Boer 1987). Thus, we can say that memory commission errors are easy to create and that the magnitude of the misinformation effect is substantial only if we are referring to the relatively peripheral details of a complex event, and/or if the subject failed to encode or is otherwise uncertain in his/her memory for the original memory for the target item. When Loftus readily generalizes these findings from misinformation suggestion to suggestion in psychotherapy she greatly overstates the data and demonstrates more of her own "confirmatory bias" than established scientific fact.

In generalizing misinformation-suggestion findings to the domain of psychotherapy, Loftus and Coan (in press) speak of "created" false memories. A similar view is advocated by Lindsay and Read (1994) in their use of the phrase, "illusory memories of traumatic life experiences" (p. 294). The problem with this strategic, and not entirely unintentional, use of language is that it distorts what we actually know and oversimplifies the mechanisms involved in suggestive influence. Within the literature on the misinformation effect there is an ongoing and rather sophisticated research debate about the underlying mechanisms of the misinformation effect. There are six identified factors that contribute to the overall variance of the misinformation effect:

1. Memory alteration: Loftus's interpretation of the data is that the memory representation for the original target event is permanently altered (Loftus 1975, 1979a,b, Loftus and Hoffman 1989). Such memories are considered "synthetic" or "blended" recollections (Loftus 1979b).

2. Nonretention: An alternative position is that no alteration occurs. Since Loftus's research design failed to account for whether or not the original target event was actually encoded in memory, the post-event misinformation cannot be said to alter a memory that never existed (Frischholz 1990).

3. Response bias: Loftus's original forced-choice recognition test makes subjects choose between original and post-event misleading information. McCloskey and Zaragoza (1985) point out that there is no way to rule out that subjects aren't simply being

biased by the experimental context to favor the post-event response in their report.

4. Memory coexistence: It may be the case that both the memory for the original target item and the memory for the post-event misinformation item coexist and that either might be accessible under certain conditions (Hammersley and Read 1986, Morton et al. 1985, Wagenaar and Boer 1987).

5. Source misattribution: It may be that the subject is simply making a source misattribution error, attributing the memory to the wrong source. The subject may genuinely come to believe that s/he "saw" the suggested post-event item as part of the original stimulus presentation instead of reading about it after the fact (Lindsay and Johnson 1989).

6. Source credibility: The false report may have nothing to do with a change in the memory representation per se but may simply be a function of social persuasion by a highly credible and authoritative source (Scheflin et al. in press, Smith and Ellsworth 1987).

There are many factors operative in the misinformation effect. Increasingly sophisticated research designs have been developed to apportion the variance contributed by each of these factors to the overall misinformation effect (Belli 1989, Frischholz 1990, Mc-Closkey and Zaragoza 1985, Wagenaar and Boer 1987). Two consistent findings emerge from this research: (1) the misinformation effect represents a complex interaction of *many* factors, and (2) the portion of the overall variance contributed by an actual change or alteration in the memory representation per se is consistently quite small (Belli 1989, Frischholz 1990, Tversky and Tuchin 1989) and sometimes negligible (McCloskey and Zaragoza 1985, Wagenaar and Boer 1987). Thus, when Loftus, Lindsay and other memory scientists speak of false memories or illusory memories, respectively, they are seriously overstating the data. Such terms imply that we are talking about a change in the memory representation per se, over and against a consistent body of data that at best very weakly supports this position. A correct position would be to say that we are talking about a false *report*, although such a report in many instances may have very little to do with the memory representation per se (Zaragoza and Koshmider 1989). Thus, while Loftus and other memory scientists are quite aware of complexity of these issues and sometimes debate them within the memory literature (e.g., Loftus and Hoffman 1989) they curiously fail to refer to the literature representing the complexity of this debate in most of their articles about suggestion effects in psychotherapy.

It is also curious that most of the literature on the misinformation effect and its application to psychotherapy, with a few exceptions (Dodd and Bradshaw 1980, Smith and Ellsworth 1987), fails to cite several decades of research on persuasion and attitude change. A reasonable hypothesis is that a lot of the variance of the misinformation effect is accounted for by social influence factors intensively studied years ago by social scientists. The only thing new is that some contemporary memory scientists now call classic persuasion effects memory suggestion effects, even in the face of the growing evidence that very little of the variance is due to a change in the memory representation per se.

A second source of data on the misinformation effect comes from experimental studies on children. The earliest studies generally applied the original Loftus paradigm to children (Cohen and Harnick 1980, Dale et al. 1978, Duncan et al. 1982, Marin et al. 1979, Zaragoza 1987, 1991). These laboratory simulation studies with children are reviewed and interpreted by Cole and Loftus (1987) in a manner similar to the adult studies. However, child researchers have developed innovative research paradigms that are a significant departure from the Loftus original paradigm. In an effort to adapt the research strategy to children's concerns some researchers dropped the viewing of video or slide presentations in favor of recall of stories read to children (Ceci et al. 1987, Saywitz 1987).

The greatest innovations in research design, however, were developed by Gail Goodman and her associates. In an effort to investigate "children's concerns" more directly Goodman and colleagues (1990) constructed a series of experiments in which the experimental event incorporated many of the elements found in reports of alleged child sexual abuse. These events were designed to meet certain criteria — they must capture the child's interest, must be personally meaningful to the child, and must evoke strong emotions. One set of these studies has become known as the *Simon Says Studies*. Typically, children of selected age groups interact with a male stranger in an unfamiliar setting. The central action involves play sequences. Some of these actions involve nonsexual touch, like playing Patty Cake. Some days after the play sequence, the children return to the laboratory. Memory performance is measured by free narrative recall of the play sequence followed by response to a series of specific, accurate, and sometimes inaccurate post-event questions about the play sequence. Inaccurate post-event questions sometimes directly address abuse-related issues such as sexual touch ("Did he touch you in your private parts?" "Did he make you take your clothes off?") (Goodman and Aman 1990, Goodman, Aman, and Hirschman 1987, Goodman and Reed 1986, Goodman et al. 1990, Goodman et al. 1991, Rudy and Goodman 1991). Many of these studies differentiate between children who passively witness and those who actively participate in the action. Many of these studies also differentiate between the type of post-event misinformation suggested, for example, for central, plot-related actions, for minor objects in the environment, and for the physical descriptions of the people involved. In this sense, the child studies are usually much better designed than the adult misinformation studies.

Another set of such studies are known as the *events of impact* studies (King and Yuille 1987). These studies utilize real-life stressful events, specifically stress that involves painful bodily experiences, such as an inoculation, a venipuncture procedure, or a gynecological examination at the pediatrician's office. Following the upsetting medical procedure children of selected ages are tested at various retention intervals with free recall and specific questions about their memory. In the experimental group, some of the post-event questions contain misleading information (Goodman et al. 1990, Goodman, Bottoms, et al. 1991, Peters 1987, 1991, Saywitz et al. 1991).

The results of the Simon Says and events of impact studies are highly consistent across experiments. (1) In free recall older children recall significantly more information than younger children, that is, they make fewer memory omission errors. While preschool children generally have a relatively incomplete verbal memory for the event, their memory is nonetheless reasonably accurate for the event. (2) In response to specific, accurate post-event questions, older children answer a greater portion of the questions correctly than do younger children. (3) Memory omission errors are more likely than commission errors across all age groups. (4) In response to various categories of misleading post-event questions, younger children are more suggestible than older children. Overall, neither preschool or school-age children make a great number of memory commission errors, especially in their memory for central actions and for events in which they directly participate. In these studies (with the exception of the Ceci studies, which will be reviewed separately) the commission error base rates consistently run about 3 to 5 percent. (5) Regarding misleading abuse-like questions like, "Did he touch you in your private parts?" older children and most younger children are "highly resistant" to suggestive post-event misinformation about fictitious abusive actions (Goodman et al. 1990, Rudy and Goodman 1991). Goodman, Aman, and Hirschman (1987) summarize the findings across these studies:

> The results of this study do not support the notion that stress interferes with a victim's memory. . . . [Children's] suggestibility is greater for characteristics of the room in which an event occurred than for actions that took place or the physical characteristics of the "culprit." Interestingly, across these studies children never made up false stories of abuse even when asked questions that might foster such reports [p. 690]

While these results are consistent across studies the conclusion that children are generally resistant to post-event misinformation, especially about abuse, is probably dependent upon the type of social interaction used in the study; that is, the findings may be limited to a "benign interview environment" (McGough 1991, p. 167) and may not be generalizable to an interview context where various types of interpersonal pressure are directly used.

INTERROGATORY SUGGESTIBILITY

Much stronger research support for memory commission errors comes from extensive forensic and some child experimental research within the domain of interrogatory suggestibility. In the forensic studies, for example, the base rates for commission errors might be as high as 42 to 76 percent. In the child experimental studies, likewise, the rates range from 37 to 72 percent. Moreover, some of these studies have included ways to distinguish between those subjects who give a false report as a consequence of compliance with the social demand (but who do not otherwise alter their memory representation) and those who actually alter their memory representation. Therefore, the forensic studies on interrogatory suggestibility, while rarely cited by the false memory advocates, actually do much more to advance our understanding of possible false-memory production in psychotherapy than the misinformation suggestion studies.

In a special edition of *Social Behavior* Gudjonsson and Clark (1986) outline their basic theoretical model for interrogatory suggestibility and distinguish it from misinformation suggestibility. In that same edition Schooler and Loftus (1986) argue that interrogatory suggestibility is not essentially different from misinformation suggestibility. In my opinion, there *is* a difference between these two types of suggestibility, at least in terms of the aspects of suggestibility that each emphasizes. In their review of research on suggestibility in children Ceci and Bruck (1993) describe two categories of variables that affect suggestibility — cognitive factors and social factors. The difference in emphasis between misinformation suggestibility and interrogatory suggestibility is important, in that the former primarily measures cognitive factors in suggestibility (like encoding status, type of post-event misinformation, the nature of retrieval strategies, etc.) and the latter addresses not only cognitive factors but a variety of social factors operative in suggestibility. Research on misinformation suggestion has done little to advance our understanding of the complex social factors operative in human suggestibility. Since these social factors may contribute more than cognitive factors to the high base rate of memory commission errors (with the exception of hypnotizability, to be reviewed subsequently), a detailed review of interrogatory suggestibility is warranted. Moreover, since psychotherapy is mainly a social interaction, the studies on interrogatory suggestibility are more directly relevant to understanding suggestibility in therapy than the misinformation suggestibility studies per se.

Interrogatory suggestibility is best understood as *misinformation suggestibility plus*, that is, misinformation suggestibility plus a constellation of social influence factors ranging from response bias, to source credibility, and especially to some sort of "interpersonal pressure" in a closed social interaction. The concept of interrogatory suggestibility evolved from detailed studies of police interrogations and from interrogation manuals written in the 1980s to guide these interviews (Inbau et al. 1986, Irving 1980). Through a detailed analysis of police interrogations Gudjonsson and Clark (1986) were able to extract the basic elements of "interpersonal pressure" from such questioning that consistently led to a very high rate of confession.

The concept of interrogatory suggestibility in a certain sense pertains to the nature of interpersonal pressure brought to bear upon the interviewee. Gudjonsson and Clark (1986) describe six basic elements of interrogatory suggestibility: (1) Interrogatory suggestibility involves a *closed social interaction* in which the flow of information is strictly controlled. The interrogator controls the setting, the rules of discourse, the information provided, and the type of response allowed. The one-way exchange of information does not allow the interviewee to entertain alternative hypotheses to the interrogator's premises about the event in question. Furthermore, the social interaction involves a clear power differential between interrogator and interviewee. (2) Interrogatory suggestibility involves a *questioning procedure* that specifically focuses on memory for some past experience. During the interrogation the interviewee's expectations and coping resources interact with the interrogator's tactics, the outcome of which is that the interviewee becomes either more or less suggestible than before the interrogation. The interviewee's degree of uncertainty about the past event in question, the interrogator's expectation or demand that the interviewee is able to remember the event, and the degree of trust between interviewee and interrogator all contribute to increased suggestibility. Moreover, the systematic manipulation of rewards and punishments, like kindness and threats, greatly contribute to the effectiveness of interrogation procedures. (3) Interrogatory suggestibility involves *suggestive stimulus questions*. The interrogator presents the subject with plausible premises about the past event in question, often in the form of leading and misleading questions. (4) A positive response to an interrogatory suggestion implies that the subject "accepts" the suggestion, which means that the suggestive stimulus has *altered the subject's memory representation* for the past event in question. (5) Interrogatory suggestibility also involves a *behavioral response*, typically in the form of an oral or written confession and sometimes in the form of a public testimonial. (6) After the subject has responded to the interrogator's premises, positive or negative *emotional feedback* is given "to strengthen or modify subsequent responses of the witness" (Gudjonsson and Clark 1986, pp. 93–94).

The social influence factors characteristic of many police interviews go far beyond the more cognitively based misinformation suggestions characteristic of laboratory research on the misinformation effect. These factors include the closed nature of the social interaction, the interpersonal pressure used as part of the questioning procedure (such as systematic rewards and punishments), the systematic introduction of repeated leading and misleading information both within and across interview sessions, and the demand for a behavioral response in the form of a confession. The rates of memory commission errors in misinformation and interrogatory suggestibility differ markedly. While the rates are generally under 25 percent in most misinformation studies (and as low as 3 to 5 percent), the confession rates across the studies on interrogatory suggestibility ranges from 42 to 76 percent (Gudjonsson 1992). In other words, about one-half to three-quarters of suspects interviewed by the police in the "right way" make a confession. It is impossible to know for sure which of the confessions are genuine and which are false (Gudjonsson and MacKeith 1988). We can say with some degree of confidence that the procedures of interrogatory suggestion make the subject far more willing to give a distorted report about a past event about which his/her memory is uncertain. A significant portion of these reports may be seriously confabulated.

A second aspect of interrogatory suggestibility is that it is a personality trait. Gudjonsson's model for interrogatory suggestibility looks at suggestibility both as a personality trait and as a style of interpersonal pressure. Thus, some people are vulnerable to making memory commission errors because they possess the trait of high suggestibility. Others, less suggestible, can be pressured into making memory commission errors if the right pattern of interpersonal pressure is applied. To investigate the trait of interrogatory suggestibility Gudjonsson (1984) developed the Gudjonsson Suggestibility Scale (GSS). It consists of a simple story about a woman whose handbag is stolen while she is on vacation. The story is read to a subject. Immediately after hearing the story, and again after some delay, say 50 minutes, the subject is asked to freely recall as much of the story as possible (out of forty scorable details). Then, the subject is asked twenty post-event questions about the story, five of which are accurate and fifteen of which are inaccurate. The subject then is told in an authoritative and disapproving manner that s/he has made a number of errors and must answer the questions more accurately a second time. The scale measures (1) immediate memory recall, (2) delayed memory recall, (3) memory misinformation suggestibility — how many of the fifteen misleading questions are incorporated into the subject's report (Yield score), and (4) how much the subject alters his/her answers after the negative emotional feedback (Shift score). Factor analytic studies have shown that the scale is essentially composed of two independent factors, one roughly corresponding to misinformation suggestibility but with a greater ratio of misleading-to-accurate post-event information (Yield score), and the other corresponding to the negative emotional feedback manipulation (Shift score).

Extensive research using the GSS has shown that there are important individual differences in interrogatory suggestibility. Some people are highly suggestible; others are highly resistant to even a large number of misleading suggestions and/or explicit negative emotional pressure. Gudjonsson (1987) found that suggestibility and memory capacity were negatively correlated, that is, the less information recalled about the story, the greater the suggestibility. Furthermore, the rate of memory decay (difference between total number of details recalled immediately as compared with a 50-minute delay) was significantly correlated with suggestibility — the more rapid the rate of forgetting, the greater the suggestibility. Explicit negative emotional feedback (Tata and Gudjonsson 1990) and systematic repetition of misleading post-event information (Gudjonsson 1992) also increase memory commission errors.

Gudjonsson tested the validity of the GSS by administering it to two groups of subjects. The first group of "alleged false confessors/retractors" made confessions under the pressure of police interrogations but later retracted them. The second group of "deniers" persistently denied any involvement in the crime despite interrogatory pressure and despite substantial circumstantial evidence that caused them to be charged with the crime. As predicted, alleged false confessors/retractors were significantly more suggestible and deniers significantly less suggestible on all the suggestibility subscales of the GSS. A subsequent study replicated these findings and demonstrated that significant differences in suggestibility between deniers (low), normals, and alleged false confessors/retractors (high) were independent of intelligence and memory capacity. Analysis of the relative contribution of each score to the group differences between deniers and alleged false confessors demonstrated that a greater portion of the overall variance was contributed by the scores on the negative emotional feedback (Shift score) and second set of misleading questions (Yield-2 score) than by the first set of post-event misleading questions (Yield-1 score). In other words, *vulnerability to interpersonal pressure*, empirically defined as negative emotional feedback and repeated misleading questioning, contributed much more to the difference between these groups than the simpler misinformation effect per se.

These studies demonstrate that false-memory production is more a matter of the type of interpersonal pressure applied than the type of misinformation supplied (Gudjonsson 1989, 1991). Kassin and Wrightsman (1985) and Gudjonsson and MacKeith (1982, 1988) make a distinction between three types of confessors: (1) *Voluntary confessors* offer a confession without any interrogatory pressure. (2) *Coerced-compliant false confessors* make a confession after a great deal of interpersonal pressure, but usually retract it. These individuals do not alter their memory representation and simply comply with the social demand inherent in the interrogation. (3) *Coerced-internalized false confessors* actually undergo a transformation of their memory representation. The resultant "pseudomemory" is sometimes quite stable.

Some of the laboratory studies on suggestibility in children re-create some of the basic elements of interrogatory suggestibility, especially the work of Stephen Ceci and his associates. Ceci believes that memory scientists need to take a "broader view of suggestibility" (Ceci and Bruck 1993, p. 404) than is represented in the misinformation studies, and study a range of social influence factors in addition to the cognitive factors typically measured in the misinformation experiments. Ceci's studies experimentally manipulate interviewer and interviewee expectations, and the systematic repetition of misinformation within and across interview sessions. In what is known as the Sam Stone study, children's expectations were manipulated. Children in an experimental group were presented with a series of twelve stereotyped stories over four weeks about a man named Sam Stone who was very clumsy and got into accidents. After the pre-event misleading information, Sam Stone came to the children's day care class while a story was being read to the children. He did little more than say hello, walk around the perimeter of the classroom, and leave. Afterward the children were asked questions about the encounter with Sam Stone over five interview sessions conducted over a ten-week span. One group of children was asked accurate questions; another group was asked some misleading questions about the visit, for example, "Did he rip the book?" "Did he soil the Teddy bear?" About 10 percent of the preschool-aged children made memory commission errors in the control condition (no pre-event stereotyped information, no misleading post-event questions). A total of 53 percent of the preschool-aged children erroneously reported that Sam Stone ripped the book or soiled the bear in response to repeated misleading post-event questions about the event. An impressive 72 percent made similar memory commission errors in an experimental group that combined the pre-event stereotyping and the post-event misleading information. Interestingly, the rate of commission errors was extremely low across all conditions and ages when the interviews entailed free narrative recall of the staged event (Ceci 1994, Leichtman and Ceci in press).

The most notable study from Ceci's laboratory has come to be known as the Mousetrap study (Ceci 1994). The experiment addressed the issue of repeated rehearsal of false information. Preschool-aged children were randomly assigned to one of two conditions—an actual memory condition and a fictitious memory condition. In the actual memory condition the children repeatedly thought about actual, known events from their distant pasts, like injuring themselves and requiring stitches. In the fictitious memory condition the children selected a card about a fictitious event that described, for example, someone getting his/her finger caught in a mousetrap and going to the hospital. Over ten interview sessions, subjects in both groups were asked to "think real hard" about the event by making a mental image and rehearsing it and to "tell me if this ever happened to you" (p. 28). A total of 58 percent of the experimental children produced a false belief about one or more of the fictitious events and 25 percent produced false beliefs about the majority of the ten fictitious events. These children came to believe, but only after extensive rehearsal of the misinformation over repeated sessions, for example, that they had actually gotten their own fingers caught in a mousetrap at some earlier time in their lives.

The Ceci studies demonstrate that a relatively high base rate of memory commission errors (ranging from 37 to 72 percent) can occur in normal children who are subjected to various combinations of interrogatory suggestive elements, like the manipulation of expectations, and systematic interrogation with the same type of misinformation repeatedly within and across a number of interview sessions. The studies fail to demonstrate what portion of these children actually alter their memory representations in response to the interrogatory pressure, and what portion do not alter the memory representation but give a report as if this were so, in compliance with the interpersonal pressure of the interview.

There is as of yet no convincing evidence that adults develop false memories for entire fictitious events. Loftus's work on misinformation suggestion has been criticized because it merely demonstrates that subjects make memory commission errors for details peripheral to the central action of the stimulus event. In response to this criticism Loftus and Coan (in press) reported their shopping mall study. Five subjects, three children and two adults, were told by a trusted adult that they had been lost in a shopping mall or similar store when they were 5 years old. All five subjects reported actually experiencing the fictitious event. Loftus and Coan conclude that "it is indeed possible to suggest to adults complete childhood memories for events that never happened." The reader should note, however, that only five subjects and no control subjects were used and they were "all friends and relatives of our research group." This seriously flawed study shows little more than Loftus's own confirmatory bias. At best it simply replicates an old principle in social psychology, namely the persuasive influence of a credible source. To assume that the report illustrates an implanted memory, or anything about a change in the memory representation for that matter, is a serious overstatement.

COERCIVE PERSUASION OR THOUGHT REFORM

Coercive persuasion (also known as thought reform or brainwashing) is defined in terms of "programs of social influence capable of producing substantive behavior and attitude change through the use of coercive tactics, persuasion, and/or interpersonal and group-based influence manipulations" (Ofshe 1991, pp. 212–213). There have been "two generations of interest" in thought reform programs (Ofshe and Singer 1986). The first generation consisted of studies on Soviet and Chinese Communist thought reform programs. The goal of these governmental programs was ideological conversion and behavioral control. The prototypical Soviet program utilized extended periods of detention and isolation to make prisoners more vulnerable to subsequent interrogation tactics. The interrogation sessions were often very lengthy. Extreme interpersonal pressure was used centering around systematic punishments alternating with a "friendly" approach. The later Chinese Communist thought reform program added extensive peer group pressure to the arsenal of coercive persuasion tactics. Unlike the Soviet prisoners, the Chinese prisoners were rarely isolated. They lived in cells with up to eight other prisoners, some of whom had been successfully brainwashed and served as peer examples of the desired ideological conversion. Both programs were characterized by *total milieu control*—control of the physical environment through detainment, control of the information supplied to the prisoner about his suspected "crime," and control of the social environment. These programs also utilized techniques for *psychophysiological destabilization* through the disruption of biological routines like eating, sleeping, and elimination and through the infliction of physical punishment (Hinkle and Wolff 1956, Lifton 1956, Sargeant 1957, Schein 1956).

The second generation programs used more sophisticated group and psychological tactics of control because, unlike the earlier Communist government-based programs, they could not imprison subjects. Contemporary religious, political, and therapeutic cults more effectively use systematic peer group pressure and altered states of consciousness induced by hypnosis, meditation, and mind-altering drugs. According to Ofshe and Singer (1986), these programs are effective because they attack core elements of the self, such as identity and self-esteem, and are not limited to an attack on peripheral aspects of the self, such as political beliefs.

Do thought reform programs actually lead to a radical and stable transformation of fundamental beliefs? Considering the vast number of people who were subjected to the Communist brainwashing technology, the results are unimpressive. The great majority of prisoners reverted back to their original political beliefs and worldview within a few weeks after being released from prison and returning home (Hinkle and Wolff 1956, Schein 1956). A much smaller group of prisoners were, however, effectively "brainwashed." Ofshe (1991) describes coercive persuasion as "situationally adaptive belief change" (p. 23) to emphasize that the ideological conversion is largely dependent on being maintained in a tightly controlled environment. A larger portion of survivors of second-generation cults often maintain their new beliefs even after leaving the cult, presumably because of the more psychologically sophisticated coercive techniques used, especially the use of altered states of consciousness and extensive peer group pressure. How are these findings on thought reform relevant to the debate about false-memory production in therapy? They imply that milieu control, especially extreme information control, experience with certain altered states of consciousness, and above all, extensive peer pressure significantly contribute to the development of stable fictitious beliefs, at least in a select population of individuals.

HYPNOTIC PSEUDOMEMORY PRODUCTION

False memories, or pseudomemories, produced through hypnotic suggestion have been known about for a century since Bernheim's (1888) discovery of retroactive hallucinations. Bernheim age-regressed a good hypnotic subject to an evening of a previous week and asked her to reexperience going to sleep, sleeping, and then waking up in the morning. He suggested in the trance that she had awakened several times during the night to go to the bathroom and on one occasion had fallen and injured herself. Upon awakening from the trance the subject reported the fictitious injury as part of her memory. Laurence and Perry (1983) essentially replicated the Bernheim study in the laboratory using highly hypnotizable subjects who were age-regressed to reexperience an evening's sleep and were given false suggestions that they heard two loud noises during the night. A total of 48 percent of these highly hypnotizable subjects incorporated the suggestion into their memories for the evening. A later replication of the study compared pseudomemory production in both high- and low-hypnotizable subjects and demonstrated that pseudomemory production occurred most frequently among high-hypnotizable and rarely among low-hypnotizable subjects (Labelle and Perry 1986).

Like the misinformation suggestion studies, the great majority of the hypnotic pseudomemory studies are limited to suggestions for relatively minor details and not for central events. High-hypnotizable subjects are known to embellish their pseudomemory reports (Mc-Cann and Sheehan 1988). At least with some high-hypnotizables it is possible to hypnotically suggest illusory memories for entire, complex events. The most dramatic illustration is Herbert Spiegel's (1968) hypnotic suggestion of a communist conspiracy plot at the height of McCarthyism to a highly hypnotizable subject, who on national television greatly embellished the fictitious story and specifically named innocent individuals as being part of the plot.

Recently, more sophisticated research designs have been used to ascertain the relative contribution of various factors to the overall hypnotic pseudomemory effect. Essentially, these designs compare groups across several conditions: high versus low hypnotizability, waking versus hypnotic induction procedure, and hypnosis versus simulation of hypnosis. Simulator designs have been used extensively in hypnosis research in order to determine the portion of the overall variance contributed by hypnotic effects and the portion contributed by nonhypnotic, contextual effects. Simulators are subjects who are not hypnotizable but who are told to act as if they are hypnotized according to the social demand of the situation. These studies have consistently demonstrated that hypnotizability (a trait variable) contributes significantly to hypnotic pseudomemory production, but that hypnotic induction and/or various hypnotic procedures contribute very little to the overall variance of pseudomemory production. In other words, the rates of pseudomemory production in high hypnotizables is about the same whether a formal hypnotic procedure is used or whether the suggestion is given in the waking state (Barnier and McConkey 1992, McConkey et al. 1990, Spanos and McLean 1986, Weekes et al. 1992). It is also clear that social, contextual variables substantially increase the rates of hypnotic pseudomemory production beyond what would be expected of the contribution of hypnotizability alone (Lynn et al. 1989, McConkey et al. 1990). Pseudomemory production increases, for example, in a hierarchical relationship and decreases in a more egalitarian, permissive hypnotic relationship (Barnier and McConkey 1992).

In summary, hypnotic pseudomemory production is best seen as an interaction between hypnotizability (a trait) and social influence. Since these studies consistently show that hypnotic procedures contribute relatively little to the overall variance of pseudomemory production, claims by false-memory advocates that hypnosis or memory recovery techniques (including hypnotic procedures) contribute to illusory memories (Lindsay and Read 1994, Loftus 1993) are misleading and overstated. High, relative to low, hypnotizables produce pseudomemories because of the manner in which they process information. They have a greater access to both fantasy productions and personal memories and have a harder time distinguishing between fantasy and memory relative to less hypnotizable subjects. The degree to which they are able to distinguish between fact and fiction depends to a large extent on the nature of the social interaction. They are more vulnerable to social suggestion than are others (Putnam 1979, Spanos et al. 1989). Yet, subjects can also sharpen their capacity to distinguish fantasy from memory in a permissive hypnotic relationship that encourages free narrative recall instead of leading inquiry, and fosters a critical attitude in the subject to learn to discriminate fact and fiction (Brown 1995).

THE RELEVANCE OF RESEARCH ON SOURCES OF SUGGESTION TO THE FALSE-MEMORY DEBATE

The essential argument of false memory advocates is that patients in psychotherapy are vulnerable to therapeutic suggestions of illusory memories of childhood sexual abuse that never happened, and that this kind of suggested false memory for abuse is happening with alarming frequency. While few would argue with the contention that false beliefs sometimes do occur as a result of psychotherapy, the false-memory argument is grossly oversimplified. Figure 3–1 presents a summary of all of the variables within the domain of human suggestion that have been identified in the available research. The table is organized around two major categories—traits and situational variables. The situational variables are arranged along a continuum—what is called the situational suggestive continuum—

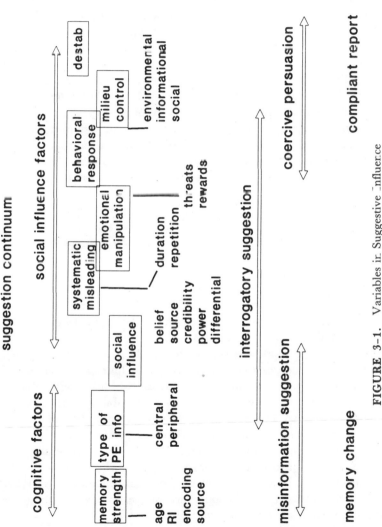

FIGURE 3-1. Variables in Suggestive Influence

from less to more suggestive. The situational variables include the strength of the memory trace (age, encoding status, source attribution, and retention interval); the type of post-event information (central versus peripheral, plausible versus discrepant, simple versus complex, neutral versus emotionally arousing); expectations (response bias, interviewee's beliefs, interrogator bias); social influence (source credibility; expectation—subject expectation, interrogatory bias, and power differential of the relationship); systematic misleading (extended duration of interviews; systematic repetition of misleading questions within and across sessions; emotional manipulation, e.g. threats of rewards, coaching and other interrogatory tactics); demanding a behavioral response (peer modeling, dissonance-reducing behaviors, compliance with hypnotic suggestion; making an oral or written confession); milieu control (environmental, informational, social); and psychophysiological destabilization (disruption of sleep and eating routines, physical affliction, systematic attack of peripheral or core aspects of the self).

An examination of Figure 3-1 makes it clear why the false memory argument is oversimplified. Loftus (1993) argues that false memories for childhood sexual abuse (CSA) are the result of therapeutic suggestion. As evidence she cites several decades of laboratory research on the misinformation effect, not the strongest source of evidence on suggestibility to make the case for therapeutically suggested false memories. This research merely shows that some subjects, whose memory strength for the original item is poor when given post-event misinformation primarily about minor details, give false reports about their recollections of the original information. Her research designs rarely include measurement of any of the various social influence variables that affect suggestibility. She rarely mentions trait differences in suggestibility in her writings on psychotherapy. Her research falls more on the left side of the situational suggestion continuum where suggestive effects are the weakest and where commission error base rates are generally low, except for minor details for which the person is uncertain. The genuine value of Loftus's research on the misinformation effect is her clear demonstration that people are suggestible when they are uncertain about the event in question.

Richard Ofshe, another outspoken advocate of the false-memory position, bases his argument on years of research on thought reform. His research falls more on the extreme right side of the situational suggestion continuum. Therefore, his argument is too extreme, unless we are to accept that what he calls memory recovery therapy is a form of brainwashing. Most psychotherapy does not utilize milieu control procedures. Psychotherapy is rarely an example of extreme information control, in that even where a therapist may have a strong bias about suspected abuse a patient is exposed to alternate sources of information outside of psychotherapy. The value of Ofshe and Singer's (1986) work is that it reminds us that total immersion in a peer cultural group can be a very powerful source of indoctrination. When research on coercive persuasion is used to understand suggestion in psychotherapy, it becomes clear that peer group influences such as peer self-help groups for abuse survivors, probably serve as a much more powerful source of suggestion of illusory reports than does individual therapy.

To understand illusory memory production in individual psychotherapy the most relevant areas of suggestion are those two other areas of suggestibility research that Loftus, Ofshe, and other advocates of the false memory position usually fail to emphasize, namely (1) trait effects and (2) interpersonal pressure. First, there is compelling evidence for a trait of suggestibility. Pseudomemory production is quite common in high-hypnotizable subjects at least for minor details, and is rare in low-hypnotizables (Laurence and Perry 1983). In the forensic field alleged false confessors (who later become retractors) are likewise highly suggestible, while deniers are not very suggestible on the GSS. High hypnotizables process information in a way that makes it difficult to distinguish between an actual memory and a fantasy. Those high on the GSS are vulnerable to systematic and repeated misinformation and/or manipulation of negative emotional feedback. It is not entirely clear if there is a unitary trait of suggestibility or several related traits, although Register and Kihlstrom (1988) found that hypnotizability and interrogatory suggestibility were relatively independent. It is clear that a small subgroup of the overall population is quite vulnerable to suggestion, and specifically memory suggestion, under most conditions. Whether or not and to what extent they produce a false memory probably still depends upon the situation. It is disturbing that the literature claiming that therapeutically suggested false memories rarely mentions trait differences in suggestibility. It is even more disturbing that the false memory argument is being used in the courts by expert witnesses to dismiss abuse allegations on the grounds of a hypothetical argument without ever bothering to objectively assess the suggestibility of the parties involved.

There is a curious logical fallacy in the false-memory argument. Those associated with the False Memory Syndrome Foundation often cite as "evidence" of a false-memory syndrome the existence of a group of "retractors." These are former psychotherapy patients who are said to have recovered memories of alleged CSA in psychotherapy and who later, typically after contact with those associated with the False Memory Syndrome Foundation, retract their abuse stories and claim that the memory for the alleged CSA was falsely suggested in therapy. It is illogical to assume that the report after retraction is somehow historically more accurate than the report made during psychotherapy. On what grounds? Gudjonsson's data comparing deniers and alleged false confessors/retractors demonstrates that retractors simply are very highly suggestible individuals. If the false memory advocates want to argue that certain people are highly vulnerable to therapeutic suggestions of illusory memories of CSA, then, logically, these highly suggestible people are equally as vulnerable to posttherapeutic influences, not the least of which are the often quite substantial interrogatory pressure of a disapproving family and the massive literature disseminated by, and sometimes the legal coaching recommended by, the False Memory Syndrome Foundation or its local affiliates. In other words, the so-called retractors are probably very highly suggestible individuals who have unfortunately been drawn into the center of a highly politicized debate, where the only thing being demonstrated is their continued vulnerability to exploitation.

Also, memory commission errors markedly increase in an interrogatory suggestive situation. The suggestive situation includes the strength of the original memory trace, the type of post-event information that is supplied (what Ceci and Bruck [1993] call "cognitive factors"), the nature of the expectations, the power differential in the interview relationship, the use of emotional manipulation, the use of systematic repetition of misinformation within and across interviews, the nature of the milieu and information control, and so on (what Ceci and Bruck call "social factors"). A pattern across all sources of research on human suggestibility is that false reports about past events significantly increase when a number of suggestion variables are combined and when the constellation of suggestion variables utilized in a given situation falls more on the right end of the situational suggestion continuum, that is, within the interrogatory or coercive persuasion range. The key is the strength of the systematic pressure applied to the interviewee.

Thus, there are two main contributing factors to the risk of therapeutically suggested false memories — a trait and an interrogatory suggestive situation. False recollection is very likely for a small subgroup of individuals who are highly suggestible. For those in the moderate range of suggestibility, false reports may or may not be likely depending on the suggestive situation. False recollections for minor details is reasonably easy to demonstrate for those moderately suggestible. Stable false recollections for entire, complex events like CSA that never happened are not so easy to demonstrate in the great majority of people within the moderate range of suggestibility, unless a specific constellation of interrogatory tactics are used systematically over time, like systematic rewards and punishments, the manipulation of expectations, and the systematic repetition of misleading information over sessions. Those measuring low in suggestibility probably will resist post-event misinformation under most circumstances.

The combination of a highly suggestible individual plus a form of psychotherapy that utilizes a number of interrogatory or coercive tactics is a clear risk for false-memory production. However, this is a very specific set of conditions, which most psychotherapy, unless it is very bad, fails to approximate. I disagree with the false-memory position that such highly suggestive therapy frequently occurs. Most professional trauma treatment is not at all conducted like a police interview, although I agree with certain of the false-memory arguments that some self-help treatment conducted by poorly trained, overidentified therapists and some investigations of allegations of child sexual abuse meet these criteria (Ceci and Bruck 1993, Gardner 1992). The lesson learned from the false-memory debate is that therapists should consider assessing suggestibility in some standardized way in their patients, especially when abuse is suspected, so as to identify those genuinely at risk for memory suggestion. Therapists should also assess their own therapeutic conduct so as to refrain from obvious interrogatory excesses like rewards and punishments, systematic repetition of misleading information about abuse, and so on (Brown 1995).

The false-memory speculation that so-called memory recovery techniques lead to illusory memories is not supported by the available research data. Memory recovery techniques are said to include imagery, hypnosis, dream work, journaling, and body work (Lindsay and Read 1994, Ofshe and Watters 1993). The false-memory advocates offer no scientific evidence to justify why these diverse methods should be considered together. Hypnosis research has shown that under certain conditions high-hypnotizable subjects shift their decision criteria and have a harder time than low-hypnotizables distinguishing fantasy from actual memory. However, a number of independent and well-designed studies have demonstrated that hynotizability, not a specific hypnotic procedure, is a risk factor for pseudomemory production. These data demonstrate that a hypnotic procedure, if considered a type of memory recovery technique, does not necessarily pose a risk for pseudomemory production, and that the false-memory argument, at least with respect to hypnotic procedures, is simply wrong. However, a highly hypnotizable individual engaged in a specific type of hypnotherapeutic situation that utilizes a number of interrogatory suggestive tactics would be at considerable risk, but most of these suggestive tactics have much more to do with nonhypnotic social influence factors and little to do with specific hypnotic procedures per se.

Moreover, it cannot be readily assumed that guided imagery contributes to false-memory production in therapy. Geiselman and colleagues (1993) developed a forensic cognitive interview to enhance memory recovery. This interview utilizes waking free association, imagery, and context reinstatement methods. The numerous studies conducted with the cognitive interview have clearly demonstrated that more complete (and not necessarily less accurate) memories are recovered with this method. Before false-memory advocates prematurely dismiss a variety of clinical methods like hypnosis and guided imagery (Lindsay and Read 1994, Loftus 1993, Ofshe and Watters 1993), they need to conduct research to support their hypotheses, or at least demonstrate why the available data on guided imagery and memory that contradict their claims should be dismissed in favor of an unsupported hypothesis (cf: also Malpass and Devine, 1981).

Another major problem with the false memory argument is that memory scientists like Lindsay and Loftus, as well as other false-memory advocates like Ofshe, repeatedly use language that overstates their argument with respect to memory. Loftus (1993) persists in her use of the phrase "false memory" and elsewhere speaks of "creating" or "implanting" false memories (Loftus and Coan in press). Lindsay and Read (1994) use the phrase "illusory memory." The problem with this more political, less scientific choice of words is that these words imply that the patient's memory representation has been changed. We have reviewed a rather long controversy within the misinformation research about Loftus's alteration hypothesis. These data demonstrate consistently that the magnitude of memory interference is quite small, sometimes negligible, and that a much greater portion of the variance of the misinformation effect is contributed by factors other than a change in the memory representation per se. So why don't the memory scientists reflect these data more accurately as good scientists would do when they hypothesize about suggestion in psychotherapy? Why don't they speak about false *reports* or *misbelief* about CSA and refrain from talking about false memories or illusory memories?

The available data imply that false reports about CSA, if they do occur, are less often reflective of changes in memory, and more often an example of giving a compliant report in a particular social interaction. Gudjonsson's data on forced-compliant versus forced-internalized false confessions is consistent with this view. In short, the data on misinformation, interrogatory, and coercive suggestion are all quite consistent. Of all the individuals who give a distorted report about the past, the great majority give a rather unstable report in compliance with the immediate social situation, which is largely reversible upon leaving the situation. A smaller group, perhaps very small, produces a stable change in the memory representation that may be relatively intractable over time. At any rate the memory scientists who repeatedly speak of false memory or illusory memory continue to seriously overstate the data.

In summary let's return to the question of memory commission error base rates. The false memory advocates wish the reader to believe that the rates are quite high; my own view is that they are quite low in professional trauma treatment, although higher in lay treatment and self help, especially in group therapy. There are no available data drawn from psychotherapy to support either speculation. What does the data from the laboratory research on suggestion say? Table 3-1 summarizes the base rate data across the different sources of suggestion. A pattern emerges. The base rates in the adult studies on the misinformation effect are highly variable, ranging from 0 to 27 percent in Loftus's studies. When response bias and source misattribution is controlled, the rate drops to 0 to 5 percent. The base rate in Goodman's child studies runs consistently about 3 to 5 percent. The base rates in the adult forensic studies on interrogatory suggestibility are much higher, from 42 to 76 percent. Ceci's child studies, where a combination of social influence factors are manipulated, are also high, ranging from 37 to 72 percent. The base rates in the hypnotic pseudomemory studies run about 25 percent in high hypnotizables when social factors are controlled, and increase up to 80 percent under the combination of hypnotizability and certain forms of social influence. In the literature on investigation of allegations of child sexual abuse, the base rates for false reports show a similar bimodal pattern—4 to 8 percent of all allegations of CSA are false, but 28 to 36 percent of reports within the context of a custody dispute are false, presumably because the child is very vulnerable to making a false report due to coaching or other interrogatory pressure by a parent (Benedek and Schetky 1987, Green 1986, Jones and McGraw 1987).

TABLE 3-1
Base Rates of Memory Commission Errors

Source:	Misinforma-tion	Hypnotiz-ability	Hypnotizability plus Social Influence	Interrogatory Suggestion
		4–6%		
adult:	0–5%*	[25%]**	25–80%	42–76%
child:	3–5%			37–72%

	General Population			Custody Disputes
child sexual abuse investiga-tions:	4–8%			28–36%
		Trait		Suggestive Situation

*when social influence like response bias and source credibility is factored out of the overall variance

**25% of high hypnotizables, or 4–6% of the general population

What do these statistics demonstrate? They support the view taken in this chapter that false reports (not necessarily false memories) for entire, complex events like CSA *can* occur in psychotherapy under very specific characteristics and conditions: (1) in an individual who is very highly suggestible; (2) in an individual who is less highly suggestible (but not on the low end of the suggestion continuum), and who is subjected to a variety of systematic interrogatory tactics, or (3) in an individual who is both suggestible and subjected to systematic interrogation. Furthermore, the data also imply that the more the suggestible influences are drawn from the social and not the cognitive domain, the greater the likelihood that the false report is simply a compliant response to social demand, and the less likely is it an example of a change in the memory representation per se. If the false-memory advocates wish to talk about high commission error base rates, they are going to have to replace phrases like "false memories" and "illusory memories" with "false beliefs" or "false reports," because neither the misinformation nor interrogatory data support any claim about high base rates for change in the memory representation per se.

The false-memory argument is more problematic when applied to a particular patient who has recovered memories. To advance the argument that a given patient has indeed recovered "false" or "illusory" memories, memory scientists like Loftus and Lindsay are going to have to produce a different kind of data than a general argument about therapeutic suggestibility (Lindsay and Read 1994, Loftus 1993). They will need to demonstrate that the given individual in question is indeed highly suggestible (trait difference) and/or that the particular psychotherapy in question did indeed utilize a constellation of very specific interrogatory or coercive tactics (not necessarily memory recovery methods). Otherwise, the essential false-memory argument remains an interesting speculation, but an idea that is neither substantially supported by the relevant sources of data on suggestibility, like interrogatory and hypnotic suggestibility, and certainly not by the particulars of a given clinical or forensic case until the person's suggestibility has actually been measured.

REFERENCES

Barnier, A. J., and McConkey, K. M. (1992). Reports of real and false memories: the relevance of hypnosis, hypnotizability, and context of memory test. *Journal of Abnormal Psychology* 101:521–527.

Belli, R. F. (1989). Influences of misleading postevent information: misinformation, interference and acceptance. *Journal of Experimental Psychology — General* 118:72–85.

Benedek, E. P., and Schetky, D. H. (1987). Problems in validating allegations of sexual abuse. Part 1: Factors affecting perception and recall of events. *Journal of the American Academy of Child and Adolescent Psychiatry* 26:912–915.

Bernheim, H. (1888). *Hypnosis and Suggestion in Therapy.* New York: Jason Aronson, 1973.

Briere, J., and Conte, J. (1993). Self-reported amnesia for abuse in adults molested in childhood. *Journal of Traumatic Stress* 6:21–31.

Brown, D. (1995). Pseudomemories, the standard of science, and the standard of care in trauma treatment. *American Journal of Clinical Hypnosis* 37:1–24.

Brown, D., and Fromm, E. (1986). *Hypnotherapy and hypnoanalysis.* Hillsdale, NJ: Lawrence Erlbaum.

Ceci, S. J. (1994). *Cognitive and social factors in children's testimony.* Presented at the Annual Meeting of the American Psychological Association, August.

Ceci, S. J., and Bruck, M. (1993). Suggestibility of the child witness: a historical review and synthesis. *Psychological Bulletin* 113:403–439.

Ceci, S. J., and Loftus, E. F. (1994). Memory work: a royal road to false memories? *Applied Cognitive Psychology* 8:351–364.

Ceci, S. J., Toglia, M. P., and Ross, D. F. (1987). *Children's Eyewitness Memory.* New York: Springer-Verlag.

Christiaansen, R. E., and Ochelak, K. (1983). Editing misleading information from memory: evidence for the co-existence of original and postevent information. *Memory and Cognition* 11:467–475.

Cohen, G. (1989). *Memory in the Real World,* Hillsdale, NJ: Lawrence Erlbaum.

Cohen, R. L., and Harnick, M. A. (1980). The susceptibility of child witness to suggestion. *Law and Human Behavior* 4:201–210.

Cole, C. B., and Loftus, E. F. (1987). The memory of children. In *Children's Eyewitness Memory,* ed. S. J. Ceci, M. P. Toglia, and D. F. Ross, pp. 178–208. New York: Springer-Verlag.

Corrigan, J. D., Dell, D. M., Lewis, K. N., and Schmidt, L. D. (1980). Counseling as a social influence process: a review. *Journal of Counseling Psychology Monograph* 27:395–441.

Courtois, C. A. (1992). The memory retrieval process in incest survivor therapy. *Journal of Child Sexual Abuse* 1:15–31.

Dale, P. S., Loftus, E. F., and Rathbun, L. (1978). The influence of the form of the question on the eyewitness testimony of preschool children. *Journal of Psycholinguistic Research* 7:269–277.

Dood, D. H., and Bradshaw, J. M. (1980). Leading questions and memory: pragmatic constraints. *Journal of Verbal Learning and Verbal Behavior* 19:695–704.

Dritsas, W. J., and Hamilton, V. L. (1977). Evidence about Evidence: Effects of Presuppositions, Item Salience, Stress, and Perceiver Set on Accident Recall. Unpublished manuscript, University of Michigan.

Duncan, E. M., Whitney, P., and Kunen, S. (1982). Integration of visual and verbal information in children's memory. *Child Development* 83:1215–1223.

Frankel, F. H. (1993). Adult reconstruction of childhood events in the multiple personality literature. *American Journal of Psychiatry* 6:954–958.

Frischholz, E. J. (1990). Understanding the Postevent Information Contamination Effect. Unpublished doctoral dissertation, University of Illinois at Chicago.

Gardner, R. A. (1992). *True and False Accusations of Child Sex Abuse*. Cresskill, NJ: Creative Therapeutics.

Geiselman, R. E., Fisher, R. P., MacKinnon, D. P., and Holland, H. L. (1993). Eyewitness memory enhancement in the police interview: cognitive retrieval mnemonics versus hypnosis. *Journal of Applied Psychology* 70:401–412.

Goodman, G. S., and Aman, C. (1990). Children's use of anatomically detailed dolls to recount an event. *Child Development*, 61:1859–1871.

Goodman, G. S., Aman, C., and Hirschman, J. (1987). Child sexual and physical abuse: children's testimony. In *Children's Eyewitness Memory*, ed. S. J. Ceci, M. P. Toglia, and D. F. Ross, (pp. 1–23). New York: Springer-Verlag.

Goodman, G. S., Bottoms, B. L., Schwartz-Kenney, B. M., and Rudy, L. (1991). Children's testimony about a stressful event: improving children's reports. *Journal of Narrative & Life History* 1:69–99.

Goodman, G. S., Hirschman, J. E., Hepps, D., and Rudy, L. (1991). Children's memory for stressful events. *Merrill-Palmer Quarterly* 37:109–155.

Goodman, G. S., and Reed, R. S. (1986). Age differences in eyewitness testimony. *Law & Human Behavior* 10:317–332.

Goodman, G. S., Rudy, L., Bottoms, B. L., and Aman, C. (1987). Children's concerns and memory: issues of ecological validity in the study of children's eyewitness testimony. In *Knowing and Remembering in Young Children*, ed. R. Fivush and J. Hudson, pp. 249–284. New York: Cambridge University Press.

Green, A. H. (1986). True and false allegations of sexual abuse in child custody disputes. *Journal of the American Academy of Child Psychiatry* 25:449–456.

Gruneberg, M. M., Morris, P. E., and Sykes, R. N., eds. (1978). *Practical*

Aspects of Memory, London: Academic.

Gudjonsson, G. H. (1984). A new scale of interrogative suggestibility. *Personality and Individual Differences* 5:303–314.

―――― (1987). The relationship between memory and suggestibility. *Social Behavior* 2:29–33.

―――― (1989). The psychology of false confessions. *Medico-Legal Journal* 57:93–110.

―――― (1991). Suggestibility and compliance among alleged false confessors and resisters in criminal trials. *Medical Science and the Law* 31:147–151.

―――― (1992). *The Psychology of Interrogations, Confessions, and Testimony*. New York: Wiley.

Gudjonsson, G. H., and Clark, N. K. (1986). Suggestibility in police interrogation: a social psychological model. *Social Behavior* 1:83–104.

Gudjonsson, G. H., and MacKeith, J. A. C. (1982). False confessions, psychological effects of interrogation. A discussion paper. In *Reconstructing the Past: The Role of Psychologists in Criminal Trials*, pp. 253–269. Deventer, Holland: Kluwer.

―――― (1988). Retracted confessions: legal, psychological and psychiatric aspects. *Medical Science and the Law* 28:187–194.

Hammersley, R., and Read, J. D. (1986). What is integration? Remembering a story and remembering false implications about the story. *British Journal of Psychology* 77:329–341.

Herman, J. L., and Schatzow, E. (1987). Recovery and verification of memories of childhood sexual trauma. *Psychoanalytic Psychology* 4:1–14.

Hinkle, L. E., and Wolff, H. G. (1956). Communist interrogation and indoctrination of "Enemies of the States." *American Medical Association Archives of Neurology and Psychiatry* 76:115–174.

Inbau, F. E., Reid, J. E., and Buckley, J. P. (1986). *Criminal Interrogation and Confessions*, 3rd ed. Baltimore: Williams & Wilkins.

Irving, B. (1980). *Police Interrogation: A Case Study of Current Practice*. Research Studies No. 2. London: HMSO.

Jones, D. P. H., and McGraw, J. M. (1987). Reliable and fictitious accounts of sexual abuse to children. *Journal of Interpersonal Violence* 2:27–45.

Kassin, S. M., and Wrightsman, L. S. (1985). Confession evidence. In *The Psychology of Evidence and Trial Procedures*. ed. S. M. Kassin, and L. S. Wrightsman, pp. 67–94. London: Sage.

Kihlstrom, J. F. (In press). Exhumed memory. In *Truth in Memory*, ed. S. J. Lynn and N. P. Spanos. New York: Guilford.

King, M. A., and Yuille, J. C. (1987). Suggestibility and the child witness. In *Children's Eyewitness Memory*, ed. S. J. Ceci, M. P. Toglia, and D. F. Ross. New York: Springer-Verlag.

Labelle, L., and Perry, C. (1986). *Pseudomemory creation in hypnosis*. Paper presented at the 94th Annual Convention of the American Psychological Association, Washington, DC, August.

Laurence, J.-R., and Perry, C. (1983). Hypnotically created memory among highly hypnotizable subjects. *Science* 222:523-524.

Leichtman, M. D., and Ceci, S. J. (In press). The effects of stereotypes and suggestions on preschooler's reports. *Developmental Psychology*.

Lifton, R. J. (1956). "Thought reform" of western civilians in Chinese prisons. *American Journal of Psychiatry* 110:732-739.

Lindsay, D. S., and Johnson, M. K. (1989). The eyewitness suggestibility effect and memory for source. *Memory and Cognition* 17:349-358.

Lindsay, D. S., and Read, J. D. (1994). Psychotherapy and memories of childhood sexual abuse: a cognitive perspective. *Applied Cognitive Psychology* 8:281-338.

Loftus, E. F. (1975). Leading questions and the eyewitness report. *Cognitive Psychology* 7:560-572.

––––– (1979a). *Eyewitness Testimony*. Cambridge, MA: Harvard University Press.

––––– (1979b). The malleability of memory, *American Scientist* 67:312-320.

––––– (1993). The reality of repressed memories. *American Psychologist* 48:518-537.

Loftus, E. F., and Coan, J. A. (In press). The construction of childhood memories. In *The Child Witness in Context: Cognitive, Social, and Legal Perspectives*, ed. D. Peters. New York: Kluwer.

Loftus, E. F., and Hoffman, H. G. (1989). Misinformation and memory: the creation of new memories. *Journal of Experimental Psychology — General* 118:100-104.

Loftus, E. F., Miller, D. G., and Burns, H. J. (1978). Semantic integration of verbal information into a visual memory. *Journal of Experimental Psychology — Human Learning & Memory* 4:19-31.

Loftus, E. F., and Palmer, J. C. (1974). Reconstruction of automobile destruction: an example of the interaction between language and memory. *Journal of Verbal Learning and Verbal Behavior* 13:585-589.

Loftus, E. F., and Zanni, G. (1975). Eyewitness testimony: the influence of the wording of a question. *Bulletin of the Psychonomic Society* 5:86-88.

Lynn, S. J., Weekes, J. R., and Milano, M. J. (1989). Reality versus suggestion: pseudomemory in hypnotizable and simulating subjects. *Journal of Abnormal Psychology* 98:137-144.

Malpass, R. S., and Devine, P. G. (1981). Guided memory in eyewitness identification. *Journal of Applied Psychology* 66:343-350.

Marin, B., Holmes, D. L., Guth, M., and Kovac, P. (1979). The potential of children as eyewitnesses *Law & Human Behavior* 3:295-306.

McCann, T., and Sheehan, P. W. (1988). Hypnotically induced pseudomemories—sampling their conditions among hypnotizable subjects. *Journal of Personality & Social Psychology* 54:339–346.

McCloskey, M., and Zaragoza, M. (1985). Misleading postevent information and memory for events: arguments and evidence against memory impairment hypotheses. *Journal of Experimental Psychology–General* 114:3–18.

McConkey, K. M., Labelle, L., Bibb, B. C., and Bryant, R. A. (1990). Hypnosis and suggested pseudomemory: the relevance of test context. *Australian Journal of Psychology* 42:197–205.

McGough, L. S. (1991). Commentary: Assessing the credibility of witnesses' statements. In *The Suggestibility of Children's Recollections*, ed. J. Doris, pp. 165–167. Washington, DC: American Psychological Association.

Morton, J., Hammersley, R. H., and Bekerian, D. A. (1985). Headed records: a model for memory and its failure. *Cognition* 20:1–23.

Munsterberg, H. (1908). *On the Witness Stand*. New York: Doubleday.

Ofshe, R. (1991). Coercive persuasion and attitude change. In *The Encyclopedia of Sociology*, ed. E. Borgatta and M. Borgatta. New York: Macmillan.

Ofshe, R., and Singer, M. T. (1986). Attacks on peripheral versus central elements of self and the impact of thought reforming techniques. *Cults Studies Journal* 3:3–24.

Ofshe, R., and Watters, E. (1993). Making monsters. *Society*, March/April:4–16.

Peters, D. P. (1987). The impact of naturally occurring stress on children's memeory. In *Children's Eyewitness Memory*, ed. S. J. Ceci, M. P. Toglia, and D. F. Ross, pp. 122–141. New York: Springer- Verlag.

——— (1991). The influence of stress and arousal on the child witness. In *The Suggestibility of Children's Recollections*, ed. J. Doris, pp. 60–76. Washington, DC: American Psychological Association.

Pettinati, H. M., ed. (1988). *Hypnosis and Memory*. New York: Guilford.

Putnam, W. H. (1979). Hypnosis and distortions in eyewitness memory. *International Journal of Clinical and Expimental Hypnosis* 27:311–341.

Register, P. A., and Kihlstrom, J. F. (1988). Hypnosis and interrogative suggestibility. *Personality and Individual Differences* 9:549–558.

Reisberg, D., Scully, J., and Karbo, W. (1993). *The laboratory creation of false memories: how generalizable?* Paper presented at the Annual Meeting of the Psychonomic Society, Washington, DC.

Ross, B. M. (1991). *Remembering the Personal Past: Descriptions of Autobiographical Memory*. New York: Oxford University Press.

Rudy, L., and Goodman, G. S. (1991). Effects of participation on children's reports: implications for children's testimony. *Developmental Psychology* 27:527–538.

Sargeant, W. (1957). *Battle for the Mind: A Physiology of Conversion and*

Brain-washing. London: Heinemann.

Saywitz, K. J. (1987). Children's testimony: age-related patterns of memory errors. In *Children's Eyewitness Memory,* ed. S. J. Ceci, M. P. Toglia, and D. F. Ross, pp. 36–52. New York: Springer-Verlag.

Saywitz, K.J., Goodman, G. S., Nicholas, E., and Moan, S. F. (1991). Children's memories of a physical examination involving genital touch: implications for reports of child sexual abuse. *Journal of Consulting and Clinical Psychology* 59:682–691.

Scheflin, A. W., Brown, D., and Hammond, D. C. (In press). *Memory, Therapy, and the Law.* Des Plaines, IL: American Society of Clinical Hypnosis.

Scheflin, A. W., and Shapiro, L. (1989). *Trance on Trial.* New York: Guilford.

Schein, E. H. (1956). The Chinese indoctrination program for prisoners of war: a study of attempted "brainwashing." *Psychiatry* 19:149–172.

Schooler, J. W. (In press). Cutting towards the core: the issues and evidence surrounding recovered accounts of sexual trauma. *Consciousness and Cognition.*

Schooler, J. W., and Loftus, E. F. (1986). Individual differences and experimentation: complementary approaches to interrogatory suggestibility, *Social Behavior* 1:105–112.

Smith, V. L., and Ellsworth, P. C. (1987). The social psychology of eyewitness accuracy: misleading questions and communicator expertise. *Journal of Applied Psychology* 72:294–300.

Spanos, N. P., and McLean, J. (1986). Hypnotically created pseudomemories: memory distortions or reporting biases? *British Journal of Experimental Hypnosis* 3:155–159.

Spanos, N. P., Gwynn, M. I., Comer, S. L., et al. (1989). Are hypnotically induced pseudomemories resitant to cross-examination? *Law and Human Behavior* 13:271–289.

Spiegel, H. (1968). Facts or fiction [film] F. McGee, producer. NBC News.

Tata, P. R., and Gudjonsson, G. H. (1990). The effects of mood and verbal feedback on interrogatory suggestibility. *Personality and Individual Differences* 11:1079–1085.

Terr, L. (1994). *Unchained Memories: True Stories of Traumatic Memories, Lost and Found.* New York: Basic Books.

Tversky, B., and Tuchin, M. (1989). A reconciliation of the evidence on eyewitness testimony: comments on McCloskey and Zaragoza (1985). *Journal of Experimental Psychology: General* 118:876–890.

Wagenaar, W. A., and Boer, J. P. A. (1987). Misleading postevent information: testing parametered models of integration in memory. *Acta Psychologia* 66:291–306.

Weekes, J. R., Lynn, S. J., Green, J. P., and Brentar, J. T. (1992).

Pseudomemory in hypnotized and task-motivated subjects. *Journal of Abnormal Psychology* 101:356–360.

Yapko, M. D. (1994). *Suggestions of Abuse*. New York: Simon & Schuster.

Zaragoza, M. S. (1987). Memory, suggestibility, and eyewitness testimony in children and adults. In *Children's Eyewitness Memory*, ed. S. J. Ceci, M. P. Toglia, and D. F. Ross, pp. 53–78. New York: Springer-Verlag.

―――― (1991). Preschool children's susceptibility to memory impairment. In *The Suggestibility of Children's Recollections*, ed. J. Doris. Washington, DC: American Psychological Association.

Zaragoza, M. S., and Koshmider, J. W. (1989). Misled subjects may know more than their performance implies. *Journal of Experimental Psychology-Learning, Memory, and Cognition* 15:246–255.

4

Hypnosis, False Memories, and Guidelines for Using Hypnosis with Potential Victims of Abuse

D. CORYDON HAMMOND

What do we seem to know about memory in general? Memory recall, especially for details, is malleable, reconstructive rather than reproductive, and has potential for inaccuracy (Loftus 1993). At the same time, however, there is also clear evidence suggesting that emotional memories seem to be encoded differently (Cahill et al. 1994, Christianson 1992a, Horowitz and Reidbord 1992, LeDoux 1992, 1994, McGaugh 1992, Nilsson and Archer 1992, Pitman 1994, Saporta and van der Kolk 1992, van der Kolk 1984, 1987, 1988, van der Kolk and Saporta 1993, van der Kolk and Van der Hart 1991), may be relatively accurate with regard to central details, and may be better retained and less susceptible to forgetting (e.g., Christianson, 1992c,d). There are also indications that suggest that more intense, violent, life-threatening trauma, or more than one type of abuse might be associated with an increased probability of dissociative amnesia (Briere and Conte 1993, Feldman-Summers and Pope 1994, Herman and Schatzow 1987, Shore et al. 1986, van der Kolk et al. 1994).

There is also abundant other evidence for the existence of

traumatic amnesia following natural disasters, accidents, war-related incidents, kidnapping, and physical or sexual abuse (summarized in Hammond et al. 1995). Although there are methodological short-comings in studies like those of Briere and Conte (1993), Williams (1992), Herman and Schatzow (1987), and Feldman-Summers and Pope (1994), I believe that the overall pattern of evidence strongly indicates that traumatic or dissociative amnesia, and what is being called robust repression (Spiegel and Scheflin 1994), clearly exists. The issue about which there is still uncertainty is the base rate of occurrence of traumatic amnesia in different abuse populations. For instance, is the realistic base rate for traumatic amnesia 59 percent (Briere and Conte 1993), 40 percent (Feldman-Summers and Pope 1994), 38 percent (Williams 1992), or just 19 percent (Loftus et al. 1994) in abuse cases?

Some of the difficulty in the current debate stems from methodological differences and emphases in studies. Some re-searchers are focused on the persistence and relative accuracy of memory (e.g., Christianson 1984, Heuer and Reisberg 1990, Reis-berg et al. 1988, Yuille and Cutshall 1986), while other academicians concentrate on inaccuracy and deterioration of memory over time (e.g., Clifford and Hollin 1981, Loftus and Burns 1982, Neisser and Harsch 1990). Loftus, for example, has done excellent research focused on the malleability of normal memory, but is considered by some of her colleagues as taking an extreme position in current memory debates (Christianson 1994, Yuille 1994), and she is not generally regarded as one of the authorities on traumatic or emo-tional memory (e.g., Christianson 1992b,c, Freyd 1994, Terr 1988, 1991, van der Kolk and Saporta 1993, van der Kolk and van der Hart 1991).

HYPNOSIS AND MEMORY

Most academic studies have found that the use of hypnosis will not improve normal memory in normally functioning persons for non-meaningful information (e.g., Erdelyi 1994). Research has demon-strated that memory in hypnosis is imperfect, just as it is in a nonhypnotic state. Some research suggests that persons in hypnosis relax their criterion for what is reported, allowing both more accurate and inaccurate information to emerge (Erdelyi 1988). We know that people distort information, confabulate and fill in gaps, and can be influenced by leading questions in hypnosis or out of hypnosis.

Unfortunately, some persons are unscientifically overgeneralizing beyond the population of normally functioning college students who are studied in a laboratory as they try to remember nonemotional, nontraumatic, and nonpersonally meaningful material (e.g., nonsense syllables, paired-associate words, numbers, word lists). White and colleagues (1940) stressed that the recall results of hypnosis experimenters were dependent on the type of stimulus used and that hypnosis would not facilitate recall for nonmeaningful material. And yet many of the academic studies throughout the next five decades have continued to use relatively meaningless, and especially personally nonrelevant stimuli, in hypnosis and memory experiments. For instance, fifty-two years after White's findings, Dinges and colleagues (1992) still persist in using 5-second exposures to slides of black-and-white line drawings of common objects as their outcome measure in hypnosis and memory research. This is reminiscent of a similar state of affairs in the investigations of memory retrieval from hearing under chemical anesthesia. In an effort to obtain experimental rigor, many studies used the recall of such things as unrelated nonsense syllables, poetry, music, or common words as their outcome measures, and generally failed to replicate clinical reports and studies demonstrating the hypnotic recall of and influence of suggestions given under chemical anesthesia. However, analysis of studies shows that when more meaningful information has been used as a criterion measure, patients tend to recall far more (Bennett 1988), and that part of the time suggestions given under anesthesia have an impact and result in implicit memory for which the patient has conscious amnesia (Bonke et al. 1990). Fascinatingly, there is also research evidence (Bennett 1988, Levinson 1969, 1990, Rath 1982), and many clinical cases demonstrating that sometimes hypnotic methods may pierce these amnestic barriers and recover chemically dissociated memories.

Good science does not permit generalization from a normal college student population to trauma, crime, and abuse victims—a population that has not been studied with regard to hypnotic recall! Reviews of the hypnosis and memory literature (Hammond et al. 1995, Kanovitz 1992, Relinger 1984, Scheflin and Shapiro 1989,

Scheflin et al. 1995, Smith 1983, Weitzenhoffer 1953) have reached the same basic conclusion that hypnosis will not enhance memory for meaningless stimuli, but that it may sometimes enhance the recall for meaningful and emotion-laden material. Laboratory research that too often bears only a limited resemblance to the real world would be better regarded as a beacon that illuminates, rather than a restrictive barrier that dictates the path for clinicians to follow (Frankel 1988).

There is evidence that the closer hypnosis research is in design to the clinical, real world uses of hypnosis, the greater will be the likelihood that hypnosis is found to facilitate memory without increased errors (Geiselman and Machlovitz 1987). In fact, Geiselman and colleagues (1985) discovered that when hypnosis interviews were conducted by experienced persons, they produced 35 percent more correct facts than police interviews, and as much as a nonhypnotic guided memory interview (that took twice as long and included three times as many questions). Geiselman and Machlovitz determined that while it might be possible for a hypnotherapist to encourage confabulation or be ineffective, their evaluation of thirty-eight experiments did not support this hypothesis, and they found that the differences in experimental design and methods were what predicted the success or failure of hypnosis-facilitated recall. Thus, as McConkey (1992) concluded in his review of hypnosis and memory, "The varying findings that have been reported in the literature appear to have as much to do with the experimental methods used as they do with the phenomena being investigated. This is an important point to underscore" (p. 411). It seems rather startling how little academic researchers have learned and changed since White and colleagues' (1940) observations!

Some academic researchers who study non-traumatic memory, like Erdelyi (1994), believe that memory enhancement may occur with hypnosis and without hypnosis. He believes that "hypnosis does not uniquely add to (or subtract from) hypermnesia" (p. 386), and that repeated efforts at retrieval are what is responsible for hypermnesia (enhanced memory) effects, whether obtained through hypnosis or through cognitive interviews. However, when a correction for a repeated recall effort was included in the statistical analysis by Hofling and colleagues (1971), they found the ratio of memories obtained by hypnotic age regression versus waking memories was 4.25/1. "This ratio, 4.25:1, represents the superiority of the hypnotically regressed recall over what would presumably have been the amount of recall of the subjects in the hypnotic group if their second attempts had been made in the ordinary waking state" (p. 378). This study of personally meaningful memories provided compelling data to challenge Erdelyi's (1994) contention that hypnotic hypermnesia only produced the kind of enhancement that any repeated recall effort would produce. Instead of the 11 percent for repeated recall efforts, hypnotic enhancement efforts produced an improvement of 46.9 percent, and after correcting for the inclusion of a repeated recall effort, there was a 42.5 percent improvement in memory. Erdelyi's (1988, 1994) reviews of hypnotic hypermnesia literature did not include Hofling and colleagues' (1971) study where hypnotic recall for personal life material was found to dramatically exceed simply repeated recall efforts. But the Hofling study possesses much more ecological validity than most of the studies reviewed by Erdelyi. However, even if repeated retrieval efforts that are part of hypnotic techniques are what accounts for enhanced memory, it seems immaterial whether one uses a cognitive interview or hypnosis (depending on one's expertise and training), so long as it may encourage hypermnesia.

Some hypnosis academics (e.g., Orne, Perry, Kihlstrom, Frankel), who are also associated with the False Memory Syndrome Foundation, believe that hypnotically retrieved memories are likely to include distorted and more inaccurate information than accurate information, rendering hypnotic recall untrustworthy (e.g., Dinges et al. 1992, Whitehouse et al. 1988). For these reasons, they have insisted that all forensic interviews must be fully videotaped to evaluate potential contamination. In the laboratory, however, researchers holding this view have not applied these same exacting standards to their own hypnotic and nonhypnotic contacts with research subjects. Their work has thus inadequately controlled for the potential contamination that a cynical perspective might have in biasing experimental outcomes (Watkins 1993). In this regard, many laboratory studies of hypnosis and memory have failed to even publish the specific suggestions given to subjects, thus not allowing adequate scientific evaluation concerning possible contamination from unrecognized experimenter bias and poor technique.

Another substantive flaw in laboratory research is that it does not differentiate between the broad concept of hypnosis and the many types of suggestions and techniques that may be used in hypnosis. This parallels the shortcoming in general psychotherapy research that for many years simply discussed the outcomes of "psychotherapy," without specifying individual techniques or suggestions used in each study.

There is one finding that appears with some consistency in hypnosis and memory research. Often, following hypnosis, subjects have false feelings of confidence for both accurate and inaccurate material that is elicited (Sheehan 1988). However, when one examines the nature of the suggestions used in these studies (when they are available) it appears that waking and hypnotic suggestions may have potentially altered subject expectancies and may be what is responsible for creating the enhanced confidence effects. If someone is told, "Everything is recorded in your unconscious mind, and you will now be able to fully and accurately remember everything," might this not create artificial confidence? Further clarifying research is needed, but the findings that increased confidence *may* be produced have important implications for clinical practice that will be discussed shortly. In the meantime, however, it must be realized that despite the possibility that hypnosis may in some instances increase confidence, this is not always the case (e.g., Mingay 1986, Putnam 1979, Sanders and Simmons 1983, Spanos et al. 1989, Yuille and McEwan 1985, Zelig and Beidelman 1981), and research has demonstrated that hypnotic techniques do not seem to immunize subjects, as Orne (1979) suggested, against the effects of cross-examination (e.g., Spanos et al. 1989, Spanos, Quigley et al. 1991). However, there is documentation from real world cases that demonstrate that hypnotic techniques clearly can improve recall of forgotten or repressed material at times (e.g., Block 1976, Kaszniak et al. 1988, Kroger and Douce 1979). For instance, there are several reports (As 1962, Benedikt 1894, Felkin 1890, Fromm 1970, Orne 1951) documenting hypnotic recall of a forgotten childhood language. Fromm (1970), for example, found during an age regression that an adult unable to speak his early childhood language (Japanese) began speaking it as a child would. Thus, there is a need for academic research to conduct studies with improved ecological validity to determine why and when memory is enhanced with hypnosis. Many of us believe that hypnosis is a controlled dissociation (e.g., Hilgard 1986, Spiegel 1993), and there is evidence that trauma and abuse victims are prone to entering trance-like, dissociative states during and after trauma (e.g., Eth and Pynoos 1985, Krystal 1993, Terr 1991). Therefore, when an emotional and dissociative context is re-created through hypnotically facilitated psychotherapy, this may facilitate the recovery and working through of traumatic memories (Spiegel 1993).

Thus, a national task force on hypnosis and memory, following a review of existing literature, concluded (Hammond et al. 1995) that hypnosis may assist in the recall of emotional and meaningful events, perhaps especially in real life situations where emotional trauma has created a block to memory. This may occur due to the state-dependent nature of some memories, the manner in which the encoding context and mood may be re-created hypnotically, and where early traumatic memories were encoded in visual images more than in verbal form (Terr 1988).

It should also be noted, however, completely separate from the issue of memory recall, that hypnotic ego-strengthening, hypnotic reframing and reinterpretation, and the use of suggestive hypnosis for symptom management have been found to be of particular therapeutic value in reducing symptoms in abuse victims and in ultimately working through trauma. Hypnotic techniques have many areas of clinical application (Crasilneck and Hall 1985, Hammond 1990, 1994), and hypnotic exploration is only one of them. There are many instances when a suggestive hypnotic approach is recommended as at least the initial level of intervention (and where it may be the only type of intervention required), rather than insight-oriented hypnosis (Hammond et al. 1995).

It is vitally important that therapists (and the public) view hypnosis realistically. Material evoked through hypnotic exploration may include accurate information, partially accurate information, and confabulation. Memory is not perfect in or out of hypnosis, and is subject to being influenced by the process of daily living, waking suggestions, peer influence, or any type of retrieval effort. A law review article reached the following conclusion after reviewing hypnosis and memory research:

> Psychodynamic psychotherapies use techniques to uncover the past that are slower than hypnosis and provide no superior guarantee that memories recovered are accurate. . . . . "Talking" psychotherapies are as capable of implanting false memories of childhood sexual abuse as

hypnotic ones. . . . There is as much opportunity for memory alteration to occur in nonhypnotic psychotherapies as in hypnotic ones.
[Kanovitz 1992, pp. 1243, 1246, 1251]

The beliefs that a subject brings to the hypnotic interview are
definitely known to influence what occurs in hypnosis (e.g., Baker
1982, Council et al. 1983, Council et al. 1986, Johnston et al. 1989,
Kirsch 1991, Kirsch et al. 1987, Spanos, Menary, et al. 1991,
Wickless and Kirsch 1989), and there is evidence that people in
general have in the past perceived hypnosis as something that
enhances memory recall (McConkey and Jupp 1985, McConkey et
al. 1989, Wilson et al. 1986). When such a situation exists, it may
inappropriately enhance the confidence that a person holds in the
veracity of information uncovered in hypnosis. Despite the fact that
recent media coverage of the controversy over false memories has
portrayed hypnosis negatively and the public image of hypnosis may
now be different, therapists need to more carefully evaluate patient
expectations about hypnosis prior to using it. Efforts must also be
made to create realistic and neutral expectations, and to educate
patients that information elicited in hypnosis may consist of accurate,
partially accurate, and/or confabulated material, which must be
corroborated before it can be known to be accurate.

DOES HYPNOSIS INCREASE FALSE MEMORIES?

Laboratory research with college students shows that false memory
for details concerning nontraumatic events may be produced in
students who score high or moderately high in hypnotizability (e.g.,
Barnier and McConkey 1992, Labelle et al. 1990, McConkey et al.
1990, Sheehan et al. 1991a,b). The research thus shows that it *may* be
possible to create a false memory report in a laboratory, but, often
the majority of subjects do not accept suggestions for false memories.
The very fact that the rate of pseudomemory production in higher-
hypnotizable subjects in the studies varies from 0 to 80 percent
demonstrates that research design (e.g., the nature of the testing
circumstances and of the suggested false memory, and the demand
characteristics of the experiment) plays a major role in whether false
memories or reports are produced or not.

However, hypnosis is not what appears as the important

variable in the production of pseudomemories (Brown 1995, Mc-Conkey 1992). Rather, the intrapersonal quality of moderate to high hypnotizability, social influence or persuasion processes, and uncertainty about the past seem to leave a person more open to the possibility of creating a pseudomemory. Thus, for example, individuals with high hypnotic capacity are more vulnerable for creating pseudomemories and responding to leading questions (Sheehan et al. 1993), whether or not they are in hypnosis. But, on the other hand, when hypnotic suggestions like we use clinically are given for age regression and to reexperience a past event, this has been shown *not* to be a variable associated with the creation of pseudomemories (Lynn et al. 1991).

Increased vulnerability for pseudomemory creation is also seen in persons who maintain personal beliefs that are compatible with the subsequently altered belief, and who expect to find something compatible with this belief (Spanos, Menary, et al. 1991). Thus, for example, if someone believes in reincarnation and anticipates that the explanation for their psychological distress resides in an event from a past life, during a hypnotic effort to find the source of their problem such persons may produce a pseudomemory congruent with their beliefs and expectations (Baker 1982). Furthermore, when an event is not verifiable (Lynn et al. 1989, 1992; McCann and Sheehan 1987, 1988) and is perceived as having a high probability of occurrence (Weekes et al. 1993), this also seems to influence pseudomemory production. It thus appears that pseudomemory reports are complexly determined events to which hypnosis makes no unique contribution, but which may be readily produced in nonhypnotic (Garry and Loftus 1994, Loftus and Coan in press) as well as hypnotic modalities, with social influence appearing to be the primary facilitating factor.

There are problems, however, with extrapolating too readily from the laboratory to the real world. One serious limitation is that the criteria for the existence of a pseudomemory in some studies (e.g., Labelle et al. 1990, Laurence and Perry 1983) have simply consisted of an expression of uncertainty or confusion. This has been challenged as artificially inflating pseudomemory rates when, in fact, this kind of criteria can just as easily be interpreted as an absence of a pseudomemory (Barnier and McConkey. 1992). Furthermore, suggested false memories of such details as hearing a phone ring or a pencil drop are unremarkable, everyday events that would hardly compare with a traumatic memory.

You will note that I have also used the term *pseudomemory report* at times in this discussion. The reason is that the laboratory is not always representative of the real world. For example, the research on hypnotic pseudomemory clearly indicates that instead of being a genuine distortion or alteration in a memory, pseudomemory reports may often exemplify a response bias that stems from social psychological variables and experimental demand effects that were not adequately controlled (Lynn et al. 1994, McCloskey and Zaragoza 1985, Murrey et al. 1992, Zaragoza and Koshmidir 1989). We thus find in the laboratory that most people in hypnosis, even when they are highly hypnotizable, can distinguish suggested fantasy scenarios from genuine occurrences. For example, when subjects have been motivated to provide honest, unbiased descriptions of their experience, pseudomemory reports seem to be minimized (e.g., Lynn et al. 1989, Murrey et al. 1992, Spanos et al. 1989), in the same way that they are when subjects are evaluated afterward away from the compliance pressure associated with the experimental testing context (e.g., McConkey et al. 1990). This is why pseudomemory rates vary so profoundly in the laboratory depending on experimental variables. These findings also correspond with what Bernheim (1888/1973) concluded from his uncontrolled experiments over a century ago: "The memory of the suggested event does not appear to be as persistent as the memory of the real event" (p. 177) and "there is nothing in induced sleep which may not occur in the waking condition" (p. 179). We also know that pseudomemories can be broken down when the person is confronted with evidence of the nature of the original events (e.g., McCann and Sheehan 1987, 1989), and pseudomemory rates are low when the focus of the pseudomemory suggestion is something that can be verified publicly (Lynn et al. 1992, McCann and Sheehan 1987, 1988).

The findings we have on pseudomemory production also have interesting implications for the situations we see in media interviews with "retractors" who now disbelieve that they were ever abused, and who now accuse a previous therapist of implanting beliefs of abuse. The very persons that research shows would be most vulnerable to developing a false memory — persons with high hypnotizability, who are vulnerable to social influence, and who cannot readily verify past events — are also the very persons most vulnerable to changing their beliefs in response to the social influence and group pressure effects of family members and false-memory movement representatives. The American Psychiatric Association (1994) statement on memories of sexual abuse acknowledges that "hesitancy in making a report, and recanting following the report can occur in victims of documented abuse. Therefore, these seemingly contradictory findings do not exclude the possibility that the report is based on a true event" (p. 24).

In the current politically and legally charged climate, we must realize that there are many therapists who have lacked sophistication concerning research on memory and some who may have unwittingly made suggestions that encouraged a patient to believe that he or she may have been abused, or reinforced such preexisting beliefs. This may be true particularly when a therapist assumes that certain psychological symptoms (e.g., bulimia, lack of interest in sex) mean a patient must have been abused. Simultaneously, however, we must acknowledge that there is a false-memory movement where some persons have an agenda of discrediting memories of abuse, protecting themselves from potential prosecution (often resulting from changes in statutes of limitation permitting repressed memory cases to be prosecuted many years later), and of blaming therapists and making it too costly in terms of liability for them to want to treat victims of abuse. Such persons have a vested interest in wanting to increase the number of "retractors." Thus, some persons associated with the false-memory movement, as well as parents (some of whom may have been falsely, and some validly, accused of abuse), may have a strong investment in actively seeking to alter the beliefs of individuals recalling memories of abuse. Furthermore, when the possibility of financial gain from lawsuits enters the picture, there is the same kind of added secondary gain we see in divorce child custody cases involving allegations of abuse, where there are found to be a larger number of false-positive allegations.

But, there is no greater reason to believe that a retractor is telling the truth than to believe that an abuse victim is telling the truth. Both may have been exposed to social influence processes (written materials, videos, interpersonal influence, therapy) that may have contaminated memory. Whenever an excessively strong ideology exists — either of expecting always to find memories of abuse,

or that repressed memories or abuse of a certain kind do not exist —
undue influence may occur through methods of social influence, and
wittingly or unwittingly create the expected conclusion. Memory is
malleable in both directions, and we do not have a litmus test for
truth. Furthermore, the very type of person most vulnerable to
pseudomemory creation is also the person most vulnerable to
changing his or her beliefs when the winds of social influence blow in
a different direction. Thus, I now know of a case of a retractor, who
has retracted her retraction!

RECOMMENDATIONS FOR CLINICIANS USING HYPNOSIS

The intensity of rhetoric in discussions of both false memories and
the nature of hypnotic memory retrieval seems characterized by
dichotomous reasoning. People have gone to extremes, suggesting
either that hypnosis invariably corrupts memory and that hypnotic
recall is always untrustworthy, or that it magically reproduces
memories as if one were replaying a videotape. Neither extreme is
justified by the evidence. Memory is imperfect, whether hypnosis is
used or not, and may be altered, for instance, through interviewing,
day-to-day living, social or family interactions, interrogation, or
hypnosis. Undue suggestion may influence memory no matter what
the modality of communication or therapy. Recent reviewers, however, have concluded that current research evidence does not justify
the targeting of hypnosis for restrictive treatment (Hammond et al.
1995, Scheflin 1994a,b). Interactive interviews, therapy groups, or
hypnosis may all be conducted in a way that includes undue
suggestion. Therapists in general must exercise greater caution in
avoiding undue influence when a patient is trying to remember
events of the past. However, it is not that hypnosis (or psychotherapy) is inherently distorting, but rather the issue should be the
manner in which one conducts psychotherapy or uses hypnotic
techniques, which may contribute to the potential for distortion of
memory. False memory reports may be readily created without
hypnosis (Garry and Loftus 1994).

I will leave it to other writers to discuss the avoidance of undue
suggestion in general psychotherapy. But, specifically with regard to
using hypnosis in psychotherapy, in the remainder of this chapter I

will provide an abbreviated summary of the recommendations made by the American Society of Clinical Hypnosis (ASCH) (Hammond et al. 1995), which may be obtained for more detailed study from the ASCH, 2200 E. Devon Avene, Suite 291, Des Plaines, IL 60018; (708) 297-3317. The best liability protection for therapists in this era where lawsuits are being actively encouraged by many in the false-memory syndrome (FMS) movement is to maintain the highest standards of practice. The following recommendations seek to clarify principles of practice that should generally meet the needs of most patients, but these recommendations should not be construed as absolute rules that are completely inclusive of all proper methods, since unique circumstances require individualization of psychotherapeutic work. The ultimate judgment regarding the care of a particular patient must be made by the therapist in light of all the circumstances presented by the patient. These recommendations are also not intended as a legal standard since standards of care can only be determined on the basis of all the conditions involved in a particular case, and change as scientific knowledge and practice patterns evolve. Neither should these recommendations be applied retroactively to evaluate the practice of therapists before these recommendations were formulated. The ASCH Committee on Hypnosis and Memory, however, believes that these recommendations reflect the state of knowledge at the current time.

PROFESSIONAL PREPARATION AND INFORMED CONSENT

Contemporary controversies require that therapists must now become more knowledgeable about research literature on the topic of memory (e.g., Christianson 1992b,c, Freyd 1994, Loftus 1993, Terr 1988, 1991, van der Kolk and Saporta 1993, van der Kolk and van der Hart 1991), and, for those using hypnosis, on hypnosis and memory (Hammond et al. 1995, McConkey 1992, Pettinati 1988). It is also vitally important for psychotherapists using hypnosis to be able to document adequate training, and it is strongly recommended that they obtain certification through ASCH and afterward consider working toward advanced certification by taking diplomate board examinations in clinical hypnosis. Clinicians using hypnosis should be able to document a minimum of sixty hours of thorough and systematic training in hypnosis (Hammond and Elkins 1994), and should only use hypnosis within their areas of expertise. Therapists who have personally experienced abuse are particularly admonished to carefully evaluate their own expectations and the possibility of biased countertransferential responses.

It is recommended that informed consent should be received from all patients prior to using therapeutic hypnosis—a sample informed consent form may be found in Hammond and colleagues (1995)—except in unusual emergency situations (e.g., a medical emergency in an emergency room). One should be familiar with legal precedents on the admissibility of hypnotically refreshed testimony (Scheflin and Shapiro 1989) in one's state in order to help protect the rights of patients to testify in court. Many jurisdictions will not allow people to testify in court concerning events when hypnosis has been used to review the events in question unless careful forensic guidelines have been scrupulously followed.

A brief example will illustrate this point. I was asked to be an expert witness in a case of alleged rape. A woman with a psychiatric history told her therapist and family about having been raped, but only divulged limited details. Many months later, a relatively newly licensed therapist with minimal training in hypnosis hypnotized the patient. He used a highly leading script from an Ericksonian book that basically suggested that things believed to be true can be realized to be different than we thought. Following this leading hypnotic intervention, the woman significantly altered her story and accused a relative of the rape. After listening to a tape recording of the hypnosis session, I testified that serious contamination and undue suggestion had occurred, and given the nature of legal precedents in the state, no testimony following the hypnotic session should be admitted. The judge's finding supported this opinion and he ruled that the patient would not be allowed to testify at trial (and she was the only witness). In another case on which I was consulted, a well-meaning social worker used hypnosis to calm a boy and refresh his recollection the week before the trial of a man accused of molesting him. Because forensic guidelines were not followed, the boy lost his right to testify against the accused perpetrator, and only his deposition could be admitted.

It is vitally important to inform patients of the potential limitation of their rights to testify if hypnosis is performed. I suspect that I was the first person to begin doing this, with some misgivings at first. But, in three and one-half years of obtaining formal informed consent, I have had only two cases where hypnotherapy could not proceed because someone was involved in potential or actual legal proceedings, and patients have not responded negatively to the procedure. If I had not discussed this issue briefly with patients while educating them about hypnosis, I may have limited the rights of these two patients and at the same time incurred possible liability.

As part of informed consent, I also elicit patient expectations about the nature of hypnosis, structure neutral and realistic expectations concerning the possible uncovering of further information, and educate the patient concerning the nature of hypnosis. This education also includes a discussion about hypnosis and memory, and that one cannot know whether material elicited in hypnosis is accurate unless it is independently confirmed. The patient is told that if insight-oriented hypnosis is used, any material that may be elicited should be considered as only one further source of information that cannot be relied on as being more accurate or necessarily superior to material he or she already consciously knows. Therefore, any further information that is obtained is simply data to be critically evaluated in therapy along with what is already consciously known. I also emphasize my belief that it is inappropriate to institute litigation or to confront someone based solely on information retrieved under hypnosis. Through the years, I have never advocated confronting alleged perpetrators. I believe that this practice, along with the increased vulnerability of abuse perpetrators because of the changes of statutes of limitations in many states, are two of the primary factors that have encouraged the false-memory movement to flourish.

Lay hypnotists have proliferated and are often seeking to circumvent laws and to use hypnosis to work with psychological and medical problems. Cases of lay hypnotists using or advertising to use hypnosis to work with abuse and trauma (or other medical-psychological problems) may be referred to state regulatory bodies for possible prosecution as practicing medicine and psychology without a license.

ASSESSMENT AND CREATING NEUTRAL EXPECTATIONS

Hypnosis should not be used until the patient has been appropriately evaluated. Therapy should be individualized, with techniques used by indication and contraindication. Hypnotic uncovering is not only unnecessary in many general therapy cases, but age regression and abreaction of emotional or traumatic memories are relatively contraindicated with some patients (Hammond et al. 1995). As someone astutely observed (originally referring to encounter groups and the wisdom of individualizing treatment), we must realize that not everyone needs to "let it all hang out." Some patients already have so much "hanging out" that they have difficulty "tucking it all back in" (Parloff 1970). Thus, a severe borderline with some thought disorder, emotional lability, and poor ego-strength is not the type of patient we want to destabilize by loosening already tenuous controls through hypnotic uncovering and an abreactive experience. Such patients may, however, benefit from hypnotic ego-strengthening and learning self-hypnosis for symptom control and management.

When the patient expresses the belief during evaluation that he or she may have been abused, the source of this belief should be thoughtfully explored. Was this idea suggested to the patient by someone else, including previous therapists or the referral source? Has the expectation stemmed from reading, television, or participation in a twelve-step group or class? Any potential contaminant must be considered in an objective evaluation, although none of these things necessarily invalidates a memory, since they may have simply provided a contextual cue that elicited a genuine memory.

FMS proponents suggest that our cultural environment probably creates an expectancy in persons entering therapy that they may have repressed memories, and that these expectancies may then make the patient vulnerable to creating a false memory. But, interestingly, when I have routinely asked new female sex therapy patients, who do not have a history of physical or sexual abuse, what they believe the probability may be that they might have a "repressed memory of sexual abuse" that they do not recall, the average estimate has been 3.9 percent, with 66 percent rating the probability as zero. Thus, based on my clinical data and experience, I believe that probably the largest proportion of patients with no recall of having ever been abused do not hold expectations that abuse may have occurred but is repressed. Exceptions might be seen in patients coming from a generally abusive background, or who may have a friend who has recalled a repressed memory of abuse. However, we must be open to the possibility that even when a patient does not believe there are repressed memories in his/her background, this could potentially be altered if a therapist confidently expressed the hypothesis that repressed sexual abuse likely accounted for his/her symptoms. Thus, therapists should be cautious about sharing such hypotheses that could potentially alter a patient's expectancies.

To avoid errors of overconfidence, therapists likewise should not create an expectancy that everything is recorded in the patient's mind and that hypnosis will unerringly uncover whatever is there. As a way of avoiding contamination and increasing confidence in whatever might be uncovered in hypnosis, it is vitally important for the therapist to seek to create neutral expectations in the patient before hypnotic exploration or age-regression work. Unless I am age regressing a patient to a specific traumatic event that he or she is already aware of, when I use methods of hypnotic exploration (e.g., Brown and Fromm 1986), the possibility that a past event might be associated with current symptomatology is only one of six or seven dynamic areas (Hammond and Cheek 1988) that I explore. It is my philosophy that most psychological disorders (e.g., depression, in-hibited sexual desire) stem from multiple etiologic factors. Thus, I typically explore various potential unconscious adaptive functions or purposes served by symptoms or problematic behavior, or whether the patient is unconsciously identifying with someone else or is punishing herself by having a symptom, before even inquiring about the possibility of a past event being associated with a problem. Prior to doing any insight-oriented hypnotic work, I suggest to the patient that there *may* be something that the patient is not consciously in touch with, *or there may not*, and that we will simply see if there might be anything we should take into account (encouraging neutral expectations). Patients should also be told before beginning hypnotic exploration that any questions that are asked should not be regarded as suggestions, but simply as requests for possible information, and that "I don't know" is a satisfactory response.

Prior to age regression to a specific, known event, it is important to suggest that the patient may or may not remember anything else, and to note that if something extra is recalled, it may or may not be accurate, and would simply be further grist for evaluation in the therapeutic mill. This also causes the patient to reflect back on the initial education about the nature of hypnosis that included discussion of hypnosis and memory, and the imperfection of memory recall. It is important not to suggest that everything is recorded in the patient's mind and he or she will now recall everything perfectly, since such a suggestion would be anticipated to potentially encourage confabulation and increase patient confidence in whatever was recalled.

ASSESSMENT OF HYPNOTIC RESPONSIVITY

Clinicians with limited training in hypnosis have a tendency when they use hypnosis to simply launch immediately into hypnotherapeutic work. I believe that this is generally a mistake, especially with victims of abuse. Many therapists utilize such a passive style of hypnosis, often stemming from their own lack of confidence, that they do not elicit hypnotic phenomena of known difficulty level to ascertain the hypnotic capacity and talents of their patient (e.g., Erickson 1952). At a minimum, this should be done informally with patients alleging abuse. It is my recommendation that in the current atmosphere of allegations of inducing false memories, that it is wise to use a formal scale of hypnotic responsivity with this population (e.g., the Stanford Hypnotic Clinical Scale, the Hypnotic Induction Profile, and the Harvard Group Scale of Hypnotic Susceptibility are the most practical instruments to use). In addition, with my abuse patients, I now take part of one interview to administer the Gudjonsson Scale of Interrogative Suggestibility (Gudjonsson 1984, 1987, 1992), which evaluates how easily a patient's memory is influenced by leading questions in an interview context.

Why may such measures be useful? Such formal scales alert us to higher-hypnotizable patients who may be more prone to developing pseudomemories (in or out of hypnosis), and who may be highly responsive to social influence in general. This may prompt us to work extra cautiously with such a patient. Furthermore, if the parents of a patient who scored lower on these scales were to allege that the therapist created false memories, these measures would confirm the low probability that this occurred. Although such measures cannot directly judge the validity of a memory of abuse, they provide evidence that the therapist takes these contemporary issues seriously and objectively evaluates factors relevant to these concerns. These measures objectively assess the possibility that a suggestion has been accepted, although only independent corroboration may determine the veridicality of a memory. When we are seeking to critically evaluate the possible source of a memory, these scales provide us with further data. For example, a highly hypnotizable person may enter spontaneous trances during interviews, interrogations, or in response to "guided imagery" (that some clinicians may not define to the patient as hypnosis and obtain informed consent, but that are hypnotic and may be considered such in court). Thus, very highly hypnotizable individuals may enter a hypnotic state without a formal induction technique. On the other side of the coin, someone scoring lower in hypnotizability may be judged as less likely to have accepted suggestions offered by a therapist even if an induction ceremony was performed, so that courts have held (e.g., *People v. Caro* 1988) that despite the use of an induction technique, the person could not be considered to have been hypnotized. In court and forensic cases, recent rulings (*Daubert v. Merrell Dow Pharmaceuticals, Inc.* 1993) will probably encourage greater use of standardized hypnotizability evaluation.

AGE REGRESSION, QUESTIONING IN HYPNOSIS, AND WORKING THROUGH

As indicated earlier, hypnotic suggestions for age regression and to reexperience a past event, almost as if one were there living it again, have been found *not* to be associated with the creation of pseudomemories (Lynn et al. 1991). However, once suggestions have been given for age regression, it is vitally important to avoid undue suggestion and leading questions. Initially, following age regression, it is recommended (Hammond et al. 1995) that the patient be permitted to engage in free recall with only occasional comments that acknowledge hearing him and provide minimal encouragement to continue, or questions that simply focus on the affective response associated with the memory. After the memory has been completely explained by the patient, cautious nonleading questions may be used concerning the event. In this process, it is important for therapists to always remain aware that information elicited under hypnosis, even when it is accompanied by strong affect, may not be accurate and may only represent something that the patient may believe. Likewise, patient confidence in what is recalled does not mean the material is accurate, and the therapist should not reinforce patient beliefs in the veridicality of retrieved material. There currently are no known ways to distinguish an accurate from a partially accurate or false memory. Patients must be apprised of this, and following hypnosis it is incumbent on us to assist the patient to critically evaluate the material evoked under hypnosis as part of the cognitive integration and working through process.

There are a variety of specialty age regression techniques designed to modulate affective intensity so as to not overwhelm the patient who has gone through trauma (Hammond 1990). While the intent of these techniques is therapeutic, these methods (e.g., seeing a rape scene from a greater distance, or experiencing the content of a memory without feeling the emotion) may have the potential to add some degree of distortion to what is remembered. No research exists on this point. Thus, it is suggested (Hammond et al. 1995) that until such research is available, therapists should weigh the well-being of the patient against the need for potentially greater accuracy. If the alleged perpetrator of abuse is deceased, has been convicted in regard to the trauma, or the abuse has always been remembered, then using a dissociative regression technique such as suggesting time distortion or using the fractionated abreaction (Kluft 1990) may be appropriate.

Therapists should, however, avoid techniques that imply that the patient, through the use of hypnosis, may be able to exceed ordinary physiologic capacities, such as using the metaphor of having a zoom lens on a camera (Reiser 1980). Such techniques encourage confabulation and provide an authorized sanction for the patient to freely use imagination and fantasy.

SUPPORTIVE THERAPEUTIC NEUTRALITY

Victims of sexual abuse, rape, and abuse by priests (Burkett and Bruni 1993) have too often suffered when other people disbelieve them. A stance of silent objectivity by a therapist may be perceived as rejection and cause iatrogenic effects (Yalom and Lieberman 1971), or at a minimum result in the patient perceiving the therapist as not being empathic or caring (Hammond et al. 1977) and result in premature termination. On the other hand, despite the excesses of radicals in the FMS movement, there is validity to some of what they say, and many of us have seen cases where persons developed inaccurate beliefs concerning abuse. We do not want to harm family members or patients. Therefore, the ASCH Committee on Hypnosis and Memory (Hammond et al. 1995) made several recommendations.

First, be supportive and empathic of the patient, while at the same time assisting the patient in nonhypnotic interviews to critically evaluate hypnotically elicited material. I believe we can indicate to patients that we believe abusive events like they have recalled do happen, but simultaneously tell them that memory is imperfect and that because we were not present in the original situation, we are not in a position to be able to know what or what parts of what was "remembered" is accurate.

Milton Erickson (Erickson and Rossi 1981) wisely counseled us that a problem with hypnotic exploration techniques is that they "are sometimes accepted uncritically as some sort of ultimate 'truth' " (p. 115). But, he explained, there was no reason to accept unconscious material as any more valid than rational thinking or conscious knowledge. It could be another source of valuable information that the patient had blocked from awareness, and this might assist a confused patient. But, hypnotically elicited information should not be used as the sole source of data for decision making, and should be balanced by appealing to common sense and overall understanding. The hypnotized patient is not inclined to evaluate information in a critical manner, and so it is necessary for us to assist the patient in subsequent interviews to do so. Might the material be metaphoric? May the patient be inclined to believe it because it is congruent with certain perceptions or beliefs, or because of any secondary gains? Therapists ourselves must remain open, and we must encourage patient openness, to considering any other explanations for "memories." For instance, "flashbacks" are a genuine phenomenon and symptom clearly associated with posttraumatic stress disorder, but how can we reliably differentiate between a flashback and obsessional, intrusive images? We must remember that independent corroboration is the only sure way of validating a memory. In the absence of corroboration, therapists should not encourage patient confrontation or litigation. In fact, therapists are well advised to assist patients to realize the many negative consequences that may accrue from the confrontation of alleged perpetrators.

The recent Ramona case in the California courts illustrates the folly of encouraging confrontation. A patient already had some "memories" of sexual abuse. She was pursuing additional potential details through sodium amytal interviews. However, her therapists then encouraged the patient to confront her father and invited him to meet with them, the mother, and the daughter. By asking a family member to come to a therapy session (which is actually recommended by many in the false memory movement and by Yapko (1994), the court held that there was a duty owed to the family member, even though he was not formally a patient. Thus, a therapist's legal liability will undoubtedly increase through involving family members and encouraging confrontation.

We (Hammond et al. 1995) have also encouraged careful chart documentation in abuse cases. For example, I suggest noting discussions concerning the nature of memory, hypnosis and memory, the obtaining of informed consent (and that the patient actually read the informed consent document), efforts to establish neutral expectations, and discussions encouraging critical evaluation of hypnotically elicited memories. Chart documentation should include that the patient has been admonished and cautioned about confronting alleged perpetrators, breaking off all contact with family members, or taking any impulsive actions based on information elicited through hypnosis or therapy.

CONCLUSION

In conclusion, I believe we know several things. Although traumatic memory may be more accurate for central details, memory in general is imperfect and we have no scientifically established way to differentiate genuine from false or partially accurate memories at present. Hypnosis has been unfairly singled out for criticism by some individuals in the false-memory movement. Hypnosis, while not magical in producing hypermnesia, will likely enhance recall for personally meaningful or emotional material, but hypnotically elicited memories cannot be assumed to be accurate without independent corroborating information. Hypnotically facilitated psychotherapy, like virtually any other form of therapy, may be conducted in a manner that may encourage distortions of memory. Thus, therapists are encouraged to obtain certification in hypnosis from the American Society of Clinical Hypnosis and to follow its recommendations for the use of hypnosis with memory in order to maintain the highest standards of therapeutic work.

REFERENCES

American Psychiatric Association. (1994). *Statement on memories of sexual abuse.* Washington, DC. APA.

As, A. (1962). The recovery of forgotten language knowledge through hypnotic age regression: a case report. *American Journal of Clinical Hypnosis* 5:24–29.

Baker, R. A. (1982). The effect of suggestion on past-lives regression. *American Journal of Clinical Hypnosis* 25(1):71–76.

Barnier, A. J., and McConkey, K. M. (1992). Reports of real and false memories: the relevance of hypnosis, hypnotizability, and context of memory test. *Journal of Abnormal Psychology* 101(3):521–527.

Benedikt, M. (1894). *Hypnotismus und Suggestion. Eine Klinisch-Psychologische Studie.* Leipzig: M. Breitenstein.

Bennett, H. L. (1988). Perception and memory for events during adequate general anesthesia for surgical operations. In *Hypnosis and Memory,* ed. H. M. Pettinati, pp. 193–231. New York: Guilford.

Bernheim, H. (1888/1973). *Hypnosis and Suggestion in Psychotherapy.* New York: Jason Aronson.

Block, E. (1976). *Hypnosis: A New Tool in Crime Detection.* New York: David McKay.

Bonke, B., Fitch, W., and Millar, K., eds. (1990). *Memory and Awareness in Anaesthesia.* Amsterdam: Swets & Zeitlinger.

Briere, J., and Conte, J. (1993). Self-reported amnesia for abuse in adults molested as children. *Journal of Traumatic Stress* 6(1):21–31.

Brown, D. (1995). Pseudomemories, the standard of science, and the standard of care in trauma treatment. *American Journal of Clinical Hypnosis.*

Brown, D.,, and Fromm, E. (1986). *Hypnotherapy and Hypnoanalysis.* Hillsdale, NJ: Lawrence Erlbaum.

Burkett, E., and Bruni, F. (1993). *A Gospel of Shame.* New York: Viking.

Cahill, L., Prins, B., Weber, M., and McGaugh, J. L. (1994). B-adrenergic activation and memory for emotional events. *Nature* 371:702–704.

Christianson, S.-A. (1984). The relationship between induced emotional arousal and amnesia. *Scandinavian Journal of Psychology* 25:147–160.

———— (1992a). Remembering emotional events: potential mechanisms. In *Handbook of Emotion and Memory*, ed. S.-A. Christianson, pp. 307–340. Hillsdale, NJ: Lawrence Erlbaum.

———— (1992b). Emotional stress and eyewitness memory: a critical review. *Psychological Bulletin* 112(2):284–309.

———— ed. (1992c). *Handbook of Emotion and Memory*. Hillsdale, NJ: Lawrence Erlbaum.

———— (1992d). Emotional memories in laboratory studies versus real-life studies: Do they compare? In *Theoretical Perspectives on Autobiographical Memory*, ed. M. A. Conway, D. C. Rubin, H. Spinnler, and W. A. Wagenaar, pp. 339–352. Dordrecht: Kluwer Academic.

———— (1994, July 25). Personal correspondence to D. Corydon Hammond.

Clifford, B. R., and Hollin, C. R. (1981). Effect of the type of incident and the number of perpetrators on eyewitness memory. *Journal of Applied Psychology* 66:364–370.

Council, J. R., Kirsch, I., and Hafner, L. P. (1986). Expectancy versus absorption in the prediction of hypnotic responding. *Journal of Personality & Social Psychology* 50:182–189.

Council, J. R., Kirsch, I., Vickery, A. R., and Carlson, D. (1983). "Trance" vs. "skill" hypnotic inductions: the effects of credibility, expectancy, and experimenter modeling. *Journal of Consulting & Clinical Psychology*, 51:432–440.

Crasilneck, H. B., and Hall, J. (1985). *Clinical Hypnosis: Principles & Applications*, 2nd ed. Boston: Allyn & Bacon.

Daubert v. Merrell Dow Pharmaceuticals, Ind. (1993). 125 L.Ed. 2d 469.

Dinges, D. F., Whitehouse, W. G., Orne, E. C., et al. (1992). Evaluating hypnotic memory enhancement (hypermnesia and reminiscence) using multitrial forced recall. *Journal of Experimental Psychology: Learning, Memory, and Cognition* 18(5):1139–1147.

Erdelyi, M. H. (1988). Hypermnesia: the effect of hypnosis, fantasy, and concentration. In *Hypnosis and Memory* ed. H. M. Pettinati, pp. 64–94. New York: Guilford.

———— (1994). Hypnotic hypermnesia: the empty set of hypermnesia. *International Journal of Clinical & Experimental Hypnosis* 42(4):379–390.

Erickson, M. H. (1952). Deep hypnosis and its induction. In *Experimental Hypnosis*, ed. L. M. LeCron, pp. 70–114. New York: Macmillan.

Erickson, M. H., and Rossi, E. L. (1981). *Experiencing Hypnosis: Therapeutic Approaches to Altered States*. New York: Irvington.

Eth, S., and Pynoos, R. S., eds. (1985). *Post Traumatic Stress Disorders in Children*. Washington: American Psychoanalytic Association.

Feldman-Summers, S., and Pope, K. S. (1994). The experience of "forgetting" childhood abuse: a national survey of psychologists. *Journal of*

Consulting & Clinical Psychology, 62(3):636–639.

Felkin, R. W. (1890). *Hypnotism or Psycho-Therapeutics*. Edinburgh: Y. J. Pentland.

Frankel, F. H. (1988). The clinical use of hypnosis in aiding recall. In *Hypnosis and Memory*, ed. H. Pettinati, pp. 247–264. New York: Guilford.

Freyd, J. J. (in press). Betrayal-trauma: traumatic amnesia as an adaptive response to childhood abuse. *Ethics and Behavior*, 4(4).

Fromm, E. (1970). Age regression with unexpected reappearance of a repressed childhood language. *International Journal of Clinical and Experimental Hypnosis*, 18(2):70–88.

Garry, M., and Loftus, E. F. (1994). Pseudomemories without hypnosis. *International Journal of Clinical and Experimental Hypnosis* 42(4):363–378.

Geiselman, R. E., Fisher, R. P., MacKinnon, D. P., and Holland, H. L. (1985). Eyewitness memory enhancement in the police interview: cognitive retrieval mnemonics versus hypnosis. *Journal of Applied Psychology* 70:401–412.

Geiselman, R. E., and Machlovitz, H. (1987). Hypnosis memory recall: implications for forensic use. *American Journal of Forensic Psychology* 1:37–47.

Gudjonsson, G. H. (1984). A new scale of interrogative suggestibility. *Personality and Individual Differences* 5(3):303–314.

_____ (1987). A parallel form of the Gudjonsson Suggestibility Scale. *British Journal of Clinical Psychology* 26:215–221.

_____ (1992). *The Psychology of Interrogations, Confessions and Testimony*. New York: John Wiley & Sons.

Hammond, D. C., ed. (1990). *Handbook of Hypnotic Suggestions and Metaphors*. New York: Norton.

_____ (1994). *Medical and Psychological Hypnosis: How It Benefits Patients*. Des Plaines, IL: American Society of Clinical Hypnosis.

Hammond, D. C., and Cheek, D. B. (1988). Ideomotor signaling: a method for rapid unconscious exploration. In *Hypnotic Induction and Suggestion*, ed. D. C. Hammond. Des Plaines, IL: American Society of Clinical Hypnosis.

Hammond, D. C. and Elkins, G. R. (1994). *Standards of Training in Clinical Hypnosis*. Des Plaines, IL: American Society of Clinical Hypnosis.

Hammond, D. C., Garver, R. B., Mutter, C. B. et al. (1995). *Clinical Hypnosis and Memory: Guidelines for Clinicians and for Forensic Hypnosis*. Des Plaines, IL: American Society of Clinical Hypnosis.

Hammond, D. C., Hepworth, D., and Smith, V. G. (1977). *Improving Therapeutic Communication*. San Francisco: Jossey-Bass.

Herman, J. L., and Schatzow, E. (1987). Recovery and verification of memories of childhood sexual trauma. *Psychoanalytic Psychology* 4:1–14.

Heuer, F., and Reisberg, D. (1990). Vivid memories of emotional events: the accuracy of remembered minutiae. *Memory and Cognition* 18:496–506.

——— (1992). Emotion, arousal, and memory for detail. In *The Handbook of Emotion and Memory*, ed. S.-A. Christianson, pp. 151–180. Hillsdale, NJ: Lawrence Erlbaum.

Hilgard, E. R. (1986). *Divided Consciousness: Multiple Controls in Human Thought and Action.* New York: Wiley-Interscience.

Hofling, C. K., Hey, B., and Wright, D. (1971). The ratio of total recoverable memories to conscious memories in normal subjects. *Comprehensive Psychiatry* 12(4):371–379.

Horowitz, M. J., and Reidbord, S. P. (1992). Memory, emotion, and response to trauma. In *The Handbook of Emotion and Memory: Research and Theory*, ed. S.-A. Christianson, pp. 343–358. Hillsdale, NJ: Lawrence Erlbaum.

Johnston, J. C., Chajkowaski, J., DuBreuil, S. C., and Spanos, N. P. (1989). The effects of manipulated expectancies on behavioural and subjective indices of hypnotisability. *Australian Journal of Clinical and Experimental Hypnosis* 17:121–130.

Kanovitz, J. (1992). Hypnotic memories and civil sexual abuse trials. *Vanderbilt Law Review* 45:1185–1262.

Kaszniak. A. W., Nussbaum, P. D., Berren, M. R., et al. (1988). Amnesia as a consequence of male rape: a case report. *Journal of Abnormal Psychology* 97:100–104.

Kirsch, I. (1991). The social learning theory of hypnosis. In *Theories of Hypnosis: Current Models and Perspectives*, ed S. J. Lynn, and J. Rhue, pp. 439–466. New York: Guilford.

Kirsch, I., Council, J. R., and Mobayed, C. (1987). Imagery and response expectancy as determinants of hypnotic behavior. *British Journal of Experimental and Clinical Hypnosis* 4:25–31.

Kluft, R. P. (1990). The fractionated abreaction technique. In *Handbook of Hypnotic Suggestions and Metaphors*, ed. D. C. Hammond, pp. 527–528. New York: Norton.

Kroger, W. S., and Douce, R. G. (1979). Hypnosis in criminal investigation. *International Journal of Clinical and Experimental Hypnosis* 27:358–374.

Krystal, H. (1993). Beyond the *DSM-III-R*: therapeutic considerations in posttraumatic stress disorder. In *International Handbook of Traumatic Stress Syndromes*, ed. J. P. Wilson, and B. Raphael, pp. 841–854. New York: Plenum.

Labelle, L., Laurence, J.-R., Nadon, R., and Perry, C. (1990). Hypnotizability, preference for an imagic cognitive style, and memory creation in hypnosis. *Journal of Abnormal Psychology* 99:222–228.

Laurence, J.-R., and Perry, C. (1983). Hypnotically created memory among high hypnotizable subjects. *Science* 222:523-524.

LeDoux, J. E. (1992). Emotion as memory: anatomical systems underlying indelible neural traces. In *Handbook of Emotion and Memory*, ed. S.-A. Christianson, pp. 269-288. Hillsdale, NJ: Lawrence Erlbaum.

_____ (1994). Emotion, memory and the brain. *Scientific American* 270(6):50-57.

Levinson, B. W. (1969). An examination of states of awareness during general anaesthesia. Unpublished thesis for the degree of Doctor of Medicine, University of the Witwatersrand, South Africa.

Levinson, B. W. (1990). The states of awareness in anaesthesia in 1965. In *Memory and Awareness in Anaesthesia,* ed. B. Bonke, W. Fitch, and K. Millar, pp., 11-18. Amsterdam: Swets & Zeitlinger.

Loftus, E. F. (1993). The reality of repressed memories. *American Psychologist* 48(5):518-537.

Loftus, E. F., and Burns, T. (1982). Mental shock can produce retrograde amnesia. *Memory and Cognition* 10:318-323.

Loftus, E. F., and Coan, J. (In press). The construction of childhood memories. In *The Child Witness in Context*: *Cognitive, Social, and Legal Perspectives*, ed. D. P. Peters. Dordrecht, Netherlands: Kluwer.

Loftus, E. F., Polonsky, S., and Fullilove, M. T. (1994). Memories of childhood sexual abuse: remembering and repressing. *Psychology of Women Quarterly* 18:67-84.

Lynn, S. J., Milano, M., and Weekes, J. R. (1991). Hypnosis and pseudomemories: The effects of prehypnotic expectancies. *Journal of Personality and Social Psychology* 60:318-326.

_____ (1992). Pseudomemory and age regression: an exploratory study. *American Journal of Clinical Hypnosis* 35(2):129-137.

Lynn, S. J., Rhue, J. W., Myers, B. P., and Weekes, J. R. (1994). Pseudomemory in hypnotized and simulating subjects. *International Journal of Clinical and Experimental Hypnosis* 42(2):118-129.

Lynn, S. J., Weekes, J. R., and Milano, M. J. (1989). Reality versus suggestion: pseudomemory in hypnotizable and simulating subjects. *Journal of Abnormal Psychology* 98:137-144.

McCann, T., and Sheehan, P. W. (1987). The breaching of pseudomemory under hypnotic instruction: implications for original memory retrieval. *British Journal of Experimental and Clinical Hypnosis* 4:101-108.

_____ (1988). Hypnotically induced pseudomemories—sampling their conditions among hypnotizable subjects. *Journal of Personality and Social Psychology* 54:239-246.

_____ (1989). Pseudomemory creation and confidence in the experimental hypnosis context. *British Journal of Experimental and Clinical Hypnosis* 6(3):151-159.

McCloskey, M., and Zaragoza, M. (1985). Misleading postevent information and memory for events: arguments and evidence against memory impairment hypotheses. *Journal of Experimental Psychology* 114(1):1–16.

McConkey, K. M. (1992). The effects of hypnotic procedures on remembering: the experimental findings and their implications for forensic hypnosis. In *Contemporary Hypnosis Research*, ed. E. Fromm, and M. R. Nash, pp, 405–426. New York: Guilford.

McConkey, K. M., and Jupp, J. J. (1985). Opinions about the forensic use of hypnosis. *Australian Psychologist* 20:283–291.

McConkey, K. M., Labelle, L., Bibb, B. C., and Bryant, R. A. (1990). Hypnosis and suggested pseudomemory: the relevance of test context. *Australian Journal of Psychology* 42:197–205.

McConkey, K. M., Roche, S. M., and Sheehan, P. W. (1989). Reports of forensic hypnosis: a critical analysis. *Australian Psychologist* 24:249–272.

McGaugh, J. L. (1992). Affect, neuromodulatory systems, and memory storage. In *Handbook of Emotion and Memory*, ed. S.-A. Christianson, pp. 245–268. Hillsdale, NJ: Laurence Erlbaum.

Mingay, D. J. (1986). Hypnosis and memory for incidentally learned scenes. *British Journal of Experimental and Clinical Hypnosis* 3:173–183.

Murrey, G. J., Cross, H. J., and Whipple, J. (1992). Hypnotically created pseudomemories: further investigation into the "memory distortion or response bias" question. *Journal of Abnormal Psychology* 101(1):75–77.

Neisser, U., and Harsch, N. (1990, February). *Phantom flashbulbs: false recollections of hearing the news about Challenger.* Paper presented at the Emory Cognition Project Conference on Affect and Flashbulb Memories, Atlanta, Georgia.

Nilsson, L.-G., and Archer, T. (1992). Biological aspects of memory and emotion: affect and cognition. In *Handbook of Emotion and Memory*, ed. S.-A. Christianson, pp. 289–306. Hillsdale, NJ: Lawrence Erlbaum.

Orne, M. T. (1951). The mechanisms of hypnotic age regression: an experimental study. *Journal of Abnormal and Social Psychology* 46:213–225.

———— (1979). The use and misuse of hypnosis in court. *International Journal of Clinical and Experimental Hypnosis* 27:311–341.

Parloff, M. B. (1970). Sheltered workshops for the alienated. *International Journal of Psychiatry* 9:197–204.

People v. Caro. (1988). 46 Cal.3cd 1194, 255 Cal. Rptr. 569, 767 p.2d 1047.

Pettinati, H. M. (1988). *Hypnosis and Memory.* New York: Guilford.

Pitman, R. K. (May, 1994). *Hormonal modulation of traumatic memory.* Scientific paper presented at the annual meeting of the American Psychiatric Association, Philadelphia, Pennsylvania.

Putnam, W. H. (1979). Hypnosis and distortions in eyewitness memory. *International Journal of Clinical and Experimental Hypnosis* 27:437–448.

Rath, B. (1982). The use of suggestions during general anesthesia. Unpublished doctoral dissertation, University of Louisville, Louisville, KY.

Reisberg, D., Heuer, F., McLean, J., and O'Shaughnessy, M. (1988). The quantity, not quality, of affect predicts memory vividness. *Bulletin of the Psychonomic Society* 26:100-103.

Reiser, M. (1980). *Handbook of Investigative Hypnosis.* Los Angeles: Law Enforcement Hypnosis Institute.

Relinger, H. (1984). Hypnotic hypermnesia: a critical review. *American Journal of Clinical Hypnosis* 26:212-225.

Sanders, G. S., and Simmons, W. L. (1983). Use of hypnosis to enhance eyewitness accuracy: Does it work? *Journal of Applied Psychology* 68:70-77.

Saporta, J. A., and van der Kolk, B. A. (1992). Psychobiological consequences of severe trauma. In *Torture and its Consequences*, ed. M. Basoglu, pp. 151-181. New York: Cambridge University Press.

Scheflin, A. W. (1994a). Forensic hypnosis and the law: the current situation in the United States. In *Hypnosis and the Law: Principles and Practices,* ed. B. J. Evans and R. O. Stanley. Heidelberg, Victoria, Australia: Australian Journal of Clinical and Experimental Hypnosis.

Scheflin, A. W. (1994b). Forensic hypnosis: unanswered questions. *Australian Journal of Clinical and Experimental Hypnosis* 22(1):23-34.

Scheflin, A. W., Brown, D. P., and Hammond, D. C. (1995). *Repressed Memory, Hypnotherapy and the Law.* Des Plaines, IL: American Society of Clinical Hypnosis.

Scheflin, A. W., and Shapiro, J. L. (1989). *Trance on Trial.* New York: Guilford.

Sheehan, P. W. (1988). Confidence, memory, and hypnosis. In *Hypnosis and Memory*, ed. H. M. Pettinati, pp. 95-127. New York: Guilford.

Sheehan, P. W., Garnett, M., and Robertson, R. (1993). The effects of cue level, hypnotizability, and state instruction on responses to leading questions. *International Journal of Clinical and Experimental Hypnosis* 41(4):287-304.

Sheehan, P. W., Grigg, L., and McCann, T. (1984). Memory distortion following exposure to false information in hypnosis. *Journal of Abnormal Psychology* 93:259-265.

Sheehan, P. W., Statham, D., and Jamieson, G. A. (1991a). Pseudomemory effects over time in the hypnotic setting. *Journal of Abnormal Psychology* 100:39-44.

_____ (1991b). Pseudomemory effects and their relationship to level of susceptibility to hypnosis and state instructions. *Journal of Personality and Social Psychology* 60: 130-137.

Shore, J. H., Tatum, E. L., and Vollmer, W. M. (1986). Psychiatric reactions to disaster: the Mount St. Helens experience. *American Journal of Psychiatry* 143:590-595.

Smith, M. C. (1983). Hypnotic memory enhancement of witnesses: does it work? *Psychological Bulletin* 94:387–407.

Spanos, N. P., Gwynn, M. I., Comer, S. L., et al. (1989). Are hypnotically induced pseudomemories resistant to cross-examination? *Law and Human Behavior* 13:271–289.

Spanos, N. P., Menary, E., Gabora, N. J., et al. (1991). Secondary identity enactments during hypnotic past-life regression: a sociocognitive perspective. *Journal of Personality and Social Psychology* 61:308–320.

Spanos, N. P., Quigley, C. A., Gwynn, M. I., et al. (1991). Hypnotic interrogation, pretrial preparation, and witness testimony during direct and cross-examination. *Law and Human Behavior* 15(6):639–653.

Spiegel, D. (1993). Hypnosis in the treatment of posttraumatic stress disorder. In *Handbook of Clinical Hypnosis*, ed. J. W. Rhue, S. J. Lynn, and I. Kirsch. Washington, DC: American Psychological Association.

Spiegel, D., and Scheflin, A. W. (1994). Dissociated or fabricated? Psychiatric aspects of repressed memory in criminal and civil cases. *International Journal of Clinical and Experimental Hypnosis* 42(4):411–432.

Terr, L. (1988). What happens to early memories of trauma? A study of twenty children under age five at the time of documented traumatic events. *Journal of the American Academy of Child and Adolescent Psychiatry* 27:96–104.

———— (1991). Childhood traumas: an outline and overview. *American Journal of Psychiatry* 148:10–20.

van der Kolk, B. A. (1984). *Post-Traumatic Stress Disorder: Psychological and Biological Sequelae*. Washington, DC: APA.

———— (1987). *Psychological Trauma*. Washington, DC: APA.

———— (1988). The trauma spectrum: the interaction of biological and social events in the genesis of the trauma response. *Journal of Traumatic Stress* 1(3):273–290.

van der Kolk, B. A., and Saporta, J. (1993). Biological response to psychic trauma. In *International Handbook of Traumatic Stress Syndromes*, ed. J. P. Wilson and B. Raphael, pp. 25–34. New York: Plenum.

van der Kolk, B. A., and Van der Hart, O. (1991). The intrusive past: the flexibility of memory and the engraving of trauma. *American Imago* 48(4):425–454.

van der Kolk, B. A., Vardi, D. J., Eisler, R. E., et al. (1994). *Traumatic versus autobiographical memory*. Scientific paper delivered at the American Psychiatric Association annual meeting, Philadelphia, Pennsylvania, May.

Watkins, J. G. (1993). Dealing with the problem of "false memory" in clinic and court. *Journal of Psychiatry and Law* 297–317.

Weekes, J. R., Lynn, S. J., Green, J. P., and Brentar, J. T. (1992). Pseudomemory in hypnotized and task-motivated subjects. *Journal of*

Abnormal Psychology 101(2):356–360.

Weekes, J. R., Lynn, S. J., and Myers, B. (1993). *Pseudomemory and hypnosis: the impact of stimulus factors.* Unpublished manuscript, Ohio University. Cited in Lynn, S. J., & Nash, M. R. (1994). Truth in memory: ramifications for psychotherapy and hypnotherapy. *American Journal of Clinical Hypnosis* 36(3):194–208.

Weitzenhoffer, A. M. (1953). *Hypnotism: An Objective Study in Suggestibility.* New York: John Wiley.

White, R. W., Fox, G. R., and Harris, W. W. (1940). Hypnotic hypermnesia for recently learned material. *Journal of Abnormal and Social Psychology* 35:88–103.

Whitehouse, W. G., Dinges, D. F., Orne, E. C., and Orne, M. T. (1988). Hypnotic hypermnesia: enhanced memory accessibility or report bias? *Journal of Abnormal Psychology* 97:289–295.

Wickless, C., and Kirsch, I. (1989). The effects of verbal and experiential expectancy manipulations on hypnotic susceptibility. *Journal of Personality and Social Psychology* 57:762–768.

Williams, L. (1992). Adult memories of childhood abuse: preliminary findings from a longitudinal study. *The Advisor* 5:19–20.

Wilson, L., Greene, E., and Loftus, E. F. (1986). Beliefs about forensic hypnosis. *International Journal of Clinical and Experimental Hypnosis* 34:110–121.

Yalom, I. D., and Lieberman, M. A. (1971). A study of encounter group casualties. *Archives of General Psychiatry* 25(1):16–30.

Yapko, M. D. (1994). *Suggestions of Abuse: True and False Memories of Childhood Sexual Trauma.* New York: Simon & Schuster.

Yuille, J. C. (1994). Personal correspondence to D. Corydon Hammond, August 9.

Yuille, J. C., and Cutshall, J. L. (1986). A case study of eyewitness memory of a crime. *Journal of Applied Psychology* 71(2):291–301.

Yuille, J. C., and McEwan, N. H. (1985) Use of hypnosis as an aid to eyewitness memory. *Journal of Applied Psychology* 70(2):389–400.

Zaragoza, M. S., and Koshmidir, J. W. (1989). Misled subjects may know more than their performance implies. *Journal of Experimental Psychology: Learning, Memory, and Cognition* 15:246–255.

Zelig, M., and Beidelman, W. B. (1981). The investigative use of hypnosis. *International Journal of Clinical & Experimental Hypnosis* 29:401–412.

PART III

Professional Practice: Selected Issues

5

Incestuous Sexual Abuse, Memory, and the Organization of the Self

HELENE KAFKA

Debate on whether early memories of survivors of incest be false or true, while focusing on possible malfeasance of therapist and/or client, misses the point. Adult victimization of children has disastrous lifetime effects on normal emotional and physical development, including memory (Blume 1990, Briere 1989, Courtois 1988, Gelinas 1983, Meiselman 1990, Shapiro 1993). Repressed memories are but a symptom of pervasive memory dysfunction. Early sexual abuse is like a malignancy. Its disintegrative workings unseen, it discolors the self-image, disrupts the organization of personality, and interferes with almost every aspect of life. These consequences are evident and treatable, even were specific memories never to be recalled.

Although clinicians might not be able to substantiate traumatic content, they can use memory functioning itself as an index of personality disorder consequent to sexual abuse. In my view, the most important point is that there is an essential link between incest in childhood, memory, and organization of the survivor's self.

The observable phenomenon is that in those who have suffered early molestation, memory deviates from its normal operative modes

(Courtois 1992, Horowitz 1986, Spiegel 1989, van der Volk 1987). Registration of experience malfunctions in the traumatized child (Perry 1992). At stages in development when children are most vulnerable, adult sexual abuse overwhelms aspects of awareness that normally are free from conflict (Gil 1988). To cope with the assault, the dual coding of verbal and imaginal experience (Paivio 1971a) is often dissociated. The domains of memory registration — behavior, affect, sensation and knowledge are deconstructed (Braun 1988a,b). Healing requires their reintegration (Kafka 1992). To search for the verity of particular traumatic memories when memory's crucial organizing operations have become dysfunctional is ignoring gross memory losses that can provide far more certainty that the person has been abused. If you want to see a strange animal, why hunt for an aardvark when there is an elephant in the zoo? It is as if mammoth distortions have become mundane because of frequency and proximity.

I contend that psychoanalysts have more clinical acumen in recognizing sexual abuse and working with survivors than the controversy would have us believe. My premise is that memory patterns of survivors, not only recovery of traumatic memories, can help therapists grasp the clients' realities and guide their treatment. Therefore, one way to ascertain that the patient's narrative truth is not stranger than fiction is to examine the tasks that memory performs for most people and then compare these with memory functioning in survivors. Such analysis reveals that for these traumatized people memory is dysfunctional in discernible and characteristic ways that disrupt personality organization. This information alerts us to pathology indicative of early incestuous abuse. Awareness of memory disorder informs analytic work just as do symptoms of a reactive depression. Both occurrences provide clues to the ramifications of the disorder and its possible causes. Consequently, we need not fear that analytic inquiry will foment untrue stories or unduly influence our analysands. When we attend to memory dysfunction, we discover that we, along with our clients, know more than we are aware of knowing.

In this chapter, I review three primary functions of normal memory that influence self-regard and cohesion. I discuss the ways they are dysfunctional in survivors of childhood incestuous abuse and illustrate this malfunctioning with case vignettes.

THREE BASIC FUNCTIONS OF MEMORY AND THEIR DISRUPTION IN SURVIVORS OF SEXUAL ABUSE

Memory Helps Organize the Self and Maintains Inner Cohesion

Memory Phenomenon. There are many interactive factors that determine what normally becomes memorable. Most basic to memory induction are internal events and the person's level of physiological development. Intent, motivation, and purpose heighten the valence of an experience, while sensory and affective excitation increase its vividness. State of consciousness plus family/ social/cultural contexts are integral to the occasion of memory representation. At the same time, memory "updates" experience (Loftus and Loftus 1980), seasoning its initial registration with ensuing life events and interpersonal transactions. These inter-twining elements of an experience are always in play.

Whether memories be factual, repressed, embellished or con-fabulated, they influence the ongoing development of the child. From birth, memories support the infant's cohesion and continuity of the self in the physical world. The newborn has command of all the basic faculties of memory, These include sensory registration, imagery, attention, learning, forgetting and recall (Cernoch and Porter 1985, Piaget and Inhelder 1973). Initially, memory of sensory and body states is primary, providing behavioral knowledge of experience (Brainard and Ornstein 1991, Chi and Koeske 1983). Such body recall enables the baby to regulate inner states in accord with self and caregiver needs. These memories are embedded (often with affects) in every interpersonal transaction. Body recall provides a relative self-sameness through time, helping establish the person's continuity in the past, present, and future. It facilitates inner constancy, despite the travails of life in the passing epochs.

Memories, be they conscious or unconscious, influence percep-tion, bolster new learning, motivate behavior, and affect self-esteem. Learning and recall are necessary building blocks of identity. Typically, a child's recall of events is in accord with family needs, desires, and values. This helps develop attitudes, mores and beliefs that become part of "character" (Allport 1960). While such integra-tions are fundamental to the individual's reservoir of recollections, they are not exact reproductions of single episodes.

Memories are dynamic and malleable, possibly condensations, amalgams, or representations of internalized, generalized experience (Courtois 1992, Stern 1988). Nevertheless, they are reiterated as parts of the self. Based on infant research, Beebe and Lachmann (1988) note, "Interaction structures are characteristic patterns of mutual regulation which the infant comes to remember and expect." Relational experiences are internally stored and recalled, providing the "basis for emerging symbolic forms of self- and object representations" (p. 305). Memories, therefore, are essential components in the articulation of personality.

> There was a child went forth every day,
> And the first object he look'd upon, that object
> he became.
> And that object became part of him for the day or
> a certain part of the day,
> or for many years or stretching cycles of years.

Walt Whitman, *Leaves of Grass*

Intellectual Competence: Learning and Recall.   Are these self-organizing functions of memory impaired in those who have been severely sexually abused? It depends. Studies suggest different faculties are diversely affected. Consider the following:

For survivors of childhood incestuous abuse, some of these roles of memory not only organize but sustain self-cohesion. Dissociative defenses, while repressing disturbed sides of the self, often preserve a responsive core available for ongoing development. Such processes enable learning and recall of neutral content to be unimpaired, and frequently superior (Davies and Frawley 1993, Kafka 1994, Ross 1989, Summit 1992). Competence in school and at work can be outstanding. Experimenters call this memory function, variously, "procedural" or "explicit" (Singer 1990).

Too often, however, these capacities are not within the conflict-free sphere of the self; they are protectively employed in the struggle to maintain inner control. Excellence is not empowering, but experienced as a compulsive demand for perfection. This faculty—retaining discrete memory despite dissociative lapses—highlights the "apparent paradox of a child who can turn the most crippling experience into spectacular outward achievement, but at the cost of genuine self-awareness and self-esteem." Summit (1992, p. 14) so describes the incestuously abused Miss America of 1958, the exemplar of most of the subjects of his study. Incest survivors apprehend that superiority obfuscates anxiety and recall of painful traumas. Proficiency feels like a mask, a split-off part of the self, Sullivan's (1953) "not me." Recall and learning are not prime integrators of the self, but in the service of its fragmentation. Gelinas (1983) reports that success may precipitate self denigration and masochistic acts.

The analyst, recognizing the pyrrhic struggle between high functioning and self-annihilation, becomes suspicious of a dissociative dynamism rooted in early sexual trauma. In my view, such self-destructiveness may be mobilized by the survivor's unconscious fear that were she successful, she would betray and abandon the more vulnerable, traumatized sides of herself. She fears repeating the disregard of the perpetrator and perhaps of neglectful parents who ignored her pain. An example:

> To avoid this "perfidy," a client on the fast track in high finance, quit her job before seeking help. She believed success in her career was preventing her from attending to her intense anxieties. She told me, "I had to finally listen to the shame and terror that have haunted me as long as I can remember." This woman did not go back to work until she felt "like a whole person."

Sensori-Affective-Motor Memories.   Other organizing facets of memory do not function even this well for people sexually victimized when young. Memories triggered by the sensorium, rather than promoting cohesion and continuity, can foster panic and emotional disruption. Memories also can be played out through somaticization (Gelinas 1983).

> A woman, who had felt suffocated by her father's body during forced fellatio at ages 6 to 10, in adult life develops an ongoing anxiety pattern with sexual activity. During intercourse, she feels painful pressure in her chest, is unable to breathe, and sobs uncontrollably on its completion. It was after three years of treatment for narcissistic problems that she consciously recalled her father's abuse. Only then did she integrate her

physical reactions with lifelong memories of her father's exhibitionism, seductiveness, and sexualized taunting. This analysand also suffered with severe hives and asthma since early childhood.

Learning from Experience.   Recall of past incidents that can guide the self is another organizing function of memory. For most people, pleasant or painful memories influence perception and promote future expectations. Analysts are familiar with the role that anticipation plays in both self-fulfilling prophecies and projective identifications common to both therapist and client. These can promote adaptation in new and/or anxiety-laden experiences. But for survivors, remembrances can be so horrendous that they both consciously and unconsciously are avoided.

When there has been prolonged abuse, "memories are often confused, contradictory, fragmented — specific times and dates, places, and even the identities of perpetrators are mixed up, forgotten, conflated with dreams and fantasy" (Wylie 1993, p. 28). Dissociative processes create amnesias not only for events but for parts of the self. Time itself can be lost. All these lapses discredit the person's self and diminish self-constancy and self-esteem. A result is the discontinuous self that Bromberg (1993) describes. The survivor seems destined to repeat, rather than to remember, calling attention to internal turmoil through sado-masochistic encounters at work and in relationships.

Memory as Figure or Ground: Selective Inattention.   Without selective attention to our memories, we would be bombarded by recollections, information, perceptions, and feelings that would prevent focus on present concerns and tasks. The appropriate balance between fragmentation and recall is required to maintain normal life. Selective inattention is as necessary as selective attention (Sullivan 1953). The stimulus barrier so necessary to adaptive life needs to exist for internal as well as external events.

Among survivors, there are those who keep their childhood abuse in constant awareness. The traumatic memories here are germane to the organization of self. In contrast to those described above with debilitating memory fragmentation, this cadre of survivors selectively attends to early trauma; abuse becomes the "figure" in their perceptual/affective experience. All else is "ground." For this minority of incest survivors, recall of childhood ordeals provides rootedness and buttresses self-regard. Deliberately keeping memories of exploitation alive, they rally with "NEVER AGAIN!" groups to eradicate victimization. Similar to Holocaust survivors, they politicize their resistance to "gain purchase over fate."

There are conditions, however, when even this capacity can run amok. Some individuals cultivate disasters, requiring repeated brutalization to experience a separate identity and, paradoxically, prevent suicide. They perpetuate an inner stalking of the self in order to feel alive, for to some, "Pain is life — the sharper, the more evidence of life" (Charles Lamb). Afflicted with hypermnesia, they seemingly refuse to relinquish memories of ravage from consciousness. Recall organizes the self around an identity as victim, which at least provides self-constancy in a fragile personality. The past is memorialized by obsessive, repetitive images or by daily mini-victimizations that repeat and confirm childhood traumas. This dynamism proves to be a desperate, convoluted attempt to maintain an identity that is separate from and unvanquished by the original perpetrators. The analyst recognizes and is often confounded by the incest survivor who refuses to "inattend" to the memories of childhood abuse.

Laurie could be called a Spitz hospitalism baby who survived . . . barely. Compounding infantile abandonment and neglect was sexual abuse by her father and uncle beginning at about age 2 and continuing through her adolescence. She was in perpetual, pathologic mourning, unconsciously both berating and satisfying the hated and yet much-needed parental introjects. She neglected serious physical problems and was incessantly battered by masochistic encounters, real or imagined.

One day, as she related yet another story of her exploitation, I had a fantasy which I told her. "There was this Jewish woman in Nazi Germany who had to wear a yellow star in childhood before being herded to a concentration camp. She survived. But when she came out, she did not go to Israel or America. She went back to Germany, and everywhere she went she wore her yellow star."

Laurie said, "I know why, because that's just what I do. I can't let them forget. As long as I keep my rage going I know I exist and will exist. It's their shame, their vileness. I am not them; I am different, the superior one. Whatever they did to me, they could never get me to give in." With a wry smile, she added, "It's pretty stupid, isn't it? That's just asking for it. Surely there must be another way."

This self-observation became predictive of the next phase of our work. As we shifted focus from her daily mini-persecutions, ironically, both Laurie and I experienced ourselves as Nazi and Jew within our transference/countertransference enactments. Through this "acting-in" of her childhood traumas in our "moment," she began to exorcise traumatic memories from so-called real life. We also employed adjunctive behavioral modification techniques. She consciously began to selectively inattend to memories of past brutalities. They gradually yielded to her efforts to wrest identity through more purposive behaviors that she willfully initated. "Becoming is being," say the existentialists.

To review, I have detailed several normal organizing functions of memory: intellectual and sensorial learning, recall, learning from experience, and selective attention. These facets of memory foster self-cohesion, continuity, constancy, competence, trust, self-esteem, and the capacity for intimacy. I cited case examples of incest survivors to demonstrate that such organizing qualities of memory frequently are disrupted in survivors.

Since memory dysfunction both reveals and increases personality disturbance, I suggest that the analytic dyad actively attend to signs and signals of disordered memory. These indicate areas of distress and possible dissociation. The damaged self has been organized around efforts to dissociate, fragment, reify, and selectively inattend to parts of experience in order to cope with reality that was too horrendous to remember as real. The aim is that by attending to memory disturbance, "dissociated states of mind may find access to the analytic relationship and be lived within it (Bromberg 1994). In the course of such analytic work with the dissociated regions of the self, specific traumatic memories, while not the focus, are more apt to be retrieved.

When recovery of delayed memories becomes the goal of

treatment (McCann and Perlman 1990), the therapeutic work is as deleteriously skewed as were the dissociative coping strategies of incest survivors. I maintain that analysis of the damaged self must be integrated with attention to the multiple ways memory is disordered. The survivor's self-esteem and stability are shaken by her recurrent memory disturbances. When these occur, they, like any other symptom, serve a compromise function. They defend against enormous anxiety, while leading to the areas of distress. In the course of analytic inquiry that addresses both memory aberrations and personality dysfunction, specific traumatic memories may arise. These become part of the ongoing synthesis of the disparate parts of the survivor's self.

Memory Soothes the Self

Memories Romance the Self.   An important self-sustaining operation of memory is that of romancing the self. It protects from harsh and unwanted realities. From the earliest study of memory, people have been found to recall pleasant memories almost twice as often as unpleasant or neutral recollections (Carter 1935). Conscious memories may be vivid, detailed, indelible, or hazy and evanescent. Often, the factual combines with the confabulated, the repressed, and the nostalgic to create a reality that is bearable, even likable. Memories can be embellished to dramatize personal and social truths that impinge, kindly or otherwise, on the self. Outstanding examples of such beneficent creativity are the filmic memoirs of Barry Levinson's *Avalon* or Fellini's *Amarcord.*

Written memoirs, be they journals or a chronicle such as that of the Nazi collaborator, filmmaker Leni Reifenstahl, can save face and enhance self-esteem, while blaming away the opprobriums of self and society. Reveries and reminiscences are able to soothe the self, especially when people are failing through age or organicity. Their impotence and perplexity are relieved by conflated, even plagiarized stories, that compensate for present lapses and fill gaps in the past. Unfortunately, the survivor of relentless sexual abuse does not allow the self surcease with fabricated memories. Shame, humiliation, guilt, self-loathing—all demand that memory blanks be left empty or filled with even worse imaginings.

Victims of childhood sexual abuse do not forgive themselves

nor the perpetrators with pleasant memories and embellished truths. Unbidden, uncontrolled memories more darkly stalk their consciousness. They reveal themselves in cataclysmic flashes, terrorize in dreams, convulse with sobs in the dark of a theater, releasing emotions with the arousal of the known forgotten.

One woman who suffered from psoriasis since age 10 had this kind of tormenting revelation on seeing the film *The Piano*. She too, she wailed, like the film's heroine, was maimed for all to see, for refusing to surrender her passion and indomitable will. Memories of incestuous sexual abuse were released with this awareness. In the ensuing work, she realized that despite repression, these memories had been influencing her actions and choices lifelong.

Reveries Quiet the Self.   Reveries are another facet of memory that offer comfort to a self beleaguered by life's misadventures. Conscious awareness is allowed to relax somewhat while reminiscences emerge. In *The Magic Lantern,* Ingmar Bergman (1988) writes, "I can still roam through the landscape of my childhood and again experience lights, smells, people, rooms, moments, gestures, tones of voice, and objects. These memories seldom have any particular meaning, but are like short or longer films with no point, shot at random" (p. 13). But, in those damaged by early, brutal sexual abuse, reveries are supplanted by trance states. In this altered state of consciousness, events are relived as if happening at the moment, or behaviors are enacted without conscious awareness or intent. At such times, whether or not the contents of memory are precise or conflated is irrelevant. The person's psyche is contorted by mind bends and time bends. She is in enormous terror and pain, involuntarily consumed by the retrieved memory.

Jane, a talented executive, whose 10-years-older brother had sadistically abused her from 18 months to age 15 (corroborated by her mother) falls spontaneously into trance when she begins to talk of him. She curls up in a ball, cries, whimpers, holds her arms tightly around her, crosses her legs under her, screams and falls silent, sniveling, mucus dripping from her nose.

This nonverbal memory became part of the history she and I both needed to know and absorb before Jane was able to integrate the multiple parts of her personality. Such memories, rather than organizing and romancing the self, were too tormenting to bear. She had to compartmentalize them, to close off awareness in order not to suicide. Together, we devised techniques for her to remain in control when she would think of her brother's savage sexual assaults.

Loss of the Ability to Self-soothe.   Without memories that romance and soothe, can there be healing? A pernicious consequence of such failed capacity to romantically reminisce or indulge in controlled reveries is the loss of the ability to self-soothe. I agree with van der Kolk's (1987) focus on annihilation anxiety in the sexually abused. He emphasizes that incest survivors have little access to memories of safe interpersonal attachment. To comfort the self requires internalization of experience with a protective person who shows and teaches the child self-care and the means of easing stress. When incestuous sexual abuse occurs, this interpersonal schemata is seriously violated. Desire for connection becomes linked with humiliation, despair, and betrayal.

Often when incest occurs between parents and their young children, life-threatening abuse is intermixed with tenderness. This proves pernicious for future attachments and intimacy. I suggest that for the survivor, the possibility of kindness (given and received) becomes disremembered along with the events of betrayal. All aspects of the early attachment are derealized and depersonalized to escape unbearable emotional dissonance and false hope. The self becomes further fragmented with these conscious and unconscious efforts to forget. In treatment, paranoid despair protects the early childhood victim from feeling tenderness for or from her therapist. Threats/acts of self-mutilation and intense negative therapeutic reactions intercept the incest survivor's desire for attachment. She attempts to both penetrate and destroy the analyst lest she again be exploited and discarded by a supposed protector.

The analysand fails to remember or absorb episodes with the analyst that demonstrate mutual caring, concern or constancy. At its worst, the survivor crashes the mutual holding environment so necessary to any therapeutic pursuit (Kafka 1994). This helps explain what Courtois (1988) voices for all analysts of the sexually abused: it is notoriously difficult to form an alliance with traumatized clients. Survivors must actually be taught how to self-soothe and control self-harm under stress. Frequently, analysts break neutrality to give these analysands pictures of themselves, write them postcards during vacations, recall past interactions — all to sustain continuity and constancy of the relationship. I suggest memory for benign attachment must be concretely reinforced to assist its integration in the personality. Such reinforced memories foster identification and help to heal the ravaged self of the survivor.

To review, for survivors the soothing functions of memory are diminished. They cannot ease the self with confabulated reminiscences or altered-state reveries. On the contrary, memory's harsh, relentless stalking of the self renders these recollections potentially terrorizing. Unbidden trance states may precipitate delayed memories or flashbacks that not only repeat past cruelties but destroy boundaries of time. These impinge on consciousness as present trauma rather than recall. The dissociated part of the self becomes primary, inaccessible to present reality, to adult identity. Such failure of memory to soothe the pain of the past is matched by the client's inability to comfort the self and develop trust in the analytic engagement. Once more, memory dysfunction is both a symptom and a cause of intransigence of the survivor's personality disturbance.

Unconscious Memory Keeps the Self Honest

Unconscious Memories are the Narrative Truth of the True Self. Unconscious memories are as unverifiable and unreliable as their conscious counterparts, but are less prone to be romanticized. I believe they keep us honest. In whatever ways they get stored, whether it be through the interweaving of interpersonal experience with body/mind states suggested by Stern's (1988) RIG (representations of internalizations generalized), or through repressive familial, cultural, and political forces (Kaminsky 1993), or through the protective, defensive mental mechanisms that create splits in the personality (Kluft 1990, Ross 1989), unconscious memories represent aspects of the self that are most consonant with a person's temperament and nature.

Analysts and clients alike have much evidence of the ubiquity and potency of unconscious memories. Such memories may take circuitous routes to announce their presence but they will not be ignored. We discern their proximity in metaphors, symbols, and slips; images, fantasies and dreams, even screen memories. Knowingly, analysts ask for earliest memories with mother, father, for repetitive dreams and nightmares. Unconscious memories are drawn into awareness through feelings, images, the sensorium as with Proust's famous "petite madeleine" or even through anhedonia. They are triggered by associations, serendipitous happenings, and often within transference/countertransference enactments. Indeed, Paivio (1971b) asserts such recall matches the original dual coding of experience in verbal and sensorial processes.

Incest survivors may unconsciously recollect events in obsessive, murderous thoughts toward the perpetrators or even in mysterious, seemingly unrelated behaviors, such as reactions to social and political events. A startling example of the unwitting "return of the repressed" occurred in my practice during the Persian Gulf War (Kafka 1991). With the war's onset, more than half a dozen women who had been sexually molested in childhood showed regressive behaviors, for examle, hiding, taking to bed, and fighting with partners. All were glued to CNN, some stopping normal daily activities to do so. Their symptoms were typical for posttraumatic stress disorder (PTSD); they included insomnia, weeping, distrust, hypervigilance, depression, depersonalization, and dissociation.

> One distraught woman declared. "I feel like I am Israel . . .passive . . . plotting . . . afraid to fight back and lose whatever protection I can get, hating myself for appeasement, knowing I'll be attacked again . . . sitting on my own power. I feel ashamed and humiliated at my compliance."

The full power of unconscious memories is revealed when they engulf the consciousness of incest survivors, submerging awareness of present reality. Flashbacks of brutal events match in their ferocity the force of all the person's efforts at dissociation, denial, and depersonalization. They assail consciousness. These memories atomize the person's sense of control, time and personhood. They charge the survivor to confront the truth and pain.

Unconscious Memories Are Open Gestalts that Demand Closure.
Open gestalts create a tension for closure that prompts the person to
confront hidden aspects of experience and the self. They function
similarly for survivors as for anyone else. The difference for victims
of childhood abuse is that unconscious memories may hold happenings so horrendous and painful, potentially so disrupting to relationships and adaptation, that even suspicion of their presence is
terrorizing. Horowitz (1986) discusses ways to take advantage of this
"completion tendency," balancing terrorizing intrusions with control,
even denial, to best desensitize the unconscious traumas and facilitate their integration.

*Relationship Between Demand of Unconscious Memories and Recover-
ing Early Traumas.*   It is because unconscious truths *insist* on being
heard, that the question whether we should *probe* for memories of
early sexual abuse may not be the most relevant. To misquote Freud,
I believe life is a compromise formation, a condensation created by
the push of all the present forces of everyday living and the pull of
unconscious memories to keep the person true to the self. The
person's consequent struggles and symptoms, bafflements and impossible behaviors, self-induced entrapments, like flares in the night,
lead us to that which demands recall.

In my opinion, the client is the guide. During certain periods of
the treatment, even though conflicted and terrified, the person might
want to learn of the past as much as she can. Despite shame and inner
repulsion, she returns to the struggle, desiring but fighting recall all
the way. At other times, she has had enough. The woman abused by
her brother now attests she need know no more than what she already
remembers to be able to get on with her present life. She is married,
expecting a second child and changing careers. She claims for the
first time in her life, at age 36, she can sleep at night, feels happy,
calm, knows who she is, and is not suicidal.

> In contrast, Nancy insists on knowing all, rebuking me con-
> stantly for failing to help her regain her past. This compulsively
> controlled woman, tortured and tormented by drug-addicted
> parents, is emotionally frozen and withdrawn, with amnesias
> for significant segments of her life. She regulates every mo-
> ment of her waking life with schedules that permit no devia-

tion. Before she even met me, she had been reading everything published on sex abuse, suspecting therein lies the avenue to the softer sides of her numbed self.

Her unconscious memories indeed keep this woman honest, in touch with her true self. Emotions and deeds of all kinds are rampant in her dreams. Terror, passion, sadism, treachery of persecutors appear along with the vulnerability, incontinence and primitive neediness of an abandoned, endangered infant. These are repeated themes that prove clues to dissociated memories. She also allows herself to play in her dreams and take many different roles, a dreaming function that releases her from the stasis of her more rigid, waking state (Bulkeley 1993). Integrating her split-off unconscious with her waking reality is a continuing process for the two of us.

To my mind the pertinent questions are: When the client's memory functioning, personality disorganization, and life difficulties point to unknown hurts and secrets, does she want us jointly to try to discover or uncover them? I ask myself, Do I have a right to start an exploration that en route may cause enormous pain, anguish, and alienation, without her agreement and foreknowledge of the journey's hazards and purposes? And then, of prime importance, How much is it necessary to know, really, for healing to occur?

Claudia, a photojournalist, has never recalled consciously any specific incident of childhood sexual abuse. Before her analysis, however, she lived in a dissociated, schizoid state, filled with fantasies and dreams that depicted life-threatening sexual cruelties to young children. She had been involved with a married man who sexually and verbally abused her. On separating from him, she felt compelled to film stories of the Holocaust. When she finished treatment a while ago, she left for Cambodia to work with women and children raped by the Khmer Rouge. She went to bear witness and report with her photo stories a criminality she felt had to be documented. She left home feeling powerful and whole, she told me, integrating her values and political beliefs with the essence of an inner experience, although ineffable, that had affected her entire life.

Claudia, exhilarated, said that she wanted to throw open her arms and dance.

To review, unconscious memories are true to us, in their fashion. They help keep us honest to ourselves. No matter how nefarious their routes, how terrible their contents, they press us to deal with them, one way or the other, in order to make peace with ourselves. This is true, but more so, for victims of childhood sexual abuse, where words might not even be the medium of memory of their early childhood incestuous experiences. But even this process becomes disturbed by uncontrolled flashbacks that bend both time and the minds of the therapeutic dyad.

CONCLUSIONS

Memory is a Recombinant Phenomenon.   Memory is both an individual and interpersonal experience. From infancy, body recall provides a relative self-sameness through time, helping establish the person's continuity in the past, present and future. There is always, however, a familial, cultural, and political context for what should be remembered, how it is to be recalled, and whether indeed it is to be recalled at all.[1]

When there are malevolent traumatic events, however, the memory process itself becomes faulted. The sensory-cognitive modalities in which memories are stored and their access to recall are fused with many intense feelings that foster dissociative processes. While this is true for all survivors of trauma, such as victims of the Holocaust and brutalities of warfare, such horrendous events do not disorganize the development of the self in like manner to the young incested child. In the child whose body and psyche have been ravaged by a known betraying adult, the organizing, soothing and unconscious operations of memory become dysfunctional. They create havoc with the person's sense of constancy, continuity, integration, self-esteem and capacity for intimacy.

---

[1] In our cultural-political context, where it is "politically correct" to respect the rights of children and women, it has become permissible to recall early victimization. And for those accustomed to exploit and be exploited, it even becomes fashionable to tell stories to the radio and television talk show hosts, the "paparazzi" of journalists.

Traumatic memories, false or true, are not the data we seek. They are symptomatic of a more pervasive memory dysfunction resultant from adult betrayal and penetration of the child's self. We more readily can learn about the possibilities of abuse, be it true or false, from the ways in which dysfunctional memory foments disorganization of the survivor's personality, from attending to memories that haunt rather than soothe the self, and from heeding the unconscious messages that manifest themselves in strange behav iors, dreams, and feelings.

We observe these disturbances along with paramount symptoms and the subtlest clues; they inform us that early traumatic damage is affecting our client's present life. Above all, when in doubt whether to explore the past for sexual trauma, we remember the analysand is an essential part of the decision. We can ask our clients what they might want to do at any specific time. And we can listen. Whether to probe for repressed traumatic memories — whether healing requires such recall become clinical/ethical dilemmas that only our clients can help us resolve.

Analytic work with all analysands is much the same, be the person severely abused or not. We weave a narrative with strands of the present and of our interactions, with those from conscious and unconscious memories. Clients' stories are created from their and our own necessities to make sense of the mystification of life. Together, we embroider the story, employing twisted threads of memory, fantasy and experience, ours with theirs, to enhance the person's cohesion, surety and self-regard, to diminish shame, humiliation, and guilt, to overcome loneliness and alienation, so that they might, in their lives, go well.

I end with a poem that expresses for me an essential analytic goal with all analysands, especially those survivors of childhood traumas. It is taken from Maya Angelou's poem, *On the Pulse of the Morning*, dedicated to the nation at President Clinton's inauguration.

> History, despite its wrenching pain,
> Cannot be unlived, but if faced
> With courage, need not be lived again.
>
> Lift up your eyes
> Upon this day breaking for you,
> Give birth again.

REFERENCES

Allport, G. W. (1960). *Personality and Social Encounter.* Boston: Beacon.

Angelou, M. (1993). *On the Pulse of Morning.* New York: Random House.

Beebe, B., and Lachmann, F. (1988). The contribution of mother-infant mutual influence to the origins of self- and object representations. *Psychoanalytic Psychology,* 5(4):305–347.

Bergman, I. (1988). *The Magic Lantern.* New York: Viking Penguin.

Blume, E. S. (1990). *Secret Survivors: Uncovering Incest and its Aftereffects in Women.* New York: John Wiley.

Brainard, C., and Ornstein, P. A. (1991). Children's memory for witnessed events: the developmental backdrop. In *The Suggestibility of Children's Recollections: Implications for Eyewitness Testimony,* ed. J. Doris. pp 10–20. Washington DC: American Psychological Association.

Braun, B. (1988a). The BASK model of dissociation, part I. *Dissociation 1:4–15.*

———— (1988b). The BASK model of dissociation, part II: treatment. *Dissociation* 1:16–23.

Briere, J. (1989). *Therapy with Adults Molested as Children: Beyond Survival.* New York: Springer.

Bromberg, P. (1993). Shadow and substance: a relative perspective on clinical processes. *Psychoanalytic Psychology 10(2):147–168.*

Bulkeley, K. (1993). Dreaming is play. *Psychoanalytic Psychology* 10(4), 501–514.

Carter, H. (1935). Effects of emotional factors on recall. *Journal of Psychology* 1:49–59.

Cernoch, J. M., and Porter, R. H. (1985). Recognition of maternal axillary odors by infants. *Child Development* 56:1593–1598.

Chi, M. T. H., and Koeske, R. H. (1983). Network representation of a child's dinosaur knowledge. *Developmental Psychology* 19:29–39.

Courtois, C. (1988). *Healing the Incest Wound: Adult Survivors in Therapy.* New York: Norton.

———— (1992). The memory retrieval process in incest survivor therapy. *Journal of Child Sexual Abuse 1(1):15 -31.*

Davies, J. M., and Frawley, M. G. (1993). *Treating the Adult Survivor of Childhood Sexual Abuse.* New York: Basic Books.

Gelinas, D. (1988). The persisting negative effects of incest. *Psychiatry* 46:313–332.

Gil, E. (1988). *Treatment of Adult Survivors of Childhood Abuse.* Walnut Creek, CA: Launch.

Horowitz, M. J. (1986). *Stress Response Syndromes,* 2nd ed. Northvale, NJ: Jason Aronson.

Kafka, H. (1991). Effect of the Persian Gulf War on survivors of childhood abuse. *Psychologist–Psychoanalyst* 11:23–24.

——— (1992). To cure or to heal? *International Forum of Psychoanalysis.* 1:110–118.

——— (1994). *Survivors of childhood incest, vicarious traumatization and the dual process of containment.* Paper presented at The International Forum of Psychoanalysis, Florence, Italy, May 10.

Kaminsky, M. (1993). Discourse and self-formation: cultural studies toward a post-structuralist psychoanalysis. Unpublished manuscript.

Kluft, R. P., ed. (1990). *Incest-Related Syndromes of Adult Psychopathology.* Washington, DC: American Psychiatric Press.

Loftus, E., and Loftus, G. (1980). On the permanence of stored information in the human brain. *American Psychologist* 35:409–427.

McCann, L., and Perlman, L. (1990). *Psychological Trauma and the Adult Survivor: Theory, Therapy, and Transformation.* New York: Brunner/Mazel.

Meiselman, K. (1990). *Resolving the Trauma of Incest: Reintegration Therapy with Survivors.* San Francisco: Jossey Bass.

Paivio, A. (1971a). *Imagery and Verbal Processes.* New York: Holt Rinehart.

——— (1971b). *Mental Representations: A Dual Coding Approach.* New York: Oxford University Press.

Perry, N. W. (1992). How children remember and why they forget. In: *The Advisor,* 5(3):1–2, 13–16. American Professional Society on the Abuse of Children.

Piaget, J., and Inhelder, B. (1973). *Memory and Intelligence.* New York: Basic Books.

Ross, C. (1989). *Multiple Personality Disorder: Diagnosis, Clinical Features, and Treatment.* New York: John Wiley.

Shapiro, S. (1993). *Incest as chronic trauma.* Paper read at William Alanson White Clinical Services Case Conference. New York.

Singer, J. R., ed. (1990). *Repression and Dissociation: Implications for Personality Theory, Psychopathology and Health.* Chicago: University of Chicago Press.

Spiegel, D, (1989). Hypnosis in the treatment of victims of sexual abuse. *Psychiatric Clinics of North America* 12:295–305.

Stern, D. (1988). The dialectic between the "interpersonal" and the "intrapsychic" with particular emphasis on the role of memory representation. *Psychoanalytic Inquiry* 8:505–512.

Sullivan, H. S. (1953). *The Interpersonal World of Psychiatry.* New York: Norton.

Summit, R. C. (1992). Misplaced attention to delayed memory. In: *The Advisor,* 5(3):1–2, 13–16. American Professional Society on the Abuse of Children.

van der Kolk, B. (1987). *Psychological Trauma.* Washington, DC: American Psychiatric Press.

Wylie, M. S. (1993). The shadow of a doubt. *Family Therapy Networker.* September/October:19–73.

6

Memory and Imagination: Placing Imagination in the Therapy of Individuals with Incest Memories

EVELYN PYE

One of the problems with the current debate about delayed versus false memory is that it sets up a bifurcation between memory and imagination. Certain images arise and the question becomes, Are they "real" or "imagined"? But this disregards the rather complex relation between memory and imagination. Perhaps the question is not one of imagination versus memory, but rather what is the *form* of *both* imagination and memory. Building on the work of Klein, Winnicott and others, it is possible to distinguish forms of thought, emotion, imagery, memory and bodily experience that are persecutory from structures or states of mind that are agentic. It is possible to differentiate these states of mind as they occur in the present and to work in therapy toward a dynamic dialectic between them. In the delayed versus false memory debate there is tremendous pressure about the question of history, about what "really happened." Significant difficulties can develop, however, when the therapy rises or falls on the question of determining the true content of memory or history, not the least of which is the pressure for the therapist to have authority about events he or she never witnessed. In this chapter an approach is offered that can circumvent some of those difficulties by focusing on contemporary experience, analyzing the ways the individual structures his or her current intrapsychic and interpersonal life and feels impelled by those structures.

An underlying premise of this chapter is that the goal, or one of the goals, of psychotherapy is the development or retrieval of the capacity for reverie and that psychological symptoms arise when the capacity for imagination is lost or ruptured — when the psychological can only become manifest through the literal. A second premise is that reverie or what Winnicott (1971) refers to as potential space is only possible with certain more agentic, less persecutory states of mind. For some individuals the experience of the imagination as an ongoing ground of being, as a place of restoration and vitality and as the carrier, along with the body, of the self is precarious or absent. For such individuals the work of repairing or developing the capacity to enter potential space and developing the agentic structure of mind that underlies that capacity can be the central focus of the therapy. In this way of thinking about therapy, the primary goal is not to ascertain the truth of memory as such, but rather to help the patient to move out of a rigidly persecutory, victimizing structure of mind into states that include the agentic and the imaginal. Thus, the work of creating space for dreaming and of repairing the capacity for reverie, the metaphoric and the nonliteral can be that which guides the therapist's thinking about the therapy. The repair of imagination can be as important as, indeed can lead to, the integration of memory.[1]

---

[1]Analysts working from a relational theoretical base have also focused on the analysis of the contemporary structuring of experience (e.g., Bromberg 1993, Ehrenberg, 1992, Mitchell 1988). For example: "Further, I suggest that the way analysts conceptualize reality in terms of past and present is also changing. The clinical focus is not as much on discovering past roots of current problems — as though past experience and present experience are discretely stratified in the memory bank of a unitary 'self' — as on exploring the way in which the self-states comprising a patient's personal identity are linked to each other, to the external world, and to the past, present and future" (Bromberg 1993, p. 150). Or: "If one views the analysand's experience of the analysis and the analyst as fundamentally interactive, as an encounter between two *persons*, the analysand is struggling to reach *this* analyst. . . . The problem is no longer past significant others, but how to connect with, surrender to, dominate, fuse with, control, love, be loved by, use, be used by, *this* person" (Mitchell 1988, p. 300). These approaches share in the project of locating the

"GOOD ARTISTS COPY; GREAT ARTISTS STEAL"

A 3-year-old was playing with her father. As part of the game she said, "Daddy you be dead." So the father played dead for a few minutes and then sat up. The daughter said, "No, no, Daddy. You be dead, and I'll go over here and dream about it." The father fell back on the grass and the little girl went over to another part of the yard, sat down, and began to sing a mournful dirge.

In this exchange between father and daughter a piece of imagination was made. Certainly a make-believe story was enacted. But more than that the girl made the father into a "ghost" in her own mind. She became an "orphan" with a memory-father. What had been the literal father was transmuted into a spirit father, a mental or psychological father for whom the child "grieved." But importantly, it was all in play. It is equally crucial for the making of imagination that the child was able to "kill" her father and that they both knew he never died. For imagination to be made the father/other must not literally be killed; the real cannot override the symbolic—that would be trauma. For imagination to be made the child must be able *to fantasize* killing her father/other and to experience the grief and anxiety that entails. And for imagination to be made, a mutual relationship with actual others must exist where the child can experience herself as shaping and being shaped by the form of their play. These three aspects about the making of imagination are central to this chapter: to carve out space for imagination takes both desire and aggression (artists must steal to create); the development of imagination is linked with the development of agency; and imagination is destroyed by the traumatic.

THE USE OF AN OBJECT

Winnicott (1971) makes the distinction between object relating and object usage. In object relating there is a steady stream of projection

---

therapeutic action in the current exchange in the therapy dyad and in the patient's current structuring of his or her experience. They do not, however, place the imagination as such in quite as central a position as I am suggesting here or as it has had with Winnicott's (1971) work on potential space and Segal's (1957, 1991) on the symbolic.

and introjection from the self to and from the other. The other is not truly other but a bundle of projections. The self gives over to the other something of herself. sometimes ideal or beneficent parts of the self, sometimes hateful parts of the self are ejected into the other. Primarily through projective identification (Klein 1946, 1955, Malin and Grotstein 1966, Ogden 1982, 1986, 1989) the other is omnipotently controlled. She is shaped and maneuvered into being what is needed at the moment. In object usage, on the other hand, the other is recognized as having a reality of her own beyond the projective control of the self. The other is over there and actual with capacities and motivations that are independent of the self. While there is a loss in omnipotence and symbiotic perfection (and persecutory perfection) in the move from object relating to object usage, there are great gains on two fronts. Now that the other is apart from the self she can actually have something to offer the self; it becomes possible to receive something from the other and to depend on her (hence the word usage). And now that projective control is transformed it becomes possible for the subject to see her own projective or imaginative life as distinct from the omnipotent shaping of the other. Imagination is born.

In Winnicott's description of the move from object relating through transitional space to object usage, the role of aggression is crucial. It is when the individual recognizes that she has banged herself or her ideas into the other, and that the other has essentially maintained her integrity that the other comes to be truly other, that is, to be located outside the omnipotent control of the self. Winnicott uses the term *survival of the object* to refer to this crucial point where the individual comes to recognize her own aggression and the independence of the other. He depicts the self as unconsciously saying to the other, " 'While I am loving you I am all the time destroying you in (unconscious) *fantasy*.' Here fantasy begins for the individual" (Winnicott 1971, p. 90 italics in original). While "survival of the object" may seem to imply survival by the other of destructive aggression, it is also the survival of the aggression of desire, wanting to consume the other and love the other "to bits."

THE DEPRESSIVE POSITION

Winnicott's concept of object usage is built on Klein's work on the depressive position. Klein (1935, 1940, 1946, 1955) delineates the development from the paranoid-schizoid position where interaction is based on projective identification, splitting, and omnipotent control of the other to the depressive position where interaction is based on the recognition of the subjectivity of the other; recognition of one's own capacity to do harm through rapacious love, hate and envy; and the desire to repair what one has (in fantasy) destroyed. With the depressive position comes the sense of oneself as a subject and author located in history as opposed to being the victim of incommensurable forces (Ogden 1986). And with the depressive position comes the capacity for symbolization and metaphor (Segal 1957, 1991) and the ability to be reflective, to take a psychological perspective on events, to engage in reverie. Winnicott was building on Klein's work in recognizing the crucial role of aggression and desire in getting to a psychologically based worldview and a capacity for reverie. However, Klein focuses a bit more than Winnicott on the simultaneous process of mourning as part of the process that allows for movement into subjectivity (hence the term *depressive position*). She sees that it is not only the recognized act of (fantasized) aggression against and consumption of the other and the other's survival that creates psychological space, but it is also the ability to bear the anxiety and grief one feels about the damage one (fantasizes one) has done and the desire to repair and resuscitate the other that makes the symbolic and reveried possible. Thus, for her, in the example of the 3-year-old with her father, it is not only the "killing of the father" but also the "mournful dirge" that allows for the child's experience of "dreaming about it," that is, reverie that is recognized as daydreaming. To get to reverie, one must be able to contain and tolerate *both* the anxiety of seeing oneself as destructive through one's love and hate *and* the anxiety of loss.

Ogden (1982, 1986, 1989) has built on the work of Winnicott, Klein, and other Kleinians (e.g., Bion 1956, 1957, 1959, Segal 1957) in a number of ways. Two of these are most relevant here. He has expanded on Klein in recognizing that projective identification is not only a means of defense, but also a form of communication. Thus, the therapist's process of containing (Bion 1962) and ultimately giving back to the patient in a symbolic rather than enacted form the patient's projective identifications can be a fundamental means of helping the patient to bear what is unbearable and to transform what is unsayable into conscious, symbolic (i.e., depressive) form. Ogden (1986, 1992) has also pointed out that Klein's paranoid-schizoid and depressive positions or Winnicott's object relating and object usage are not simply ontologically defined developmental steps. They are categories or structures of thought and experience that are always present in adult life in a constant dialectical interplay with each other. Thus, the individual may shift over the course of an analytic hour back and forth between the positions of being a hapless victim and of being one who is involved in the making of her own life and world and who is affected by that world.

OMNIPOTENCE VERSUS "HAVING HANDS"

In the move from object relating to object usage or from the paranoid-schizoid to the depressive position there is a change in the form of agency for the individual. In a paranoid-schizoid structure there is simultaneously a profound experience of impotence — one feels shunted about by incommensurable forces from within and without, *and* there is tremendous effort toward gaining control of these forces through omnipotent and magical means. There is simultaneously victimization and tyranny. Moods, memories, thoughts, images, and bodily states just appear and take one over and then shift or disappear just as arbitrarily. It is a violently fluctuating world in which feelings, thoughts, images, and the body are all experienced as the enemy. At the same time, the individual treats his psychic life just as tyrannically and arbitrarily. He acts as if he could simply shift the reality of what he feels, thinks, or sees however he wishes, as if by executive decision. States that are potentially unbearable are simply evacuated or unfelt. They are "disappeared." It is a structure in which a fundamental experience of impotence is overlaid or defended against by omnipotent, magical means.

Perhaps paradoxically, as one enters a depressive state it becomes possible to recognize both the autonomy of the other and the interchange of effects between oneself and others. The depressive anxiety about the destructive power of one's own aggression, greed, and desire carries with it the implicit knowledge that one is able to affect others. As one struggles with this anxiety, it becomes bearable to see one's effects on others and how one is affected by them. At the same time, a more mutual relationship develops with one's own psychic life. It becomes bearable to make links, to see the parallels between outer events and inner states and between different inner states. One can see, for example, the connections between a certain emotion and a certain bodily state, or between a dream or fantasy and a particular way one treats one's thoughts or emotions when awake. A mutuality of influence becomes possible, where respect for the actuality of one's psychic life goes hand in hand with a developing awareness of how and where effects and transformations are possible. In this way Winnicott's concept of object usage is relevant on both the interpersonal and intrapsychic planes.

The shift from paranoid-schizoid to depressive, thus, involves a shift from a solipsistic kind of agency where the individual copes with intrusions from the inside or outside by action on his own mind to a kind of agency where the individual is in a relatively mutual relationship of affecting and being affected by the other, where "the other" is both actual persons and one's own psychic life. There is a shift from a world of evacuations and splittings and disappearances to one where both grief and influence are possible. It is a movement from magical thinking to "having hands" (von Franz 1972).

MEMORY AND IMAGINATION

Memory and imagination are intimately intertwined. Much of the time, but not always, we remember through imaginative, imagistic means. The capacity to have memories at all, to have sufficient continuity of experience to have historicity, is dependent on our developing ability to engage in reverie and to imagine (Klein 1935, 1940, Ogden 1986, Segal 1957, 1991). And when we do come to have memories as such, those memories are by necessity structured by the shape of our imaginative and projective processes both at the time of the original experience and at the moment we are remembering. As we develop in our capacity for reverie and self-reflection, our view of our memories and the significance those memories have for us can evolve. The *form* of our memory at any particular time speaks to the form of our imaginations and vice versa.

Adler (1985) explicates specific developmental aspects of the interrelation between memory and imagination. He builds on the work of Piaget (1937) and Fraiberg (1969) in making the distinction between recognition and evocative memory. In recognition memory there is no ability to conjure up an image of people or objects when they are not present. There is no object permanence, and the individual tends to have a persecutory relationship with his own memory, both feeling waylaid by it and treating it tyrannically. With evocative memory, on the other hand, there is object permanence, the capacity to evoke the image of the absent person. A trace of the other stays with us when we part. Evocative memory implies the ability to introject aspects of the other, commingled with our projections onto them. It is evocative memory that provides the continuity of experience that we usually think of as memory. And evocative memory is based on the ability to imagine — to conjure an image, usually visual, sometimes auditory, conceptual, or proprioceptive. *It is only as we come to be able to imagine that we come to be able to remember.*

Evocative memory is subtle, if powerful. On the one hand, we can with intent conjure up a memory. On the other hand, memories come to us outside our conscious control, through associational and reveried means. There is something soothing in and of itself about evocative memory, about what it conveys of the continuity of our existence, about the "going-on-being" (Winnicott 1965) that is fundamental to us with no conscious intent or effort on our part. When evocative memory is not present either temporarily or as an ongoing state of affairs, when the individual is operating in a paranoid-schizoid manner with only recognition memory available, these two aspects of memory as evocation and association become more extreme. On the one hand, memory is experienced as intruding and subjecting the self to its own exigencies. On the other hand, there can be an attempt to control memory omnipotently — the individual treats her memory tyrannically, forcing images out of and into view as a means of controlling her own emotions. Memory itself becomes an abuser, ready to pounce and overwhelm at any moment. With this persecutory form of memory there is the feeling that there is something inside of the individual that will sneak up or crash in from behind and take control. There is also the feeling that memory cannot be relied upon. A memory of an event, person, feeling, or thought unpredictably intrudes on the individual and then is just as suddenly forgotten, utterly disappeared from mind. There is a manhandling of memory and imagination and an experience of being manhandled by memory and imagination. Memory and imagination become a place of assault — both the individual's assault on his own psychic life and the assault of his feelings, images, and body on the self. Both reverie and evocative memory are impossible. In this struggle between being overwhelmed by one's memories or having to gain omnipotent control over them, there is a loss of the life of memory. To "remember" may fill one with dread or intrusive imagery, but the transmutation of that remembering into a world that is alive, of people and events remembered, cherished, hated, and/or mourned is foreclosed. To remember in the way we usually use the word, one must be able to entertain "ghosts," to allow oneself to dwell with feelings, images, thoughts, and/or bodily sensations in ways that allow the mind to wander. Aspects of experience come to mind and coalesce, new links are made and others dissolve. When this is not possible, memory can become reified. There is pressure toward memory as singular, a univocal thing that either is or is not true. It is impossible to reflect on memories, to allow them to be ambiguous, to cohere, and to differentiate. The individual experiences herself as at the mercy of harrowing terrors, which she can only fend off by magical and tyrannical means. Reverie is impossible.

PSYCHOTHERAPY OF THE BROKEN IMAGINATION

The work of therapy can be to help patients to have flexibility between the states of mind described thus far and, therefore, to be able to enter potential space and the full humanity of their imaginations. The process of coming to be able to have both imagination and memory is dependent upon transformation of the entire psychic structure of which imagination and memory are crucial parts. This involves the work of recognizing the shifts back and forth between persecutory and agentic structures and it involves analyzing what constellates those shifts in mind. Part of what keeps an individual locked in a persecutory paradigm is a set of omnipotent, magical defenses that protect against the overwhelming sense of powerlessness. The analysis of this defensive structure involves containing and transmuting anxiety about linking that which has been sundered and makes it possible gradually to bring the patient's split-off aggression and desire into the therapy. This in turn makes possible the transformation from a solipsistic kind of agency into object usage . At the same time the work of entering into "having hands" (von Franz

1972) also allows for potential space and the development of the patient's capacity for reverie. Each aspect of this work will be discussed in turn.

Analyzing Anxiety About Making Linkages

In a persecutory structure of experience there is no history (Ogden 1986, 1989). There are no links between events. Each emotional event is a cataclysm unrelated to the last or the next. Working to build links between moments of time and between states of mind in the present is central to helping the patient to develop hands — and imagination and memory. It is important to bear in mind that these attacks on linking (Bion 1959) are a *defense*. They are intended to ward off an even greater terror that would come if those links were maintained. Thus, the therapist needs to recognize the omnipotent defenses *as* omnipotence, that is, as a form of magical thinking that is intended to ward off this high anxiety. The work of analyzing the patient's fears of linking one moment to the next, analyzing her fears about the power of her omnipotent fantasies, and analyzing her fears about the significance of her altered states to events in the current therapy exchange all serve to return the patient's mind to her. And with the return of her mind comes the return of memory and imagination.

    To take a hypothetical example: a patient reports that she has had a terrifying flashback the night before the current therapy hour, a "delayed memory." She saw and experienced things she has never quite been aware of before. She was in an altered state and felt "done-to" by all that she was seeing and feeling. She is still very shaken. One choice would be to go into the content of the images that were revealed. But this leads to a slippery slope of deciding the status of those images. Are they memories? Are they screen memories and condensations? Are they dreams? Is their truth purely psychological or also literal? A different direction is to analyze the process that compelled the patient into such an altered state of mind where she lost her own subjectivity and became the object of her psyche rather than a coauthor with it. Such an analysis focuses on what could have been the event of the previous day's therapy session that propelled the patient into such a state. In one case it is something the therapist said that seemed to miss the patient; in another it is something the therapist said that was all-too-correct and brought the therapy dyad into an intimacy that was terrifying for the patient. In another case it is a simmering rage the patient feels but dares not express about the therapist's recent or impending vacation. In another case it is the intensity of the patient's feelings of love, hate, or love-hate for the therapist at a particular moment. The work is to recognize that to speak directly of such things feels terrifying to the patient, as if to tell the therapist her love, anger or disappointment would kill the therapist (either the actual therapist or the therapist in the patient's mind) and explode the therapy. Rather than kill the therapist and all that has felt valuable in the therapy, the patient kills her own mind. Naming this terror of her own omnipotent fantasies and making the link between the moment where the patient experiences the process of her own agency as murderous and the moment where she destroys her own mind are essential to bringing these experiences into a human register.

There are two parts to this kind of interpretation. First, there is making the link between a state in which the patient has lost her subjectivity and is experiencing herself as the object of abuse (e.g., episodes of self-mutilation, dissociation, delayed memory, flashbacks) and a current event, usually one within the therapy known to both parties. Second, there is interpreting the patient's anxiety about her response to the current situation and the magical fantasies contained within that anxiety (e.g., that her anger or desire would damage the therapist or the value of the therapy), which is what has propelled her into the dissociative state. This kind of linking interpretation makes it possible for the patient gradually to resolve her anxiety, which derives from a persecutory paradigm where to affect someone is equivalent to victimizing him or her. When, for example, the patient tells the therapist about last night's flashback/delayed memory, the therapist recognizes that the psychic material is coming in a form that leaves the patient split-off and groundless. She traces with the patient the progression from the last therapy hour to this most recent episode until it becomes clear when the moment in the therapy hour occurred where the patient also felt split-off and groundless, even if it was at a much less intense level. The therapist links these two moments and considers what was so frightening to the patient in the therapy moment that her mind split apart. As this anxiety is named and contained within the therapy, the need to protect against it through omnipotent defenses lessens.

This transformation built up over many hours of making such linkages is part of what gradually shifts the patient out of a persecutory paradigm. She begins no longer to need to be either a victim or tyrant, intrapsychically or interpersonally. She no longer needs to kill her own mind in order not to kill the other, either literally or within herself. It becomes bearable to see both how she is affected by the therapist and how she both affects and is afraid of affecting the therapist. What has been a self-destructive, volatile, and solipsistic form of agency becomes converted into a human dimension.

Analyzing Negative Transference

Linking interpretations involving the patient's aggression and experience of negative transference are particularly crucial and particularly difficult. With individuals caught in a rigidly persecutory paradigm, there are often extremes of abuse and victimization with little center ground. Feelings of disappointment, disavowal, anger, and hate toward the therapist are seen by the patient as unspeakably dangerous. There is an omnipotent belief that to speak such things will cause irreparable harm. The boundary between conveying a feeling or fantasy and enacting it literally becomes murky. The danger is not only to the actual therapist but also to the therapist and the therapy as positive values within the patient's mind. It feels as though to entertain the negative feelings would destroy all that is felt to be positive. To protect the therapy the patient keeps overt signs of negative transference out of the office and enacts those feelings out of view, often against her own mind and body. The break in linkage can be so thorough that any connections between horrendous acts of self-violence and -victimization outside the therapy would never be associated with thoughts or feelings about the therapy or therapist. It feels to the patient as if she is simply swept into desperate states where she must enact self-mutilations of one form or another rather than explode or dissolve. Such situations are structured as if *both* patient and therapist are helpless victims. Finding the way out of this interpersonal and intrapsychic persecutory structure is crucial and it involves finding a way to address the patient as the *author* of aggression rather than the *object* of it.

The countertransference experience in this kind of situation is twofold. On the one hand, the therapist can feel as impotent as the patient in the face of self-destructive acts committed during altered states. How can you engage with someone to stop an action when the individual feels entirely the victim of herself? On the other hand, there can be a countertransference strain around the therapist's own aggression, as if to interpret the patient's split-off aggression would be a retraumatizing assault on the skinless victim-patient or a trigger that starts another cycle of extreme self-abuse and -derision. The therapist needs to come to terms with her own fear (not unlike the patient's) that to speak of these things will cause unredeemable harm. It is important for the therapist to recognize the aggression involved in the patient's attacks on herself and to interpret the patient's anxiety about bringing the negative feelings into the therapy (Ogden 1991). The patient, for example, cuts herself in order to protect the therapist from the patient's rage. As the therapist speaks about the cutting as an expression of the patient's anxiety about the harm her rage could do both intrapsychically and interpersonally, she is implicitly conveying that there is room within the therapy for those feelings. And as the therapist links each episode of self-destructive behavior with events in the therapy and with anxiety about negative transference feelings, those self-destructive acts transform from being arbitrary events governed by their own invisible and unknowable rules to being an aspect of the human exchange between patient and therapist.

Analyzing Solipsistic Communication

This work on negative transference is part of transforming a solipsistic process into an interpersonal one. When the patient converts her rage at the therapist into attacks on her own body and mind outside the therapy, she is engaged in a kind of magical thinking. At first such events may appear to be involuntary impulses devoid of premeditation or communicative value. But with analysis it becomes evident that these events occur in response to something that has happened in the therapy and that they are based on an unconscious or preconscious assumption that somehow they are doing something or communicating something to the therapist magically. There is an unconscious assumption that somehow these acts will affect the therapist without their meaning or emotion ever having to be spoken. It is an aspect of a persecutory paradigm where the individual is unable to take overt action and so instead takes action autistically and magically within and on herself. Interpreting this magical thinking helps to bring it into the realm of interpersonal communication and thus to make the experience of affecting another tolerable for the patient, rather than being experienced as tantamount to murder. What has been a solipsistic kind of agency is gradually converted into a form of communication and directed aggression within the therapy relationship.

Gradually space is made within the therapy to contain feelings of loss and rage and to allow direct, symbolized communication about such feelings and fantasies. It becomes possible for both parties to distinguish two kinds of communicating that are indicative of two distinct states of mind. In one kind the patient is in a closed loop. It is a form of autistic self-inscribing that unconsciously is predicated on magical thinking as the means of communication. For example, the patient may engage in self-destructive acts or withdraw from the therapy in order "to get back at" the therapist without ever saying explicitly, even to herself, that this is what she is doing. The other kind of communication involves making a bridge between therapist and patient, where the patient is able to communicate through explicit and symbolic means. As this differentiation becomes a part of the vocabulary of the therapy, it becomes possible to trace the shifts from one state to the other and to understand what allows and what precludes the move toward "having hands." The patient can begin to understand the difference between tolerating a discomfort or anguish by switching something within her mind so that the pain is no longer experienced ("just standing something," "hurting me instead of hurting you," "making myself disappear") from being agentic as a form of thought and communication within the therapy ("doing something about it," "telling you when I'm angry," "knowing you can stand it"). Once this distinction is clear it becomes possible to track what seems to allow for a move into the agentic and what precipitates a collapse back into the autistic. It also becomes possible to look at the anxiety about affecting the therapist or the internal image of the therapist or therapy that underlies reversion to the solipsistic. Ultimately this can lead to the patient's being able to recognize her own agency within processes that have previously seemed utterly autonomous. These are significant steps in moving from being a victim of her own mind to being one who can reflect on her mind and on shifts in her states of mind.

Object Permanence

Work on object permanence is closely related to this work on containing the negative transference and containing annihilatory anxiety about making linkages. There is a reciprocal relationship between being able to maintain an internal image or experience of the therapy as positive and a source of holding on the one hand and the need to split off negative feelings about the therapy or therapist and enact them outside the therapy on the other. The implicit fear is that if anger and disappointment with the therapist and the therapy is juxtaposed with experiences of the therapist and the therapy as holding or transmutative, then the former will destroy the latter. To protect the positive sense of the therapy from this danger, the individual may split off his aggression and enact it outside the therapy and/or he may send all positive feelings about the therapy so far away from consciousness as to be virtually unreachable (Ogden 1994). In either case, the result is the utter loss of any positive sense of the therapy, of the therapist, or of the experience of oneself in therapy. Object permanence for the therapy or therapist as helpful and soothing and for oneself as engaged in and held by the therapy is dismembered. This can all play out in terms of drastic reactions to breaks in therapy and/or in an escalating dependence on the actual person of the therapist even when there is no disruption in the regular appointment schedule. The manifest problem is a reliance on the literal, concrete therapy setup and an inability to transmute that into a psychological register, which will stay with the patient when the actual is not present.

The work that has already been described of addressing the anxiety about bringing the negative transference into the therapy is clearly crucial in the process of regaining or developing object permanence. In addition, there is work that directly addresses the patient's capacity to hold the therapy in imagination. Explicitly looking at how the patient keeps the therapy experience in mind between sessions and during longer absences can help with the articulation of a process that may otherwise be quite subliminal. The therapist's interest in the images, words, and bodily experiences that stay with the patient as signs of the therapy helps to imbue those representations with significance. The imagination becomes visible and valued. And the therapy process can come to remain present for the patient through psychological processes of imagination and not only through the concrete presence of the actual therapist. There is an ongoing analysis of presence and absence and of how the actual is able to become psychological — how the patient is able to inhabit and be inhabited by the evocation of the therapy. This is a process of helping the patient to develop a "skin," a sense of holding and a benign surround, and it is a process of helping the patient to have an interior that is alive, transmutative, and not under attack. The patient begins to have a sense of herself as located. She experiences herself both as in something — a process, a relationship, her own imagination — and as having *within* her something that is vital and alive.

This work on object permanence involves containing and analyzing rage. It also involves bearing mourning. The ghost of the other person and of the situation that stays with one is a precipitate of mourning. To hold the spirit of another within, we must be able to transmute the literal and to contain whatever grief that might entail. The failure to hold the therapy or therapist in mind when there is separation can be a manic defense against loss (Klein 1935). To be able to keep that connection involves passing through what can seem a grievous sadness about the specific rupture and all the unbearable losses of a lifetime. The therapist needs to be able to recognize the grief that is being kept at bay and to address the anxiety, that if allowed to surface, would drown the therapy. What may seem for the therapist to be a relatively benign hiatus of several days or weeks, or even a month, is a much more profound calamity for a patient who cannot maintain the imaginal thread that connects her to the therapy. Perhaps paradoxically, bearing the grief of that loss is part of what makes it possible to begin to have some glimmers of imagination that keep the therapy alive through absences of the actual.

Containing Anxiety about the Ambiguity of Potential Space

This work on object permanence is a specific aspect of the more general process of creating imagination and the capacity for potential space within the patient and in the therapy. In order for the individual to engage in the work of imagination and transmutation of the literal, it is necessary to allow ambiguity to enter the room. Addressing anxiety about this ambiguity is essential for this work to go forward. The term *potential space* (Winnicott 1971) refers to an attitude of multiple, paradoxical possibilities which by definition is ambiguous. To enter potential space or the imaginal, one must be able to tolerate some measure of such ambiguity. However, for some patients, including individuals where there is a question of abuse, the pressure to know *exactly* what is happening, to have no shadowy corner, can be paramount. The more analytic attitude of wondering, of curiosity about what might unfold, about welcoming polyvalence is anathema. Ambiguity raises the moment of waiting for abuse — will it come, how bad will it be, how can one hurry up and get it over with. There can be a tremendous countertransference pull to provide the relief of certainty that will dissolve this intense anxiety. But that move keeps the therapy hostage to an abuse scene. Perhaps by dispelling uncertainty the therapist can be a protective mother, but he has not found a way to question the basic terms of a persecutory paradigm where uncertainty equals danger. The alternative is for the therapist to work with the patient to make the paradoxical and ambiguous bearable.

Recognizing the patient's anxiety and giving voice to it early in the therapy is one step that can help give language and form to that anxiety, so that it need not impel the direction of the therapy. When one is caught in a persecutory paradigm the situation itself is uroboric — there is conflation and no space whatsoever to speak about what is happening. The process of talking about what transpires between patient and therapist shifts the exchange out of an abuse scene. Recognizing the earliest signs of this anxiety and looking immediately for what is so frightening about what is paradoxical or unknown can help significantly to contain this anxiety so that it does not spiral into the unbearable or the dissociative. The process of tracking the constellation in the hour that raises the anxiety about ambiguity involves taking a depressive attitude toward the anxiety, trying to understand its meaning rather than simply collapsing into the literal in order to expel the anxiety.

Making a Place for the Imagination

In addition to this work of analyzing the anxiety that runs counter to the polyvalence of imagination, there is also the work of establishing a place for imagination as such within the therapy and within the patient. This involves multiple aspects. Perhaps the fundamental underpinning is the therapist's own psychological attitude. If the therapist can listen to all that transpires in the hour in terms of the psychic space that is being created in the present, that can go a long way toward creating room for the imaginal within the therapy. The abuser in the patient's dream is not simply a person from the patient's past. S/he is a figure within the patient's psyche now. The relevant question is: Why has this figure appeared now? The concern is to understand how the dream reflects an abuse that is current, probably an abuse in how the patient is derisive and high-handed with his own imagination and desire and in how he feels abused by his own thoughts, feelings, and intimations. The point is that one can hear associations as communications about the dream that is happening currently in the office and one can listen to dreams not simply reductively in terms of the past but also in their own right as statements about the form of the patient's imagination in the present. The therapist's use of metaphoric language derived from the images of the patient's own associations and dreams helps those figures, landscapes, and actions to become imbued with life and meaning for the patient. And the therapist's responding to the literal with an ear for the metaphoric helps to make the therapy a place of imagination. (What did the patient imagine the sound that just happened outside the office might be? What does the patient imagine when he asks the therapist where he is going on vacation?) As the therapist speaks a language that is about the current psychology of the situation — how the patient's associations, whether memories or not, reflect an up-to-the-minute report on the way the patient is structuring his experience in the present — a psychological mindedness is established as the basic coin of the therapy. This is not to undermine historicity or to question the facticity of remembered events one way or the other. It is, however, to recognize that only certain states of mind have history and to help the patient to find his way into those states of mind.

Winnicott (1954) gives a detailed description of one way in which the therapist can help to make a place for imagination within the therapy. He distinguishes between "withdrawal" (essentially dissociation), where the patient is in a schizoid state devoid of imagination, and "regression," where imagination is present and reverie is possible. Regression is the state where images can arise, be entertained, and transmute. Winnicott delineates the ways the therapist can help to turn a dissociative state into reverie by helping the patient to feel contained within some form of holding. He assumes that in order for the patient to have reverie, there must be a surround to the imagination that is safe and steady. We must feel encompassed to imagine. When such holding is precarious or only barely visible as an implicit glimmer, Winnicott helps to make it explicit. He describes a series of moments from the analysis of one man over a period of months where the patient experienced himself as withdrawn, somnolent, far away from the present situation in the therapy. In each case Winnicott either helped to make conscious a surround to that withdrawn state or interpreted the absence of such a holding. For example, in the second reported episode, the patient withdrew from the therapy into somnolence and then reported that he remembered no dream. But then when Winnicott spoke to the pain of being exactly between waking and sleeping, the patient was able to have the idea of being curled up, which he indicated by moving his hands in front of his face to show where the curled up position was and that he was moving while in it. This curled up position was entirely imaginal; his literal position was flat on his back. At this point Winnicott (1954) interpreted, "In speaking of yourself as curled up and moving round, you are at the same time implying something which naturally you are not describing since you are not aware of it; you imply the *existence of a medium*" (p. 256, italics in original). The patient understood Winnicott's meaning ("Like the oil in which wheels move") and what might have been a moment of schizoid withdrawal and absence in the therapy became a moment of imagination.

The same process also worked in reverse, where Winnicott interpreted the absence of a safe medium. For example, when the patient in another withdrawal had an image of rain beating down on his naked body, Winnicott interpreted that the patient was experiencing himself as a newborn baby in a ruthless environment. It is important to recognize that Winnicott is not saying that this image is a memory of something that literally happened. Rather, he is saying that in one structure of adult reverie there is both the sense of a vulnerability, tenderness, or emergence identified as a self and a sense of a surround or encompassing medium. When either aspect of this structure is in abeyance or hostile, he interprets that fact as a means to help the patient out of dissociation and into a state of reverie, where both aspects of the structure are present and the medium around the emergent image is enabling or benign rather than assaultive. It is important to note that Winnicott is not simply providing an image of a medium from his own imaginition. If there is a glimmer of such an experience in the patient's own imagining, he makes that sprout explicit. If there is no such glimmer, he makes the absence or hostility explicit. *This work is entirely of the imagination.* It is not about determining the truth or falsehood of memory or adjudicating history. It is about helping the patient to be able to engage in potential space and to experience the aliveness and transformative possibilities of the imagination in its own right. In my experience, patients can come to recognize the feeling of a medium around or inside them where it has only been subliminal, and for each patient that sense comes with its own proprioceptive sensations, imagery, and language. One way to help a patient back from an episode of dissociation or to provide a calm holding when imagery or emotions are frightening is to listen for where such a medium is implicit in the patient's experience and to help to make it explicit.

In the vignette of the 3-year-old who "killed" her father in order to "dream about" him, we can appreciate that in her "dreaming" about him his literal presence is being transmuted into something psychological, something of imagination. It is a transformative moment. There are moments like this in almost any therapy, moments of dreaming while awake and with another person. Often these moments are quite brief and subtle, and they can all too easily pass unnoticed by both patient and therapist. If the therapist has an eye and ear for such moments and picks them up as they occur, a gradual building of the transmutative and imaginal can become a central process in the therapy. The image that arises—a bird, a darkness, a polished stone, a lake, a metal form, swimming, digging, a bodily sensation, a proprioceptive gesture—that little piece of dreaming, can be brought into awareness and given its significance and place. Certain images become emblematic of the therapy. Their aliveness in this regard speaks to the aliveness of the patient. While the content of the image may be analyzed for its import, the very fact of having such imaginings in and of itself is therapeutic. It is a gaining or regaining of imagination and, thus, of mind and selfhood.

Case Example

The following case example speaks to the interplay among imagination, aggression, and agency. It shows the transformation of an experience of victimization into one of agency and how that transformation both involved bringing rage into the therapy and resulted in the ability for imagination and symbolic, depressive communication.

> A patient, who was 5 years old and in her second year of therapy, constructed play when she heard someone screaming in the field behind my office. She ran to the window, in what I thought was a labile way, but then said, "Someone is being raped." She began to take care of her baby and told me to come sneaking into her house. She began to yell at me and tell me that I shouldn't rape people, that someone could get hurt and I could wake up the baby. She replayed this scene in several transmutations, all of which allowed her to yell at me extraordinarily passionately that I shouldn't rape people. I did what I could to allow her to continue, staying circumspect in my actions while also saying, for example, "But I like to rape people," or, "But I don't want to stop raping people." Eventually she moved the scene to her "office." She sat at my desk and I came and stood next to it, still the rapist. She opened the drawer and took out a penny (which she knew she was allowed to do from previous sessions). She handed it over to me and said, "Here, take this and go find another girl." She then called the police, who came and arrested me. Then she had me return as her boyfriend and she told me about her day, recapitulating the whole scene now as a narration.

This session was the culmination of months of ongoing work — most of it about mothers, babies, abandonment, and care. Although occasional sessions touched on men who hurt or stole children and many sessions involved nonspecific aggression, the explicit issue of sexual abuse did not come up. The session reported here was remarkable for the level of the patient's passion and clarity and for the degree to which she allowed her directed rage into the play — all the time clearly knowing it was play. It was important that she be allowed to turn the screams from outside the office into what she needed and that she *not* be reassured about the benignity of what was literally going on. There was a gradual escalation of intensity, from scolding me that I could wake the baby (i.e., her own needs for dependence and comforting, which actually would not have helped her in this scene) to increasing rage about rape. (I was not sure at first that she knew the meaning of the word, but it became clear that she did.) It was not a scene about danger or her fears (there had been plenty of those previously); it was about passionate insistence that this should never happen. The culmination when she gave me the penny was momentous. It was an act of sending away from herself this violation, this fate, this identification as victim. And it required that *another* little girl be hurt. There was something fundamentally aggressive about it, perhaps immoral, but clearly of life. It required that in order for her to live she had to be willing to let someone else (someone of her imagination) be hurt. The ruthlessness required to slough off the rapist and his potential effect on someone else was an achievement. In some sense, the "other girl" is a part of the patient herself, and this scene could be interpreted as repression-in-the-making; the abuse and the abused child are being sent away to the farther reaches of the unconscious. But I think, more importantly, "go find another girl" is about the passionate force needed to carve out a space *within* the patient, between herself and the abuser (or the persecutory paradigm) within her. It is about the ruthlessness needed to make that space.

When this patient had entered therapy there had been a bifurcation between split-off aggressive acts that had no ideational content (e.g., torturing animals, stomping on play dough in the office) and scenes of terror and victimization (e.g., hiding under my desk because "the cops are coming"). By the time of the session reported here, she knows what she is stomping and the terrorized space under the desk has transformed into a whole "office." She now sits *at* the desk. The space within her is no longer a retreat from persecution but rather it is a space large enough for creation, where she is the executor. The final part of the session I think confirms this understanding. The abuse scene is not shunted away either by evacuation or manic defense. Rather, the girl remembers exactly what has transpired and understands its significance. She consolidates her achievement by telling her boyfriend (a transformation of the abuser) what she has done. It is a move to another, a triadic, order of symbolization within the play—there is now the narrator, the audience, and the experience being symbolized (Segal 1957, 1991).

MEMORY AND IMAGINATION: II

So this story will not finish with some tomb to be visited in pious memory. For the smoke that rises from crematoria obeys physical laws like any other: the particles come together and disperse according to the wind, which propels them. The only pilgrimage, dear reader, would be to look sadly at a stormy sky now and then.

André Schwarz-Bart, *The Last of the Just*

The recovery of memory is of a piece with the recovery of mind, which also includes imagination, agency and desire. For many people the process of building memory is gradual. There are some things one has always known about oneself. Over time new images come to mind that support or subtly shift what has always been known. Some of these images seem to be of actual events as perceived by the individual. Other images seem to be more metaphoric, speaking of a psychological truth through a narrative framing that is not literal, the way a dream speaks of what is true. There is a process of sifting. Some of what has always been known is seen in a different light, takes on new meaning. Aspects of oneself and one's experience that never seemed related become joined, make sense vis-à-vis each other. Themes, narratives, struggles emerge that seem to have always been with one and to have taken different forms and weightings during different periods of one's life. The nature of one's fantasies, what one can imagine for oneself and others, the shape of one's desires and antinomies are all part of this evolving sense of oneself, which even with its shiftings and conflicts has a certain coherence over time. One can recognize oneself in different moments and different memories.

Sometimes, however, the recovery of memory and the building of a life is not so gradual. Images or feelings or bodily states arise that are radically different from anything one has ever known about oneself. Something new arrives and much that one thought about oneself, much of who one thought oneself to be is turned over. The act of remembering is not a gradual filling of lacunae, which provides meaning and sense. Rather it is a jolt, a shock of major proportions that turns everything upside down. Remembering itself is traumatic. The kind of sifting where one considers images and their possible metaphoric, contemporary and interpersonal meanings is impossible. In this kind of situation the act of remembering is dismembering to the individual's mind.

When one speaks of "delayed memory" it is usually some variant of this second form of remembering that is meant. In the more gradual kind of remembering, where reverie *about* memory is possible, things that have not previously been thought may come to mind, but it does not have the disjunctive and dislodging import that is usually referred to as part of delayed memory. When images are coming in the assaultive, persecutory way of the second kind of remembering, the individual needs help to get her mind back so that she can undertake the kind of sifting and consideration that is part of the first kind of remembering. This sifting implies a kind of subjectivity and action with respect to the images. One weighs, one tries on different links and rejects or shifts the weighting of others. In the second kind of remembering one feels at the mercy of the images and can only respond by trying to control them "back." This is the difference at an intrasubjective level between agency and omnipotence, between having hands or object usage and magical thinking. With the first kind of remembering it is possible to "look at a stormy sky" and conjure up a world of lives, of people known, cherished, and mourned, of events lived or relived in imagination. With the second kind of remembering the looking at a stormy sky might precipitate a hail of intrusive memories with no room for reverie and no awareness of the outer event (the sky) that had let loose the barrage.

Before it is possible to decipher the psychological truth of images that have arisen in this assaultive way, it is necessary to find one's way to a more agentic structure of mind. In therapy, this involves analyzing and helping to transform the omnipotent defensive structure that overlays the terrible sense of powerlessness in the face of such harrowing recall experiences. Much of this work around agency, aggression, desire, and imagination may not appear to be overtly about memory, although it has the most profound ramifications for the building of evocative memory. However, there are certain periods of such therapies where memory itself becomes the content of the therapy. The goal of therapy as the recovery of mind, imagination, and potential space is lost. Instead the recovery of "what happened" begins to drive the therapy—both as the singular goal of therapy and as that which instills terror. In this context, it is all too easy for memory to become reified, something that must be pinned down hard and fast. There can be tremendous pressure to find out what the singular, univocal truth of memory might be. It can feel as if this is the only way to protect the patient from the persecution of images. Thus, the content of memory itself becomes the currency of exchange in the therapy. The multivalence and ambiguity of potential space is lost. In this situation it can be helpful for the therapist to bear in mind that while memory is the language that is being spoken explicitly in the therapy, the actual action of the therapy is in the realm of impotence-omnipotence and of the patient's struggles both to preserve and to get out of that defensive structure.

This structure of impotence/omnipotence regarding memory plays out in the therapy relationship in a dual way through the power of projective identification. The patient projects an omnipotence into the therapist—she is *demanded* to know things that she cannot possibly know and to have an omnipotent, pathological certainty (Adler 1994, Shapiro 1982) about her knowledge, while the patient experiences herself as diminished, without knowledge, at the mercy of her own memory and the therapist's knowledge. In essence, the patient is projecting into the therapist her own memory, as if the therapist could remember the patient's childhood. The patient is also locating her own doubt in the therapist to be solved there through omniscience. At the same time the patient is projecting into the therapist her own experience of impotence. The therapist finds that she is being asked, even demanded, to stretch herself into the untenable and exhausting position of knowing what she cannot possibly know. She also finds that her efforts to engage in an analytic inquiry into possibilities, to enter into the ambiguity of potential space, only serves to raise terrifying anxieties for the patient (Adler 1989). There is erosion of the space within which the therapist can operate without evidently creating cataclysms. To ask questions, to look at things psychologically only serves to increase the patient's anxiety. The therapist's hands become tied. To proceed in a psychologically minded way is foreclosed; indeed it seems to be a form of torture for the patient, only raising more harrowing imagery or anxiety about such imagery. At the same time the therapist can feel compelled to take on the omnipotent defense, to operate in ways and to know things that are really outside her purview. It is really not possible for the therapist to know what happened years ago when she was not present, but there can be tremendous pressure for her to do just that, as if that destruction of ambiguity would return the patient's mind to her.

The pressure may be for the therapist to make reconstructive interpretations. However, for the patient to use reconstructions he must be able to take them as hypotheses and as a possible framework to try on, modify, and/or reject. When an individual is caught in a persecutory paradigm such a metaphoric entertaining of possibilities and ambiguities is impossible. The therapist's words are treated as things and taken in as literal and absolute. The patient's mind remains passive and possibly even feels assaulted by the reconstructive interpretations. This may all happen in a rather subtle way, so that the therapist is not aware that it is going on. But the results can be damaging to the therapy process and only serve to keep the patient in an abuse paradigm. The situation can quickly spiral into panic and escalations.

If, instead, the therapist keeps a focus not on the content of memory as such but rather on the process of returning the patient to an agentic position, the emphasis will at first be on what, particularly in the therapy, constellates these episodes of assaultive imagery and dissociation. As that work proceeds along some of the lines that have been outlined here, the patient's relationship to her own memory changes. It becomes possible to reflect on memory, to have reverie around memory, and to have a sense of one's continuity of existence, body, and mind in the face of shifting memories. Reconstructive interpretations may emerge, but they come from the patient. They are not felt as coming from without or from the omniscience of the therapist, no matter how benign that may be. And such reconstructions do not become the focus of therapy, the definition of the patient's identity, nor the call to specific, literal action.

As this transformation from the persecutory to the agentic occurs, the patient's mind returns to her (or is discovered for the first time), and both evocative memory and reveried imagination become possible. The quality, the *form*, of both memory and imagination is transformed because the underlying persecutory paradigm is shifted. Images come to mind and it becomes possible to reflect on them and the multiplicity of their possible meanings. Memory (and imagination) becomes something that emerges, that shifts, that expands and contracts, that bears reflection and questioning. Images come to mind and that very fact in and of itself is reassuring, since it speaks to the humanity of the individual. The process of placing these images — as imagination, as memory, as memory filtered through imagination — becomes the weaving of an individual life rather than a life and death struggle to make things stay put and be univocal. Grief for what has been suffered may certainly be profound. But the situation is no longer desperate. The patient does not have to force herself, her own mind, or the therapist one way or the other because the abuse that was the fabric of the patient's mind in the present has transformed into different forms of agency.

SUMMARY

A distinction has been drawn between states of mind that are persecutory where the individual experiences him- or herself as the victim of incommensurable forces including his or her own memories, fantasies, emotions, and body, and states of mind that are agentic in which the individual is a subject with a history who can reflect on his or her memories and fantasies and who can engage in reverie. The work of therapy can be to help patients have flexibility between these states of mind and be able to enter potential space and the full humanity of their imaginations.

Part of what keeps an individual locked in a persecutory paradigm is a set of omnipotent, magical defenses that protect against the overwhelming sense of powerlessness. The analysis of this defensive structure gradually brings the patient's anxiety about split-off aggression and desire into the therapy and makes conscious the anxiety about the underlying fantasy that these aspects of the patient are murderous, either literally or intrapsychically. What has been a solipsistic kind of agency is gradually converted into a form of communication and directed aggression within the therapy relationship. At the same time the work of entering into agency also involves developing or retrieving the capacity for reverie, which entails the capacity to bear the ambiguity of potential space, the capacity to mourn, and the capacity to enter into the metaphoric and imaginal. In therapies where there is tremendous pressure about "delayed memories," the issue is usually that the patient is trapped in a persecutory paradigm. The patient feels persecuted by his or her memories and hopes or expects that the therapist can protect the patient omnipotently by being able to decipher what did or did not occur at times when the therapist was not present. If instead the therapist helps the patient to enter an agentic paradigm, it gradually becomes possible for the patient to reflect on memories, to allow them to be ambiguous, to cohere, and to differentiate. The pressure to make memory into something definitive and univocal subsides. While there may be much to grieve, the process of building a life and a mind can proceed with the patient as an active subject who has an evolving history and an imagination. The abuse that has been in the present is ended.

ACKNOWLEDGMENTS

I would like to thank Gerald Adler, M.D., Adin DeLaCour, L.I.C.S.W., Carolyn Hicks, Ed.D., and Thomas Ogden, M.D., each of whom generously read and responded to earlier drafts of this chapter.

REFERENCES

Adler, G. (1985). *Borderline Psychopathology and its Treatment.* New York, London: Jason Aronson.

_____ (1989). Transitional phenomena, projective identification, and the essential ambiguity of the psychoanalytic situation. *Psychoanalytic Quarterly* 58:81–104.

_____ (1994). Transference, countertransference, and abuse in psychotherapy. *Harvard Review of Psychiatry* 2:151-159.

Bion, W. R. (1956). Development of schizophrenic thought. In *Second Thoughts: Selected Papers on Psycho-Analysis,* pp. 36–42. New York: Jason Aronson, 1967.

_____ (1957). Differentiation of the psychotic from the non-psychotic personalities. In *Second Thoughts: Selected Papers on Psycho-Analysis,* pp. 43–64. New York: Jason Aronson, 1967.

———— (1959). Attacks on linking. *International Journal of Psycho-Analysis* 40:308–315.

———— (1962). *Learning from Experience.* New York: Basic Books.

Bromberg, P. (1993). Shadow and substance: a relational perspective on clinical process. *Psychoanalytic Psychology* 10:147–168.

Ehrenberg, P. B. (1992). *The Intimate Edge: Extending the Reach of Psychoanalytic Interaction.* New York: Norton.

Fraiberg, S. (1969). Libidinal object constancy and mental representation. *Psychoanalytic Study of the Child* 24:9–47. New York: International Universities Press.

Klein, M. (1935). A contribution to the psychogenesis of manic-depressive states. In *Contribution to Psycho-Analysis, 1921–1945*, pp. 282–311. London: Hogarth, 1968.

———— (1940). Mourning and its relation to manic-depressive states. In *Contributions to Psycho-Analysis, 1921–1945*, pp. 311–338. London: Hogarth, 1968.

———— (1946). Notes on some schizoid mechanisms. In *Envy and Gratitude and Other Works, 1946–1963*, pp. 1–24. New York: Delacorte, 1975.

———— (1955). On identification. In *Envy and Gratitude and Other Works, 1946–1963*, pp. 141–175. New York: Delacorte, 1975.

Malin, A., and Grotstein, J. (1966). Projective identification in the therapeutic process. *International Journal of Psycho-Analysis* 47:26–31.

Mitchell, S. A. (1988) *Relational Concepts in Psychoanalysis. An Integration.* Cambridge: Harvard University Press.

Ogden, T. (1982). *Projective Identification and Psychotherapeutic Technique.* New York: Jason Aronson.

———— (1986). *The Matrix of the Mind: Object Relations and the Psychoanalytic Dialogue.* Northvale, NJ: Jason Aronson.

———— (1989). *The Primitive Edge of Experience.* Northvale, NJ: Jason Aronson.

———— (1991). Consultation is often needed when treating severe dissociative disorders. *Psychodynamic Letter* 1(10):1–4.

———— (1992). The dialectically constituted/decentered subject of psychoanalysis. II. The contributions of Klein and Winnicott. *International Journal of Psycho-Analysis* 73:613–626.

———— (1994). Personal communication.

Piaget, J. (1937). *The Construction of Reality in the Child.* New York: Basic Books, 1967.

Schwarz-Bart, A. (1961). *The Last of the Just*, trans. S. Becker. London: Secker and Warburg.

Segal, H. (1957). Notes on symbol formation. *International Journal of Psycho-Analysis* 38:391–397.

———— (1991). *Dream, Phantasy and Art.* London, New York: Tavistock/ Routledge.

Shapiro, E. R. (1982). On curiosity: intrapsychic and interpersonal boundary formation in family life. *International Journal of Family Psychiatry* 3:209–232.

von Franz, M. L. (1972). *The Feminine in Fairytales*. Dallas, TX: Spring.

Winnicott, D. W. (1954). Withdrawal and regression. In *Through Paediatrics to Psycho-Analysis* pp. 255–261. New York: Basic Books, 1975.

———— (1965). The *Maturational Processes and the Facilitating Environment*. New York: International Universities Press.

———— (1971). *Playing and Reality*. New York: Basic Books.

Young, J. E. (1993). *The Texture of Memory: Holocaust Memorials and Meaning*. New Haven: Yale University Press.

7

Transferential Issues in the Psychoanalytic Treatment of Incest Survivors

ELIZABETH HEGEMAN

Thinking about incest trauma has been changing in the last decade, with an important merger now being effected among different psychoanalytic theories (Schwartz 1994) to embrace a relational model including dissociation. While it has been understood for some time that when trauma interferes with development, and the capacity for symbolization and verbalization are diminished, the effects of trauma on the physiological process of encoding of experience are demonstrated (van der Kolk 1989), and we now understand that dissociation lies at the extreme end of the continuum of defensive adaptations to traumatic experience.

DEFENSIVE ADAPTATION TO TRAUMA: REPRESSION VERSUS DISSOCIATION

According to Davies and Frawley (1994), repression and dissociation can be understood as different processes, with repression as an active process "in which the ego gains mastery over conflictual material," while dissociation is "the last ditch effort of an overwhelmed ego to salvage some semblance of adequate mental functioning" (p. 65). They further differentiate repression as a response that adds to a sense of mastery because it allows for ongoing internal psychic work, making the material potentially available for rediscovery in psychoanalysis, while dissociation "is experienced as an inadequate response, a submission and resignation to the inevitability of overwhelming, even psychically deadening danger." Repression applies to material that has been in awareness and can be potentially remembered and thus linked with other experiences, contributing to a coherent sense of self, while dissociation breaks connections between groups of events and their internal representations, with the apparent function of warding off awareness of trauma.

TRANSFERENCE PROVIDES ACCESS TO DISSOCIATED MATERIAL

Access to dissociated material appears to be dependent on the patient being in the ego state in which the experience occurred. This may mean that the patient is in trance or has used drugs or alcohol, or it may be that certain kinds of relationships, activities, or feeling states bring back, or "trigger," chunks of associated experience. The patient may develop elaborate ways of avoidance of these triggering cues, ways that eventually form the dissociative disorder. The relational model of analytic treatment, which includes dissociation, supposes that experience is unconceptualized at the time the incest occurs, and that it is maintained in that form to keep at bay the pain and disorganization that would be overwhelming were the experience allowed into awareness.

Approaching the treatment of the dissociated patient from any sort of traditional model of psychoanalytic work is highly problematic because it means getting the patient to confront that which she has been doing her best not to be aware of through dissociation. The difficulties of treatment do not flow just from the fact that the analyst is in the same structural position of power as the incesting parent; nor is treatment simply a case of replacing a bad object (the incesting parent) with a good one (presumably the analyst). Treatment must also modify the internal structural accommodations (the dissociative defenses) that took place to avoid the awareness of the original trauma, because they interfere with development of the self.

However, it is that very fragmented, doubting self, "with holes in it," as one patient put it, that must be mobilized to engage with and negotiate the dissociated material. Therefore maximum attention must be paid early in treatment to restoring the patient's capacity for relationship. This is especially important because dissociative defenses play havoc with analysis by complicating the patient's identity and ego functions, such as attention and emotional flexibility; thus it is not just the trauma that becomes inaccessible, but parts of the self as well. Since dissociated material has not been verbally encoded or processed internally, when it reemerges into awareness it is as terrifying and overwhelming as when it first occurred.

Transference as Trigger

In therapy or analysis, the patient is expected to establish a trusting-enough relationship to follow the basic rule of not consciously holding anything back. For the patient with trauma in her developmental history, and ongoing dissociative defenses, this may mean being expected to go from the safe numbness of dissociation back to a feeling state of vulnerability, which has been painful, disorganizing, and even dangerous to her in the past (Herman 1992). The analytic relationship, with its invitation to trust and intimate revelation, repeats the emotional conditions of the original relationship in which the betrayal trauma took place and may therefore make it possible for the patient to rework the dissociated experience. The conditions of treatment replicate the felt dangers of the original traumatic relationship, and will be experienced as a double-bind similar to the incest itself. The patient may be in terror, in a rage, or in a trance within minutes of the beginning of treatment; these states may alternate with numbness, constriction, or being frozen in affect. The bind of being expected to trust, when she has learned how dangerous that is, will be likely to trigger the dissociative patient to reexperience parts of the traumatic memories in the form of intrusive symptoms such as flashbacks and nightmares. The very act of seeking contact on the basis of emotional needs, which is a usual situation of a neurotic patient seeking treatment, is likely to throw the dissociative patient off stride, since she has usually learned (or taught herself) to shun emotional needs, sometimes shaming or punishing herself terribly for having them. The double-bind of having to seem trusting while knowing one should feel afraid, or act trusting while not feeling it, brings back the familiar traumatic situation, perhaps triggering a state of trance that will facilitate access to traumatic memory.

Paradoxically, the recognition of the reality of trauma in the patient's development may deprive the trained analyst of one of our main tools: the analysis of transference distortions. When should the therapist who is being experienced as an abuser choose to appear to accept the distortion and work within it? This use of the transitional space of the analysis, to allow the pretense or play that the analyst is the abuser, may feel too real for comfort for the patient. Analysis of transference distortions has always been regarded as the most effective path in treatment, but with the dissociative patient there is a risk of the patient becoming flooded with unmodulated traumatic experience. Or, like the cognitive behaviorists, should the therapist try to correct the distortions and risk deflecting powerful transferential feelings to objects outside the analytic relationship, such as the original abuser? This is a difficult tightrope to walk. False accusations may even stem from transference relationships that have been deflected in this way, or otherwise not been successfully analyzed and worked through to resolution.

Traumatic Transference

Herman (1992) sensitively discusses traumatic transference and countertransference in the words of survivors, drawing as well on Vietnam and Holocaust experiences that are now more accepted and therefore more familiar for the reader. She explains how the special demands the survivor makes of the therapist are understandable, sometimes even legitimate, given the helplessness and terror the survivor has experienced before in a trusting relationship, even though these demands are perhaps impossible — such as the need for an omnipotent rescuer. Herman also recommends certain extra-analytic techniques such as confrontation with the abuser, when appropriate, and reconnection with community through group therapy and political work.

Observation of the dynamics of traumatic transference led

Spiegel (1978) to define it as when the patient "unconsciously expects that the therapist, despite overt helpfulness and concern, will covertly exploit the patient for his or her own narcissistic gratification" (p 72). The patient may seem to have an attachment disorder, in which he or she experiences extreme anxiety and the need to avoid attachment or even the hope of it, due to the fear of betrayal in the future as well as in the past. One might speculate that the negative therapeutic reaction, the development of uncontained persecutory feelings and malignant rage in the transference, is the result of early betrayal trauma that has not been recognized as such in the treatment.

Transference in Ferenczi's "Mutual Analysis"

Perhaps the first analyst to recognize delayed memories for incestuous abuse after Freud and Breuer was Ferenczi (1932), in his now famous "Confusion of Tongues between Adults and the Child." Like the best analysts, he made his discoveries through feeling and observing the transference/countertransference with his patients. He noted some of the same characteristics of abused patients that have captured the attention of today's analytic thinkers as features of traumatic transference: submissive overcompliance alternated with accusations to the analyst of cruelty and lack of concern, extreme sensitivity on the part of the patient to "professional hypocrisy," the necessity that the analyst be willing to admit mistakes and explore them with the patient, and the tendency of the treatment to set off seemingly hallucination-like symptoms such as flashbacks, nightmares, and sleep disturbances that do not necessarily improve quickly with treatment.

Ferenczi even observed what we would now call dissociation and the double bind created by the abuse, although he did not use those terms; he reported that in the "traumatic trance" the abused child preserves the situation of tenderness, while introjecting both the adult as object (thereby removing the attacking object from awareness) and the guilt feelings of the adult. Ferenczi considered that this identification with the aggressor results in self-hatred and loathing for the child victim, and recognized what we would now call idealization as a necessary adaptation to the abusive caregiver. These views were denounced by mainstream psychoanalysis at the time, and Ferenczi's work was only recently ideologically "rehabilitated."

This understanding of "recovered" or "delayed" memories as arising from the breach in the dissociative barrier set off by the intensity of the therapy relationship is based on an understanding of the effects of trauma on the personality. Instead of drawing comfort and learning to soothe herself through the benign new relationship, the incest survivor will at times *feel* more panicky and distressed (Davies and Frawley 1994, Kramer and Akhtar 1991). Far from implying that the analyst suggests these memories, or that the patient is fabricating them, this view of "recovered memory" explains on the basis of transference how therapy sets off the process by which chunks of experience intrude on the self. The distress and anxiety engendered by the formation of any potentially intimate relationship, including the analytic or therapy relationship, contribute to otherwise puzzling symptoms. Painful as this process is, it makes the troubling material available to be worked on in the relationship as it has not been before.

IMPACT OF TRAUMA ON THE DEVELOPMENT OF SELF

The word *trauma* has become almost a euphemism, so vague and overused is it. The self, at whatever stage of immaturity, was usually so overwhelmed by the incest experience and unable to process and integrate its meaning that the events, together with the chaotic experience itself, seem to get "parked" in an unsymbolized form, rather than being subject to normal access and recall. As Enid Balint (1991) says,

> It is important to keep in mind that what is remembered by the patient but has never been thought — has never had words — must have been experienced by the patient in a different way from other events, the occurrence of which has perhaps been wiped out by the patient. [p. 425]

Enid and Michael Balint are among the early British analysts who struggled to understand patients who were not helped by analysis, because (they supposed) of some early failure of relatedness, and formulated the notion of the "basic fault" (M. Balint 1979) as a way of understanding that impact.

The capacity for relatedness becomes impaired due to excess reliance on dissociative defenses, whether of the numbing sort or of the intrusive sort, such as flashbacks and nightmares. As Bromberg (1993a) points out in his paper "Shadow and Substance," the analytic work with traumatized patients "thus involves periods of transition from the patient's primary use of dissociation and enactment in the transference-countertransference field to an increasing capacity to sustain the experience of internal conflict" (p. 165). He quotes Laub and Auerhahn (1993): "Because the traumatic state cannot be represented, it is unmodifiable by interpretation . . . [and] what is required initially in the therapy is not elucidation of psychic conflict but [that] the link between self and other must be rebuilt" (Bromberg p. 165). This approach is more radical a departure from past views than the concession that there may be a needed period of work for "ego repair" before "real" analytic work can begin. Bromberg and others decenter the analytic work from a primary focus on the patient, and concentrate on the relational field as the arena for study.

CONFLICT BASED INTERPRETATIONS: THE NEED FOR REEVALUATION

Traditional treatment concepts like transference neurosis or repetition compulsion imply a neurotic, or conflict-based origin of symptoms within the patient. So even if therapists know of the abuse and acknowledge it, unless they also reevaluate their techniques to incorporate work with the dissociation, they will unwittingly, but inevitably, be oriented to interpretations based on internal conflict that may not apply. Because the profound impact dissociation has on the treatment is not yet fully recognized, therapists who have the intellectual recognition of abuse dynamics may not realize that they also need to learn how to work differently with the dissociated patient. Because traditional transference interpretations presume and refer to a relatively intact self, formulations based on the neurotic model of inner conflict will very likely imply to patients who do not yet experience a relational self that they should be able to do something that they are not.

Already very prone to shame and feelings of inadequacy because of the twofold impact of abuse and dissociation, abuse survivors are likely to feel from a transference interpretation that they are bad. If they grew up in a chronically abusive situation, they probably even feel that the trauma happened because of their rage, or their "bad" erotic potential. Thus even the most correct of interpretations is likely to be experienced as a retraumatization, even if they just imply to the patient that she should be able to own or acknowledge aspects of self that she cannot. The traditional transference or conflict-based interpretation at the very least will evoke shame in the survivor who does not yet have the capacity to sustain internal conflict, is struggling with a subjective sense of damage or impairment, and doubts her ability to relate. Since dissociative patterns interfere with normal development and proliferate in the face of new developmental demands, by the time the patient has entered treatment, dissociation may have become a disorder, not just a defensive style.

For example, an analyst who had fallen ill said to her patient, who was afraid she had caused the illness, "Perhaps you feel angry with me and wish me harm, and that is why you are afraid you caused my illness." Instead of feeling relieved of the guilt over the angry feelings attributed to her, which might be expected of a nondissociative person, this patient whose self was not yet well enough developed to contain ambivalence felt (1) shame and despair that the destructiveness she feared in herself was now seen by the analyst; (2) enraged that the analyst did not see that her fear for the analyst was an expression of caring; (3) intense shame at what she felt to be her own failure of relatedness in that she had not been able to get the analyst to understand her feelings; and (4) abandonment because the analyst seemed to have dismissed her fear by interpreting it as irrational, when the patient had in fact been explicitly told by her abusers that she was harmful and destructive to others. Thus the interpretation had exactly the opposite effect from the reassurance and relief from inner tension that was intended. This example also shows how the omnipotent or grandiose aspects of the self are among the most troubling to work with in the traumatized patient, because they are so disguised.

An analytic stance that acknowledges trauma yet keeps the focus firmly on the patient as "doer" or author of events, including reenactments, and leaves out discussion of the analyst's own contributions, or the patient's lack of conscious authorship of the original trauma or more recent enactments can be experienced as blaming. Since this group of patients is overly prone to blame themselves, and feel guilty to the point of grandiosity, a conflict-based orientation can lend itself to a hidden enactment, such as when the compliant patient experiences even accurate interpretations as criticisms and changes her behavior to please the analyst. Only a full understanding of trauma, extending to relational technique and the willingness to include the analyst's own experience in the field of study, will deal with the enactment as an aspect of the interpersonal field that has been incorporated into the patient's transferential patterns and that persists in dissociated form.

This is a crucial distinction for most patients who identify themselves as survivors. Analytic work based on the assumption of inner conflict can have the effect of forcing the patient to own aspects of him- or herself that may be still dissociated — clearly an enactment of power within the analytic relationship, but that can go unrecognized if the therapist is operating with intrapsychic models and thinking in terms of transference neurosis. The patient's compliance can mask the imposition of a meaning or construction of reality that is not truly the patient's own. I mean here not just to raise again the question about timing of interpretations, but to point to a qualitatively different kind of work that may be necessary in analytic work with traumatized patients.

IDEALIZATION AND THE TRAUMATIZED PATIENT

To preserve a sense of security, survivors very often have assumed the blame for their abuse, idealizing their abusers, especially if they are parents or caregivers with whom the child must stay. Often, survivors have been told explicitly that the abuse was their fault, and they have a strong motive to believe that; it fits in with the idealizations they may need to survive emotionally. This process lays the groundwork for dissociation, however, by falsifying the child's object world, which now has self-deception at its core.

At the same time incested patients are exquisitely sensitive to what Ferenczi called "professional hypocrisy" in their analyst, as discussed above, such as when an uncertain analyst resorts to theory as a way of bolstering faltering judgment; the analyst's arrogance, self-absorption, or selfishness are taken for granted, while at the same time the patient experiences herself as the flawed object. Over and over again a patient moans, "I can't do what you want me to be able to do," meaning that she cannot tolerate the separations and fears disintegration between sessions. She is experiencing the analytic requirements (being related enough to talk trustfully, and to have enough of an internal connection with the analyst to endure the times between sessions) as a form of torture, which the analyst imposes on her by virtue of her power. Unable to recognize the analyst's real limits (which include not being available on a twenty-four-hour basis), the patient experiences her as willfully imposing impossible conditions, as the abuser did. On the other hand, it still feels like the patient's fault when she cannot manage to bear those conditions. Taking the blame and sense of fault into herself is the patient's solution to the double bind of needing to maintain the relationship with an abusive person; the consequent damage to self-esteem is great.

Valerie Sinason (1991) discusses the countertransferential omnipotence that keeps therapists and staff from naming a real condition such as a disability or abuse, for fear that naming will overwhelm or shame the patient. Yet not naming these has an even worse effect: Sinason describes how difficult it was for her to get up the courage to overcome her normal denial, or normal dissociation, of the horrible experience, in order to effectively interpret a child's repetitive play:

> Finally one day I was saner and braver and I knew it was, yet again, sexual abuse I was looking at. Nervously, and feeling awful, I said hesitantly that perhaps the white stuff she was pouring over the doll was like the white stuff that comes out of a man's penis. . . . [p. 19]

Sinason points out that when we cannot "think the unthinkable," the result is that children must hold "in their heads and bodies" the events that we must eject from our awareness. Patients are sensitive to this denial or dissociation, fearful for themselves that therapists may shame or reject them rather than face the terrible reality, and fearful for their therapists that they will suffer when they do understand.

TRANSFERENCE AND REENACTMENTS

Perhaps one reason why analysts have been slow to modify technique and recognize abuse aftereffects in the transference had to do with

the nature of enactment and reenactment. Enactment is now understood as an important form of communication of unconscious
material in any treatment, not just that of abuse survivors (Rosenfeld
1987). *Reenactment* is the term that refers to the replaying of dissociated relations in the here and now, usually at first without the
recognition of their developmental significance. These events used to
be widely dismissed by analysts as "acting out" by patients unable to
use the verbal analytic medium, and were attributed to impulsive-
ness, personality disorder, or resistance, and may even have been
treated punitively, especially in hospital settings, although the punishments were well rationalized.

In order for reenactments to be recognized as communication
rather than resistance, the analyst has to be willing and able to own
some extreme countertransference feelings and be open to looking at
the whole of the relationship, as well as understanding how trauma
truncates verbal and symbolic communication and keeps the patient
"frozen in time" (Reis 1993). In the analysis of Alice, the most
important meanings were conveyed through reenactment, and only
gradually decoded within the relationship.

ALICE

Alice was a successful black professional woman. Her friends
urged her to consult an analyst because her brother was
blackmailing her emotionally, with his threats of suicide, into
spending every weekend with him and having to be available
for phone calls at any hour. She was unable to set or keep any
boundaries with him, and her life and work were a shambles.
Whenever she hesitated to meet his demands, he would accuse
her of wishing him dead, or of letting him die; in this "collapse
of potential space" they both ignored the fact that it was he who
was threatening his life, not Alice.

Although it was clear from the outset both to her and her
analyst that this situation was a replication of the early sexual
abuse by her father, which she reported in a bland, affectless
manner, she was uninterested in exploring that. Although she
sometimes felt enraged at her brother's provocations, she felt
she had no alternative but to give in to his demands, because he

too was abused at an early age. She was passing her helplessness through to her friends by complaining to them and enlisting their sympathy, while she was unable to change the situation. She tried to involve the analyst in futile attempts both to set boundaries with the brother, and to explain her helplessness to her enraged friends. The analyst made "correct" but ineffective interpretations of her omnipotent need to rescue, her contempt for her brother expressed in her compliance, her contempt for caregivers like the analyst who keep themselves safe within their boundaries and will not show their "caring" through sacrifice, as she did. The analyst pointed out how Alice needed to have her capacity for generosity and nurturance validated, since her abuser had just taken from her.

All of these were thoughtfully accepted with apparent appreciation and interest, but without any change and with escalation of her self-destructiveness, as she began walking into traffic, seemingly in a daze. The dissociative fog that had led to the enactments between Alice and her brother had expanded to include more portions of her life, including the analysis. Finally the analyst asked, visibly moved by the despair Alice clearly was living out, but was unable to put into words, "Since you are not able to let me help you change this situation, it must be my role to be a helpless witness to your sacrifice as you destroy yourself. I guess you must think that this is the only way you can get me to understand how horrible it is for you."

The patient was shocked to see her impact on the analyst. She had not realized that she was living out the early abuse with herself in the active role of abuser of the analyst, and she was horrified. Consciously, she had been afraid to deny anything to her brother for fear that refusing him would make her a monster, as he manipulatively claimed. This was the level of psychic operation that was organized by conflict and repression, and was available to analysis and verbal discussion, without any change in the compulsive, desperate behavior. It was only when she became able to see her impact on the analyst that her actions began to have meaning to her. It was not just that she felt guilty over hurting the analyst with the horror Alice herself no longer felt that made a difference in the treatment; that was the conflict-level of functioning. What shifted was that Alice could now begin to observe how she had been making the analyst a helpless, frightened *yet aware and suffering* witness to her destructiveness, and that the analyst could stay connected to her emotionally while feeling and speaking about her feelings. When the analyst's words lifted the dissociative barrier, Alice began to be able to feel and experience her own destructiveness as real, as mattering to someone, rather than feeling indifferent, or just feeling like a victim, and she became more able to modify her living out of the early drama. Bromberg (1994) describes such moments of change as occurring when the enactment "is serving its proper function" when the dissociated aspects of the patient's experience have been sufficiently processed in the analytic relationship. The patient can now begin gradually to accept the dissociated material "that the analyst has been holding as part of himself"; the patient can now become aware of and slowly accept those aspects of self. In this way, Alice became aware of her own capacity for aggression when she could see how she had inflicted her helplessness and despair on the therapist.

THE INTERSUBJECTIVE REALITY

The example of Alice could illustrate how the building of an intersubjective reality and the inevitability of enactments are intertwined. The empathic therapist, deprived of the ability to soothe symbolically which characterizes treatment with "good" analytic patients, faced with a patient whose capacity for symbolic thinking is impaired, or for whom potential space has collapsed, will feel a great pull to be drawn into a concrete nurturant role, which may seem necessary even at times for the patient's survival, but which inevitably involves boundary violations. The well-known multiple personality disorder (MPD) cases, such as Sybil, where the therapist acted as agent in the sale of the patient's artwork and took the patient into her own home, and the therapist couple in *The Flock* (Casey 1991), who invited the patient to live with them, come to mind. But even very well-trained analysts are very likely to fall into this trap. Much of the time the therapist is conflicted enough about these bendings of the rules to keep them secret from colleagues and the world, thereby replicating the original incestuous situation, and gratifying the patient in secret, forbidden ways.

Failure to recognize enactments of transference as such can lead to horrible retraumatizations for dissociative patients. One patient who had been diagnosed as having chronic posttraumatic stress disorder, and whose childhood included a brutal incestuous relationship, reported almost proudly that five different emergency room teams had subdued and tranquilized her in a fashion identical to the original abuse conditions; in each case she was tied up and drugged exactly as she had been when she had been abused as a child. She clearly saw the other's part of the transferential implications of these enactments, and took some pride in the retrospective self-righteous revenge they gave her. In carrying out these episodes, she was illustrating her point of view about how bad and violent doctors and hospitals are, without seeing her own role in bringing about these disasters. Such a person can create havoc with a concrete approach to patient management: the patient's dissociated expectation can coincide with the felt mandate of the staff to make a mockery of the "helping" professions.

THE TRANSFERENTIAL "TRUTH" OF RECOVERED MEMORIES

Analysts are likely to acknowledge that patient and therapist may never know the full truth, because of the formidable elaborations of the press of fantasies upon the patient's inner psychic reality. Shengold (1989) calls what actually happened "irrecoverable"; what is retained in the patient's inner world is changed by "how what has happened to the patient has been registered, and what the patient is compelled from within to repeat." Furthermore, what actually happened is not the purview of analytic work. "Analytic work centers on attending to the transference of the past as concentrated and distorted in the patient's current unconscious wishes toward the analyst" (p. 319). Shengold still sees the "cure," even for the traumatized patient, as having to do with the effective analysis of the transference.

The term *delayed memory* is to some extent a misnomer; *memory* is the term applied when "normal" or nontraumatic experience can be processed, stored, and integrated by the person to whom it happens. Trauma gives rise to experience that cannot be formulated, understood, connected with other experiences or with any coherent sense of self, or communicated in words. As Bromberg (1994) says, "Trauma produces dissociation, and dissociation creates retrospective falsification of the past and retrospective falsification of one's ability to predict the future" (p. 537). According to Bromberg, the vivid and convincing quality of the material produced in connection with the trauma has to do with the fact that "experiential memory remains relatively intact" while the linear quality of time is altered "as a protective device." The condensation of time experience leaves the person with an ongoing sense of dread, and the feeling that something terrible is happening or is about to happen. Bromberg (1994) suggests that the dissociative process protects the self from the sense of disintegration, and from the sense of unpreparedness, but at a cost: the patient's ability to imagine a future safe from trauma is seriously impaired, and seemingly, in order to ensure that future trauma will at least not be unanticipated, the patient remains in a constant state of dread, often inducing the worst in this way.

Traumatic experience is chaotic and overwhelms the immature self. Later, it leads to the unwelcome intrusion upon the self of sudden inexplicable, terrifying, painful body feelings, visual flashbacks, or words heard over and over again in the mind, which feel like hallucinations. What happens to the self when the dissociative barrier fails is hardly so orderly, tame or contained that it could be called memory, and it could never be studied in any laboratory setting.

The task of the analyst, which is as taxing as it is necessary, is that of rising to the challenge of taking the patient's experience as emotionally "true" and valid, in the sense that it represents real trauma, and is an effort at representing and communicating real experience, while understanding that the patient's verbal productions may not represent any consensually validated version of reality. Thus the question "Do you believe me?" becomes a difficult negotiation for the analytic pair. At this point it is helpful to find out what really is being asked for; Bromberg (1994) believes that recognition of the dissociated speaker, wordlessly struggling with the horror of what happened, is what is ultimately curative, rather than "gratification" (as when the patient is asking for some modification of analytic boundaries). He acknowledges the exquisite difficulty of making such decisions, but bodly and wisely points out that "gratification is most often experienced by patients as an empathic abandonment because it is typically a substitute for the more painful effort at recognition" (p. 543). This point needs some elaboration. What is gratification and what is recognition? This discrimination depends largely on the analyst's estimate of the patient's capacity to hold an inner object; a younger child, or a patient who dissociatively lacks the capacity for object constancy, will clearly have much more trouble staying connected without contact during a vacation or a long break between sessions, for example. Bromberg allows that there are some patients "for whom some directly gratifying response by the analyst is the only way they can trust the analyst's concern for them" (p. 543). Recognition as used in this way means the analyst's empathic grasp of the grat frustration and difficulty the patient may experience in the treatment situation, which may feel like it calls for more than the patient can bear. Empathy with this struggle is certainly the more demanding route for the therapist, but without it, the treatment is in danger of becoming "re-parenting" rather than analysis.

TRANSFERENCE AND THE DOUBLE-BIND

Double-bind communication is a very prominent feature of interaction in therapy, especially with MPD where it is virtually guaranteed. One therapist spent hours trying to reassure a sobbing, terrified child alter who was convinced that when she died, her father would be there, just waiting to hurt her again, only to find a message on her answering machine from another alter, thanking her profusely for making it safe for her to commit suicide. Another example illustrates Bateson's definition of the double-bind communication, mistaking the abstract for the concrete; the therapist was explaining to one alter of a multiple personality patient how she had been working with another alter who became frightened by the image of a cave they had developed as a metaphor for a safe, secure space. "So how did you get her out?" asked the patient. "I carried her," replied the therapist, whereupon the adult alter began to laugh and said, "I meant, how did you persuade her?" Suddenly the therapist began to feel very foolish for having taken the child alter's fear concretely, and having reacted to the shared metaphor as the child did, becoming more involved and more concerned for the frightened child part than the patient was herself. This experience of being left "holding the bag" is reminiscent of the case in *The Fifty Minute Hour* by Robert Lindner entitled "The Jet-Propelled Couch," in which the analyst had become so taken up with the patient's delusions that he was still involved with them after the patient had given them up. Judith Nenner (personal communication) puts it aptly: "You lit the fire, you ran out of the room, and now you ask why I'm hot?"

Adapting to the double-bind communication implicit in abuse sets the stage for dissociative formations; the primary double-bind is what the abuser says or implies: "I am now exploiting you, and you are to pretend that it is not happening." Spiegel (1978), who has written extensively about dissociation, points out that in hypnosis, the most effective trance inductions involve benign double-binds, and suggests that this form of communication during or around the abuse facilitates the child's development of dissociative operations. The dissociated part of the relationship cannot be accessed by the patient except under trance conditions, so transference interpretations aimed at uncovering the patient's expectation of being exploited may be met with bewilderment, or worse; the patient will feel again that he or she is being accused, shamed, or punished for having "bad" feelings. Often hidden, these transferential reenactments will color and confuse any treatment, but especially one where the analyst is adamant or rigid about theory and technique, or unaware of the nature of dissociation.

TRANSFERENCE AND MULTIPLE PERSONALITY DISORDER/DISSOCIATIVE IDENTITY DISORDER

When trauma is in the picture, whatever the analyst does, he or she may be experienced as abusive, in either an intrusive or a neglectful way. The intensity of both these extremes is hard to get comfortable with, but it is inevitable if the work is to be successful. The magnitude and intensity of reliving trauma, with all reality distortions and annihilation anxiety, are likely to be much greater than the therapist is prepared for; punitive diagnoses like "borderline" may ensue, reenacting both sides of the abuse in the treatment.

Davies and Frawley (1994) not only recognize the importance of the relational model to analytic work with traumatized patients, they also expand and amplify work with traumatic transference and countertransference to include technique of accessing dissociated "ego states." They recognize the essential part dissociation plays in preserving a living core of self, but in their excellent descriptions of technical issues with dissociated patients they stop short of the most extreme form; the persistent and chronic pattern of dissociation and consequent fragmentation of the self is a fundamental defense that leads to the syndrome of multiple personality disorder, now known as dissociative identity disorder. Reis (1993) reviews analytic understanding of MPD and suggests that the British school of object relations offers the best model for empathic holding of the patient's material "without the attendant pain and terror that precipitated annihilation anxiety in the past" (p. 316). Reis cites B. L. Smith (1990) as describing dissociative disorders as "collapsed potential space" and suggests that the MPD patient has failed to achieve and use transitional object phenomena at a phase-appropriate time; consequently, "fantasy objects are experienced not as illusory but as real" (p. 312). If true, this process would certainly complicate the reconstruction of "reality" for both patient and analyst.

Schwartz (1994) has taken the crucial step of integrating a relational analytic point of view with trauma/dissociation theories, including useful elements from cognitive-behavioral theorists. He describes the clinical picture of the MPD patient as arising from a trauma where the mind has tried to "get rid of itself," to flee its own subjectivity, to evacuate pain in order to adapt to the chronic and early trauma that is believed to lead to MPD. In this clinical picture, delayed memory is only one of the problematic issues in treatment:

> The MPD child, mummified in layers of complex false-self organiza-
> tion, becomes embedded in a secret, tormented world where frag-
> ments of self-experience alternately dominate each other and vie for
> supremacy in the name of survival. [p. 192]

OMNIPOTENCE AND GRANDIOSITY
IN THE TRANSFERENCE

It is not uncommon for the patient to have a hidden agenda of rescuing and rehabilitating the abuser. Like the poor minister in

Somerset Maugham's play *Rain*, who tries to convert a wanton Sadie Thompson and is instead seduced himself, this omnipotent goal leads directly to the transferential retraumatization of abused patients in current relationships, and very likely in the treatment as well. A confusing projective-introjective system of counteridentifications develops that complicates the identities of all parties.

For Alice, the omnipotent goal of rescuing her brother from his destructiveness, and the shame she experienced from her failure, served to obscure a fresh source of pain and shame that would come from the awareness that someone who (supposedly) loves her would be treating her in this way, forcing her to prove her love for him by sacrificing her own well-being and the integrity of her life to gratify him, even while he is attacking her. Thus her subjective affect of guilt is multidetermined; it helps her idealize him as she did her father, and is certainly preferable to the shame of seeing his denigration and hostility toward her more clearly. Alice believes she should have been able to make things right for him, and if he isn't happy, she's to blame. This conviction captured her experience of rescuing her father emotionally as he incested her, and kept her sadomasochistically involved with her brother, as she replayed the past relationship with her father in the present.

In attributing omnipotence to the analyst, nothing short of constant contact will suffice; this mirrors the inner world of desire for attachment so intense it is cannibalistic, a theme that comes up frequently in these treatments. The attachment hunger is intense and it is never experienced simultaneously with an equally strong attachment aversion, in which the contact with the analyst is feared and shunned. This attitude is contained in the multiple by the "protector alters," parts who hold what would have been healthy aggression in a normal developmental picture, but who are scornful of attachment and attachment figures, given to dangerous or foolish counterphobic behavior, and who think they know better than adults and have contempt for them. These parts of the self attack the self for any felt need for contact.

Grandiose elements in the personality of incest survivors represent identifications with the part of the parent that felt above the law, even the ancient and universal prohibition against incest. These children experienced the "specialness" of being chosen by a parent, often chosen over the parent of the same sex, so they are not just "oedipal victors" but even more grandiose and entitled pre-oedipal victors, since the abuse and the family dysfunction that supports it generally begins far younger than oedipal strivings are thought to arise.

THE THERAPIST'S SELF

To counteract these grandiose elements, traumatized patients as a group may need even more than any other group of patients for the analyst to be able to be wrong; not just to tolerate projections, but to be able to be completely off-target, without getting discombobulated or losing face. The analyst has to "leave space," because having to be too right, or having to know better than the patient about herself, or interpreting experience before the patient has felt it, can be experienced as a form of domination. Bromberg (1991) has stated this most eloquently in his paper "On Knowing One's Patient Inside Out," which is beautifully evocative of the need for balance and mutual attunement in the analytic pair, and of the need for modesty and self-forgiveness.

Because dissociated material is unformulated and not yet admitted to the verbal or conscious domain, the therapist who is working effectively may find herself taking on shifting roles through enactment, having to endure a patient's abusive behavior long enough for both to understand it, and having to own warded-off sadistic aspects of self. She will probably have to tolerate experiencing some very dystonic aspects of herself rather than working in the more comfortable ego-syntonic verbal domain of traditional therapy and analysis. Here is an example:

> A deeply traumatized patient, in crisis over a past abandonment and anticipating her therapist's imminent vacation, has been haranguing her therapist for weeks for being uncaring, for setting impossible limits (not allowing the patient to hurt herself during sessions). Apropos of the therapist's supposed lack of concern, the patient says, "I'd like to take a gun — what would you do if I shoot myself right here, so you'd have to see my blood and have it all over your carpet!"

The therapist, reeling from the context of a session in which violence and hatred had overflowed, replied to the very real threat she felt: "I'd have to call the police to come and take your body away." Upon a moment of reflection the therapist realized that the patient had induced a fear that the fantasy was real, and noticed how sadistic and hurtful she had felt in saying that. The therapist apologized, and asked the patient whether she had meant to really threaten, or whether she had given voice to a fantasy. The patient was able to acknowledge that the image of shooting herself had been a long-standing fantasy of having some impact on her father, and cried for a few minutes in recognition of relinquishing the possibility of acting on it.

The patient could only tolerate this moment of shared grief for a short time, however. She then said calmly and quietly that she would have to leave therapy now because the therapist had not been able to tell the difference between fantasy and reality, and she could not feel safe under those conditions. She then walked out, this time reenacting the role of her abandoning father and leaving the therapist feeling terrible anguish, guilt, inadequacy, despair and loss, not knowing when or if she would be back, just as the patient had felt as a child when her father had left.

This passage shows how the job of the analyst with the traumatized patient may be much more active and taxing than analysis of neurosis; the analyst must simultaneously lend herself to the full reexperiencing of the terrible events with which the patient is still struggling. At the same time the therapist must keep her head well enough to process the events at the verbal level, and decide whether to contain or reinterpret them to the patient. All this is usually too much to do at one and the same time, and so there is often an "out-of-synch" quality to the work. Such work is often counterintuitive for the analytically trained therapist. In the terms of the double-bind, she has to be able to allow herself to experience being attacked, while not being retaliatory; she must "go crazy" enough to capture the felt emotion while staying sane enough to think, and has to allow herself the freedom to be and feel sadistic or abusive, while trying not to act on those feelings, and while still trying to be capable of caring about the patient.

Sometimes analysis of the transference-countertransference is only possible after reenactment; extremes of rejection, abandonment, domination, and sadistic/masochistic positions precede recognition by either party that action replicates past events and experiences. The patient above was impelled to take over the transitional space of the analytic relationship and enact a real abandonment or threaten an action that drew the therapist into retaliation or domination; only after the dust has settled can there be understanding of that dissociated material, and recognition or interpretation can occur.

Bromberg (1993a) points out that the "acting out" that contributes to enactments is the result of dissociative avoidance of inner conflict. The patient may not yet be organized enough internally to be capable of an ambivalent state that can at once hold all of these, and so may cycle between the need to make contact, knowing that the therapist will permit contact, and the ability to hold back from calling, out of an acceptance that the analyst has real limits.

When dissociative defenses are being overused in response to intrusive symptoms, the patient is cut off from self-feelings, as under a bell jar, and feeling unreal. A young woman explained to me recently that before she was raped, "I used to be able to count on myself—I could ask questions, be curious, I could know how things were. But now I can't feel anything so I don't know what's what; I guess I sound and even look the same to other people, but I don't *have myself* anymore." Things are not so unbearable when one is totally numb, but "not feeling real" seems to be so unpleasant that it drives people to drugs and alcohol abuse, or self-mutilation.

I would like to extend Bromberg's position to ask whether we may not be inflicting a particular type of trauma on the patient if we do not recognize the dissociative mode enough to reconsider our technique. By continuing to interpret to the supposed inner conflicts, we may be imposing a false appearance of relatedness, even a false self. The alternative Bromberg (1993a) proposes is "rather a process of addressing individual subnarratives, each on its own terms, and enabling negotiation to take place between them" (p. 161). The analyst who fails to accept this preliminary work with the patient is risking being an abuser of our special type of power—the imposition of meaning.

REPETITION COMPULSION, DISSOCIATION, AND REENACTMENT

The successful analysis of an abuse survivor necessarily moves from an initial state in which the patient inevitably re-creates with the analyst the original abusive situation in many forms, automatically, without recognizing it. The intersubjective position is a natural basis for restoring the capacity for relatedness, since it is based on the shared experience of the session, and allows the patient to move to a state in which the felt inequities and problems in the analytic relationship are real enough to be talked about and worked through. Dissociated material tends to re-create abusive situations in the patient's life, as does repetition compulsion, in which the dynamic arises from repressed experience. However, patients tend to report a dreamlike, automatic quality when in the grips of a dissociated pattern; the awareness of choice is absent.

One occasion for the patient to experience a repetition of the sense of abuse arises around the problem of asking questions about it. Both patient and analyst are likely to be highly reluctant to address the trauma, even if it has been a premise of the treatment, that is, the patient comes to the treatment "with memories," and identifies him- or herself as having experienced abuse. The analyst under these conditions is walking a tightrope; by not taking the initiative in discussing the abuse, the neutral analyst can come to be experienced as the neglectful parent who colludes with the abuser, leaving the patient in despair.

This was how one patient, Sam, frequently experienced me: without being able to say so, he was waiting for me to bring up the abuse, experiencing me as cold and uninvolved when I did not. Taking the lead by focusing on himself, guiding and even controlling the session by taking the initiative, was not possible for him. On the other side of the dilemma, if I were to bring up the traumatic experience, such as by referring to the abuse, he would wince and I felt I was risking reenacting the role of intruder, forcing a shocking and shameful view of him on a patient who wasn't expecting it. This has happened frequently during the course of the analysis. Or, if I departed from neutrality in the interests of fostering the dissociated patient's relatedness, I must then worry about burdening the patient and shifting the focus of the treatment. The problem also arises of the meaning of any departures from neutrality. This set of dilemmas applies especially to self-disclosure.

Most patients are intensely ambivalent about acknowledging the abuse, because it means accepting those "not me" ego states into the self. Those who have memories generally want to believe that they imagined it; those who don't, feel an urgency about "finding the truth" and are often preoccupied with gimmicks like heterohypnosis or sodium amytal so as to "find out what really happened." These techniques are most likely to create reenactments of the abusive situation, since they generally involve the fantasy of submitting to some power outside the self.

SAM

This case material comes from the fifth year of a four-to-five times weekly analysis, in which the patient moved from a state of frozen numb unrelatedness, with islands of self floating in a sea of dissociation, to a state of capacity to observe himself enough to maintain an intimate relationship. When we began he was connected to the world almost exclusively through his intellectual competence and competitive drive; he was the youngest person ever promoted to receive a certain high achievement in his chosen artistic field, but his loneliness was almost unbearable. He lived in the state of driven intensity of the posttraumatic stress disorder (PTSS) patient who has become adapted to a high level of adrenaline: working far too much, drinking to relax, traveling on business to as many as three cities in one day, blocking out physical discomfort as a sign of needed health care until serious health problems developed.

The patient had always "known" factually that he had been incested by his father, but had not known this in a feeling way until his mid-twenties when he began to have intrusive flashbacks of violent rape. These sometimes occurred as body sensations but more frequently as vivid visual and emotional pictures with intensely painful physical sensations. But they were always partial in some way — if he had visual images, there were no body sensations; if he had body sensations, he had to force himself, if asked, to speculate on the events that might have engendered them. Like so many incest survivors he had some adolescent years of compulsive promiscuity and drug use with no conscious emotion attached. So in no instance were all the components of memory present at the same time: knowledge, emotion, sensation, visual image, and reenacted behavior. The overall meaning that the symptoms represented was always disguised; one and one and one and one remained a series of numbers, not adding up to four. This kind of thinking allowed him to minimize the importance of the abusive contact.

Before I realized the pervasiveness of his dissociation and was still thinking about our work in terms of transference and conflict, I thought I represented the self-absorbed mother who ignored his desperate need for contact. He couldn't even be the one to begin speaking because the inner fantasy of violent physical abuse was dissociated but underlying even the most benign-seeming interactions. Frozen in fear, he spoke in a monotone and was only able to say a few sentences in each session. He didn't look at me, but away — or through me, which was more chilling. To begin a session with his own concerns, or to spontaneously say whatever came to mind, was a form of initiative that was out of the question for him; it would be too violent an intrusion.

It was only after years of treatment that we began to understand that this fear was the outcome of, in Ferenczi's terms, a true "confusion of tongues." When he had crawled onto his father's lap as a toddler, seeking tenderness or comfort for a hurt, it had triggered the father to see and use him sexually. So if he was feeling needy, I was either the father who misinterpreted his gestures as sexual and made use of what was his by intruding exploitatively, or the mother who was barely aware of his existence. The enactments we studied for the first three years of treatment were related to these two positions.

Not being able to remember much of his childhood, and only a few visual flashes of the occasions of incest, was both shameful and frustrating to Sam; it was an assault to his formidable need for complete control over himself and his surroundings. On the other hand, like so many survivors, he was terrified of what he might find out if he did remember, and feel even more damaged by the fuller picture of what happened. We were both concerned that the traumatic memories might overwhelm him and disrupt a very demanding work schedule. As it happened, memories of all sorts generally followed some breakthrough in the relationship between us.

A breakthrough came in the second year of treatment. I realized that he was going into trance in the sessions and asked about it; he didn't know what I was talking about. When I probed for how he prepared himself for important games in tennis, a sport at which he excelled, he recognized the altered state and we began a project of bringing this ability more under his conscious control. In a few months he was able to use his autohypnotic abilities to put himself into a state of deep relaxation before critical presentations at work, and as a relief from the extreme stress. This collaboration between us began a period of Sam's use of his trance abilities to allow memories to come up, and very gradually over time we both became more able to comment on our relationship.

This material comes from a session in the fourth year of treatment, at a point when the patient was just beginning to paint again, after a long period of being unable to engage with the work he loved. The session shows the patient moving back and forth between using dissociative defenses, in the form of putting himself into trance, body feelings — numbness, heaviness, and so on — but also beginning to be able to verbalize his inner conflicts, which he was just now able to recognize.

Sam began the session by saying that he had a feeling this was going to be a hard session. He had been able to be very alive in working with his paints that weekend, and able to stay present (meaning not go numb or dissociated) more than ever before, but he had begun feeling strange this evening, before the session — heavy, like it would be hard to move. We both recognized these as the beginnings of trance or dissociative feelings. I asked when that heavy feeling had started, and he said he had been so open, and it felt so good, and then he began to think about what we'd been talking about, that the moment he begins to feel carefree and unguarded is the moment when he begins to feel that the worst thing can happen. I asked if he was still feeling strange now, and he said yes, kind of numb, and that he was afraid I would disapprove of him for being so free, so impulsive. I reflected that that was the way he had felt yesterday when we were considering the pros and cons of jumping into the painting. He confirmed that he was worried I would see him as aggressive. He said that he knew intellectually that I would not condemn him, but was afraid anyway, and quite anguished about needing my approval. He wished he didn't feel this way, that it was hard to feel like an adult when he was feeling so needy. I asked what he imagined me feeling. He said he imagined me being critical, condemning him for taking the initiative. I said that it seemed that he was picturing me as attacking him when he was feeling most vulnerable, hurting him with words. (I was feeling that in having this fantasy at that moment he was getting me to be the aggressive one, rather than engaging with his fear of becoming the hurtful, dangerous one through being bold with the paint.) After a short silence, he became agitated and said that he was really angry, so angry that he wanted to break something right now; he had realized he was taking the blame yet again for what his father had done to him. From the mixture of intense feelings in his voice I understood him to be feeling a loss, realizing with regret how this special moment had been spoiled for him by the encroachment of his fear. He asked mournfully why was it that he needed to feel so *bad*. I thought about the continuum from active to passive that had been so hideously compressed for him, and replied that the alternative to feeling like the bad one must have been to feel utterly helpless. He thought, then said, "Yeah, but why do I have to feel *so* bad?" I said that I guessed it was better than feeling something else. In the silence he sighed, regretfully, then said that he could sort of see that now, but not completely. He became angry again about what had been taken from him, and talked about wanting to break something again. What could he break? He didn't really want to, but not doing it meant keeping all this tension in his body. I talked about what it was like having to hold himself in. He said he couldn't stand that tension — but that it got easier as we talked. He wondered why he was having these numb feelings now when he was all right this afternoon for a while. I wondered if maybe there was something about being with me that brought them on. He confessed that he had a dread about having me know: he felt so confused, *knew* I wouldn't think he was too pushy, but felt afraid anyway. He wished that I could show him somehow that it was okay to paint so boldly, and okay to have feelings freely. I commented that then I would be taking the lead, showing that I could be pushy. He agreed. After a pause he said that he felt this funny feeling, like dread, about me, and laughed. Maybe this feeling was that I didn't know yet what trouble I was in for. I replied that I was going to be the helpless one now, and he could feel powerful, knowing what I was in for. He laughed again and said that maybe he would find out something bad about me.

In this session I found myself sticking very close to his feelings, mirroring the body feelings as well as the ideas and feelings, and not interpreting much so Sam could find his own meanings. The heavy feeling in his body and the numbness faded during the session, as they tend to do when we have a full exchange, meaning that we each take on all of the roles available to abuser and abused. I take this shift to mean that his need to push away his hurt and terrified, helpless self has lessened for that moment, and that he can begin to tolerate for a brief time the reality of the trauma without "leaving" dissociatively. His capacity to bear the unbearable, to say the unspeakable, to know the unknowable will make it possible gradually for Sam to "stay here" more and more, and to dissociate less and less.

REFERENCES

Balint, E. (1991). Commentary on Philip Bromberg's "On Knowing One's Patient Inside Out." *Psychoanalytic Dialogues* 1:423–430.

Balint, M. (1979). *The Basic Fault.* New York: Brunner/Mazel.

Bateson, G. (1978). Toward a theory of schizophrenia. In *Beyond the Double Bind*, ed. M. Berger, pp. 38–74. New York: Brunner/Mazel.

Bromberg, P. (1991). On knowing one's patient inside out. *Psychoanalytic Dialogues* 1(4):399–422.

—— (1993a). Shadow and substance. *Psychoanalytic Psychology* 10(2):147–167.

—— (1993b). *Resistance: obstacle or stepping stone?* Discussion presented at W. A. White Institute 50th Anniversary Celebration, November 13.

—— (1994). "Speak! that I may see you"; Some reflections on dissociation, reality, and psychoanalytic listening. *Psychoanalytic Dialogues* 4(4):517–547.

Casey, J. F. (1991). *The Flock: The Autobiography of a Multiple Personality*. New York: Knopf.

Davies, J. M., and Frawley, M. G. (1994). *Treating the Adult Survivor of Childhood Sexual Abuse*. New York: Basic Books.

Ferenczi, S. (1932). *Confusion of tongues between adults and the child*. Paper presented at the Twelfth International Psycho-Analytic Congress, Wiesbaden, September. (Reprinted in *Contemporary Analysis* 1988, pp. 196–206.)

Herman, J. (1992). *Trauma and Recovery*. New York: Basic Books.

Kramer, S., and Akhtar, S. (1991). *The Trauma of Transgression: Psychotherapy of Incest Survivors*. New York: Jason Aronson.

Laub, D., and Auerhahn, N. C. (1993). Knowing and not knowing massive psychic trauma: forms of traumatic memory. *International Journal of Psycho-Analysis* 74:287–302.

Lindner, R. M. (1955). *The Fifty Minute Hour*. New York: Rinehart.

Price, M. (1994). Incest and the idealized self: adaptations to childhood sexual abuse. *American Journal of Psychoanalysis* 54:21–36.

Reis, B. (1993). Toward a psychoanalytic understanding of multiple personality disorder. *Bulletin of the Menninger Clinic* 57:309–318.

Rosenfeld, H. (1987). *Impasse and Interpretation*. New York: Routledge.

Schwartz, H. L. (1994). From dissociation to negotiation: a relational psychoanalytic perspective on multiple personality disorder. *Psychoanalytic Psychology* 11(2):189–231.

Shengold, L. (1989). *Soul Murder: The Effects of Childhood Abuse and Deprivation*. New Haven: Yale University Press.

Sinason, V. (1991). Interpretations that feel horrible to make and a theoretical unicorn. *Journal of Child Psychotherapy* 17(1):11–24.

Smith, B. L. (1990). Potential space and the Rorschach: an application of object relations theory. *Journal of Personality Assessment* 55:756–767.

Spiegel, D. (1978). *Trance and Treatment: Clinical Uses of Hypnosis*. New York: Basic Books.

van der Kolk, B. A. (1989). The compulsion to repeat the trauma. *Psychiatric Clinics of North America* 12:389–411.

8

Time as the Missing Dimension in Traumatic Memory and Dissociative Subjectivity

BRUCE E. REIS

All our experiences, inasmuch as they are ours, arrange themselves in terms of before and after, because temporality, in Kantian language, is the form taken by our inner sense, and because it is the most general characteristic of "psychic facts." But in reality . . . we have already discovered, between time and subjectivity, a much more intimate relationship.

M. Merleau-Ponty, *The Phenomenology of Perception*

Much of the current attention paid to the subject of traumatic memory surrounds the epistemic issues (knowing, doubting, truth and falsity). This chapter takes a decidedly different approach to these phenomena in illustrating the ontologic disturbances produced by the phenomenal experiencing of traumatic memories. Examination of these issues is critical for the clinician working with psychically traumatized adults.

So-called reliving phenomena represent the central component of phenomenally experienced traumatic memory. With the return of the memory the patient experiences, often in full force, the affective charge of the past experience while sitting in the present. Often the person experiences visual, auditory, somatic, even olfactory sensations that were experienced at the time of the trauma. Reliving phenomena experienced by adult survivors of childhood sexual abuse disturb the adequate maintenance of adult relationships, such as in the case of a highly dissociative married woman, who had been raped by both her father and grandfather between ages 6 and 12, when she described that during sexual intercourse, her husband's penis "feels like my grandfather's." The experience is intense, and quite striking for those witnessing it for the first time. The phenomenal reexperiencing of dissociative memory can so overwhelm perceptual orientation within the present that the lived experience is one of the past superimposed (or even superseding) the present.

In this mode of experiencing, the reliving of trauma is experienced as a real and contemporary event (Chu 1991). Not uncommonly the patient in session will double over with pain, crying out, as she experiences the somatic genital sensations of past abuse. Patients will report the movie-like clarity of visual images of the abusive experiences: "I'm standing off to the side of that pull-out bed and I can see him there naked, it's disgusting the way he looks and how fat he is." Clinically, when working with the patient experiencing traumatic memory phenomena, a shift will occur so that the patient comes to use the present tense in describing her memory of abuse. In flashbacks, dissociative reenactment phenomena, body memories—the stuff of phenomenally experienced traumatic memory—what is experienced is the past trauma occurring within the present reality.

In our practices with psychically traumatized patients we often hear descriptions of their traumatic experience in a distorted time sense. As a component piece of a derealization process patients describe experiencing the event happening in slow motion, or the experience of time having completely stopped during the trauma. A police officer whom I recently evaluated, in describing having been shot eleven years ago, commented, "May God strike me dead if I didn't see the bullet leave the gun and travel this slow," tracing his finger in slow motion in the air. The pioneering investigations of van der Kolk (1991) have strongly suggested that the particular brain structures within the limbic system responsible for temporalizing and contextualizing experience into memory are rendered nonfunctional during trauma (and that serotonin reuptake inhibitors are often helpful in reregulating these brain structures).

Remarkably little attention has been paid to the assaults on the experience of time following traumatization. The only notable exception is Terr's (1983) descriptive study of thirty children and adults, some of whom experienced alterations in the perception or memory of time duration, and others who experienced confusion in sequencing or in orienting themselves in time. In other research, semantic memory systems (involved in the acquisition and utilization of language) have been differentiated from episodic memory systems (responsible for temporally contextualizing events) (Tulving 1983). Waites (1993) has noted episodic memory to be particularly vulnerable to traumatic disruption "perhaps because it involves the location of events in time, and time perception is itself often distorted during periods of extreme stress" (p. 28). Schacter and colleagues (1982) have suggested that episodic memories are organized around personal identity and that when episodic memory systems become dissociated from personal identity, the frame of reference for organization is thus absent. Waites and others have noted that while traumatized individuals sometimes report memory loss with an intact sense of identity, in other cases memory persists clearly and eidetically (such as in a flashback) and it is the sense of personal identity that is experienced as disturbed or different. It is the thesis of this chapter that the disturbances in time experience represent a central component in posttraumatic memory phenomena with alterations in perception or memory of time duration and confusions in sequencing and orientation (of the self) in time being intimately tied to dissociative, "not-me" disturbances of subjectivity.

Trauma theory informs us that traumatic experiences are encoded in state dependent memories (van der Kolk and van der Hart 1989) that, when dissociated from other conscious operations, contain the sensorimotor sensations, affect, and knowledge of past experiences. To access these states is to often access these unmodulated, unsymbolized experiences that once again may overwhelm the subject. Experienced clinicians who work with patients who have been sexually traumatized recognize that they continually alternate across self states. Less severely dissociatively disordered patients describe what has been understood as the posttraumatic sequelae of reexperiencing the original trauma as if it were presently occurring. On the extreme end of the dissociative continuum, dissociative identity-disordered patients often lose or seem to confabulate, orientation to present reality, experiencing themselves existing in another time, or physical location.

Clinicians inexperienced in working with dissociatively disordered patients may fail to recognize more subtle switching across self states, or misdiagnose such shifts when they are of a more dramatic form. Behaviors performed within dissociated states have come to be misunderstood by clinicans as psychotic or hysterical productions, borderline splitting phenomena, masochism, and/or forms of acting out or in rather than as memory phenomena. A wonderful illustration of this is contained in Alfred Hitchcock's 1945 classic film *Spellbound*, in which Gregory Peck dissociatively reexperiences and reenacts a variety of posttraumatic memory phenomena. Peck skillfully portrays these symptoms and amnesias that his analyst Ingrid Bergman understands as a trauma reaction, but that her supervisor is sure are the behaviors of a violent schizophrenic.

Traumatic memory of early abuse often does not present as the form of memory we are most accustomed to or acquainted with. Remembered as the perception of an event, it is expressed that way too. Unsymbolized it cannot be articulated and is often enacted instead. Often it is the enactment, however, that simultaneously covers and reveals the memory. Traumatic memory locks in patterns of self-other interaction that are reenacted and replayed with a different cast of characters, on a different stage. Those of us who grew up following the travails of Bruce Wayne in the comics knew of the character's witnessing of his parents' murders as the genesis of the development of his "alter ego," Batman, who compulsively hunted and was often revictimized by Gotham's criminals.

The reexperiencing and reenactment of traumatic memory is not a new subject to psychoanalysis. Freud took up the theme over the course of his writings, noting early on that, upon reemerging, a traumatic memory "will operate as though it were a contemporary event" (Freud 1896, p. 154), and commenting on the often visual "hallucinatory reproductions of the fright itself" during reliving experiences (Freud 1886, p. 152). In "Remembering, Repeating and Working Through" (1914), Freud understood behavioral reenactment qua memory phenomena, noting the disturbances of memory (i.e. amnesias) associated with traumatic reenactment: "He reproduces it not as a memory, but as an action; he *repeats* it, without, of course, knowing that he is repeating it" (p. 150); and later, "As long as the patient is in the treatment he cannot escape from this compulsion to repeat; and in the end we understand that this is his way of remembering" (p. 150). Freud (1937a) would again revisit the subject of reenactment observing that the patient will repeat his "modes of reaction . . . right before our eyes" (p. 341) and giving prime importance to these phenomena, which constitutes "half our analytic task" (p. 341). Later I will illustrate Freud's avant-garde approach to the understanding of what is currently thought of as the delayed memory of trauma.

Conceptualization and treatment from trauma theory often is cognitive-behaviorally based and many times resembles straight stimulus-response behaviorism, such as in the conceptualization of a "trigger" reaction. I believe that a contemporary psychoanalytic approach to traumatic memory phenomena provides a more comprehensive understanding, one that informs a treatment approach that allows the patient to rework his experiences on a more profound level of meaning. As dynamic clinicians, it is our task to reconceptualize our patients' experiences in experience-near analytic understanding so as not to simply transpose trauma theory into the psychoanaltyic work and thereby adopt simplistic models such as the "trigger." To this end I have attempted here to reconceptualize what has popularly been referred to as the "delayed" quality of traumatic memory, arguing that it is the disruption of the experience of time that goes to the heart of the dissociative disturbances of subjectivity.

CASE EXAMPLE

Ms. A. was a severely dissociative woman who experienced frequent, often uncontrolled switching between alter personalities (i.e., self states) and attendant amnesias ("losses of time"). She suffered frequent flashback experiences to her early abusive experiences that overwhelmed her with violent physical sensations, visual images, and smells of what had occurred. The patient was a single Caucasian teacher in her mid-twenties. Ms. A., who had been from infancy incested by her father, and, after the father's death, by her older brother through her adolescence, expressed immediate uneasiness at the gender of the therapist and asked for continued reassurances around the frame of treatment (e.g., that I not leave my chair during session) for fear of revictimization. Despite her hypervigilant expectations of attack, Ms. A. seemingly worked well in discussing her early incest experiences, relying emotionally on the therapist as a surround of trust and safety appeared to develop within the transference relationship.

One year into the treatment, during the course of several weeks, Ms. A. seemed obviously troubled, wishing to ask me something, but felt unable to do so. Eventually I learned what was troubling her: recently after having left our sessions she would return home to find that her brassiere was undone. This experience occurred repeatedly over the course of several weeks. The patient reported no memory of how this could have occurred, and became terrified that the therapist now had assumed the role of the next trusted male who would abuse her sexually. She began to become angry at me, not only accusing me of doing this to her, but also somehow for having allowed this to happen to her again. The enactment created an apparent impasse in the treatment. Ms. A.'s reality of the therapist was that he was abusive and sexually retraumatizing. She was experiencing in the present, in relation to me, the terror bound with past object relationships, as she compliantly represented herself twice weekly.

But this was not all of her experience. In speaking with other alter personalities, and eventually with the internalized abusers, I was to learn that a group of internalized bad objects (alters) had observed Ms. A.'s continued work and developing feelings of trust and safety within the treatment. The co-conscious experience of having felt cared for without having felt concomitantly abused caused these personalities in concert to reassert their incestuous loyalty and to sabotage the development of the relational space. The sentiments expressed were that Ms. A. does not deserve to feel cared for and that above all she must continue to suffer. Consequently, when different aspects of her internal world began to become engaged in the positive transference, they enacted a concretizing, defensive reaction of abuse utilizing the amnestic structure to protect against the affective experience of object relating.

DISCUSSION

Dissociative patients are always to one degree or another simultaneously "in" the present of other ego-states as well as "in" the (i.e., "our") present. For instance, when an alter within a multiple personality system experiences existing as a different gender, or in a different geographical location, he or she continues in this mode of experiencing even when that alter is not "out." When a posttraumatic stress disorder (PTSD) patient remains hypervigilant months or years after the trauma, he or she is simultaneously responding in the past and the present. While analytic theory has adopted the concept of dissociative state shifts, it has not yet adopted the model of co-conscious mental operations that accompanies vertical splitting and has been discussed in the trauma literature since the pioneering investigations of Morton Prince (1978/1906). Such a model not only advocates for shifting states but holds that such states also occur simultaneously in the person's experience. Where a model of shifting states would be analogous to an either/or mental operation, a model of co-conscious states is one of both/and.

Although it is initially difficult to imagine this, being mired in the structural model such as we are, consider the following example. I am driving in my car. At the same time I am listening to the baseball game on the car radio. I am concentrating on the game, on the wind up and the delivery of the pitch, the description of the swing. At the same time I am driving appropriately, staying in lane, regulating speed. It is only when a toll booth appears that I "snap out of it" and attend fully to driving (slowing down, searching for change), only at that time does the state shift from one to the other. I believe an example such as this one is the closest that many of us who are not highly dissociative can come to understanding the phenomenal experience of co-consciousness that predominates the mental lives of dissociative patients. However, since we are able to experience these decenterings, we are able to meet our patients within these jointly created spaces to do the therapeutic work.

Ogden (1994) has spoken of the importance of the analyst's use of reverie (Bion 1962) in symbolic transformation of the patient's unarticulated experience. In fact it is my contention that descriptions of analytic intersubjective space (e.g., Bromberg 1993, Ogden 1994) resemble descriptions of dissociative modes of experiencing. Ogden, for example, has noted that, "In this state, the dialectical interplay of consciousness and unconsciousness has been altered in ways that resemble a dream state" (Ogden 1994, p. 12). It has been my experience that dissociative patients are adept not only at inducing autohypnotic states but also inducing in the therapist dissociative countertransference states either through their repeated traumatizations of the therapist (by the retelling of the multiple, horrific trauma stories or assaults on the frame of treatment) or through projective forms of interpersonal communications. Loewenstein (1993) has commented on how the therapist may experience a host of perceptual alterations (e.g. depersonalization, trance-like states, countertransferential "spacing out," and the inability to think) as a result of the intensity of the patient's dissociative projective identifications.

Through repeated exposure the therapist becomes overwhelmed, feels helpless, numbed, employs denial and has it fail, and may experience a host of other posttraumatic and dissociative states as he is invaded via enactment with the patient's trauma. Such counter-trance-ference states are, I believe, essential to understanding the multiple transferences and multiple subjectivities present in working with such patients. Working from these states, the therapist needs to maintain the dialectic of relating to the patient's discontinuities of experience by holding a psychic image of a continuous subject who exists only as a potentiality, while at the same time containing and relating with the patient's multiple versions of self in a manner described by Mitchell (1993) and Bromberg (1994). It is through such necessary, logically illogical action that the therapist assists the patient in temporalizing the therapeutic "space." From this therapeutic vantage, the patient is not simply seen as amnestic for their experience but can be understood to know and not know simultaneously (Laub and Auerhahn 1993).

It is because our patients are often locked in these intersections of dissociation, after having suffered attacks on psychic "linking functions" (Bion 1993), that their experience of their experience is assaulted. Often they cannot feel the emotions they know they feel, often they remain temporally adrift, at times unable to differentiate what is presently happening to them from the incestuous experiences that occurred decades earlier and often dissociating their current symptomatic state from their past traumatic experiences. The fact that the trauma is displaced (i.e., misplaced) in time to the present is evident in these patients' consistent presentations of autonomic hyperarousal (Perry 1994), numbed states, and hypervigilance. Terr (1983) has noted that among victims of psychic trauma there is an indistinct differentiation between actual perception and memory of perception. As the philosopher Merleau-Ponty (1962) observed, "A preserved perception is a perception, it continues to exist, it persists in the present, and it does not open behind us that dimension of escape and absence that we call the past" (p. 413). Following Freud's guidance then, the therapeutic aim in cases of traumatic memory phenomena may involve "liberating the fragment of historic truth from its distortions and attachments to the actual present day and in leading it back to the point in the past to which it belongs" (Freud 1937b, p. 370).

Perceptual overlays are often elicited by and become enmeshed within the transference. Relationally oriented analysts have begun to express an appreciation for the role of dissociative enactment phenomena and argued for modifications in technique (Davies and Frawley 1994). Enactment, from a relational perspective,

> involves a need to be known—in the only way possible, intersubjectively—through playing out with the analyst, in some mutually creative way that is different from the old and fixed patterning of self-other interactions, a version of the situation that led to the original need for dissociation; and through this relational act of sameness and difference to construct jointly an act of meaning [Bruner 1990] that allows the dissociated threat of potential trauma to be cognitively processed. [Bromberg 1993, p. 154]

In the case of Ms A. an enactment was performed in a dissociated state. In mobilizing my own anxieties, Ms A. communicated the terror of her own experience by inducing such feelings in me. The trauma literature has for years recognized the abused patient's formation of traumatic transferences (Kluft 1984, Spiegel 1986). Authors from this school have illustrated the abused patients' invocation of abuser, victim, and rescuer roles as they continually and inevitably shift between therapist and patient. Psychoanalysts, too (Casement 1982, Karon 1984) have commented on the "tyrannizing transferences" (Ogden 1992) relived within the abused/abusive patient's relationship to the analyst. Until recently, these reenactments within the transference were viewed largely as the delusional productions of borderline and schizophrenic patients, rather than as predominantly memory phenomena of a dissociative nature.

Dissociative states often co-occur in time. The clinician who works with dissociative patients is aware that the multiple transferences that are formed are simultaneous, in addition to shifting (Putnam 1989). For instance, it is quite common that alter B will react to conversations the therapist was engaging in with alter A. Amnestic barriers are often permeable and continually shift around, often depending on what's being discussed. Multiple states are contacted at the same time by the therapist who works with dissociative patients, and these multiple states are not (multiple Cartesian) subjects who stand outside of the flow of experience, but facets of the patient's total consciousness. Thus, with these patients a multiplicity of transferences is interactively present. This is why many trauma-oriented therapists utilize contracts between alters and the therapist as a containing device across therapist–patient relational patterns. The notion that there is a one-to-one correspondence in representation (e.g., a patient to abusive father schema) is overly simplistic and fails to capture the multiple/simultaneous dialectics of the inter- and intra-actions contained within the experience of the dissociative patient's subjectivity.

Ms. A.'s enactment was an aggressive and ruthless action against the therapist. Her behavior allowed Ms. A. to be both victim and perpetrator of her enactment simultaneously. Certainly her enactment with the male therapist was within the paternal transference. But also the communicative aspect (i.e., the attempted engagement via enactment with the unseeing mother) was seen to be simultaneously occurring with the maternal transference. Rather than the one-to-one correspondence of schematic representation, we see here several relational paradigms enacted simultaneously (e.g., patient in relation to father, with therapist being father; patient in relation to father with patient being father; patient in relation to [absent] mother).

Through the simultaneous creation of both victim and perpetrator roles the event itself was re-created within the transference-countertransference matrix. Within Ms. A.'s enactment, for instance, I experienced confusion, anger, shame, fear at being aggressed upon, and strong anxieties around my own potential for malevolence. The patient's internalized abusing objects had re-created and forced into me through a projective identificatory process these aspects of the patient's early abusive experience for me to "know." The use of the therapist in a parent–child configuration ultimately represents her potential to engage new objects and consequently to rework experience into memory. From a relational perspective Ms. A.'s enactment may be understood as a therapeutic opportunity to disengage prematurely experienced and brutal forms of adult sexuality from arrested preoedipal needs for maternal holding (e.g., safety and consistency) and good-enough parenting.

Hegeman (1993), for one, has noted the potentially damaging effects that a traditionally interpretative mode may have in treatment with a trauma survivor in its neglect of the interpersonal context of trauma and subsequent implication that the basic fault lies in the internal dynamics of the patient herself. She says, "Recurrence of the relational trauma can either confuse and confound the issues, as it does when the analyst fails to recognize that the transference is influenced by trauma, or it can offer the patient a chance to rework the relational aspects of unresolved earlier trauma" (p. 4).

I would suggest that one aspect of recognizing the influence of trauma on the transference involves attending to the perceptual backflow of time into the present relationship. This phenomenon is understood to be different from the commingling of past, present, and future dimensions within the transference not effected by severe trauma, as in that condition the sense of present is not foreclosed by the collapse of this temporal dialectic. This emphasis differs from traditional, drive based notions of an eroticized transference and is reconceptualized in trauma patients to represent flashback transfer-ences (Loewenstein 1993) where memory is experienced (to varying degrees) as current relational reality. In another clinical example, Bigras (1990) regarded a patient's disorientation in time within the session as "her sense of experiencing the original trauma in the here and now in such an intense way that time seemed to have stopped" (p. 185). This experience became enmeshed within the transference-countertransference matrix when the patient handed over to the analyst control of (session) time, which Bigras interpreted as "making me into the abuser who alone had the power to release her from the torture of the sessions" (p. 185). The differences from classically analytic approaches in the use of the analyst/therapist proposed are consistent with Winnicott's (1955, 1963, 1974) description of the patient's needing to be able to experience in the present with the analyst "the extremes of feeling which belonged to an early traumatic experience but which had been 'frozen' because of being too intense for the primitive ego to encompass *at that time*" (Casement 1982, p. 284).

TEMPORALITY

The element of temporal transposition is central to an understanding of delayed traumatic memory and reliving experience. Freud's (1895) concept of *Nachträglichkeit*, that "a memory is repressed which has only become a trauma after the event" (p. 356), reflects a clinical appreciation of posttraumatic reliving phenomena within a temporally nonlinear framework. "The introduction of the *Nachträglichkeit* indicates those moments when Freud leaves aside the model of mechanical causality and a linear temporality on the past and present vector for a dialectic concept of causality and a 'spiral' model of temporality where future and past condition and signify each other reciprocally in the structuring of the present" (Baranger et al. 1988, pp. 115–116). Freud's concept of *Nachträglichkeit*, poorly translated by Strachey as the deferred or delayed action of traumatic memory has been redefined as a theory of "subsequentiality" by Modell (1990, p. 2) within a psychology of cyclic rather than linear time. Modell takes the concept of *Nachträglichkeit* to mean "that the ego is a structure engaged in the processing and reorganizing of time" (p. 4). Winnicott's conception of traumatic experience which is 'frozen' because it could not be assimilated and accommodated by the ego illustrates Modell's approach, as it places such experience outside of the temporal dialectic where past and immediate future fold into themselves and each other in order to create a sense of the present. The patient continues to be occupied by traumatic events that belong to the past Winnicott (1974) observed, because "the original experience of primitive agony cannot get into the past tense unless the ego can first gather it into its own present time experience and into omnipotent control now" (p. 105). As such the quality of reliving explicit in traumatic "memory" (in quotes because it is not exactly one's own memory yet) illustrates what Merleau-Ponty (1962) referred to as the experience of the reversability, or back flow, of time.

Reenactments within this state have been viewed clinically (van der Kolk and van der Hart 1991) as a present living within the unremembered past, and Spiegel (1993) has observed that during reliving experiences it is subsequent history that is dissociated, as the individuals are not aware that they have already survived the traumatic experience. It is of little surprise therefore that so many of our patients who experience these disturbances of time as a result of trauma additionally feel their futures are foreshortened. If, following Modell's contemporary reinterpretation, the dynamic relationship in the experience of past, present, and future time has been disrupted as a result of trauma it seems a misnomer then to use a phrase such as "delayed memory" to describe the lived experience of the trauma survivor. For in this condition trauma has overwhelmed the synthetic capacity of the ego to contextualize the experience of time, not allowing the event to become a part of one's past and throwing the individual into a pathological state of timelessness (Bromberg 1991). These clinical observations appear well grounded in modern psycho-biological investigations (see van der Kolk, Chapter 2 in this volume).

The element of temporal back flow is central to an experience-near clinical understanding of these traumatic memory phenomena and resulting changes in subjectivity. The continuous nature of consciousness depends to a great extent upon the ordering of events in time, a succession mediated by several major brain components that contribute to memory (Edelman 1989). Van der Hart and colleagues (1993) noted that during a flashback, for instance, "the trauma survivor is usually still relatively aware of his or her current surroundings and situation (but) there is a kind of doubling of consciousness, i.e., of reliving the past (to which the person also begins to respond) while at the same time partially staying in the present" (p. 164). Within the context of the therapeutic relationship it is easy to see how such a process may become linked up with the transference and how the individual may to varying degrees lose mooring within present reality (i.e. experience multiple simultaneous realities [Bromberg 1993, Modell 1990] and experience the therapist as either abusive himself, as Ms. A. did, or in the extreme as the original abuser (as in Casement 1982).

In treatment it may be said that memory is created for the first time by the narrative reordering, within a temporal dialectic, of previously amnestic, unsymbolized, or enacted trauma. In the patient's process of translating fragmented somatic and cognitive perceptions into narrative memory, the vicissitudes of dissociation are often revealed. The victim's original sense of helplessness and confusion, which contributed to the need to dissociate slowly, comes under the ego's omnipotence, as, with the help of the therapist, symbolization occurs.

> Nancy, a previous patient, had always "known," for instance, that her uncle had penetrated her vaginally when she was a child, though she had never discussed his repeated abuse with anyone. When Nancy described in session her memories of what her uncle had done to her she writhed in pain, clutching her groin. Over several subsequent sessions I asked Nancy what she understood her uncle had done to her; she seemed not to know what was obvious. With a quizzical expression she looked at me and repeatedly asked, "Was that rape?" Moments later, with a flash of recognition Nancy quietly declared, "Oh my God, he raped me." For Nancy, the wordless pain had ceased to be a primitive agony. Language had given it a shape that had become tragically understandable to her. It is as if Nancy's understanding of her experience had been frozen in its original unspeakable confusion, and then released for her adult self to claim. The memory was assembled.

The very fact that these fragmented perceptions bear the signature of past trauma in their unique and readily identifiable posttraumatic presentation displays the history of the patients not yet narrated, not yet their own. As clinicians we must recognize that we work with the transformations of traumatic memory. This work then entails a narrative reordering of experience, a releasing of the temporal displacement of enactment, yielding to a reflective symbolization of the content of experience. This is done within the context of a therapeutic holding environment where the patient may feel the necessary degree of safety that allows her to experience strong (previously dissociated) affect in relationship to the therapist, without the necessity of having to be defensively psychically absent (Casement 1982).

One should not be misled by the spatial metaphor of integrating an existing memory or dissociative self state "into" the total personality. As Brierley (1944) recognized in her discussion of dissociation fifty years ago, "Integration is not mere summation." The clinical work with dissociative patients does not involve putting together fragmented pieces to make one whole person. These pieces do not fit together and if somehow put together would not then make the assumed (cohesive) person. Integration is a spatial metaphor based on a structural model, when what is discussed here is not solely a structural, but a temporal, model (see Mitchell 1993). For Bigras (1990) the analyst becomes "a representative of the law" (Laplanche and Pontalis 1973, p. 440) in Lacan's terms. "By reinstating the taboo of incest, the analyst begins the work of establishing the 'Symbolic'" (Laplanche and Pontalis 1973, p. 439). Destroyed inner space begins to be knit together or overlaid with coordinates of time, of ethics, and eventually of desire" (Bigras 1990, p. 191). With Ms. A., it was only after discussing the enacted event as an "analytic third" (Ogden 1994) that the patient was able to verbalize in the present her own longings for the parent/therapist, to grieve the absence of the good father and protecting mother, and most important to become aware of the conflict inherent in her own experience.

CONCLUSIONS

Winnicott (1960) expressed, in his experience-near formulation around traumatic impingements, that the alternative to being is reacting, and that reacting interrupts being and annihilates the continuous experience of consolidated subjectivity. Repetitive retraumatization by flashbacks, body memories, and reenactments forecloses the individual's ability to remain conscious of one's consciousness. A collapse of subjectivity results because it is only through a sense of temporality that there can "be" a subject of subjectivity, a rhythm to one's being.

In many ways the goals of our work with (especially these) patients are ontologic (although it is the epistemic question that has received the lion's share of attention from clinicians). We attempt to help our patients to stop reacting and to be more continuously, or, as Bromberg (1993) has suggested, to enact new ways of being. With this goal, treatment is successful when, in the words of Merleau-Ponty (1962) "past and future withdraw of their own accord from being and move over into subjectivity in search, not of some real support, but, on the contrary, of a possibility of non-being which accords with their nature" (p. 410). When the patient reclaims her own history, says Herman (1992), "Time starts to move again. . . . the traumatic experience truly belongs to the past. At this point, the survivor faces the tasks of rebuilding her life in the present and pursuing her aspirations for the future" (p. 195).

ACKNOWLEDGMENTS

The author would like to express his appreciation to the following for their helpful comments on earlier versions of this chapter: Laurie Pearlman, Sue Grand, Judie Alpert, Michelle Price, Bill Pinney, and Jodie Wigren.

REFERENCES

Baranger, M., Baranger, W., and Mom, J. M. (1988). The infantile psychic trauma from us to Freud: pure trauma, retroactivitiy and reconstruction. *International Journal of Psycho-Analysis* 69:113–128.

Bigras, J. (1990). Psychoanalysis as incestuous repetition, some technical considerations. In *Adult Analysis and Childhood Sexual Abuse.*, ed. H. B. Levine, pp. 173–196. Hillsdale, NJ: Analytic Press.

Bion, W. R. (1962). *Learning from Experience.* New York: Basic Books.

——— (1993). Attacks on linking. In *Second Thoughts, Selected Papers on Psycho-Analysis.* Northvale, NJ: Jason Aronson.

Brierley, M. (1944). Notes on metapsychology as process theory. *International Journal of Psycho-Analysis* 25(3, 4):97–107.

Bromberg, P. M. (1991). On knowing one's patient inside out: the aesthetics of unconscious communication. *Psychoanalytic Dialogues* 1(4):399–422.

——— (1993). Shadow and substance: a relational perspective on clinical process. *Psychoanalytic Psychology* 10(2):147–168.

——— (1994). *"Speak! That I may see you."* Paper presented at the second annual Bernard N. Kalinkowitz Memorial Lecture, New York University, February 25.

Bruner, J. (1990). *Acts of Meaning.* Cambridge, MA: Harvard University Press.

Casement, P. J. (1982). Some pressures on the analyst for physical contact during the reliving of an early trauma. *International Review of Psycho-Analysis* 9(3):279–286.

Chu, J. A. (1991). The repetition compulsion revisited: reliving dissociated trauma. *Psychotherapy* 28(2):327–332.

Davies, J. M., and Frawley, M. G. (1994). *Treating the Adult Survivor of Childhood Sexual Abuse: A Psychoanalytic Perspective.* New York: Basic Books.

Edelman, G. M. (1909). *The Remembered Present: A Biological Theory of Consciousness.* New York: Basic Books.

Freud, S. (1886). Sketches for the "Preliminary Communication" of 1893: early drafts on hysteria. *Standard Edition* 1:145–154.

Freud, S. (1895). Project for a scientific psychology. *Standard Edition* 1:281–397.

—— (1896). Heredity and the aetiology of the neuroses. *Standard Edition* 3:141–156.

—— (1914). Remembering, repeating, and working through. *Standard Edition.*

—— (1937a). Analysis terminable and interminable. In *Collected Papers*, ed. J. Strachey, 5:316–357. London: Hogarth, 1953.

—— (1937b). Constructions in analysis. In *Collected Papers*, ed. J. Strachey, 5:358–371. London: Hogarth, 1953.

Hegeman, E. (1993). *Resolution of traumatic transference: two cases.* Paper presented at the W. A. White Institute 50th Anniversary Celebration, Nov. 14.

Herman, J. (1992). *Trauma and Recovery.* New York: Basic Books.

Karon, B. P. (1984). A type of transference based on identification with an abusing parent. *Psychoanalytic Psychology* 1(4):345–348.

Kluft, R. P. (1984). Aspects of the treatment of multiple personality disorder. *Psychiatric Annals* 14:51–55.

Laplanche, J., and Pontalis, J. B. (1973). *The Language of Psycho-Analysis,* trans. D. Nicholson-Smith. London: Hogarth.

Laub, D., and Auerhahn, N. C. (1993). Knowing and not knowing massive psychic trauma: forms of traumatic memory. *International Journal of Psycho-Analysis* 74:287–302.

Loewenstein, R. J. (1993). Posttraumatic and dissociative aspects of transference and countertransference in the treatment of multiple personality disorder. In *Clinical Perspectives on Multiple Personality Disorder*, ed. R. P. Kluft, and C. G. Fine, pp. 51–85. Washington, DC: American Psychiatric Press.

Merleau-Ponty, M. (1962). *Phenomenology of Perception.* London: Routledge and Kegan Paul.

Mitchell, S. A. (1993). *Hope and Dread in Psychoanalysis.* New York: Basic Books.

Modell, A. H. (1990). *Other Times, Other Realities: Toward a Theory of Psychoanalytic Treatment.* Cambridge, MA: Harvard University Press.

Ogden, T. H. (1992). Consultation is often needed when treating severe dissociative disorders. *Psychodynamic Letter* 1(10):1-4.

———— (1994). *Subjects of Analysis.* Northvale, NJ: Jason Aronson.

Perry, B. D. (1994). Neurobiological sequelae of childhood trauma: PTSD in children. In *Catecholamine Function in Posttraumatic Stress Disorder: Emerging Concepts,* ed. M. M. Murburg. Washington, DC: American Psychiatric Press.

Prince, M. (1978/1906). *The Dissociation of a Personality: The Hunt for the Real Miss Beauchamp.* Oxford, England: Oxford University Press.

Putnam, F. W. (1989). *Diagnosis and Treatment of Multiple Personality Disorder.* New York: Guilford.

Schacter, D., Wang, P., Tulving, E., and Freedman, M. (1982). Functional retrograde amnesia: a quantitative case study. *Neuropsychologia* 20:523-532.

Spiegel, D. (1986). Dissociation, double binds, and posttraumatic stress in multiple personality disorder. In *Treatment of Multiple Personality Disorder,* ed. B. G. Braun, pp. 61-78. Washington, DC: American Psychiatric Press.

———— (1993). Dissociation and trauma. In *Dissociative Disorders: A Clinical Review,* ed. D. Spiegel, pp.117-131. Lutherville, MD: Sidran.

Terr, L. C. (1983). Time sense following psychic trauma: a clinical study of ten adults and twenty children. *American Journal of Orthopsychiatry* 53(2).

Tulving, E. (1983). *Elements of Episodic Memory.* Oxford, England: Clarendon.

van der Hart, O., Steele, K., Boon, S., and Brown, P. (1993). The treatment of traumatic memories: synthesis, realization, and integration. *Dissociation* 6(2/3):162-180.

van der Kolk, B. A. (1991). The biological response to psychic trauma: mechanisms and treatment of intrusion and numbing. *Anxiety Research* 4:199-212.

van der Kolk, B. A., and van der Hart, O. (1989). Pierre Janet and the breakdown of adaptation in psychological trauma. *American Journal of Psychiatry* 146:1530-1540.

———— (1991). The intrusive past: the flexibility of memory and the engraving of trauma. *American Imago* 48:425-454.

Waites, E. A. (1993). *Trauma and Survival: Post Traumatic and Dissociative Disorders in Women.* New York: Norton.

Winnicott, D. W. (1955). Metapsychological and clinical aspects of regression within the psycho-analytical set-up. *International Journal of Psycho-Analysis* 36:(1):16-26.

———— (1960). The theory of the parent–infant relationship. *International*

Journal of Psycho-Analysis 41:385-395.

_____ (1963). Dependence in infant-care, in child-care, and in the psycho-analytical setting. In *The Maturational Processes and the Facilitating Environment*. New York: International Universities Press.

_____ (1974). Fear of breakdown. *International Review of Psycho-Analysis* 1(1, 2):103-107.

9

Incest and the Intersubjective Politics of Knowing History

SUE GRAND

We psychoanalysts are practicing in a paradoxical historical moment, full of extraordinary contradiction and exciting potential. We are developing a view of the analytic situation as a rich field of relational play, a world of mutually constructed meanings and intersubjective truths. These truths are explored in an egalitarian, two-person relationship in which, at long last, the patients are permitted to "see and know" the analyst, to have and possess their own perceptions of the analytic reality. However, at the very moment we relinquish the pursuit of historical truth, we are simultaneously attempting to integrate trauma theory and research into psychoanalysis (Alpert 1994, Davies and Frawley 1994).

But here we have a contradiction and a conundrum—the treatment of all trauma is predicated on a shared conviction between analyst and patient that the trauma actually occurred. The establishment of the actual historicity of trauma is particularly necessary with incest. Incest is a trauma uniquely characterized by the falsification of reality; it has invariably occurred secretly, in family systems that deny its very existence. Survivors of other forms of trauma, such as war, kidnappings, natural disasters, all receive the profound support of consensual validation from survivor cohorts and the larger culture.

The incest survivor has been robbed of reality and of history; cure requires its restoration. Admittedly, the restoration of a clear sense of history is a problematic process in many cases of possible incest, in which memory may dissociated; it is nonetheless necessary. Ideally, the patient needs to know, Was I or wasn't I a victim of incest? I believe we are without an adequate epistemological paradigm in psychoanalysis that will allow us to integrate both the nature of the incest trauma and the merits of the new constructivism in a unified psychoanalytic theory. I would suggest that this is the reason that the burgeoning field of trauma theory and research is essentially alienated from contemporary psychoanalysis.

Unlike the one-person, classic, archaeological model, the new social constructivism releases the incest survivor to repossess her own perceptions and experiences, rather than to defer the definition of perception to authority/analyst/parent. This is vital to her recovery. However, she finds herself once again lost in funhouse mirrors if she seeks to resolve the historical reality of her ambiguous, dissociated memories of incest in an analysis operating on this constructivist model. While there is endless empathic space for analyst and patient to "converse" as Spezzano (1993) says, about the patient's desire for historical truth, the actual facts of trauma would be considered inaccessible, lost forever in what Spence (1982, 1993) describes as the endless embellishments and distortions of language, time and memory, leaving only what Geha (1993) calls the fictions of the mind. Much of our contemporary psychoanalytic epistemology reflects just this type of radical hermeneutics espoused by Gadamer, and criticized by Habermas, for its abandonment of the pursuit of objective knowledge (Baynes 1989).

For the psychoanalytic treatment of incest survivors to be effective, there must be some epistemological paradigm that is neither positivist nor constructivist, some psychoanalytic model that retains the context of relational mutuality and intersubjectivity without negating the significance and accessibility of historical truth. We must return to an awareness of what Sampson (1992) calls a person's innate, primary, and powerful interest in reality. As Sass (1993) says, "It is the patient's life that is at stake, and the sheer undeniable reality of his or her emotions and memories may well make the patient less than enthusiastic about the prospect of engaging in some kind of aestheticist or deconstructive game" (p. 251).

We all know, as human beings living our ordinary lives that reality is not entirely mutually constructed, that truth is not merely narrative. The real puzzle is to find some way to locate and define the elusive interplay of historical and narrative truth. If we can allow ourselves to explore this epistemological problem, informed both by the dilemma of the incest survivor and by the data available from trauma research, we have the potential to attain yet another new paradigm for psychoanalysis. Such a paradigmatic shift would allow for the more effective psychoanalytic treatment of incest survivors, while undoubtedly enlivening psychoanalysis in general.

As we approach this knotty problem, it is imperative that we stay in touch with the tragic and paradoxical dimensions of the false memory controversy. We must never forget the nightmarish specter of the parents who have indeed been falsely accused and had their lives destroyed, nor can we ignore the existence of incompetent therapists who proffer incest as the only explanation for every symptom. I would suggest that such cases are much rarer than is currently presented by the media and the False Memory Association. Herman and Harvey (1993) estimate that false accusations account for approximately 3 to 8 percent of all accusations of incest.

Simultaneously, we must recall that the incest survivor's life has been doubly destroyed—first by the trauma of incest, and second by the negation of its existence. It is a particularly paradoxical controversy, in that almost all incest perpetrators lie about the incest, protesting outraged innocence, portraying themselves as the victim, and threatening retaliation when exposed. Thousands of accused perpetrators have now created an entire social movement to protest their innocence, to disavow incest, and to punish and discredit those who uncover it—patients and therapists alike. How to tell which parent is actually innocent when all perpetrators lie? In this context, issues of historical versus subjective truth are fraught with the potential for human destruction on both sides of the question, and we must exercise great caution.

Just as we begin an exploration of the integration of trauma theory and psychoanalytic theory (Alpert 1994, Davies and Frawley 1994) we are met with the powerful, repressive external counterforce of the false-memory controversy. The potential for lawsuits in this area is escalating rapidly; the fear this induces may succeed in turning us away from grappling with difficult clinical questions and the epistemological issues behind them, particularly since Loftus's critique of memory may seem to resonate all too well with our new constructivist view of mind.

Loftus's (1991, 1993) view of the suggestibility and mutability of memory sounds remarkably similar to the views of memory promulgated by many of our contemporary theorists. Ogden (1990) for example, says, "What is of importance is the way in which the patient constructs his symbolic representation of the past. The past no longer exists and is absolutely irretrievable. The patient in the present creates his own history" (p. 241). Geha (1993) writes, "Mind-made realities constitute for human beings their sole realms of existence, and that it is only about these realms that anything at all can be known. No other knowable realities exist" (p. 209).

Loftus is not an adherent of our radical form of social constructivism. As a rationalist pursuing primarily laboratory-based research, she believes that intense affect destroys accurate memory; since trauma is characterized by intense affect it should really never be possible to retain an accurate memory of it. If we read only Loftus's work, or, worse, the media's presentation of Loftus's work, it becomes all too easy to turn away from the excavation of traumatic memories of incest for the second time in our psychoanalytic history, once again suppressing the truth about incest at the very moment when it has begun to emerge, once again utilizing the rationalizations provided by whatever metapsychology is current to conceal our legitimate terror of incest and all of its emotional, cultural, and legal ramifications.

Loftus's view of memory fails utterly to take into account other memory research, and in particular the research on traumatic memory by Herman (1992), Herman and Harvey (1993) and van der Kolk (1987, 1994). Contrary to Loftus's view, Herman and van der Kolk find that the essence of traumatic memory is retained intact, although it is often dissociated. The intensity of affect contributes to the retention of memory, although this same affect may necessitate dissociation. According to these authors, traumatic memory does not exist in the linear verbal form in which we retain nontraumatic memory; it is sensory, pictorial, and enacted through a consistent constellation of posttraumatic stress disorder (PTSD) symptoms and signs. Loftus (1991) herself courageously reveals a clear, compelling, and unchallenged delayed memory of being sexually abused as a young child. Remarkably, her own memory appears exempt from the types of memory distortions she reviews in her book. Her own memory is, in fact, an excellent example of the persistence of traumatic memory as described by Herman. If we credit the validity of traumatic memory research, either to the exclusion of, or in addition to, the research by Loftus, we find ourselves suspended in a critical epistemological no-man's land.

As human beings we are all living in this no-man's land. Ours is a strange age that radically deconstructs reality and evidence while simultaneously witnessing a rampant escalation of dehumanized violence. Our entire nation witnessed the Rodney King videotape; what more "objective evidence" could be obtained to demonstrate police brutality? Yet this evidence was subjected to endless hermeneutic interpretation and reinterpretation, resulting in a nonguilty verdict by twelve sincere jurists. Neo-Nazis proliferate, as does the view that the Holocaust never really happened (Lipstadt 1994). What is the meaning of our collusion in the radical deconstruction of memory, history, and evidence? How to define truth and memory when they are neither simply objective nor simply subjective?

I believe that a consideration of the political aspect of truth is vital to the evolution of such a new epistemological perspective. What do I mean by the political aspect of truth? As a good relational psychoanalyst, I believe that we must contextualize our definitions of truth in relationship, rather than merely in philosophy. I suggest that the definition of truth shifts, depending on the distribution of power in a relationship.

In a relationship of mutual recognition, one may safely relinquish rigid adherence to objective truth and play with continually shifting realities. The relationship itself provides the ground that makes this possible. We must recall, after all, that not all truth is the safe intersubjective truth of mutuality; some truth is the harsh objective truth of oppression. In a relationship of domination, power is maintained in part by the authority's exclusive right to define objective reality, and to label the unwillingness of subordinates to accept this version of truth as "resistance" or, currently, false-memory syndrome.

But powerless people can only liberate themselves by differentiating between actual truth and the lies that perpetuate the needs and objectives of the oppressor, by repossessing the truth of their own condition. The oppressed are often accused of false memory at the very moment they are discovering the truth. The False Memory Syndrome Foundation reveals this tactic insofar as the attribution of suggestibility of memory is used in a unidirectional manner, to cast doubt only on the credibility of survivors' memories, while treating the protestations of parental innocence as accurate memory, free of distortion and suggestive influence. In *1984,* George Orwell (1949) penetratingly describes this process of memory falsification by the incestuous parent when he writes of doublethink.

> The process has to be conscious or it would not be carried out with sufficient precision, but it also has to be unconscious or it would bring with it a feeling of falsity and hence of guilt. To tell deliberate lies while genuinely believing in them, to forget any fact that has become inconvenient and then, when it becomes necessary again, to draw it back from oblivion for just so long as it is needed, to deny the existence of objective reality and on the whole to take account of the reality which one denies — all this is indispensably necessary. Even in using the word doublethink it is necessary to exercise doublethink, for by using the word one admits that one is tampering with reality; by a fresh act of doublethink one erases this knowledge; and so on indefinitely with the lie always one leap ahead of the truth. Ultimately, it is by means of doublethink that the party has been able to arrest the course of history. [p. 36]

I believe this falsification of memory obtains in any relationship of domination, whether it is a political system or an incestuous family. The original one-person model of psychoanalysis was a subtle analogue of this power relation; ultimately it became too repressive and stagnant for analysts and patients genuinely interested in healing and mutuality, and an egalitarian model evolved. It was not the pursuit of historical truth per se that was the problem in psychoanalysis; it was the exclusive pursuit of historical truth in the original authoritarian relationship that was the problem. I believe that it is no accident that the technique of reconstruction and the pursuit of historical truth was originally embedded in an authoritarian, one-person psychoanalytic paradigm, and that the repudiation of historical truth in preference for intersubjective truth and meaning occurred *after* an egalitarian treatment model had emerged out of interpersonal and relational theory. I would argue that we have not completed our evolutionary movement away from an authoritarian model in psychoanalysis, and that, oddly enough, the remnants of this authoritarian model can be found in our theoretical conviction that relational mutuality and intersubjectivity cannot coexist with the pursuit of historical truth. To complete this movement we must restore the concept of historical truth, but place it, this time, in the patient's hands, in a relational context of mutuality.

In a certain sense, my perspective resonates with significant aspects of Foucault's (1980) view of the embeddedness of power and knowledge. According to Foucault, all cultural discourse (political, familial, analytic, etc.) invariably involves a dominant unitary knowledge, which is disseminated throughout the culture as "objective knowledge," while other knowledges (or truths) are subjugated, dissociated, deviant, and not known. The dominant, unitary truths of a culture serve both to constitute and create meaning and identity, while simultaneously subjugating, alienating, and disenfranchising other forms of discourse, and the persons who hold these forms of knowledge. Therefore, from Foucault's perspective, all truth and knowledge is inherently political and imbued with power relations, something that White and Epston (1990) feel analysts rarely acknowledge. Such an appreciation of the intrinsic power aspects of truth and knowledge is vital to any psychodynamic understanding of the incestuous relationship, and of its mirror image, the false-memory controversy. It is also vital to the creation of a new epistemological frame for psychoanalysis.

TRANSFERENCE-COUNTERTRANSFERENCE DILEMMAS

I will now examine the nature of the object tie between the incestuous parent and the victimized child, and the role that the obfuscation of memory and the politics of knowledge have in the maintenance of this tie. I believe that this object tie is manifested quite clearly in the very nature of the false-memory controversy itself, as well as in the transference–countertransference enactments that result from this controversy.

Benjamin's (1988) work on the psychology of domination and submission is extremely useful in understanding the nature of the object tie between perpetrator and survivor. According to Benjamin, psychological development occurs through the dynamic interplay of the need for self-assertion and recognition. Self-expression can acquire meaning and significance only by the recognition of a separate, subjective other, never through the coerced recognition of an objectified other. The evolution of mutuality versus domination is based on the evolution of a process of mutual recognition between two subjects. Domination results from various failures of this process and involves a relation between subject and object. From my perspective, I would emphasize that a recognized and autonomous experience of the immutability of one's own history and memory is a vital dimension to the ability to experience oneself as a separate subject, rather than as a subjective object. Loftus (1991) acknowledges this when she describes her deliberations about whether to testify against the Treblinka survivors who identified Ivan the Terrible. As a Jew, she cannot bear to engage in discrediting the memories of these survivors; she writes, "How can you separate a man from his memory? If you take the memories away, haven't you also stripped him of his past . . . without his memories, wouldn't (he) fold up and die, an exterior scaffolding that has lost its inner structure and suddenly collapses in upon itself" (p. 231).

I would suggest that during incest, the child's subjectivity is simultaneously annihilated and defined. In this very moment of destruction resides the birth of the child's most authentic secret self; as Benjamin states, however, it can have no meaning unless it is recognized by a subjective parent. In many ways, the incestuous relationship mirrors Benjamin's concept of the relationship of domination. The incest survivor is object to the parent's subject; the parent coerces recognition from the child without having to recognize the subjectivity of the child in return. Part of the perpetrator's coercive annihilation of the child's subjectivity is to demand that the child submit to the incest and to simultaneously collude in an elaborate maze of doublethink, in whatever false, mercurial definition of reality the perpetrator prefers at the moment.

While Benjamin's analysis of the master–slave relationship differs in many respects from that of the survivor to her perpetrator, it is similar in one critical respect. The only hope the survivors have had (prior to treatment) of regaining their subjectivity has been to receive recognition by their perpetrators, and only by their perpetrators. Only the perpetrator has known them, and has been known by them, in their most secret moment of violation, Further, because of the nature of most incestuous relationships and the incestuous family system, it is often the perpetrator whose parental subjectivity is most accessible to the child; as Benjamin states, recognition will only have power if obtained from a subjective parent. Thus, the perpetrator becomes at once the survivor's only beloved, her only hope of being known and found as a subjective self, and at the same time, her greatest terror and tormentor. This explains, to some extent, the common fantasies in incest survivors of symbiotic merger with an idealized parent/perpetrator described by Price (1992). Paradoxically, it is only by participating in the lies and the not-knowing that the child can sustain the attunement with the beloved tormentor, avoid further retaliations and/or abandonments, and persist in the hope and longing for the recognition that only he can provide. From Benjamin's point of view, it would never be sufficient, or really possible, for the survivors to know what happened *by themselves*; like all other childhood experience, this would require the recognition of a strong subjective other. This type of conceptualization is helpful in understanding the meanings of lawsuits by patients against perpetrators.

1984: THE ANNIHILATION OF HISTORY AND SUBJECTIVITY

Orwell's *1984* provides a penetrating analysis of this bond of domination that exists between perpetrator and victim. It is also a chilling parable about the false memory controversy. It is a tale of the falsification of memory and history, of oppression and of the annihilation of human subjectivity. It also provides a dark satire of the extreme consequences of adhering to a view of truth that is exclusively intersubjective and ahistorical, in a world of violation and domination.

Oceania is a bleak and merciless totalitarian state in which the human soul is on the verge of extinction. Thought and subjectivity are legislated; hatred flourishes, and love is punishable by death. All human bonds are forbidden. Even as Big Brother annihilates one's soul, he is experienced as the sole parental protector, the only beloved.

In this dark place, Winston is the singular man who has retained his soul; he lives in an agony of loneliness and despair. He is an old-fashioned existential man; he is not a constructivist. He believes in the immutability of history, of memory, and of truth. He knows that in a world of oppression, one cannot compromise on the truth; there are only truth and lies. One must hold onto memory and truth because without memory there is no interiority, a condition for the integrity of the human soul. He knows, as Sass (1993) says, that "to experience the more intense and full-blooded emotions — love and hate sadness and simple joy — may require a sense of existential rootedness that is inconsistent with radical fictionalism; namely a grounding in the lived-body, feelings of connection with solid objects and living human beings, and an awareness of finitude of finality and of risk" (p. 252). Like the incest survivor, this very knowledge places Winston at risk for terrible retribution. Winston works in the Ministry of Truth, where all recorded history is rewritten daily in accordance with the latest Party lie, so that there will never be any documentary evidence about "what really happened." Doublethink is practiced so that the workers in the ministry know and don't know that history has been altered; they are able to know they are lying and yet believe the lie seamlessly. Winston alone grasps the enormous implications of the destruction of history, "If the party could thrust its hand into the past and say of this or that event it never happened — that surely was more terrifying than mere torture and death" (p. 32). Winston understands that with torture and death, the human soul may remain alive, but the annihilation of one's history and of one's capacity to know reality results in what Shengold (1989) calls, "soul murder." Where history and memory are completely mutable and in the hands of one's oppressor, one is emptied of will, autonomy, and humanity. Even as Winston is desperately trying to retain his memory of history, while he attempts to locate any source of evidence that history is not what the Party says it is, he finds himself lost in the ambiguous fog of memory that characterizes the incest survivor: "The past, he reflected, has not merely been altered, it had been actually destroyed . . . everything melted into mist. Sometimes, indeed you could put your finger on a definite lie, but you could prove nothing. There was never any evidence" (p. 33).

Winston has received the early recognition of his loving mother, and so, unlike the incest survivor, he is capable of knowing the truth in complete solitude, but he cannot bear the agony of living a mechanical false life without ever having been known. Risking arrest and death, he forms two relationships of love: one with Julia and one with O'Brian. With Julia he shares an exquisite rebellion of private sensuality, tenderness, and warmth. But he cannot share his concern about the eradication of history and memory with her; she is not interested and doesn't understand its significance; when he speaks of it, she falls asleep. Because of this, her subjectivity seems limited, ephemeral, and transient; ultimately he cannot be fully known by her. (In a sense, this is a metaphor for the fatal flaw of the social-constructivist context for psychoanalysis; it provides a vibrant field in which to experience one's aliveness, but it is unconscious with regard to the importance of actual memory.) This is the fatal flaw in Winston's relationship to Julia, which drives him into the arms of inner party member O'Brian.

For many years, Winston and O'Brian have studied each other without speaking. In O'Brian's face Winston perceives his soulmate: a deeply intelligent man, full of compassion and suffering, secretly antagonistic to the party, and the only living person with whom Winston can share his concern about the immutability of memory. In Winston's deep longing to be known, he gradually relinquishes his vigilant knowledge that O'Brian is a dangerous inner party member, much as the incest survivor idealizes her parent and denies what she knows. Winston persuades Julia that they should reveal themselves to O'Brian in the hopes that O'Brian will connect them with the underground, and for one extraordinary moment this indeed seems possible. Knowing that they may be arrested at any time, Winston and Julia agree that although they will undoubtedly say anything under torture, it will not constitute a betrayal of one another unless they stop loving one another. This they believe is impossible, for how can anyone get inside of you like that?

The next day, Winston and Julia are arrested and Winston discovers that O'Brian is his personal torturer and interrogator. So begins Winston's most intimate relationship, one in which he is completely known and completely violated: tortured, comforted, understood, and annihilated. These are the moments of incest. O'Brian remains awake and engaged during Winston's courageous discourses about history; he very much shares Winston's conviction that without immutable history there is no survival of the human soul. Winston can endure tremendous pain and abuse without losing himself, because the pain is inflicted by his beloved, who recognizes him fully even though he tortures him. But Winston is seeking mutuality; O'Brian is seeking dominance and power. Winston cherishes the immutability of memory because it makes him human; O'Brian must destroy it. Like the incestuous parent, O'Brian knows he will only gain absolute power when he has eradicated Winston's autonomous conviction about memory; when he has seduced and terrorized Winston into willing surrender of both his subjectivity and his history.

The seduction of Winston's soul and his voluntary submission to a falsified reality is achieved through the simultaneous promise of exquisite recognition and the threat of annihilation terror; this precisely replicates the dynamic of incest. Mere pain is inadequate; O'Brian takes Winston into Room 101, where he meets his greatest terror: carnivorous rats. Winston can survive starvation and brutality; he does not fear death. But here he is subjected to disintegration anxiety. In a desperate effort to avoid the rats, he cries out: "Do it to Julia." He feels it—he wishes they would do it to her instead. In the same moment he has betrayed Julia and lost her he has relinquished his soul forever. He is empty and can be filled with the party's lies and love of Big Brother. Once O'Brian has successfully broken Winston, dissolved his resistance and his memory, the bond between them ends much as the perpetrator's interest in the child would dissolve if the child were a dead thing, incapable of human response, of sexuality, of fear and resistance.

Winston can no longer offer O'Brian the recognition that O'Brian has coerced from him. Winston retains only the memory of his own betrayal of himself and of Julia in Room 101; he cannot remember the long chain of abuse; he loves Big Brother. Indeed, O'Brian has gotten inside of him in ways Winston had never believed possible, but that O'Brian had predicted, "Things will happen to you from which you could not recover, . . . Everything will be dead. . . . We shall squeeze you empty and then we shall fill you with ourselves" (p. 211). The incest survivor had indeed been squeezed empty, and is filled only with the perpetrator. Unlike the ultimately annihilated Winston, the incest survivor sustains a deeply buried living wish to be recognized and to have her subjectivity restored; like Winston's search for O'Brian, the incest survivor must always return to the perpetrator in her hope for restoration.

CASE MATERIAL

"Do it to Julia." I am haunted by this phrase, this image, the way it exquisitely captures the devastation of betrayal in a reign of terror. I am haunted by the fear that I will commit such a betrayal, and become, like Winston, one of the hollow men. Any analytic exploration of possible incest is fraught with opportunities for awesome human courage and devastating betrayals, with the anxieties and shifting sands of the projective identificatory process described by Davies and Frawley(1994) and Price (1992). I have weathered this type of treatment many times. But now, in the maelstrom of the false-memory controversy we move beyond an identification with the terrified inner child described by Davies and Frawley; now the perpetrator can really get us, too. He can enter our real lives and wreak destruction. How does this controversy effect the transference-countertransference enactments with the incest survivor?

I would like to discuss a moment in an analysis with a possible incest survivor, a moment when I find myself in Room 101. The patient I am about to describe may or may not be a survivor of father–daughter incest; she is certainly the victim of his sexual inappropriateness. She suffers profound anxiety that incest has either already occurred or is imminent. (I would like to note that this case material has been disguised to protect patient confidentiality.)

> In the second year of her analysis, an intelligent outspoken young woman tells me the following dream: "Literature comes to my house in an envelope. There are pornographic pictures inside and pamphlets about incest. One of the pamphlets is about a seminar that has already passed; the second is in October. It hadn't come yet. In the pornographic pictures there is a girl who looks like me, around age 11 or 12. I am not sure what is happening in the picture. I think the girl is posing nude. I have long hair at 12, the pictures are like me in my early teens. There is writing next to the picture of the girl but I am

not sure what it says. I was terrified." At this point, my patient begins sobbing and says, with fear and tentative conviction, "Did my father do this to me, take these pictures?"

Let us move back in time in her analysis, to the evolution of this moment. This woman entered treatment because of panic attacks and disturbing memories of having been sexually abused by a female neighbor when she was 5. She had never repressed this memory. As we worked on this experience, and began investigating the larger context of her life, we moved into a long period revealing profound anxiety and rage in relation to men. In addition to her panic attacks, she had night terrors and nightmares, extensive, shifting somatic complaints, inexplicable rage storms at her otherwise beloved husband, chronic fears of rape and of looking womanly in front of men. She gained weight and began to dress to obscure her feminine beauty. She recalled a long period of engaging in degrading promiscuous sexuality at the behest of abusive boyfriends, and two date rapes. Her stepfather (the patient never knew her natural father; the mother married the stepfather when the patient was an infant) was initially presented as the preferred parent: intelligent, sophisticated, attentive, and exciting, interested in encouraging the patient in her explorations of life. She could confide in him, and he in her. While the mother provided solid basic care, she was seen as cold and dull; it was clearly the stepfather who possessed the capacity to know her. She had never revealed the sexual abuse to either parent at the time it occurred, but, as an adult she chose to tell her stepfather and not her mother.

Over time, another stepfather emerged: an alcoholic con man and pathological liar who had been arrested and jailed for embezzlement when the patient was 3, after which the parents divorced. When asked about the reason he was in jail, he lied to her, denying he had been committing these thefts, although the mother unequivocally states that he was stealing and conning over a long period of time.

My patient also revealed considerable material about her stepfather's sexual perversity — involving orgies and compulsive affairs, all of which he told her about when she was a teenager; her discovery of pornographic photos and letters about wife swapping; his insistence on kissing her on the mouth despite her obvious discomfort and attempts to evade him; the ways he related to her as his emotional wife instead of as his daughter; his efforts to take her with him to a nudist colony as a child despite her protests and humiliation; how even now he demands sexual admiration from her. When drunk at a recent party, he pulled her close and whispered seductively in her ear, "Give me a kiss." In the same period were a series of graphic sexual nightmares. She dreamt about huge penises bearing down on her face; about rape, vaginal pain and bleeding; about worms emerging from her vagina and rectum; about meeting the author of a book on incest and thanking her for writing a book "for me." In one image, she came to a party dressed in a short, tight sexy red dress (something she would never do) and was disturbed to encounter the teenage boy who had raped her. In the dream, this teenage rapist kissed her in exactly the way her stepfather does; she was mute and resistant in the same way she is with her stepfather. She has shared with me a growing suspicion that she was sexually abused by a man in her childhood, although she has no clear memories. When she talks about this suspicion, she is flooded by panic, but insists she wants to know if something happened.

On this particular day, I have read yet another media exposé on the false-memory controversy. I realize that this outspoken, serious, and assertive woman would confront her stepfather if thoroughly convinced that had incested her; this litigious volatile man would lie and very possibly sue me for "implanting" an incest memory. Her stepfather suddenly appears to me powerful, vindictive, and relentless in his retaliation; I am helpless, vulnerable, small. I feel exposed. There is a dangerous secret about what is going on in her analysis. I will be implicated. Financially ruined, professionally humiliated. I am a little girl, terrorized, with a shameful secret. Even as she weeps, she does not yet know, but she has lost me. I hear the howls of judicial accusation: Have I suggested this? How can I demonstrate that I haven't? Should I start taping to protect myself, and how to explain this to the patient? Have I allowed her to be too literal in her interpretations of her dreams and symptoms? How can I demonstrate in court that I have not led the patient into this? Suddenly I feel I must demonstrate to the patient that these images may be more symbolic than literal, expressive of other issues and anxieties. I must document my effort to explore other explanations besides incest for her dreams and symptoms. Even as she weeps, I question her differently, drawing her away from the image of actual incest. She attempts to follow me where I am going, desperate for us to stay together, willing to be confused, deflected.

Inside of my secret terror, I know I have betrayed her, I have said, "Do it to Julia." In this most critical moment of revelation, her trusted analyst-of-mutuality has been eclipsed first by a dissociated terrorized child, and then by the analyst-father-of-domination. I save myself from my intolerable state by sacrificing my patient, my child, by repudiating her knowledge of history. I am inauthentic, subtly coercive and secretly ashamed. It is one of my worst moments as an analyst. I don't want her or anyone else to see me.

The next day I receive a rare call of protest from my patient; fortunately, I have been trustworthy up until now. By the time she calls, I have worked myself through this counter-transferential moment. She says that she felt I did not believe her. She has never felt so alone and bewildered with me before. Despite my inquiry, she cannot allow herself to attribute this to any failure of mine, but rather must attribute this to her own lack of clarity and poor communication. This sophisticated woman, who is fully informed about the false-memory controversy and its attendant lawsuits, cannot access any of her knowledge about what may have actually occurred inside *me* during her session. This is familiar analytic ground for us; we have often seen a surge of panic attacks when she is refusing to know what she knows about being betrayed and in danger. In the transference, she resurrects an object tie of mendacity and submission, after I have enacted a subtle form of domination by redirecting the definition of reality about incest. She has returned to her exclusive bond with her stepfather, a bond in which all dangerous knowledge must be falsified and denied, in the hopes that she can hide from the impact of trauma and ultimately be safe and known.

In subsequent sessions, she does not mention either incest or the moment of analytic rupture I have described. Her symptoms increase. She has retreated from what she was beginning to know about him, and what she knows about me, because of the transferential reenactment of memory falsification. Her inability to know what she knows becomes the focus of her analysis. What she cannot yet afford to discover is that, unlike her father, I am willing to see myself and for her to see me, for her to see and know my betrayal, for her to be angry, for her to regain her memory and her history in this transferential moment. When she is able to discover this aspect of me, she may feel the despair and liberation of separation.

This clinical vignette is important in that it clarifies the inseparability of history and genuine intersubjectivity. In the very moment when genuine intersubjectivity is restored between analyst and patient the patient's immutable history in the transference is recovered, releasing her to know her childhood history, as well. This vignette also reveals the way this transference-countertransference byplay may be "read" for clues to the patient's sexual history. Her willingness to surrender her own perceptions and knowledge, to enter into a relationship of dominance and lies, to collude in the falsification of her own history, to conceal the secret of the parental defect and betrayal, are all familiar ground for the incest survivor. My own experience of childlike terror alternating with the experience of acting as a dominating parent who exploits and betrays her is likewise suggestive. Only arduous analysis will answer the question of whether she is indeed an incest survivor, or whether her father's sexual inappropriateness and lies about history have evoked a sense of incestuous menace that parallels the affective dilemma of the survivor.

Ultimately, we psychoanalysts must evolve some clinical and epistemological position that allows us to provide that which the incest survivor has never had: a sense of the immutability of her history in a context of genuine intersubjectivity. We must evolve clinical techniques that allow us to sustain our courage when betrayal beckons to us in the midst of this controversy. We must negotiate these controversial times without saying of our patient, "Do it to Julia."

REFERENCES

Alpert, J. (1991). Retrospective treatment of incest victims: suggested analytic attitudes. *Psychoanalytic Review* 78(3):425–435.
_____ (1994). Analytic reconstruction in the treatment of incest survivors. *Psychoanalytic Review* 78(3):425–435.
Baynes, K. (1989). Rational reconstruction and social criticism: Habermas' model of interpretive social science. *Philosophical Forum Quarterly* 21:122–145.
Benjamin, J. (1988). *The Bonds of Love.* New York: Pantheon.
Davies, J. M., and Frawley, M. G. (1994). *Treating the Adult Survivor of Sexual Abuse: A Psychoanalytic Perspective.* New York: Basic Books.
Foucault, M. (1980). *Power/Knowledge: Selected Interviews and Other Writings,* ed. C. Gordon. New York: Pantheon.
Geha, R. (1993). Transferred fictions. *Psychoanalytic Dialogues* 3(2):209–245.
Herman, J. L. (1992). *Trauma and Recovery.* New York: Basic Books.
Herman, J. L., and Harvey, M. R. (1993). The false memory debate: social science or social backlash? *Harvard Mental Health Newsletter* 9(10):4–6.
Lipstadt, D. (1994). *Denying the Holocaust.* New York: Plume.
Loftus, E. (1991). *Witness for the Defense.* New York: St. Martin's.
_____ (1993). The reality of repressed memories. *American Psychologist* 48(5):518–537.
Ogden, T. H. (1990). *The Matrix of the Mind.* Northvale, NJ: Jason Aronson.
Orwell, G. (1949). *1984.* New York: Harcourt Brace Jovanovich.
Price, M. (1992). *Incest: transference and countertransference implications.* Paper presented at the American Academy of Psychoanalysis, December.
Sampson, H. (1992). The role of "real" experience in psychopathology and treatment. *Psychoanalytic Dialogues* 2(4):509–529.
Sass, L. A. (1993). Psychoanalysis as "conversations" and as "fictions": a Commentary on Charles Spezzano's "A Relational Model of Inquiry and Truth" and Richard Geha's "Transferred Fictions." *Psychoanalytic Dialogues* 3(2):245–255.
Shengold, L. (1989). *Soul Murder: the Effects of Childhood Abuse and Deprivation* New Haven, CT: Yale University Press.
Spence, D. (1982). *Narrative Truth and Historical Truth.* New York: Norton.
_____ (1993). The hermeneutic turn: soft science or loyal opposition?

Psychoanalytic Dialogues 3(1):1-11.

Spezzano, C. (1993). A relational model of inquiry and truth: the place of psychoanalysis in the human conversation. *Psychoanalytic Dialogues* 3(2):177-209.

Stolorow, R. D., Brandchaft, B., and Atwood, G. E. (1987). *Psychoanalytic Treatment: An Intersubjective Approach.* Hillsdale, NJ: Analytic Press.

van der Kolk, B. S. (1987). Psychological Trauma. Washington, DC: American Psychiatric Press.

———— (1994). The body keeps the score: memory and the evolving psychobiology of posttraumatic stress. *Harvard Review of Psychiatry* 1:253-265.

White, M., and Epston, D. (1990). *Narrative Means to Therapeutic Ends.* New York: Norton.

PART IV

Professional Practice:
Selected Situations

10

Toward a Reconceptualization of False-Memory Phenomena

SUE GRAND

It has been the perspective of this book that dissociative processes occurring during trauma can lead to delayed, essentially accurate memory, although some peripheral details may be confabulated. Initial chapters have been devoted to research documentation of this position; subsequent chapters have focused on the type of responsible clinical practice that leads to the emergence of accurate delayed memory. No responsible book on this subject would be complete, however, without an investigation into the so-called implanted memory or false-memory phenomena. This chapter represents a work in progress, the intention of which is to critique, contextualize, and reconceptualize such phenomena, and the current levels of explanation to which they are subjected. I will begin to propose an alternate framing of the entire problem, which I believe will be more useful for responsible researchers and clinicians. Ultimately, we must generate explanatory principles that can be used to account for the frequently confabulated memory of the accused and the occasionally confabulated memory of the accuser.

At the outset, I must note that I repudiate the notion that incompetent practitioners, suggestible patients, and false accusations are widespread. I am in agreement with Berliner and Williams

(1994), Terr (1994), and Yapko (1994) that the percentage of sex abuse accusations that are wholly false is extremely low, while false denials by sex abuse perpetrators are extremely common (Gudjonsson 1992). In fact, Pezdek (1994) demonstrates that there are, in fact, no documented cases of false-memory syndrome. Insofar as we subject parental claims of innocence to the same standards of external verification to which they would subject the claims of delayed memories, there are no proven cases of false accusations. Furthermore, most adults who recover memories of incest do not do so while in therapy, and most patients who decide to confront parents while in therapy never forgot the incest (Berliner and Williams 1994, Pezdek 1994). Nevertheless, it is imperative to investigate, from a trauma perspective, those rare cases of confabulated memory of sexual abuse arising in contexts of therapeutic persuasion.

Any attempt to locate new, more respectful, levels of explanation for occasional cases of implanted memory must derive from a fundamental understanding of the psychosocial context in which this controversy has arisen. A close examination of the history of this controversy reveals certain archaic patriarchal assumptions that continue to imbue the false memory movement. As Herman (1992) argues, the history of psychological research into trauma is one of bitter controversy and "episodic amnesia." At its core, the false-memory movement represents another amnestic eclipse of incest. Herman suggests that an unwitting collusion between the innocent bystander and the perpetrator creates this cultural amnesia. I would argue that this collusion derives from a marriage between the two faces of patriarchy: the perpetrator-father conceals himself behind the mask of the "just" idealized father. As responsible clinicians, we must disembed patriarchal influences from legitimate clinical and research questions regarding the nature of memory and suggestion. This will facilitate a new examination of false memory that reduces extant polarization, moves us closer to establishing actual guilt and innocence, and lends greater credibility to the claims of incest survivors. We will become able to ask, with regard to both parent and child, accuser and accused, what is the nature of memory and suggestion? How do we know our own history?

For clinicians treating trauma, the historical trend toward discrediting victims and their advocates has created understandable resistance to acknowledging and investigating actual rare cases of confabulated memories of sexual abuse. The Ingram case (Wright 1994) and the Green case (Terr 1994) do argue persuasively that the confabulated production of sexual abuse memory can occur in a context of intense suggestion by trusted authorities. Although the Ingram family memories may not have been wholly false, it was evident that intense persuasion from religious leaders, police, and psychologists led to an escalating cycle of confabulated accusation and confession. Psychotherapy, incompetently practiced, can provide such a context of authority and suggestion. Every clinician has heard appalling clinical vignettes such as Yapko (1994) and Loftus (1993) describe in which a therapist immediately pronounces that a patient's symptoms are caused by repressed memories of sexual abuse. Blume's (1990) early pioneering literature on incest has been justly criticized (Lindsay and Read 1994, Loftus 1993) for attributing all symptoms to the single causal factor of sexual abuse, and for encouraging the assumption that an actual molestation *has occurred* when patients only vaguely identify with incest, but are utterly without memory. Lindsay and Read's review of memory research successfully argues for the occasional fallibility and suggestibility of memory, noting the quality of authenticity that can characterize the recall of implanted memory.

Many factors must be explored before we can fully account for perpetrators' false memories of innocence and patients' false memories of sexual victimization. Although this chapter primarily focuses on the accuser, it is possible to formulate a constellation of factors affecting memory that would be equally applicable to the perpetrators' false memory of innocence, as well as to the collusive denial of the innocent bystander. I have limited the scope of this chapter to two factors that may contribute to the development of patients' false accusations. I view these as necessary but not sufficient conditions for memory confabulation in therapeutic contexts. These factors are *developmentally arrested personal epistemologies*, or ways of knowing truth, and *preconscious deep and abiding hatred of the parents*, which, while not due to incest, nonetheless originated in real and severely destructive family dynamics. Ingram, for example, clearly dominated and intimidated his entire family with his sadistic authoritarian attitude (including physical abuse) and his cold neglect (see Wright 1994).

Ultimately his wife and children found an excellent forum in which to reverse the master–slave relations that permeated the Ingram home.

In families characterized by verbal, emotional and/or physical maltreatment, sexual politics are rarely healthy. Destructive familial themes of poor boundaries, sadism, dominance, cloying seduction and possessiveness, narcissistic exploitation of children, invasiveness, and so on, inform and permeate the interpersonal dialectics of family sexuality even when incestuous contact does not actually occur. At times, children sense their parents' barely successful struggle to control incestuous urges; such children suffer preconscious anxiety that incest is imminent. In such contexts, the patient's real history offers fertile ground for confabulated memories of actual sexual contact. The profoundly painful sexualized affects evoked by the patient's actual childhood can be readily attached to sex abuse imagery, as such imagery parallels and mirrors the emotional truth of destructive childhood events. An erroneous accusation of sexual abuse functions to release and organize primitive and authentic affects, while allowing an outlet for the patient's preconscious sadism toward parental authority in a reversal of powerlessness and emotional abuse. For these and other reasons it is important to relinquish the term *false memory* in favor of *confabulated memory*. My view supports Berliner and Williams's (1994) contention that, "While there is evidence based on laboratory studies for the fallibility of memory, suggestibility, and inaccuracy, it has not been proven that full-blown memories for traumatic childhood experiences can be created from nothing" (p. 385).

I will argue that the therapist utilizing persuasion techniques shares the epistemological assumptions of this type of patient. Insofar as we recognize shared epistemological positions and dissociative malice, the confabulated memory becomes a therapist–patient co-constructed act. Such acts are reflective of the patient's evolving capacities for agency and intentionality. My view of the "false" accusers robs them of the passive, childlike, misguided innocence conferred on them by the false-memory movement. They are neither irrationally vindictive nor capable of inauthentic, melodramatic abreaction. Simultaneously this view robs the ostensibly falsely accused just patriarch of his own confabulated pretensions to an ordinary, decent, family life. Instead, the therapist, patient, and falsely accused all repossess adult culpability and responsibility in a level playing field; the accuser becomes the parental peer rather than the subordinated child.

This shift in perspective will also allow us to reconceptualize the memory distortions of the denying perpetrator-parent. The denying (as differentiated from lying) perpetrator could be viewed as likewise impaired by an arrested epistemology and by dissociative malice arising from real conditions of his/her own childhood. Thus, the denying perpetrator and the wholly falsely accusing patient are both vulnerable to, and responsible for, the same types of memory distortions, although such memory distortions are much more frequent in the denying perpetrator than in the patient claiming a history of sexual abuse. I will argue that my view of the false accuser is intrinsically problematic for a false memory movement grounded in a paradigmatic relation of the just patriarch to the suggestible, dependent child.

PATRIARCHY, HYSTERIA, AND FALSE MEMORY

Before any reconceptualization of false-memory phenomena can be fully developed, it is necessary to articulate the archaic patriarchal assumptions that implicitly organize the current formulations of such phenomena. In this section, I attempt to expose these assumptions, contextualizing my critique within a historical review of hysteria and patriarchal discourse.

Foucault (1978) has argued that white men have historically retained the power to define and control all levels of discourse in Western patriarchal culture, thereby subordinating and silencing the marginalized other: women, children, and men who are not within the dominant class. According to Hartsock (1990), the historical creation of a devalued "other" was the necessary precondition for the creation of a rational transcendent subject within the exclusive purview of the dominant white male. This other is never accorded the status of subject, but remains perpetually objectified to themselves as well as to the patriarch. Forms of knowledge unique to the marginalized are not and cannot be known; one must turn to the patriarch for the linguistic forms with which to define one's own experience. Thus, one is exploited and cannot even call it exploitation.

The patriarchal view of the parent–child relationship resonates with Memmi's (1967) description of the relations between the colonizer and the colonized. The colonizer defines the colonized as everything he is not; all negative qualities are projected onto the colonized other as a means of legitimizing dominance and enslavement. The colonized is viewed as void of all culturally valued qualities, backward, not fully human, chaotic, disorganized. If given the opportunity to act independently, the colonized will express its intrinsic wickedness; the colonized must therefore remain under the morally superior judgment and control of the colonizer. In the patriarchal family the devalued others are women and children. Such a family system is characterized by a fundamental assumption that just men are morally compelled to control the minds and bodies of weak, morally defective women and children, who require the shelter of the father's rational care and judgment. The just father's moral imperative simultaneously allows him, as Struve (1990) and Jacobs (1994) describe it, the rights of sexual dominion over wife and children who have been regarded as his chattel property and whom he may dominate under the shroud of secrecy and family privacy. Herman (1992), Jacobs (1994), Masson (1984), Struve (1990), and Walker (1994) argue that patriarchal culture has variously endorsed, denied, and neglected the sexual abuse of women and children for centuries. Disclosures of childhood sexual abuse have frequently been discredited through the diagnosis of hysteria. In this view, women/female children were seen either as culpable seducers who were not really damaged by the sex abuse or as dramatic fantasizers projecting their own incestuous wishes onto the father. I will argue that this view pervades the false-memory movement and can be found, for example, in Gardner's work (1992).

The history of hysteria is a history of the relation between the colonizing father and the colonized devalued other. Historical reviews of centuries of hysteria (Bart and Scully 1979, Smith-Rosenberg 1972, Rousseau 1993, Temoshok and Atkisson 1977) find that while hysteria's specific forms may have varied, a constant theme reveals a pejorative, gender-biased illness entity characterized by sexual voraciousness, a defective moral sense, seductiveness, malingering, manipulativeness, emotional lability and inauthenticity, a tendency toward fantasy and fabrication, and a life riddled with deceit, cunning and falsehood. Describing the Renaissance period, Rousseau (1993) argues that the hysterical woman was simultaneously seen as childlike, frail, but also, "part animal, part witch; part pleasure-giver, part wreaker of destruction to avenge her own irrationality — anything but a strong rational creature resembling homo mensicus" (p. 108). Rather than viewing these symptoms as arising from the real material conditions of being female in the family and in the culture, these qualities have been considered intrinsic to the defective nature of woman.

Bart and Scully (1979) quote a theologian from the Middle Ages who epitomizes this view of the hysterical women when he advocates strict control of women because, "when a woman thinks alone, she thinks evil" (p. 356). These authors find functionally similar views pervading contemporary psychology despite their manifest elimination in the *Diagnostic and Statistical Manual (DSM)* diagnosis of histrionic personality disorder. Certainly these attitudes permeated Freud's (1914,1933) view of feminine psychology after he repudiated the seduction theory. More recently, for example, Hollender (1988) considers most hysterics to be female; both Shapiro (1965) and Hollender regard hysterical memory as intrinsically defective, as it is supposedly derived from an impulsive, selective, impressionistic encoding process. Further, they describe the hysteric's definition of truth as untrustworthy as it is based on impulsive, affect-laden hunches rather than on carefully analyzed fact. For an accurate representation of truth and history, the hysteric must defer to the obsessional, just father, in precisely the manner described by Foucault. Hysterics have received only one brief reprieve from this long history of paternalism, during the period in which Freud (and Ferenczi) embraced the seduction theory. When reports of incest were believed, hysteria emerged as a rational, symbolic language of pain and protest. Female hysterics were listened to respectfully and patiently and were regarded as intelligent, authentically suffering, and of strong character (Chodorow 1989, Herman 1992).

While Mitchell (1984) described hysteria as a "daughter's disease," a syndrome of protest against the social and symbolic laws of the father, I am in agreement with Showalter (1993), who suggests that hysteria is more truly the disease of the powerless and the silenced. She views it as the disease of the marginalized son in relation to the father as well as the disease of the daughter. Throughout its history, male hysteria has always been considered a shameful, effeminate disorder. Historical reviews cited above (Bart and Scully 1979, Smith-Rosenberg 1972, Temoshok and Atkisson 1977) indicate that the males who received this diagnosis were immigrants, blacks, working class, homosexuals, as well as the first World War I shell shock victims. Upper-class white males received other diagnoses that were considered to be either organically based or reactive to real-life stressors. To be diagnosed as a male hysteric was to become part of the devalued colonized "other": subordinated, discredited, and rendered not male.

I believe that enduring patriarchal stereotypes of the family and of hysteria suffuse the implicit assumptions of the false-memory perspective, functioning to bolster the unquestioned judgment of the father. The essence of such attitudes is found in the pervasive beliefs that parental memory and judgment is superior to the memory and judgment of the accuser; that parental memory is not susceptible to the fallacies of memory, which are considered to characterize (and discredit) the memory of the accuser; that accusers are childlike, suggestible, naive, histrionic, and readily manipulated, and as such must be removed from the influence of therapists and returned to the protective shelter of parental guidance.

To begin with, we discover patriarchal influences in the linguistic frame of this controversy. The terms *false memory* and *implanted memory* originated with the denials of accused parents in the False Memory Syndrome Foundation. These terms have permeated the media. What defines a recovered memory as false? In the absence of available external verification, it is the parental denial of incest that defines the memory as false. The very language in which this is cast reveals a patriarchal prejudice; it is parental construction of history, not the adult child's construction of history, that defines truth. This has become an acceptable aspect of the delayed memory discourse, not only in the media, but among researchers and clinicians, despite the general understanding that most perpetrators lie about incest. If our culture were truly unbiased by patriarchal influence, psychological terminology would not be defined by parents accused of incest. If incest were recognized and parents did not possess superior status, the culture would evolve a different linguistic frame that did not privilege parental memory.

The view of patients and therapists promulgated by the false-memory movement is infused with archaic images of hysteria and the colonized other. Throughout the media, as well as in clinical and research formulations, patient/accusers are implicitly or explicitly portrayed as histrionic personalities: vacuous, suggestible, dependent, compliant toward authority, capable of dramatizing extensive "false" abreactions, possessing defective memories of history, impulsively and impressionistically incapable of pursuing a rational and judicious path to truth, and too naive to be held accountable for any destructive intent (Gardner 1992, Lindsay and Read 1994, Loftus 1993, Pope 1994, Yapko 1994). Male patients who identify themselves as sex abuse victims are viewed as weak, suggestible, hysterical female children, much as marginalized hysterical men have been feminized and castrated throughout history. To view masses of patients in this manner is paternalistic, and clearly in the service of the amnestic eclipse of incest. Further, this view is fraught with internal logical contradiction. In the type of patient described by the false-memory movement (i.e., a dependent or histrionic personality) no sense of self would exist without symbiotic enmeshment in the other, self-experience would be void and amorphous, and there would be an excessive fear of autonomous activity, separation, and conflict (Bornstein 1993, Johnson 1991). Such patients would be dependent and deferential to all authority, particularly toward parents who are the original objects of their abject dependency. While such patients may falsely reinterpret their experience in accord with the therapeutic hypothesis of sex abuse, they would hardly be capable of the sustained confrontation and controversy with parental authority that is involved in these delayed memory cases. Mercurial, dependent, and compliant, they could scarcely endure the rage, abandonment and denial of their parents. Instead, they would readily mirror and adopt any new terms of self-definition proposed by their environment, continuing, chameleonlike, to reflect the most proximate, significant, and persuasive authority. Such patients would immediately recant their confabulated memory not because they know it is confabulated, but because it causes controversy with parental authority. In such cases the false-memory movement heralds recantations as proof that the memory was indeed implanted, insinuating that the patients' suggestibility exists only in relation to a therapist and ceases to exist with the parent whose just view the patients can now meet with autonomous, considered judgment. As Berliner and Williams (1994) state, "It is particularly ironic that statements from retractors are considered credible when they deny abuse and allege misconduct by therapists, but are incredible when they claim to have been abused" (p. 381). I would argue that most recantations are proof of nothing except characterological suggestibility and compliance, or perhaps, fear of the perpetrator. Obviously, this archaic mythology about hysterical patients fails to meet the phenomena of confabulation and sustained false accusation.

The false-memory movement's portrayal of clinicians treating sex abuse survivors is similarly imbued with the imprint of hysteria (Gardner 1992, Loftus 1993, Pope 1994, Wright 1994, Yapko 1994). It is relevant that the original pioneering work in this field was primarily written by women clinicians for primarily women patients (Bass and Davis 1988, Blume 1990, Courtois 1988, Herman 1981, Russell 1983, Walker 1994). As Berliner and Williams (1994) note, critics of delayed memory most often describe young professional women who enter treatment with other young professional women and suddenly emerge with constructed memories. Whereas there are certainly incompetent practitioners in this field, as in any other, the false-memory movement caricatures the vast majority of "recovery" therapists as incompetent. The very term *recovery therapy* itself derives solely from the linguistic frame of the false-memory movement, rather than from the terminology of responsible clinicians; it bears a subtle and unmistakable connotation of lack of training. This derogation of clinicians treating incest survivors can be found, for example, in Gardner's generalized reference to recovery therapists as "Ms." (p. 647) in evident contrast with himself as "Doctor."

Views of recovery therapists either embody archaic images of the "frail" misguided hysteric or images of the wicked colonized "other" hysteric acting outside the protective moral constraints of the patriarch. Thus, such a therapist is portrayed as either grossly incompetent, impulsive, impressionistic, morally negligent, and uneducated but "well intended," or as the amoral, manipulative seductress, who wreaks "destruction to avenge her own irrationality." Such a histrionic characterization rarely obtains for the incompetent practice of other, male-dominated fields such as medicine and law, where professional error is equally devastating. The "hysterical" therapist differs from the "hysterical" patient insofar as the therapist becomes, in this discourse, the woman who "thinking alone, thinks evil"; she is therefore to be held exclusively culpable for the patient's accusations. The parent is not only innocent of incest, he is considered essentially just, innocent of any profound destructiveness that might give rise to confabulation. Much as Memmi suggests that the colonizer projects all negative qualities onto the colonized, so I believe that the perpetrator-patriarch projects his own profile of abuse onto the therapist, who becomes the abuser, exploiter of the weak and dependent, manipulative, amoral, deadly. This allows the perpetrator to retain the mask of the just patriarch to whom both patient and therapist must return if they are to be redeemed in truth and in history.

Finally, patriarchal bias is evident in the ubiquitous unidirectional challenge to patient memory. Berliner and Williams (1994) critique cognitive memory research for its exclusive focus on illusory memory, rather than on how lack of recall works, even when cognitive researchers acknowledge the existence of delayed memory. Nash's (1994) work is a rare exception. He critiques proponents of pseudomemory who

> employ a curious twist of logic that if False Positives [the belief that you were traumatized when you were not] are demonstrated to occur, then the validity of False Negatives (i.e., repression, dissociation) is necessarily negated. Logically, this doesn't follow . . . if cultural and psychological factors can create the need to believe that certain events occurred when they did not [False Positive], why then can these factors not operate in such a way as to engender not remembering certain events when they did in actuality occur? [p. 347]

Research on the fallibility of memory is utilized to cast doubt on accuser memory alone. Thus, what appears to be merely science qua science is actually functioning in the service of colonization. Parental memory is implicitly viewed as exempt from memory deficits and the suggestive influences that discredit accuser memory. Yapko (1994) and Loftus (1993) make only minor references to the possibility that the parent may be suffering from a confabulated false memory of himself as innocent. At the same time, they provide lengthy discussions on the confabulation of accuser memory. Although Yapko cautions clinicians that it is impossible to differentiate between an authentic memory and an authentically felt but false confabulated memory of sexual abuse, he clearly believes the anguished protestations of innocence by the accused parents he treats.

One never reads a research study that equally applies findings about the suggestibility of memory to accused and accuser alike. Lindsay and Read's (1994) excellent review of the memory research, for example, is concerned only with suggestive influences affecting patient memory. I have read only one instance in which the suggestibility of parental memory was explored: the Ingram case (Wright 1994). But in this case, the suggestibility of parental memory is used to support parental *innocence* of incest. Reading the literature, one would naturally conclude that patient memories are infinitely suggestible to the creation of false memories of sexual abuse, whereas parental memory is primarily intact except insofar as they may be led to confess to sexual abuse that they in fact did not commit. This tendency to reify parental memory is supported by the exclusive focus on therapy (and evaluation teams) as the only significant locus of suggestion and memory tampering. As long as the false memory perspective isolates therapy as the sole locus of suggestion, the accuser's memory will always be in doubt more than the parent/accused's. Generally, the accused is not in therapy and thus his judgment is viewed as unimpaired and uninfluenced.

Is therapy the only locus of powerful, authoritative suggestion? The culture and the family system are rife with daily suggestion. One could readily argue that enculturation is suggestion; socialization without suggestion could not exist. Every systemic encounter occurs within a culture defined by authority figures; these encounters invariably involve the constrained articulation of reality, truth, and history. Such encounters organize self-experience beginning at birth. Much as Spence (1982) argues that readers cannot meet texts without *a priori* interpretative principles, so I would argue culture meets persons. These ubiquitous forms of cultural suggestion, without which life would truly be "nasty, brutish, and short," are likely to be the first cause for actual patient suggestibility. They are certainly more powerful than the forms of therapeutic suggestion that occur one or two hours a week. The suggestive influences of family and culture are most potent when the child is the exclusive province, day after day, year after year, of her parents. How much suggestion was occurring at home to cause the abused child to be raped and be unable to call it rape? How much suggestive influence was exerted in psychotherapy over the last century to persuade patients that incest memories were fantasies? How many cultural influences persuade perpetrator-parents that parents are good, and that they are up-standing members of the community? How many "false-memory therapists" continue to persuade patients that their memories are fabricated? What is the suggestive influence of the media and the legal system on our society's impressions about incest and delayed memory?

If the patriarchal prejudices of the false-memory movement were removed from the investigation of suggestive influence and memory confabulation, the field of those subject to persuasive influence would expand to include accused, accuser, as well as innocent bystander.

EPISTEMOLOGY, DISSOCIATIVE MALICE, AND CONFABULATED MEMORY

When the implicit patriarchal assumptions of the false-memory position are exposed, we see how difficult it is to locate a level of explanation for confabulated memory that transcends these assump-tions. We must, instead, take them into account in our analysis. In searching for a theory that recognizes patriarchal influences and that can begin to embrace parental and child memory within a unitary understanding, I would like to open an inquiry into the fundamental grounding relations that may obtain between epistemology, privi-lege, and dissociative malice. The question of how parents, patients, and therapists (and innocent bystanders) discover and know truth is at the core of the false-memory question. I am in agreement with Hartsock (1990) that different ways of knowing and discovering truth derive from different material conditions.

Belenky and colleagues (1986) have evolved a stage theory of women's epistemological positions, or "ways of knowing"; they compare and contrast these with the ways of knowing in college-age men as described by Perry (1970). The men investigated in the Perry study were predominantly white, middle class, and privileged; the women in the Belenky study ranged from marginal destitute minorities to the upper class, white, and privileged. The Belenky study takes into account three axes of oppression within the patriarchal culture: race, gender, and class. Belensky and colleagues find two common themes running through all levels of women's development. These themes are of vital importance to issues of memory confabulation. The first involves women's preoccupation with the metaphor of speech, dialogue, and silence in relation to self and patriarchal culture; the second involves the otherness of their relation to authorities of knowledge. While the Perry study finds similar epistemological stages, privileged men do not frame their epistemological concern in terms of finding a voice; they do not feel silenced. Regardless of their epistemological stage, these men are identified with authorities of knowledge, and see such authoritative privileged truth as their own future. Throughout women's epistemological development, they have an *other* relation to authority, perpetually retaining a view that privileged authoritative truth was the original source of their silence.

Although one must be cautious about oversimplifying for the sake of convenience, I believe Showalter's (1993) argument about hysteria is relevant here. I view Belenky and colleagues' (1986) stages not merely as the stages of women, but rather as the epistemological stages of the powerless and the silenced who struggle in search of voice and empowerment. The ensuing discussion is therefore applicable to those men who have defined themselves as sex abuse survivors. The Perry (1970) findings and the Belenky findings can be transposed to the examination of the core question of memory confabulation: How do we know and define truth?

The Belenky group finds five epistemological positions among women. Each of the last four positions reflects not only a different *way* of knowing, each implies a different type of truth that can be authentically known. While each phase attempts to know all truths within its own mode, the mode of knowing is not always adequate to the object of knowledge, rendering certain truths developmentally unknowable. I will argue that the truth of incest is one of these truths. Thus epistemological arrest would be a contributory factor to both delayed and confabulated memory in patients, therapists, and perpetrators. This view of the mind's progressive, dialectic evolution toward the attainment of truth derives historically from the work of Hegel. For Hegel (1837), the mind progresses, through new shapes of consciousness, along a natural dialectical path from phenomenal knowledge to absolute knowlege where subject and object are unified.

The first position is *silence*, in which women experience themselves as mindless, voiceless, and subject to the whims of authority. The second is *received knowledge*, in which women conceive of all knowledge, including self-knowledge, as received from external authority. They regard themselves as incapable of finding truth within or for themselves. If there is a conflict between self and other, the received knower will always defer to the other. At this phase, women are especially at the mercy of the power of authority; they know themselves only as object, not as subject. Notably, such women seem aware that their source of knowledge is always external. The type of truth that can be successfully, authentically known in the received mode would be restricted, for example, to skills and rudimentary facts. The truth of self-knowlege could not be known within this modality. I would argue that dissociated incest is unknowable in a position in which all knowlege is derived exclusively from patriarchal authority. While the received knower may have always retained memory of incest (if the patriarch gave her this knowlege), she cannot in any case know the full truth of her own incest experience.

The third position is *subjective knowledge*. For the marginalized other silenced by patriarchal discourse, this stage is a critical way station to the reclamation of freedom, truth, and subjecthood. This position represents a pivotal transitional phase in which truth and knowledge are conceived as private, subjectively known, and intuited. This position reflects a shift from passive to active, from accepting to protesting, to self as becoming. Subjective knowers are mistrustful of logical analysis and abstraction, viewing these forms of knowing truth as the oppressive and discrediting standards of white male authority. Subjective knowers have realized that many important personal and interpersonal truths and skills can only be known intuitively, within themselves. It is here that the truth of incest begins to emerge. While this phase is characterized by an increase in self-esteem and strength, Belenky and colleagues (1986) find that a small subset of subjective knowers may become rigidly and angrily entrenched in the view of things that comes exclusively from their own gut, negating the value of any analytic process, of objective information or of alternative ways of knowing. These women tend to isolate themselves with other recalcitrant subjective knowers who adhere to a singular and absolute view of truth. In essence, they may regard their own intuition in the same dualistic, authoritarian mode as they previously regarded knowledge received from male experts. The authors note that many marginalized women shift into the subjective mode after having been profoundly disappointed by male authority, frequently through some form of abuse.

The fourth position, *procedural knowledge*, is entered when subjective knowers become aware that intuitions are not infallible and that conscious, deliberate analysis is required to obtain many kinds of truth. The procedural knower is interested in accessing the mode of knowing truth that will allow them entry into the world of competence and success. There is a quest after more objective knowledge, and the emphasis on the inner voice decreases even as there is an increase in the sense of control. This position involves the acquisition of powers of reason and objective thought. Having located her own inner voice, she temporarily forsakes it to acquire 'male' ways of knowing.

The fifth and highest level of epistemological development is the *constructed knowledge* position, in which the self and the inner voice of intuition are integrated with thoughtful analysis and objective knowledge. Rational and emotive thought are integrated; the subject and object are no longer split. Experts are appreciated from a standpoint of intelligent evaluative critique. The constructed knower is a peer to those who previously posed as authority. The constructed knower possesses the capacity to know a complex range of truths. It is in this position that a patient is most able to accurately know the truth of her own incestuous past, synthesizing intuitions with careful analysis. She does not reify external objective verification, but utilizes objective information where it is accessible; where it is not, she embarks on a thoroughgoing analysis of subjective data.

For Belenky and colleagues (1986) the movement to more sophisticated ways of knowing is facilitated by relational contexts characterized by egalitarian dialogue; persuasive authoritarian approaches arrest epistemological development at the earlier stages. Privileged, educated, nonabused women from egalitarian homes are most likely to achieve the stage of constructed knowledge. Marginalized, oppressed, and abused women are more likely be epistomologically arrested in the first two positions. One of the goals of psychotherapy should be the facilitation of epistemological growth through nonpersuasive, egalitarian dialogue. Where sex abuse and the possibility of delayed memory enters as a therapeutic hypothesis, the therapist should be cognizant of the patient's arrested epistemological position and its implications for either abandoning true memories of sexual abuse or for confabulating memory of sexual abuse. Accurate recall of sexual abuse needs to be grounded in epistemological growth or the patient will never know whose memory it is and if it is real. If therapists focus their initial efforts on enhancing epistemological sophistication, a patient will gradually emerge who is a constructed knower, capable of listening to her inner voice while pursuing a careful, judicious, self-directed investigation of the sexual abuse hypothesis. Paradoxically, sex abuse may be one of the most common causes of the very silence and epistemological arrest that renders the patient prone to therapeutic influence. In such cases, therapists must work carefully back and forth between epistemological focus and sexual abuse, always utilizing egalitarian dialogue and avoiding persuasion. Therapists' capacity to work in this way is naturally constrained by their own level of epistemological development. For example, false-memory therapists who are received knowers in Perry's position of identification with just patriarchal authority would tend to persuade patients that their real sex abuse memories are false. In the subjective mode, clinicians treating survivors would encourage an intuitive, "just trust your gut" attitude, discouraging patients from slow, careful analysis.

I would argue that patients are in danger of either confabulating memories of sexual abuse or of discrediting their true memories when they are in treatment dyads in which both patient and therapist are received and/or subjective knowers. While the received knower may be prone to confabulation, I believe it is only the subjective knower suffering from preconscious, dissociative malice who will pursue a protracted false accusation.

We may conceptualize the received knower as suggestible in the sense that she considers self-knowledge to derive exclusively from external authority; she remains an object to herself, lost in the patriarchal discourse, deaf to her own voice. Seeking self-knowledge, she enters psychotherapy; she is prone, however, to internalize the therapist's beliefs. With regard to sexual abuse, she may find herself stretched between contradictory sources of external truth: her culture tells her it rarely exists; her persuasive therapist may tell her that she has repressed it. She may defer to the most proximate authority. She may begin to either deny her own experience of sexual abuse or confabulate memories of victimization, rather than listening intently to her own inner experience. This process will be quite damaging to the patient in either case, because she entered therapy to find her own voice and has been betrayed. She is not likely to pursue any type of ongoing accusation, true or false. She would readily recant, deferring to parental claims of innocence (true or false) as soon as she encounters them. This is particularly likely as she is generally aware that she is a received knower; she willingly concedes that her memory was implanted. In fact, she regards all self-knowledge as implanted; thus, she does not conceive of her sex abuse discovery as originating in her own inside.

There is a subset of the subjective knowers who may be prone to pursue a false accusation. Such a person is stronger than the received knower, more active, devoted to the power of her own intuitive knowledge, isolated from other types of epistemological positions, closed to alternate views, absolute, and full of legitimate protest and rage against the disappointments and destructiveness of parental authority. She recognizes that she has been silenced and oppressed by her previous tendency to defer exclusively to received knowledge. She has suffered, in real and profound ways, at the hands of her parents and is suffused with preconscious dissociative malice. She is vulnerable to the persuasive hypothesis of the therapist regarding repressed sexual abuse insofar as it resonates, epistemologically, with her own angry intuitive rebellion. In this treatment dyad, the persuasive clinician shares this subjectivity, repudiating careful analytic strategies, and rebelling against psychotherapy's historical betrayal and silencing of the incest survivor. This clinician may have received no training in the treatment of sex abuse issues because patriarchal education provided none. She may herself be a survivor who suffered at the hands of psychotherapists who discredited her memories; she may be angry at rational, patriarchal discourse with its demands for nonexistent external verification of secret family crimes. Identifying with the child, such a clinician cannot simultaneously view the parent as a subject who will be justifiably devastated by a confabulated accusation. The therapist sharing this subjective mode of knowing fails to recognize the patient's subjective knower position as a healthy transitional phase along the path of reclaiming truth and the subjective self; she may fail to help the patient carefully articulate her own history and the true source of her murderous feelings toward her parents. Instead, the persuasive therapist encourages the patient to "go with your gut." In such a case, one can imagine the patient succumbing to the persuasive influence of the therapist yet possessing enough autonomous fire to confront parents and sustain the confrontation over time.

CASE MATERIAL

The following clinical material exemplifies the interplay between epistemological position, dissociative malice, and vulnerability to therapeutic persuasion. I have intentionally chosen somewhat ambiguous cases in which dissociated memories of sexual abuse may or may not be a causative factor in the very epistemological arrest that creates the patient's vulnerability to persuasion. Questions of sexual abuse have been left unresolved in an effort to immerse the reader in the therapeutic assessment and facilitation of ways of knowing and the requirement to resist premature closure regarding delayed memory and incestuous history. For purposes of illustration, I limit my clinical focus to ways of knowing truth, deemphasizing psychodynamic interpretation. I will begin with the *constructed knower* to illustrate the pathway toward truth that leads to the most accurate recall of delayed memories; I will then move to illustrations of epistomological arrest that may lead to confabulation. All clinical material has been disguised to protect patient confidentiality.

Linda

Linda is a highly intelligent, uneducated young woman from an inner-city working-class family. She entered treatment in a suicidal depression precipitated by a profoundly disturbing relationship with her lover. Hidden in her deep depression and depersonalization was another Linda: deeply ethical, spunky, independent, courageous. This stronger self was a seeker of truth, despite the profound pain and loss it might entail.

Linda always recalled an incestuous relationship with her uncle from ages 15 to 18. Linda's natural parents died violently when she was a young infant; she was adopted by her aunt and uncle. Her adoptive parents divorced when she was 5, after which Linda lived with her female cousin and her cold, neglectful depressive aunt, while her male cousin lived with the uncle. At the age of 12 her deteriorating, drug-addicted aunt abandoned her entirely. Linda went to live with her cousins, her grandfather, and her uncle. Her uncle had always been intensely adoring of her, as well as explosive; unlike her aunt, he provided some love and basic care. Despite his sexual exploitation of her, there were moments of genuine mutuality. He had great respect for her depth and wisdom; they would talk intimately for hours. When she reached 15, he would tell her he lusted after her, take her out on dates and buy her romantic gifts, forbid her to call him uncle in public, kissed her on the neck, made him lie in his arms in his bed, and verbalized his sexual admiration for her legs and breasts. If she avoided sexual contacts, he would become explosive and withdrawn. There was no genital contact. Her cousin witnessed and remembers this incestuous behavior. At these times, Linda felt frozen, repelled, confused, intimidated by his incipient rages, dead, and unreal. At age 18 she finally said no to his lustful attentions and left home, having less and less contact with him over the years.

Aware of a pervasive sense of shame and self-hatred, she began to explore this relationship. Gradually, she began to suspect that he may have had genital contact with her in early childhood, although she had no memory for this. Her initial sense of this was purely intuitive. She developed a profound wish to discover the truth of her early life with him, and has embarked on an anguished journey to find it. Although Linda has come to trust many of her own feelings, she does not consider intuition alone to be a satisfactory basis for establishing such a cataclysmic truth. Rather, she sees her intuition as a point of departure for a thorough investigation. Although she feels considerable rage at him, she is not in search of revenge. She is in search of truth, freedom, and the restoration of her living, vibrant self. She knows that such a restoration cannot be founded on a false accusation; in fact she would be deeply troubled to have falsely accused him even in her own mind. She recognizes the need to carefully analyze and evaluate both subjective and objective information. She hopes to find the truth, and fears she may never know.

Aware that external verification of genital contact per se is impossible, Linda nonetheless consults others about their memories of family history. Patterns emerge of generations of incest and physical abuse; she discovers her grandfather sexually abused her cousin as well as his own daughter and was physically abusive to her uncle. Her aunt recalls that Linda was desperate and terrified about being left alone with her uncle prior to the divorce; she informs Linda that the uncle hit Linda while she was in the crib. My patient examines photos and childhood correspondence with her uncle. Although terrified, she engaged in several dialogues with him about their relationship. Expressing some remorse and guilt, he was able to acknowledge the damaging effects of his sexual attention. He claimed he never touched her genitals and was never sexually attracted to children. Initially open to the possibility that he was telling the truth, she subsequently discovered evidence that his memory was faulty; she and her cousins all recalled him lustfully showing them his child pornography when they were, variously, ages ll to 15. He maintains that he would never have done such a thing. While this did not provide proof that he had touched her genitals, it did lend support to her suspicion that he could have, and that he would deny it.

In a similarly thoughtful manner, Linda investigates more subjective internal cues, sorting through transference manifestations, dreams, sensations, images, and memories, looking for recurrent patterns that either support or negate her suspicions. She never heralds a single indicator as a definitive memory. Her process is largely self-regulatory, initiated and controlled by the patient. My role is to provide empathic holding for the intense pain aroused by her search. As her field of evidence changes and grows, Linda moves through shifting experiences of loss, doubt, fear, horror, and despair. Sometimes she ceases her search for months at a time and focuses on other issues. During these times she is able to tolerate not knowing. She never defers the definition of truth to either myself or to other authorities; rather, she consults authorities and critically evaluates their input. She knows that only she can ultimately weigh all the evidence that she has carefully and painstakingly amassed.

Linda's extraordinary strength, courage and autonomous capacity to search for truth derives to some extent from her unique relationship with her perpetrator. Unlike most perpetrators, her uncle does not require pervasive denial. He remembers a great deal, and although he accuses her of "wanting it," he allows her to see his guilt and culpability. Most importantly, their shared history of deep mutual dialogue has co-created her constructed way of knowing.

Anne

The case of Anne provides an excellent example of the *received knower* who has no memory of sexual abuse, but has some of the signs and symptoms suggestive of it. Anne is an empathic, intelligent young secretary from a middle-class Protestant family. She entered treatment chronically depressed, feeling empty and profoundly confused about her most elemental needs, feelings, and experiences. She saw herself as void of originality and felt that all aspects of her self-definition were externally derived. For example, she would regularly cry copious tears when describing her grandmother's death, giving the appearance of missing her terribly and being extremely sad. If asked what she was feeling, she would say she didn't know; she didn't even know if she loved her. If I so much as gently reflected that she looked sad and like she did miss her, she would become confused. Was she sad? Were these the tears of grief and longing? If I said so, then they must be. But were these her feelings or mine? How would she be able to know? She expressed frequent concern about mirroring my definition of her feelings and never finding her own. She was aware of her own suggestibility, and was continually alerting me to it. Far from empty, Anne was in fact full of depressive protest against received knowing and the loss of her own voice.

This extremely lost person said, more than once, that she almost wished she could remember traumatic incidents of sexual abuse. Without sex abuse memories she was left with the more vague, indefinable, but equally pernicious struggle with chronic family patterns of unrelatedness and detachment, of utter lack of empathic attunement and dialogue. For these family dynamics and the resultant pain, she had no words. Somehow, for sex abuse there would be words and visible scars with which to codify her amorphous anguish. This would legitimize her lifelong pain, offer her a cohesive identity, and allow her to receive much needed nurturant support. She feared that she was motivated to confabulate such memories. She was further confused, however, as she knew she suffered from some possible indicators of sexual abuse. These included her mute passivity regarding unwanted sex resulting in a rape in her twenties, her unvarying experience of men as rapists, her compulsive overeating and anxiety about looking womanly, her recurrent sexual nightmares, and her raging outbursts at strangers. Could she be an incest survivor, she would ask, or was she just looking for the care and recognition she imagined such victims received?

What was in the forefront of our work was to support her dawning recognition that her own inner voice was *already speaking* through its longing for subjectivity and empathic care. Treatment involved a slow, careful discovery of her own feelings and identity in an empathic, reflective egalitarian atmosphere. I supported the patient in living with ambiguity regarding sexual abuse until she could be sure that whatever truth emerged was hers.

At present, the patient possesses a much more articulated identity; she is no longer alexithymic, isolated, depressed. She can now appreciate the rigor with which she protected herself against external influence and repudiated received knowledge and false compliance. She is a healthy subjective knower, valuing needs, feelings, and intuitions, and possessing an inner core through which she discovers her own personal truth. She is not yet able to integrate her dawning subjective autonomy with objective analysis; her own emotive voice still tends to collapse as it meets rationality. She is not yet a constructed knower. She continues to dread sexual attention and to discourage it through compulsive eating and other maneuvers. At present, she cautiously initiates intermittent explorations into the question of sexual abuse. It is possible that she would have responded to a persuasive therapist by temporarily confabulating memories of sexual abuse; however, she was ultimately protected by her own healthy suspicion of external influence and by her conscious wish to find her own voice.

Larry

The case of Larry offers an illustration of a *received knower* who was more vulnerable to sustained and dramatic memory confabulation. Larry is a 45-year-old computer programmer from an Italian background. Upon entering therapy, Larry was severely depressed; he was engaged in a continual self-flagellating internal monologue. Although quite intelligent, he functioned marginally, both personally and professionally. His work functioning was severely impaired by his profound obsessionalism, his intimidation by and abject dependency on authority, his terror of making an error, his preoccupation with always being a "good boy," and his incapacity to act autonomously. Although kind and giving, he was totally isolated and socially very awkward. He suffered from a profound incapacity to grasp interpersonal cues, roles, and boundaries, and found himself continually rejected and humiliated. In his innermost core he carried secret shame about a perversion that involves being sexually dominated.

Like Anne, Larry had numerous signs and symptoms of childhood sexual abuse: in addition to his need for sexual humiliation and submission, he evidenced sexual boundary problems inside and outside the treatment. Complaining on several occasions that his stomach was bloated and painful, he unzipped his pants, put his hand in, rubbed his abdomen and moaned suggestively. On one occasion he proceeded to "dress" after a session (zipping up, replacing sweaters, lacing shoes, etc.) in the waiting room. A female patient witnessing this became concerned that we might be having sex. This naive oblivion to sexual boundaries caused him to frighten and offend women at the very moment he thought he would induce their maternal care (for his "stomachache"); their reactions induced bewildered rage, hurt, and humiliation. When I set limits on this acting out in session he was hurt; he decided to comply with my "rules" even though they were "crazy." Were Larry's enactments an effort to communicate an incestuous secret or were they indicative of noncontact sexual pathology in his home? Upon inquiry into this behavior, I discovered his utter incapacity to label sexual cues and overtures. Similar boundary violations occurring in his home emerged; for example, his mother left the bathroom door in their small apartment wide open while she defecated, knowing that her adult son was present. The mother appears seductive and cloying, wearing revealing clothing, kissing him on the mouth, and so on. The family is characterized by poor sexual boundaries: Larry's adult sister pinches his buttocks and demands that he lie in her arms on the sofa in full view of the family. The patient had one clear memory, from age 3 or 4, of being permitted to play with his mother's breasts while she laughed. He remembers this moment as playful until it was devastated by his father's subsequent rage. He had no other memory of sexual contact.

Larry's profound sense of symbiotic exploitation by his close-binding, cloying mother and his submissive relation to his dominant, castrating father provided the initial focus of the treatment. Although I wondered if the patient had been sexually molested, I felt it was dangerous to approach this directly due to his tendency toward compliance. Our work focused on family dynamics underlying his craven submissiveness toward authority. We hoped to restore a sense of self and authentic agency, to put him, as he said, "in the driver's seat." In the context of our nurturant and respectful relationship, his depression, self-abuse, and compulsion toward sexual humiliation lessened. At some point, the patient met an incest survivor and noted his resonance with her experience; he wanted to explore this more in the treatment. In response to his request from the "driver's seat," I asked him about memories of his mother's body. In answer, he produced a flood of intense, dramatic images of having his face in her vagina. He seemed quite ready to believe it was a memory *if I said it was*, recapitulating his deference to received truth. When I expressed my unwillingness to define truth for him, he was able to express his own concern that he would readily mirror whatever I thought about his sexual history.

Was this an emerging memory or was it a symbolic expression of his sexualized merger with his suffocating mother? Did he have oral sex with his mother or did he feel *as if* she wanted to keep his head in her vagina? It was too soon to know. Although we recognized that incest might have been a causal factor in his pathological relation to truth and authority, we understood together that increased clarity could only emerge from a more autonomous and considered "constructed" way of knowing. Given the patient's deference toward authority we were both concerned about the potential for confabulation. I was careful to neither dismiss nor persuade the patient about incest. I do believe that Larry was capable of creating partially confabulated memories of sexual victimization that would concretize the seductive, invasive, symbiotic merger his mother had required. He was certainly not capable of a sustained, defiant accusation of his domineering father and overbearing mother.

Arlene

In my twenty years of practice, Arlene is the only *subjective knower* I have encountered who seems capable of both confabulation and false accusation. Or perhaps she is an incest survivor who unconsciously induced disbelief in me in order to keep her secret despite her avowed wish for it to emerge. When this middle-aged professional called to request therapy, she stated that she discovered in her twelve-step group that she was an incest survivor and wanted to "find my memories." She assumed her father was her perpetrator. Recognizing that it is possible for accurate delayed memory to begin with mere instinctual feelings, I was willing to investigate her hypothesis. Like the patients above, Arlene evidenced some signs and symptoms of childhood sexual abuse. She was sexually compulsive, unable to protect herself from AIDS, a former addict, and filled with bitter hatred of all men, whom she viewed as abandoning and sexually exploitative. Her affective range and interpersonal relatedness were limited to bitter accusation and envy, resulting in a tendency to spoil all potentially nurturant contact. At our initial meeting, she seemed remarkably willing to assume she was a survivor although she lacked any memory or evidence to support this position. She revealed little anguish, conflict, or doubt about this devastating identification.

What were her actual memories? Arlene grew up in the rural midwest in a religious and isolated home. She had always recalled severely neglectful, verbally and physically abusive alcoholic parents who overexposed her to the hostile sexuality of their own relationship. Sexually flooded by this overexposure, she became hypersexual as early as age 5, masturbating compulsively to the sounds of her parents' intercourse. In adolescence, upon expressing an interest in boys, she was assaulted with accusations of being in league with Satan and of being a "whore." She received sexually paranoid injunctions against men and was required to be completely covered when permitted outside the home. While this family system possessed many characteristics of an incest family, there was never any memory of actual sexual contact. Arlene had stopped speaking to her parents many years before entering treatment, and never spoke of them without intense (and justifiable) hatred. She never expressed conflictual feelings of longing, loss, or anxiety. Belligerent and abusive both inside and outside the treatment, Arlene experienced herself solely as victim rather than as victim-abuser. Certainly, Arlene's belligerence represented an identification with the aggressor, but was it a *sexual* parental aggressor, or the paranoid, verbally abusive father she described? Efforts on my part to investigate her own abusiveness were met with great resistance, as was any therapeutic investigation into the fear, loss, and emptiness caused by the disturbing childhood events she actually did remember. She was insistent throughout that she "just knew" she was an incest survivor and wanted to just "have my memories." Over two years of treatment, no actual memory of incestuous contact emerged. She never attempted to fabricate such memories. She would, however, strain very hard in her interpretations of her occasional, ambiguous dreams and altered states. She was disappointed that she was not finding her memories; she had, after all, sought out a "sex abuse specialist." Perhaps she was a survivor and we never reached the truth; I think it is likely that she was not.

As I worked with Arlene, it began to occur to me that her intuitive "truth" was confabulated. Arlene's painful response to her abusive, chaotic, sexually overstimulating family system could have easily resonated with that of the incest survivors in her twelve-step group, without her actually being a survivor. What caused me to question her? Her lack of doubt, horror, and conflict was unlike anything I had ever seen in the survivors I've treated. More importantly, the patient gradually revealed a somewhat psychopathic sense of entitlement to restitution. She began to confabulate other damaged aspects of her identity in the service of establishing this entitlement. She would not lie, per se, just as she never actively fabricated incest memories, but she would distort, deny, and exaggerate before my eyes. These distortions then became an unquestioned intuitive "true" aspect of her self-concept, which could not be challenged or investigated. Embittered and hostile, she utilized these confabulations to exploit friends, lovers, and various institutions. Never asking for care in a respectful manner, she would manipulate others into providing for her so that she would not have to be a responsible adult. Increasingly, she sought the therapist's collusion in her manipulative efforts toward restitution. Therapy ended due to my refusal to engage with her this way.

Arlene was a subjective knower who was legitimately enraged at familial abuse and oppression, and at her childhood role of submission and silence. Associating careful analysis with the demand of the patriarch for nonexistent external verification of secret family crimes, she repudiated such methods of pursuing truth. Assuming a position of radical incendiary protest, she insisted on the exclusive and absolute truth of her own inner voice. She felt entitled to restitution, and desirous of exacting sadistic revenge on the authorities who had rendered her powerless and terrorized. She demanded a reversal of the colonizer-colonized relationship, attempting to regain subjectivity by objectifying and marginalizing any "other" who did not mirror her position. She seemed able to confabulate sex abuse memories to achieve these ends, once such an explanation was proffered to her in a therapeutic context (in this case, group). Although she may be misguided in her accusations of sexual abuse, we nonetheless find within her authentically painful sexualized affects, as well as a transitional movement toward agency and intentionality. Such a patient deserves clinical and societal recognition both as a subject and as a culpable agent. She was certainly capable of the sustained defiance of parental authority involved in a false-memory accusation. She needs to move toward Linda's type of constructed knowing, and toward a healthy resolution of her own sadism and powerlessness. She must not be met by a persuasive therapist who is him/herself a subjective knower. Such a therapist could have readily "uncovered" confabulated memories.

CONCLUSION

In this chapter, I have begun to articulate the archaic patriarchal assumptions implicit in the false-memory movement. This movement is seen as the most recent historical manifestation of the "just patriarch–fragile hysteric" paradigm that discredits the legitimate claims of sexual abuse survivors. This paradigm permeates most research and clinical formulations that challenge the existence of delayed memory.

Nonetheless, it is important for clinicians treating trauma to resist polarization and to acknowledge and investigate the rare case of memory confabulation leading to false accusations of sexual abuse. It is imperative to develop a set of explanatory principles for memory confabulation that can be equitably applied to patient, parent, and innocent bystander alike. Such principles can only be formulated once we have eliminated patriarchal assumptions from the discourse on delayed memory and suggestibility. This work in progress has begun this reformulation by proposing a nonsexist alternative view of the false accuser. I have argued that he/she is neither the fragile hysteric nor the hysteric who "wreaks destruction to avenge her own irrationality." His/her accusation arises from authentic preconscious affects deriving from a genuinely destructive family system. This patient's developmentally arrested way of knowing truth is grounded in her position as marginalized other in the family and in the culture. Upon encountering a persuasive therapist, the memory linked to these affects may be mislabeled, resulting in a confabulated memory of actual sexual contact where none may have existed. This view robs the patriarch of his bewildered protestations of an ordinary, decent family life. Thus, the patient suffering from confabulated memory of sexual abuse is not lost again in the objectification of patriarchal discourse, which discredits her as it does the vast multitude of sex abuse survivors. Rather, the angry retribution of the powerless and the silenced become known. It becomes possible to view the false memory of perpetrator innocence as likewise grounded in early destructive familial patterns and arrested ways of knowing truth.

Ultimately, we will become able to respond to patient, parent, therapist and innocent bystander in a manner that transcends the just patriarch–fragile hysteric paradigm of the false memory movement. In pursuit of this end, we must recognize that ways of knowing are just as important as the object of knowledge in establishing guilt and innocence.

REFERENCES

Bart, P. B., and Scully, D. H. (1979). The politics of hysteria: the case of the wandering womb. In *Gender and Disordered Behavior*, ed. E. S. Gomberg, and V. Franks. New York: Brunner-Mazel.

Bass, E., and Davis L. (1988). *The Courage to Heal: A Guide for Women Survivors of Child Sexual Abuse.* New York: Harper and Row.

Belenky, M. F., Clincy, B. M., Goldberger, N. R., and Tarule, J. M. (1986). *Women's Ways of Knowing*. New York: Basic Books.

Berliner, L., and Williams, L. M. (1994). Memories of child sexual abuse: a response to Lindsay and Read. In *Applied Cognitive Psychology* 8(4):379–389.

Blume, S. E. (1990). *Secret Survivors: Uncovering Incest and its Aftereffects in Women*. New York: John Wiley.

Bornstein, R. F. (1993). *The Dependent Personality*. New York: Guilford.

Chodorow, N. (1989). *Feminism and Psychoanalytic Theory*. New Haven, CT: Yale University Press.

Courtois, C. A. (1988). *Healing the Incest Wound: Adult Survivors in Therapy*. New York: Norton.

Foucault, M. (1978). *The History of Sexuality, vol. 1, An Introduction*. London: Penguin.

Freud, S. (1914). On narcissism, an introduction. *Standard Edition* 14.

———— (1933) Femininity. *Standard Edition* 22.

Gardner, R. A. (1992). *True and False Accusations of Child Sex Abuse*. Cresskill, NJ: Creative Therapeutics.

Gudjonsson, J. S. (1991). *The Psychology of Interrogations, Confessions and Testimony*. Chichester, England: Wiley.

Hartsock, N. (1990). Foucault on power: a theory for women? In *Feminism/Postmodernism*, ed. L. J. Nicholson. New York: Routledge.

Hegel, G. W. F. (1837). *Reason in History*. Indianapolis: Bobbs-Merrill.

Herman, J. L. (1981). *Father–Daughter Incest*. Cambridge, MA: Harvard University Press.

———— (1992). *Trauma and Recovery*. New York: Basic Books.

Hollender, M. H. (1988). Hysteria and memory. In *Hypnosis and Memory*, ed. H. Pettinati. New York: Guilford.

Jacobs, J. L. (1994). *Victimized Daughters: Incest and the Development of the Female Self*. New York: Routledge.

Johnson, S. M. (1991). *The Symbiotic Character*. New York: Norton.

Lindsay, D. S., and Read, J. D. (1994). Psychotherapy and memories of childhood sexual abuse: a cognitive perspective. In *Applied Cognitive Psychology* 8(4):281-339.

Loftus, E. (1993). The reality of repressed memories. *American Psychologist* 48(5):518–537.

Masson, J. M. (1984). *The Assault on Truth: Freud's Suppression of the Seduction Theory*. New York: Farrar, Straus, & Giroux.

Memmi, A. (1967). *The Colonizer and the Colonized*. Boston: Beacon Press.

Mitchell, J. (1984). Femininity, narrative and psychoanalysis. In *Women: The Longest Revolution*. London: Virago.

Nash, M. R. (1994). Memory distortion and sexual trauma: the problem of false negatives and false positives. *Applied Cognitive Psychology* 8(4).

Perry, W. G. (1970). *Forms of Intellectual and Ethical Development in the College Years.* New York: Holt, Rinehart, & Winston.

Pezdek, K. (1994). The illusion of illusory memory. *Applied Cognitive Psychology* 8(4).

Pope, H. G. Jr. (1994). Recovered memories: recent events and a review of evidence, an interview with Harrison G. Pope, Jr. *Currents in Affective Illness* 13(7).

Rousseau, G. S. (1993) . A strange pathology: hysteria in the modern world 1500–1800. In *Hysteria Beyond Freud*, eds. S. L. Gilman, H. King, R. Porter, et al. Berkeley: University of California Press.

Russell, D. E. H. (1986). *The Secret Trauma: Incest in the Lives of Girls and Women.* New York: Basic Books.

Shapiro, D. (1965). *Neurotic Styles.* New York: Basic Books.

Showalter, E. (1993). Hysteria, feminism and gender. In *Hysteria Beyond Freud,* ed. S. L. Gilman, H. King, R. Porter, et al. Berkely: University of California Press.

Smith-Rosenberg, C. (1972). The hysterical woman: sex roles and conflict in 19th century America. *Social Research* 39:652–678.

Spence, D. P. (1982). *Narrative Truth and Historical Truth.* New York: Norton.

Struve, J. (1990). Dancing with the patriarchy: the politics of sexual abuse. In *The Sexually Abused Male, vol. 1: Prevalence, Impact, and Treatment,* ed. M. Hunter. New York: Lexington.

Temoshok, L., and Atkisson, C. C. (1977). Epidemiology and hysterical phenomenon: evidence for a psychosocial theory. In *Hysterical Personality,* ed. M. J. Horowitz. New York: Jason Aronson.

Terr, L. (1994). *Unchained Memories.* New York: Basic Books.

Walker, L. E. A. (1994). *Abused Women and Survivor Therapy: A Practical Guide for the Psychotherapist.* Washington, DC: American Psychological Association.

Wright, L. (1994). *Remembering Satan: a Case of Recovered Memory and the Shattering of the American Family.* New York: Knopf.

Yapko, M. D. (1994). *Suggestions of Abuse: True and False Memories of Childhood Sexual Trauma.* New York: Simon & Schuster.

11

Knowing and Not Knowing: Paradox in the Construction of Historical Narratives

MICHELLE PRICE

In our current culture, many forms of personal trauma find their ways into public discourse, such as on television talk shows, in news magazines, and in the tabloids. Although there is a need to remove certain events like incest and childhood sexual abuse from the realms of secrecy and shame, certain types of discourses can simplify, depersonalize, and polarize complex issues, particularly those involving human betrayal, pain, and suffering. This seems to be the impact of the current debate regarding true and false memory. This debate, as it has been represented in the media and by some of its spokespeople, seems to be rather straightforward. There are two significant aspects to the debate: (1) people have either true or false memories; (2) those with false memories have had them implanted by militant and/or incompetent feminist/therapists.

The "false-memory syndrome" is defined as a condition in which a person strongly believes in the occurrence of a traumatic memory, which is false. False appears, though, to signify nonverification, rather then objective truth. Furthermore, the construction of these binaries, true and false, and their reification as concrete entities, further mystifies, rather than elucidates, the human tragedy of child abuse. As a result, the actual victims are ignored, neglected, or made into media heroes. The rhetorical devices utilized to create these positions erase the complexity and fuzziness of issues related to memory, life narratives, and trauma. Extreme positions on both sides act as if these binary positions are "real" and deciphering the truth (as if that is an inherently real category) is just a question of who you believe, victim or victimizer or hard science versus narrative constructions.

Although the need to determine the truthfulness of claims of child abuse may appear rational and reasonable in a court of law, it becomes highly suspect in a psychotherapy/psychoanalytic context. Further confusion arises from the attempt to utilize criteria developed within legal contexts to evaluate and influence psychotherapeutic treatment. Requiring psychotherapists to assist their patients in forming objectively true (beyond a shadow of a doubt) historical narratives can and often has the effect of eclipsing elements of our patients' words, affects, and images. Yet, we are in a quandary as both patients and external forces are requiring documentation of truth and the validity of child abuse accusations and/or suspicions. The lack of a semicoherent life narrative does have the potential to leave an individual feeling lost, fragmented, and chaotic (M. Kaminsky, personal communication, 1994). Despite this, some of the current demands made on therapists, in addition to the whole realm we signify as reality and truth, must be examined. What is really being requested? Is it for us to silence our patients, provide quick assessments or cures or believe that any thought or feeling related to childhood abuse is proof that it has occurred? What countertransferential impacts does this "big brother" climate have on the analytic relationship (Grand, this volume, Chapter 9) and therapeutic dialogues? I have no answers for these dilemmas, only an appreciation of some of the difficulties we face today in treating individuals who present with a history of, or suspicion of a history of, childhood sexual abuse.

In addition to challenging the category of truth, one is also confronted with the problems of memory. What is memory? Is it ever present and reliable? Or is it continuous, changing and evolving within social, cultural, and dialogic contexts? If the latter, does that mean it is not to be trusted? Is there one memory or is memory like the concept of self—multiple, existing within different registers of speech, contexts, and sensorimotor and affective states (van der Hart 1993)? What do we judge as accurate memory? If one fact is wrong or if it changes do we discard the entire story? Do traumatic events get encoded and stored as memory in different ways than nontraumatic events, as Terr (1994), van der Kolk (1987), Bucci (1994), and others suggest?

Memory appears to be as fuzzy a concept as truth or consciousness, especially if we begin to consider the impacts of power/knowledge structures and the regulatory practices of the culture on what is made available for discourse and memory. To further understand this, a critique of discursive factors and hegemonic institutions in the formation of available cultural discourses and knowledges is required.[1] The question arises as to how we can remember that which was never permitted into the family or social discourse, that which was forbidden creation by words or signifiers or more simply that which we could not talk about. Are there other forms of memory, especially for those events that have not been languaged? This would include consideration of somatic and affective memories[2] as well as the entire phenomenon of reenactment as a form of past/present merger (Terdiman 1993) and the overlapping of time sequences.

These questions necessitate a critique of some of the current

---

[1]Schachtel (1984) attempts to explore the impact of the normative practices of the culture in determining what is available for memory. He particularly attends to how particular self states and experiences are unable to be remembered, as they could potentially conflict with a conventional style of existence that the culture requires. He writes, "No experience, no object perceived with the quality of freshness, newness, of something wonder-full, can be preserved and recalled by the conventional concept of that object as designated in its conventional name in language" (p. 293).

This critique additionally suggests the power of language to constitute, rather than reveal experience and that language exists within and maintains the discursive and normative practices of the culture. For further elaboration of these concepts, see Lacan (1977) and Bakhtin (1984).

[2] Affective and somatic memories (or body memories) are problematic as well. These areas are not outside of the discursive and regulatory forces of the culture. They are constructed, organized, and signified within particular contexts and discourses. They are marked, formed by the regulatory ideals and norms that are inherent in our thinking and speaking. The cultural discourses form our ideas and interpretations regarding the body and affects. Therefore, references to the body further forms, constructs, and constitutes the body (Butler 1993).

issues being raised regarding memory to reveal political motives and biases. For example, if we question what is recorded as memory as possibly being false, we can also question that which is not remembered as having gaps or being unreliable. If memory is not a pure, reified entity and what is remembered can be challenged as false, then we can maintain the same criteria for what is not remembered. I also wonder how it is that the memory of incest victims is being challenged as potentially false, but the memories of the accused perpetuators are rarely, if ever, the object of analysis. Theirs are accurate and left out of this current discourse. What are the political and social factors that are involved in and influence the recent debates?

In considering all these factors, but particularly the possibility of the absence of memory regarding past events, I will limit this discussion to those individuals who present in a psychotherapy or psychoanalytic context with no initially obvious or clear memories, but yet have a distinct "knowledge" of their own abuse history. I will consider the possibility of this type of knowledge in the context of contemporary psychoanalytic narratives, as well as implications derived from postmodernist thinking and discourse theory. The utilization of these different texts and idealogies can assist in revealing some of the biases and political factors that influence our current conceptions of memory, knowledge, and childhood sexual abuse.

MULTIPLE SELVES AND DISSOCIATION

Historically, psychoanalysis has organized around the concept of a unitary self that is a distinct entity that proceeds along linear developmental lines. Straying from the designated developmental paths can lead to pathology in the forms of fixation, false self creation, ego or self deficits, and general maladjustment. Based on one's particular theoretical narrative, treatment proceeds as a way of correcting, uncovering, filling in, and/or reparenting the conflicts/deficits areas so that the self can be reconstituted, integrated and whole.

Contemporary psychoanalytic narratives, borrowing heavily from philosophical, feminist, and literary texts have begun to challenge the idea of the unified, unitary self and to consider the existence of multiple selves or identities (Bromberg 1993, Harris 1994, Mitchell

1992, 1993). This is in line with the increased emphasis on relational and interactional themes in constructing identity and personal meaning systems. According to Mitchell (1993), the self is no longer a finite entity, but temporal, embedded in particular relational matrixes and in our narratives regarding them. Bromberg (1991) writes about the need to address in analysis the person's individual subnarratives and to enable negotiations to take place between them. He postulates (1993) that the self does not originate as an integrated whole, but is nonunitary in origin and continues as a multiplicity of self-other configurations. The experience of wholeness or coherence, as he refers to it, is a necessary illusion. Within this new meta-narrative, an individual cannot be conceptualized except within the context of mini- and macro-cultural influences. Bakhtin (1984), the Russian literary critic, details the dialogic aspects of our linguistic utterances, revealing relational aspects in the construction of values and positions. Kaminsky (1994) makes similar claims in his ongoing work with Eastern European Jewish immigrants and contests the claim of the melting pot metaphor. In his project, he evocatively illustrates the existence of multiple self and other states contextualized in relational and cultural configurations within the superficially appearing assimilated individual.

Within the field of trauma studies, similar trends have been taking place based on work with individuals diagnosed with multiple personality disorders (Kluft 1985, 1993, Loewenstein and Putnam 1988, Putnam 1989, Reis 1993). This is not to imply that all individuals are multiple personalities, but the distinction lies in the amount of dissociation and fragmentation between multiple states, not in the existence of multiple states. As Rivera (1989) writes in her important paper on feminist theory and multiple personality disorder, the problem lies not in the multiplicity but in the dissociation. The work of analysis is to listen to those voices not as a unified choir, but as singular voices begging to be heard and recognized and simultaneously fearing such recognition (Price 1994d). "If we don't have an image of this multiplicity, we are going to wind up either missing those dimensions of our patient's experiences that enable them to grow or recreating the molds that got our patients into trouble in the first place" (Dimen 1994).

These new analytic narratives explode theoretical stories regarding personality, identity, and gender. They have serious implications for work with individuals with a history of trauma, particularly sexual abuse perpetrated in a relational context by those to whom the child's care, well-being, and very survival was entrusted. They create openings and new lenses in which to view the impact of trauma and how it is experienced, processed, and remembered. In a world where individuals are no longer constructed as singular entities, dissociation refers to a relationship not only between internal and external events, but also between internal representations, affective states, and interpretive and meaning systems. Implicit in this is a consideration of horizontal splits, as opposed to the archaeological view of the person, whereby memories, traumas, and experiences are buried in a vertical fashion, waiting for the skillful excavator/analyst to uncover them.

Dissociation replaces repression. Dissociation refers to fissures and sharp breaks between the different states of consciousness and identities. Depending on the extent and severity of trauma, the connections between multiple states will be affected and in its most extreme form severed. An individual may be unable to access particular self and other representations, events, and knowledges that are highly traumatic and potentially disruptive, particularly if they are marginalized from the dominant cultural discourses. Within this type of configuration, an absence of clear memories of traumatic events and the person's involvement in them can occur. The faint memories of these events can exist within dissociative and linguistic gaps.

This particular use of dissociation and multiplicity additionally serves as an alternative explanation of the split some people manifest between recall of traumatic events and related affective and narrative significance. Clinical manifestations of this present themselves with individuals who can recount the details of their abuse and verbalize "appropriate" reactions, but yet there is a lack of concordant affective responsiveness or awareness (Price 1994a).

> Ms. B. is a 35-year-old woman who presented herself as having difficulties in certain areas of her life, such as compulsive eating, obesity, and a fear of men and sexual activity. She had grown up the youngest child in a middle-class suburban family, with a domineering, violent father and a passive mother. Ms. B. functioned as her mother's helper in every way; homecare,

confidante, and caretaker. She had no social life and would often miss school if her mother was sick or depressed. She felt guilty if she made plans with friends. From the ages of approximately 8 to 15 she was routinely sexually and physically abused by her brother, five years her senior.

Upon entering treatment, Ms. B. proclaimed to have worked through and resolved her incest issues in a previous treatment and was interested in working on her obesity, anxiety over dating, and inability to sustain a sexual relationship with a man. Accompanying these issues were feelings of deadness and a constriction in her emotional life. Over time, it became more and more evident that what "working through" meant was that she had talked about the incest in a detached, dissociated manner, with a minimum of affective or narrative significance. Additionally, there began to be an increase in depressive symptoms, especially as we began talking about her relationship with her family, in which she continued to maintain a role equivalent to servitude. Although willing to answer any questions regarding the incest and making superficial connections between it and present difficulties, she maintained a highly guarded and distant attitude toward these stories.

One day she entered the session extremely distraught, crying and visibly shaken. She reported going to her parents for the weekend and being in the room where her brother had repeatedly raped her. Although she had been in this room many times before, something hit her this time and she began to feel the terror, shame, and pain she had experienced during those years. She connected this opening where feelings seeped out as related to our conversations and my sustained interest in that part of her life. She additionally recalled a specific memory of where her brother had forced her to have sex with him while his friend watched. She stated that she had not allowed herself to think about that before. In the next session, she brought in a ragged, stuffed animal that she slept with and held on tightly to while her brother had molested her. Since that time, she continued to sleep with this animal and felt that all his rips and tears were symbols of her traumas. His scars were her scars.

Bringing him into the session represented to her a willingness to talk about and to signify all the events and feelings that they had witnessed, that they knew but could not/would not talk about until now.

ENACTMENTS

Many authors writing on analytic work with adults with a history of childhood sexual abuse discuss the existence of dissociated multiple self and other representations and narratives constructed by the trauma victim (Alpert 1994, Davies and Frawley 1994, Ehrenberg 1992, Gartner 1993, Price 1993, 1994a, c, van der Kolk 1989). These authors provide theoretical and clinical illustrations of how these multiple states are enacted in verbal, behavioral, affective, and physiological modes in the individual's relational matrices. From this type of paradigm we are able to understand how the roles of abuser and abusee are enacted in the analysis, with patient and analyst occupying concordant and complementary positions. A powerful form of communication of multiple states is represented by the concepts of projective identification and counteridentifications and transference/countertransference, in their broadest definitions. By projective identification, I refer to the various self and other narratives that permeate the analytic field and the co-constructed dialogues of patient and analyst within that space. This relies heavily on the work of Ogden (1982) and his clinical use of this concept and its further elaboration by Tansey and Burke (1989). Projective identification encompasses nonverbal forms of communication that can function as windows into the patient's various worlds. The creation of openings, whereby dissociated identities and/or experiences can emerge and play themselves out between analyst and patient, is a crucial aspect of therapeutic work with adults with a sexual abuse history. As Bromberg (1993) writes, "In the proper analytic setting, there is a chance, with the analyst, for the dissociated domains of self to play out aspects of unsymbolized experience that will allow motoric, affective, imagistic, and verbal elements to coalesce with relevant narrative memory" (p. 163).

Utilizing these theoretical constructs, there exists the possibility of the patient knowing and not knowing the existence of a history of incest. Depending on the level of dissociation, a person can be aware of or have a sense of a traumatic history, while being disconnected from the actual concrete facts. Through the evocation of the metaphoric concept of projective identification, it allows for the analyst to possess information that the patient is consciously unaware of. The analyst's belief or disbelief in the patient's history of sexual abuse can be related to a communication of dissociated aspects of the patient who either disclaims or acknowledges her/his (hi)story (Price 1994c). The conversations between analyst and patient regarding the possibility of such a history may in and of itself be an enactment of earlier dialogues in the patient's life with the abuser or other family members. This would imply that all our patients' words are never monologues but rather are dialogues, scripts with many players' parts being recited (Bakhtin 1984, Harris 1992, Ingram 1994) within the therapeutic setting. The analyst's receptivity to these communications creates a new context for previous dissociated self and other constructions and events to be talked about and processed and formed into relevant narrative memory and truth (Spence 1982).

DISCOURSES AND MARGINALIZATION

The ideas of dialogic selves, narratives, and paradox is particularly crucial to my understanding of childhood sexual abuse, memory, and dissociated knowledges. Postmodernist, social constructionist, and hermeneutic discourses need not only be a way of contesting incest victims claims of abuse, as Grand (1991) so clearly illustrates, but can be used to complicate the concept of memory and expose the intricacies of an individual's recall or lack of information for events. Postmodernist trends in contemporary psychoanalysis provide alternative positions in examining the formation of recorded and symbolized experiences. The postmodernist era is characterized by uncertainty, heterogeneity, multiplicity, difference, and an attention to history, context, discourse, rhetoric, and revealing the arbitrary categorization and interpretation of experience through cultural configurations. It attempts to destabilize subjectivity, knowledge, and truth and locate the political and rhetorical devices that have created these illusions (Price 1994b). It signifies a diverse group of discourses that reflect certain positions within the human sciences that are a response to enlightenment claims, Cartesian dualism, and structuralism. Postmodernist texts and narratives privilege language, focus on power/knowledge factors, and attempt to decipher the existence of binary hierarchies. These aspects, as well as the locating of the regulatory practices of the culture in the creation of available and acceptable social discourses and knowledges lend much insight to analytic work.

Within postmodernist philosophy or theories, language and signification are highlighted and privileged. Language is not a fixed system, but we inhabit our words so that they begin to construct for us our meaning of events and our experiences of them. Language is relational and reflective of the hierarchal, political system that we are situated in. "Reality" and the "natural" are negotiated and constructed by language within a cultural context and its discursive practices. In line with the work of Lacan (1977), Schaefer (1992), and various philosophers and literary critics, such as Bakhtin (1984), Wittgenstein (1953), and Eagleton (1983), realities are created through language. Language games and signifiers are highlighted as opposed to the idea that language reflects or reveals prexisting and preformed ideas. There is no natural. Linguistic coding creates and transforms the substance of events, experiences, and beings rather than revealing or exposing them. Language provides us with a way of describing and signifying experiences, but simultaneously alienates us from them.

As Lacan (1977) illustrates, what is signified is always slipping beneath the signifier. Therefore signifiers can only signify other signifiers and positivist claims to true meanings are nonexistent. Meaning is created within multiple dialogues and the speaking of language is part of an activity that constructs (Wittgenstein 1953). There are many truths in the world (Derrida 1981), although some are prevented entry into the world of discourse and signification. Language, narration, and discourse are highly political, influenced heavily by power/knowledge factors, context, and culture. There is no way of separating events out of a cultural context, which is multicultural. All events and experiences occur within the context of regulatory ideals and principles and the meta-narratives that contextualize them. Cultural discourses constitute the naming and defining of experiences. There is no experience that is not contextualized within the historicity of its own norms and discursive features.[3]

Part of the analytic work, as I see it, is to create spaces for marginalized or subverted discourses to be heard, the local knowledges that have been excluded from representation by the culture's dominant, master narratives. The co-construction of multinarratives by patient and analyst (Hoffman 1992, Ingram 1994) is valued and necessary. Utilizing a social constructionist narrative located within postmodernist trends, Kamsler (1990) critiques some of the psychoanalytic and psychiatric literature on the treatment of women with a history of incest as being too focused on the incest survivor's internal pathological state. Her approach, which is influenced heavily by the family therapist Michael White (White and Epston 1990), proposes that we utilize a contextual, interactional perspective that does not see the development of difficulties as taking place inside the person. This would shift the therapeutic lens to the various relational and social contexts within which a person's difficulties may emerge (Kamsler 1990). As a result of this, analysands are seen as being under the influence of a dominant story that defines (them)selves and relationships, and constructs their problems. Therapeutic work involves the deconstruction and challenging of the dominant, usually pathological story, such as "I am damaged," to generate alternative self and other stories. The dominant story is constructed as a dialogue between the person and others in their past and present life, as well as related to ideological and political trends in the culture.

Finding Kamsler's (1990) essay particularly helpful, as well as the work of White, I believe their text analogy in conjunction with literary contributions can be further utilized to understand how individuals record events in their lives, which is signified by the word *memory*. Memory can be conceived as our relationship to the past, a way in which we register and inscribe that which has occurred (Terdiman 1993). Following from this, Terdiman postulates that forgetting is a failure of inscription, an "absence."

I propose that lack of memory or dissociation of events can be

---

[3] I would like to express my appreciation and gratitude for the conversations, colleagueship, and texts of Doug Ingram, Muriel Dimen and Carla Massey in the formation of these ideas. I additionally am grateful to the Psychoanalytic Connection for an ongoing on-line conversation on postmodernism and psychoanalysis.

attributed to the events never being allowed to be linguistically coded, symbolized, constructed and discussed. This lack of discourse may be attributed to power and discursive forces within familial, social, and cultural contexts that define acceptable conversations. Power in the family and culture is the network of practices that sustain dominance and subordination and is built into the order of the culture. It defines and constructs what is truth and what is fact (Sampson 1993). This lack of inscription of experiences in the family's or person's dominant storyline prohibits the recall of certain events. Therefore, adults with a history of incest do not forget their history, do not repress it, but were never allowed to know it in the sense that we describe knowledge. It exists in a space that Bollas (1987) in a different context refers to as the "unthought known," which expands on Freud's topographical theory, minus some of its positivism (Ingram 1994). It refers to the shadow that falls between what patients know and what they can think, due to the deprivation and trauma that has occurred in the family culture (Bollas 1987, Kaminsky 1994).

The knowledge of past events can exist without language, disenfranchised without symbolization and in the gaps and absences of an individual's speech and narratives. This additionally may explain why there has been an influx of reports of childhood sexual abuse. The creation of a context and a discourse that recognizes and acknowledges such traumas, permits individuals to identify and discuss previously foreclosed experiences and interactional events.

In other cases, the incest experience does get discussed, but it is misrepresented and defined by the perpetuator as an act of love or caring, or as punishment for the child's misdeeds. This signification creates for the child victim states of confusion and conflict, whereby that which is experienced affectively and physically as "bad," "wrong," and "hurtful" is stated to be something else by those in the power position. In other cases, the child is warned and threatened not to reveal what has occurred at the risk of serious danger to self and others. In these cases, child victims are forced to participate in their own victimization and oppression by accepting the perpetrator's explanations and interpretations of reality. This, combined with years of silence and shameful secretiveness, further contributes to individuals' lack of knowledge of their history and ability to signify it. It comes to rest in a dissociated place, in the marginal areas of the person's life history, as a subverted discourse whose voice is silenced.

Through this banishment, the perpetrator continues to control the victimized child/adult and maintain him or her in the position of the "other."

As Foucault (1974, as recorded in Terdiman 1993) writes, "Memory is actually a very important factor in struggle. . . . If one controls people's memory, one controls their dynamism. . . . It is vital to have possession of this memory" (p. 19). This co-opting of a person's memory and personal knowledges, which Shengold (1989) also discusses in regard to soul murder, is not always complete. People can maintain an awareness of what has happened but are unable to represent their personal experience of it. They simultaneously know it and do not know it. They know it, but cannot think or speak it. It exists as a marginalized discourse, which, within a different context, like the therapeutic relationship, can be brought out of exile. Within this new context and discourse, people can access areas of knowledge that they have been prohibited from recognizing. The deconstruction of the person's dominant narrative and realign ment of power, subjectivity, and agency can begin to allow for the signification and languaging of events that have been dissociated and foreclosed on. It allows for disparate storylines (Schaefer 1992) to emerge in a therapeutic context which the person can integrate into her life's narratives.

> Ms. T. is a 42-year-old divorced woman who has a history of severe drug and alcohol abuse, spanning 15 years. At the time of beginning treatment, she had been substance-free for approximately five years. She reported that during brief periods of non–drug use, she would be haunted by "knowledges" of her father's past sexual abuse of her. She would become horrified, disoriented, and confused and shortly after resume her substance abuse. While using, she would frequently place herself in extremely dangerous and destructive positions and felt that she deserved to be punished. She was uncertain as to why she deserved this punishment but always maintained feelings of being dirty and damaged, which she would confirm through self-reported promiscuous sexual activity and other events in her life.
>
> After Ms. T. became drug free and sober, she became more and more convinced that she had been abused, but was

unable to describe it in any detail. Frequently in her sessions, she would become so distraught over her lack of memories that she would wonder if she had made the whole thing up. She additionally discussed at length her fear of seeing her father as an abuser. As time elapsed Ms. T. began to have recall of certain visual images involving her and her father, such as his penis being placed in her mouth. She spoke of this and other events with the language and mannerisms of a young child, lacking the appropriate words and describing the feels, the smells, and what it looked like. For example, she would cringe over that "icky, gooey stuff in my mouth." She additionally described frequently hiding under her bed late at night, as she was afraid of that "big bad monster-man." While discussing this in session, she would quickly begin wiping off any makeup, which was related to a fear of being attractive and a wish not to be seen as a desirable woman and a "grown-up."

Over time Ms. T. began to use her and the analyst's language system and register of words to piece together her own narrative history. With the recall of these events, she began to have access to a world of affective responses that she had previously been dissociated from, such as rage, despair, sadness, and grief. Her history of drug abuse and sexual activity had served the purpose of deepening her dissociation from these events and the pain associated with them. Inherent to this was the conflict of acknowledging the roles her father directly, and her mother indirectly, played in her abuse history, thereby relinquishing much of her idealization of them. Additionally this involved the containing of multiple experiences, positive and negative, of her parents.

The marginalization of discourses from dominant narratives in individuals' lives, such as the preceding clinical vignette illustrates, is a continual occurrence within societies, history, and fields of knowledge. Due predominantly to the work of the feminist movement, we have begun to attend to the gaps in our history of female experiences and contributions. Due to the rise of multiculturalism, we are additionally attempting to deconstruct the good versus bad, hero versus villain binaries that characterize many historical accounts.

The inclusion of different voices and their counterdiscourses further complicate simplistic and smooth accounts of history and reveal their distortions and political manipulations.

Within the field of psychoanalysis, we have additionally been witness to the exclusion of alternative theoretical positions and ideas. The marginalization and banishment of the work of pioneers such as Ferenczi and Horney served to preserve and present psychoanalysis as a cohesive body of knowledge, deriving from the works of Freud and his most loyal followers. It is only quite recently that the work of Ferenczi has been taken out of the closet and allowed entry into the psychoanalytic domain. These academic and historical examples illustrate the same concept that I propose is evident in work with individuals and the construction of their past and present identities.

UNCERTAINTIES

Despite my conviction regarding the possibility of people knowing and not knowing that they had been sexually abused, there is much room for confusion and uncertainty. Maintaining the absolute binary of true versus false continues to eclipse possibilities and knowledges from evolving. Once again, the person, the patient is lost and forced into recanting a dominant self and other narrative. What I am suggesting and advocating is that we as therapists must maintain positions of paradox and possibility, concordant with our patients. A discourse with much tension is maintained between knowing and not knowing.

Ms. A., a 38-year-old woman was referred to treatment by a local women's center. She identified herself as an incest survivor and stated that she had left her previous therapist as she sought treatment with a woman who was experienced in this area. She presented her history as having grown up with an angry, volatile mother who had later been diagnosed as having psychotic episodes. Her father had been viewed as the good, nurturing parent who supported her. At the current time, he has been dead five years. Ms. A. said that most of her previous therapy had dealt with issues related to her mother and her impact on her sense of self and relationships. She defined her current problems as choosing unavailable men, lack of assertiveness, and lack of success in pursuing life goals.

Ms. A. reported discovering that she was an incest survivor approximately one year ago. She had a dream that reflected the possibility of some sexual contact between her and her father. Her previous therapist had been reluctant to consider that as evidence of incest having occurred. She then went to a local women's center that confirmed that her dream was indicative of such a history and correlated it with some of her current symptoms. The center agreed that she should see an expert and referred her to me. It quickly became clear that my being defined as an expert or experienced in the area of incest meant to her that I would definitively confirm a history of sexual abuse.

Throughout the brief treatment, I vacillated in my belief about the reality of incest having occurred, as did the patient. This vacillation was due to the fact that the patient's only idea that incest had occurred was related to a dream. Despite this, Ms. A. insisted that I confirm such a history. This included demands that I interpret her doubts as being typical of incest survivors and that these doubts themselves were proof of such a history. I viewed my own doubts and different positions of knowledge regarding the patient in line with an appreciation of paradox and not knowing. I additionally conceptualized my knowing/not knowing as possibly related to an enactment of past relational configurations and aspects of the patient's world of dissociated self and other identities. It neither confirmed nor denied the possibility of a history of abuse. Despite explanations of this, the patient would have none of it. She demanded certainty and definitive interpretations. She felt she could not work with a therapist who could not validate her or overcome her doubts or blockages to know the truth. Blockages were considered by her to be the lack of any memories about the abuse. She implied that the therapist should know more about the patient than the patient did. Not knowing on the part of the therapist was equivalent to disbelief, invalidation, and silencing her.

I, on the other hand felt that to unequivocally validate such a history meant misrepresenting myself and submitting to the patient's threats and accusations (which were quite effective). The patient was uninterested in looking at the possible enactment contained in the relational entanglement she and I were in and left the treatment. I was left feeling angry, scared, insecure, and worried about my reputation with the center that had referred her.

In this experience, as well as others that I have encountered in clinical practice and supervision, maintaining positions of paradox and ambiguity are very difficult. We and our patients often crave certainty and definitiveness, especially regarding our pasts and identities. The temptation or insistence for premature interpretations and declarations of truth, as in the above clinical vignette, can be viewed as transference/countertransference enactments that once again put the patient or the analyst in the role of being told what has happened to them and what it means (Price 1994c). At other times, it may be indicative of the therapist's lack of training or experience, which should be considered.

CONCLUSIONS

Working with individuals who either have or suspect a history of incest and/or childhood sexual abuse raises important issues and difficulties that the therapist must be willing to immerse him/herself in. It is my opinion that some of the recent postmodernist influences in psychoanalysis as well as (re)constructions of memory, life history, and truth open up, rather than close, spaces for (re)considering dissociation and the forms of recall of historical events. These constructions challenge some of the recent attention to the areas designated as repressed memory and the false-memory syndrome. It exposes the rhetorical strategies utilized and some of the political factors that are in the background of this debate. (Re)conceptualizations of memory in line with power/knowledge, linguistic, and discourse systems allow for the possibility of an individual's lack of recall of past events, particularly those of a traumatic nature. This chapter has attempted to discuss this issue and has used the concepts of dissociation and marginalization as ways of signifying and comprehending these possibilities.

This chapter further contests the ideas of a unified, unitary self and a unified memory system that accurately records all events in a linear fashion. Multiplicity in conjunction with dissociative processes allow for the marginalization and subjugation of narrative events. Bollas's (1987) concept of the unthought known further elucidates this and challenges past ways of thinking. Therapeutic dialogues and relationships involve both analyst and patient in a world of paradox, ambiguity, and relational enactments, all created and contexualized by language and the discursive and regulatory practices of the culture. The demand for certainty and the insertion of objective truth and knowledge claims limits and forecloses on an individual's ability to embrace multiple identities and experiences. It does not allow for an appreciation of the impact of context and power factors on the recall and accessibility to past aspects of one's life. These demands and claims can potentially subject a person to oppression, silencing, and the destruction of creativity and possibility. In conclusion, as therapists we are rarely, if ever, in a position to definitively know our patient's history, but we must be able to practice in a culture that allows for all possibilities, uncertainties, and certainties to mutually coexist.

ACKNOWLEDGMENTS

I am especially grateful to Vincent Giannone, Dough Ingram, Marc Kaminsky, and Muriel Dimen for their astute and significant comments on reading earlier drafts of this chapter. Their ideas and our conversations were invaluable in the construction of this text.

REFERENCES

Alpert, J. L. (1994). Analytic reconstruction in the treatment of an incest survivor. *Psychoanalytic Review* 81(2):217–235.

Bakhtin M. (1984). *Problems of Dostoyevsky's Poetics,* trans. C. Emerson. Minneapolis: University of Minnesota Press.

Bollas, C. (1987). *The Shadow of the Object: Psychoanalysis of the Unthought Known.* New York: Columbia University Press.

Bromberg, P. M. (1991). On knowing one's patient inside out: the aesthetics of unconscious communication. *Psychoanalytic Dialogues* 1(4):399–422.

⸻ (1993). Shadow and substance: a relational perspective on clinical process. *Psychoanalytic Psychology* 10(2):147–168.

Bucci, W. (1994). The multiple code theory and the psychoanalytic process: a framework for research. *Annual of Psychoanalysis* 22:239–259.

Butler, J. (1993). *Bodies that Matter: On the Discursive Limits of "Sex."* New York: Routledge.

Davies J. M., and Frawley, M. G. (1994). *Treating the Adult Survivor of Childhood Sexual Abuse: A Psychoanalytic Perspective.* New York: Basic Books.

Derrida, J. (1981). *Positions*, trans. A. Bass. Chicago: University of Chicago Press.

Dimen, M. (1994). *The third step: Freud, the feminists and postmodernism.* Paper presented at the Scientific Meeting Series of the Association for the Advancement of Psychoanalysis, April 21.

Eagleton, T. (1983). *Literary Theory: An Introduction.* Minneapolis: University of Minnesota Press.

Ehrenberg, D. B. (1992). *The Intimate Edge.* New York: W. W. Norton.

Foucault, M. (1974). Film and popular memory. In *Foucault Live (Interviews 1966–84)*, ed. S. Lotringer, trans. M. Jordin. New York: Semiotext(e); 1989.

Gartner, R. B. (1993). *Considerations in the psychoanalytic treatment of men who were sexually abused as children.* Paper presented at the spring meeting of Division 39 of the American Psychological Association, New York.

Grand, S. (1991). *Doubting and knowing: contemporary psychoanalytic dilemmas in the treatment of incest survivors.* Paper presented at the American Psychological Association, San Francisco.

Harris, A. (1992). Dialogues as transitional space: a rapprochement of psychoanalysis and developmental psycholinguistics. In *Relational Perspectives in Psychoanalysis*, ed. N. J. Skolnick, and S. C. Warshaw. New York: The Analytic Press.

⸻ (1994). *Gender practices and speech practices: towards a model of dialogical and relational selves.* Paper presented at Division 39 of the American Psychological Association, Washington, DC, April 14.

Hoffman, I. Z. (1992). Some practical implications of a social-constructivist view of the psychoanalytic situation. *Psychoanalytic Dialogues* 2(3):287–304.

Ingram, D. H. (1994). Poststructuralist interpretation of the psychoanalytic relationship. *Journal of the American Academy of Psychoanalysis,* 22(2):175–193.

Kaminsky, M. (1994). Discourse and self formation: a concept of the mensch in modern Yiddish culture. *American Journal of Psychoanalysis,* 54(4).

Kamsler, A. (1990). Her-story in the making: therapy with women who were sexually abused in childhood. In *Ideas for Therapy with Sexual Abuse*, ed. M. Durant, and C. White. Adelaide, South Australia: Dulwich Centre.

Kluft, R. P. (1985). The natural history of multiple personality disorder. In *Childhood Antecedents of Multiple Personality*, ed. R. P. Kluft. Washington, DC: American Psychiatric Press.

_____ (1993). Multiple personality disorders. In *Dissociative Disorders: A Clinical Review*, ed. D. Spiegel. Lutherville, MD: Sidran.

Lacan J. (1977). *Ecrits*, trans. A. Sheridan. New York: W. W. Norton.

Loewenstein, R. J., and Putnam, F. W. (1988). A comparison study of dissociative symptoms in patients with complex partial seizures, MPD, and posttraumatic stress disorder. *Dissociation* 1:17-23.

Mitchell, S. A. (1992). True selves, false selves, and the ambiguity of authenticity. In *Relational Perspectives in Psychoanalysis*, ed. N. J. Skolnick, and S. C. Warshaw. New York: Analytic Press.

_____ (1993). *Hope and Dread in Psychoanalysis*. New York: Basic Books.

Ogden, T. (1982). *Projective Identification and Psychotherapeutic Technique*. Northvale, NJ: Jason Aronson.

Price, M. (1993). The impact of incest on identity formation in women. *Journal of the American Academy of Psychoanalysis* 21(2):213-228.

_____ (1994a). Incest and the idealized self: adaptations to childhood sexual abuse. *American Journal of Psychoanalysis* 54(1):21-36.

_____ (1994b). *Discussion of panel on postmodernist trends in psychoanalysis*. Annual meeting of the American Academy of Psychoanalysis, Philadelphia.

_____ (1994c). Incest: transference and countertransference implications. *Journal of the American Academy of Psychoanalysis* 22(2):211-229.

_____ (1994d). Commentary on Kaminsky's "Discourse and Self-Formation." *The American Journal of Psychoanalysis* 54(4).

Putnam, F. W. (1989). *The Diagnosis and Treatment of Multiple Personality Disorders*. New York: Guilford.

Reis, B. E. (1993). Toward a psychoanalytic understanding of multiple personality disorder. *Bulletin of the Menninger Clinic* 57(3):309-318.

Rivera, M. (1989). Linking the psychological and the social: feminism, postmodernism and multiple personality. *Dissociation* 2(1):24-31.

Sampson, E. E. (1993). Identity politics: challenges to psychology's understanding. *American Psychologist* 48(12):1219-1230.

Schachter, E. (1984). *Metamorphosis: On the Development of Affect, Perception, Attention and Memory*. New York: Da Capo.

Schaefer, R. (1992). *Retelling a Life: Narration and Dialogue in Psychoanalysis*. New York: Basic Books.

Shengold, L. (1989). *Soul Murder: The Effects of Childhood Abuse and Deprivation*.

New Haven, CT: Yale University Press.

Spence, D. (1982). *Narrative Truth and Historical Truth: Meaning and Interpretation in Psychoanalysis*. New York: W. W. Norton.

Tansey, M. J., and Burke, W. F. (1989). *Understanding Countertransference: From Projective Identification to Empathy*. Hillsdale, NJ: Analytic Press.

Terdiman, R. (1993). *Present/Past: Modernity and the Memory Crisis*. Ithaca, NY: Cornell University Press.

Terr, L. (1994). *Unchained Memories*. New York: Basic Books.

van der Hart, O., et al. (1993). The treatment of traumatic memories: synthesis, realization and integration. *Dissociation* 6(2/3):162–180.

van der Kolk, B. (1987). *Psychological Trauma*. Washington, DC: American Psychiatric Press.

―――― (1989). The compulsion to repeat the trauma: reenactment, revictimization and masochism. *Psychiatric Clinics of North America* 12(2):389–411.

White, M., and Epston, D. (1990). *Narrative Means to Therapeutic Ends*. New York: W. W. Norton.

Wittgenstein, L. (1953). *Philosophical Investigations*, trans. G. E. M. Anscombe, 3rd ed. New York: Macmillan, 1968.

12

Impact of Validation of Recovered Memories on Patients' Treatment

SUE SHAPIRO

Empirical research on memory can be used to help understand how people can fail for long periods of time to remember painful, dramatic childhood events. For example, research has identified the importance of rehearsal and retelling for strengthening the sense of reality that some memories have.[1] This finding has importance for understanding the haziness and unreality people have for memories of events that were unmentionable and never spoken. As children they may have wondered if something was a truly private event as in a dream or fantasy, or if the event did occur in reality with a person they knew and saw daily but who never spoke of it. Research has also found that parental recall of child-rearing practices is inaccurate and the errors are not random. In general parents describe a course of development that is much smoother than it was and remember child-rearing practices that were more in keeping with expert opinion than reality (Robbins 1963). Unfortunately there has been little collaboration between the two cultures — that of the laboratory and

---

[1]Clinicians interested in reviewing the psychology of memory are referred to Baddeley (1990), Rose (1992), and Grossman and Pressley (1994). I am indebted to Bill Hirst and Catherine and Steve Hanson for teaching me about this perspective.

that of the consulting room. The current American Psychological Association panel consisting of equal numbers of clinicians and researchers charged with the task of reviewing the literature on evaluating memories is an important first step. Participants in the debate about childhood memories have become increasingly polarized and the level of debate has sunk.

Viewed from a historical perspective, the intensity of this debate is not surprising since controversy over the truth or falsity of memories of childhood sexual abuse has plagued psychoanalytic theorizing from the beginning (Masson 1984). In fact some have argued that psychoanalysis was born when the seduction theory was abandoned and the significance of unconscious fantasy was realized. In addition, the sexual attraction of first degree relatives is so intense, and the consequences for species survival so dire, that there has been some form of incest taboo in most cultures. European society was shocked by Freud's assertions about the sexual fantasies and feelings of children. At least as shocking, and even less frequently reported in case histories, despite its frequent conscious presence, is adults' sexual interest in children — even their own. Ironically, while psychoanalysis is itself divided on the subject of childhood abuse, the rest of our culture has linked the recovered memory specialists with psychoanalysis to launch a wholesale attack on psychoanalysis (Crews 1994a,b). This attack comes at a time when psychoanalysts have been debating whether psychoanalysis is a natural or a hermeneutic science — whether there is a historical truth that we aim to uncover or whether our interest is in making coherent narratives (Spence 1982, Wolff 1988).

Solid academic researchers who study memory and have valid questions and criticisms have been used as expert witnesses by individuals who are themselves the target of sexual abuse charges. This use of empirical research on memory in the courtroom further alienates clinicians from academic psychologists, who usually have no training in trauma. Well-meaning, but poorly trained psychotherapists make their livelihood by simplistically applying the latest clinical theories and fads in their consulting rooms. This has been the case whether the fad is a theory of penis envy, ego psychology, the inner child, or sexual abuse. When these therapists testify in court, they and the treatments they conduct are easily discredited, often this has led to discrediting all theories and treatments of emotional disturbance.

Most patients readily adapt their discourse to fit the interests and theories of their therapists, and their ensuing dialogue surely influences the narratives they produce. While we don't have fool-proof means for correlating the narratives produced in the consulting room with historical truth, most clinicians operate with the assumption that they aim for an understanding of their patient's experience of his or her history (Wolff 1988). The rules of evidence in the consulting room remain vastly different from the rules of evidence in the courtroom.

The understanding of childhood memories in general, and traumatic memories in particular, begs for a collaborative approach between clinicians, empirical psychologists and neurobiologists (Berliner and Williams 1994, Brenneis 1994, Lindsay and Read 1994, Terr 1990, 1994). In fact the false-memory controversy provides a challenge, an opportunity for psychoanalysts to study and integrate the last fifty years of laboratory research on memory. This is only one of many areas of empirical research that have deep significance in understanding people's lives and actions. We have seen significant changes in psychoanalytic treatment of infertile men and women, minorities, people with various sexual orientations, as well as changes in treatment of various symptom configurations (e.g., depression, obsessive compulsive behavior, panic attacks, psychosis) as data from biology, history, feminism, academic psychology, and anthropology alter our ideas about human experience. I see the integration of laboratory work on memory into psychoanalytic understanding as just a beginning—the start of an integrated approach to human experience, development, and psychopathology. This is an opportunity to be embraced, not responded to in a dismissive and defensive manner.

THE CLINICAL SETTING

In the consulting room it has become difficult to discuss and evaluate a particular set of memories of abuse (sexual and/or physical), given both the widespread prevalence in America today of abuse that goes unreported and the contemporary hysteria over changes in the American family and ideas about sexuality. Evaluation of claims of abuse becomes all the more difficult when secondary gain or loss is involved. Many responsible therapists and researchers know that this situation is exceedingly complex and requires sophisticated investigation and understanding. Increasingly therapists are faced with the difficult task of distinguishing what seem to be memories of real abuse, from elaborations, perhaps secondary to previous therapy, that seem to be just that—elaborations. At times these elaborations may accurately represent a person's experience—in other words, the mixture of both objective acts and expectable (under the circumstances) fantasy elaborations. In this case the person's experience needs to be worked through in such a way that its complexity is appreciated without muddling issues of culpability and agency.

For example, let's assume that many young children have fantasies about "marrying" same and/or opposite sex parents, and some children are then singled out by this parent for extra attention and then for sexual activity. These children are brought into a private secret pact with this parent, which keeps them apart from the other parent, who is often denigrated and who may have been neglectful of the child in the past, or who, once the pattern of extra attention has developed, is both neglectful and hostile. We can expect that in these instances, there will be some confusion in the child's experience between pleasure and guilt over wish fulfillment on the one hand, and on the other, fear of the intensity of the adult's behavior, as well as anger, fear, and despair over betrayal if the sexual activity was not only pleasurable but also painful. This child will also experience anxiety over pleasure and secretiveness, anger at the neglectful parent, a longing to protect the idealized parent, and so on. The elaborate entwinings of conscious and unconscious fantasy, developmental stage, family dynamics, and actual physical and psychological responses to sexual acts are all part of this child's experience and will be reworked over time through subsequent developmental stages and as relationships with the various participants in this drama change. These experiences will also be projected onto future relationships.

In therapy, as the patient's experience is explored, it is necessary to unravel these issues. It becomes critical that we clarify, and distinguish with our patients, conflictual childhood oedipal desires and fantasies from acts initiated by grown-ups with grown bodies and desires — acts that children are not responsible for even if they experienced some pleasure during the encounters. It becomes necessary to help these patients recover from what Ferenczi (1932) called "the confusion of tongues" between the language of tenderness and the language of passion. We must help these patients regain or strengthen their ability to differentiate fantasy from reality. Often patients will describe the experience of working through memories of abuse as "getting back my mind."

When unspeakable events occur, they make the difference between public and private experience harder to identify and articulate. We've all had experiences that we cannot believe are real. If we are fortunate enough to have someone we know witness the event, and that person is willing to speak about it, we feel greatly relieved, as in "pinch me so I know I'm here and not dreaming." In many families unspeakable events occur and it is not possible, in fact it is forbidden, to acknowledge and confirm that they did occur. At times these unspeakable events take the form of behaviors while intoxicated or otherwise drugged, or behaviors that occur when parents are in an altered or dissociated state. For example, I once saw the child of two Holocaust survivors. He described how sometimes his mother's face would change and he would know they were all in for trouble. At these times his mother would begin to scream and hurl terrible abuse at her husband for being a Nazi. In the morning she would not recall the events of the previous night, and it was all so horrible and uncanny that the whole episode would not be mentioned by anyone in the family.

In other families, children may witness spousal abuse and one parent's terror in the face of the other parent's violence. If the children bring up their fears, the abused parent may deny that anything frightening had occurred and might insist that it will never happen again. It may be too terrifying to mention the incident to the abusive parent lest another violent episode be precipitated. In still other families, one parent may be chronically drunk while the other parent is in continual denial. Over time, in these families, the prohibition against speaking and the development of an "official story" begins to take over and the children begin to believe the lie they have been told and are telling.

For example, one patient's father died of cirrhosis of the liver, but everyone in the family insisted that he didn't have a drinking problem. The mother denied how difficult her marriage had been and how abusive her husband was, but also chose to have no funeral or memorial service for him while insisting that she loved him and that he had been a good father. In treatment, the patient, a depressed, addictive woman with many somatic problems, recalled nightly rituals of getting drinks for her father and staying up with him as he consumed vast quantities of beer. Eventually she recalled the day the boiler blew up and they both had to escape from her room where they were taking a nap together. Over time more memories of times spent with her father, both pleasurable and abusive, emerged. The first recollections of sexual abuse occurred with body memories—for the first time in this woman's conscious experience she had vaginal sensations in the absence of direct stimulation. These sensations greatly disturbed her and led to her first images of sexual abuse by her father. She continued to doubt the extent of her abuse and chose not to confront her mother, because even when she mentioned memories of her father's drinking, memories she was not only convinced of but that other relatives corroborated, her mother would deny her stories and change the subject. The patient's sister, an obese woman in a marriage that resembled the parents' marriage, physically abused her own child. My patient was desperate for a sense of belonging and family. She feared that with direct confrontation she would lose whatever family she had. The closest she was able to come to this was when her sister visited, she had the sister drive with her to a group for sexual abuse survivors. The sister stayed in the car during the group. My patient told her the nature of the group, hoping her sister would ask a question, but no questions were asked. The patient continued to suffer from chronic doubting throughout my work with her and was beset by chronic somatic problems, bodily flashbacks, and nightmares; often she returned to self-medication and addictive behavior.

Another patient's mother was psychotic and at times had gone after her with a knife. The father was in massive denial in part out of his fear of the consequences of seeing just how bad things were. My patient, the eldest of many children, had left home as early as possible and had managed better than her siblings. Her perceptions of her mother's difficulties were repeatedly denied by her father and doubted by herself. When she began treatment she used her treatment initially as a form of supervision. She would present documents that her mother had written and needed me to offer my professional opinion. As it became clearer that her mother was indeed psychotic for much of my patient's life, more material began to emerge and it became easier for the patient to begin to talk openly with her siblings and get some confirmation of her experiences. Some of these experiences had been forgotten or repressed, others had always been available to memory but were never verbalized. Many seemed so odd that she couldn't believe they were true.

Sometimes well-meaning parents are so distressed by problems that befall their children that they can't ever discuss them and in this sense fail their children.

A patient required genital surgery during adolescence. His parents were so distressed by their inability to protect their child and by the site of the surgery that they lied about it even within their immediate family and were unable to either prepare him for the surgery or speak to him about his feelings after it was completed. The patient was completely isolated by this experience and even though in many ways it was a central organizer to his life, one that he never forgot, it took a long time before it could be discussed. Although some of the facts of his condition had always been known, many aspects of his experience had never before been formulated.

Still other patients describe events that were taken for granted at home, but were not to be discussed outside the home. Such patients are able to realize how oddly their families behaved only after they are out of the home or during treatment.

In one extended family the younger generation would often engage in sexual fondling. In one game they would gather around and blow on one boy's penis until it became erect. They played this "game" until well into their twenties. While these experiences were always recalled, they were never deemed important until one of the members of this generation began to speak about being sexually abused by a much older brother. The other members of the generation were only slightly surprised, they had always suspected something. After this material came to light, the other background sexualized behavior seemed more salient to all of them.

Sometimes experiences during childhood are so odd, or were experienced in an altered state because of fear or through an identification with a parent who was in an altered state, that they didn't seem real. Adults who grew up in exceedingly violent or chaotic homes may remember the abuse inflicted on their siblings but not that which they themselves survived. Frequently in my practice I have seen patients who describe the severe abuse a sibling experienced. When I suggest that they speak to this sibling and further their sense of personal history, they frequently are told that the sibling doesn't remember much being done to him but recalls my patient being abused. Idiosyncratic forms of punishment, like being treated as a dog and being made to eat from a plate on the floor, may seem too odd to be true, and the patient may assume this was a dream until a sibling confirms the experience.

In one family, a young man tried to save an abused parent by running to tell a priest that he had to come quickly to stop his father from hurting his mother. When the priest arrived the parents were on good behavior and the boy was subsequently punished for airing the family's dirty laundry and telling lies. The boy began to doubt his perceptions and wondered whether his parents were right—that he only said these things to get attention. These doubts about memories of abuse within his family—abuse of the mother by the father, including an incident in which the father put out cigarettes on the mother, and of all the children by both parents, continued through adulthood. The abuse was totally denied by the patient's mother during a joint session but was confirmed in meetings with the siblings. Until this confirmation was forthcoming my patient felt in danger of losing his mind whenever he would visit his family and be criticized by his parents for avoiding them for no reason.

These clinical vignettes illustrate some of the ways in which a child's family's manner of processing events affects later memory of those events. Even as adults the desire to avoid cognitive dissonance and the hope of extracting some good times and loving feelings from their family of origin keep some patients doubting their memories of abuse.

RECALL AND CONFIRMATION OF MEMORIES

All of us who work with adults who have been seriously abused in childhood, struggle with and are perplexed by the way some people have continual memories of horrible experiences while others have little conscious memory of even benign childhoods. Some traumatized people have the symptoms of posttraumatic stress disorder (PTSD) all their lives, whereas others only get these symptoms as adults when they begin to recall abuse, and in still other cases the onset of memories is heralded by PTSD symptoms. Some people have no memories of abuse until some curious chain of events opens the door and then they are flooded by memories of childhood terror and abuse, and others have the door open only to continue to stand guard and try to close it as tightly as ever despite an ongoing struggle with symptoms that would probably be alleviated if only they let themselves go further into their past.

Some patients describe the recovery of memories as "getting back my mind," while others feel that they are "losing my mind." The questions: Is this true? Did this really happen? plague everyone who doesn't have continuous uninterrupted memories of their past. Even people with continuous memories at times have trouble knowing and distinguishing memories that represent objective reality from those that are more of a screen memory. The importance of external confirmation of memories of childhood can be understood in this context. For example, one patient always had a vague memory of playing doctor with her mother and delivering babies from her. In the memory the mother is naked and the girl is doing something to her vagina. The patient didn't think this really happened, wasn't sure, but felt that this conveyed the general level of boundarylessness and overstimulation that characterized her childhood. Imagine the different experience of the patient in the following scenarios that could follow from a confrontation with her mother:

1. Mother says, "You know, I've always felt very strange about that but I didn't really know how to respond to your curiosity and I didn't want to inhibit you. I didn't want to bring it up because I didn't know if you remembered it and I didn't want to upset you."
2. Mother says, "That's crazy, I never did that and you never did that; I hope you're not telling your therapist lies like that."
3. More blandly, Mother says, "I don't remember anything like that; that would certainly have been strange."

Given the problems with personal memory I've been describing, the only response that would feel ultimately satisfying, although disturbing, is the first. The second might seem too defensive but not surprising even if the mother is telling the objective truth, given the somewhat shocking nature of the memory, and the third might seem oddly detached and therefore make the event itself seem conceivable.

Let's add another variable: The mother and daughter have many instances in which the mother's autobiographical memory during difficult times in their lives together is surprisingly deficient. I say "surprisingly" because in other domains the mother is noted for her excellent memory. But she readily admits that there are certain difficult periods in her adult life for which she has little or no recall and she is willing to accept someone else's version of history for these times.

If the mother's cognitive style is to dissociate during times of stress and subsequently have few memories of these periods, it raises the question of a biological predisposition to this defense that the daughter may have inherited. Or the daughter may have learned that her mother is made too anxious by certain events or memories that then don't get repeated or rehearsed and are therefore not reinforced—these events and memories become part of what Sullivan called the "not-me" system. Or this mother's cognitive style may be an indication that she herself was abused, tends to dissociate, and has an inadequate or pathological sense of personal boundaries.

Let's return to the first scenario in which the mother confirms the memory. What does the mother's relatively benign and emotionless confirmation do to the daughter's memory? Does the daughter wonder why she's making such a big deal of it? Does she question whether they both could be remembering the same event? Are they? In some sense no—both have symbolically elaborated the event over the intervening years in different ways and both probably experienced it quite differently initially. Although even the first response is more complicated than I realized at first. As Blechner (personal communication) pointed out, it could represent a bizarre effort by the mother to "share" her daughter's experience and express her support for the daughter's explorations, or could represent some shared fantasy. Thus we must keep in mind that support or consensual validation doesn't necessarily mean confirmation. In the remainder of this chapter I will explore the impact on patients of confirmation of memories and some of the clinical issues that surround the search for such confirmation.

Even patients who were always dimly aware of abuse events benefit greatly when other family members confirm their memories.

A 6-year-old girl and her slightly older sister were both raped by two strangers while playing in the countryside near their home. The young girl's memory focused on the humiliation of returning home without her underwear and she recalled that her mother was away at the time and that she was therefore bathed by her nanny. Her father was at home. She thinks her older sister had it worse. She has no clear memory of the penetration, but she does remember the intimidation and fear of being hit. She developed various somatic symptoms and preoccupations. She and her sister never speak of this in detail except for a few occasions as adults at the therapist's urging— they disagree on some of the details and never pursue these discussions at any length, but they both remember the general outline of the incident in the same way. The parents did not report the incident to the police and never referred to it subsequently. The overall impact in terms of pregnancy fears, sadomasochistic enactments, fears of her own aggression, and physical tension was enormous and took many years to work through. At times it seemed that if the older sister had not witnessed this event, it would be hard to keep its reality in mind. Certainly the parents' reactions to the incident were characteristic of the ongoing familial environment and were central to this person's character.

Most of the instances of abuse that my patients have continuous recall for either occurred at the hands of strangers, when they were older, or were spoken of at the time — at least to a sibling. The abuse that was repressed usually remained unspoken or was specifically banned from speech,[2] was more violent, lasted longer, started earlier, and was committed by a parent. This is consistent with findings by Briere (1989), Briere and Conte (1993), and Herman (1992).

I have seen several people who, as children, were sexually abused by their stepparents. This abuse was less frequently repressed than abuse by a biological parent, and at times was specifically communicated to the biological parent. Often the biological parent did nothing and even when there was serious subsequent acting out, including psychiatric hospitalizations, the fact of sexual abuse was not mentioned to the psychiatric staff. These patients, while always conscious of the abuse, minimized its impact in part as a way of avoiding the full force of their disappointment in their biological parent who failed to protect them and chose their mate over the well-being of their child.

One person's stepfather, when confronted, acknowledged forcing her at age 12 to perform oral sex on him. He claimed that he needed to punish her and how else could he do it? This explanation was acceptable to the patient's mother, and was not mentioned to authorities even when the patient was hospitalized for her dangerous acting out behaviors. In this case, the full extent of her abuse by both the stepfather and the

---

[2]While I am not aware of research that specifically studies the importance of verbalizing in autobiographical memories, I think this finding from my own practice is consistent with research on the importance of rehearsal in memory storage and retrieval.

neglectful mother was first consciously experienced when this woman had her first child and suddenly realized the degree of maternal neglect she had experienced. This memory of neglect and its impact was confirmed not so much by the mother's words as by the mother's continued lack of engagement around the seriousness of these past events, her continued defense of her husband, the acknowledged perpetrator, and her continued insistence that her daughter not speak of this to relatives even though these relatives could have given her the financial help she required in order to continue treatment.

In yet another instance of abuse that was continuously remembered, the victim, a young girl, recalled trying to communicate to adults — teachers, doctors, and therapists — the extent of her distress while not violating her parents' injunctions to keep silent. This led to some exceedingly bizarre behavior, some dramatic lies, and several interventions by social agencies. On each occasion, the parents, who were exceedingly intelligent, verbal, and in respected professions, were able to persuade authorities to leave the family alone and the most severe interpretation they got was the statement that their interactions seemed almost incestuous. The bizarreness of her home environment was alleviated by an intense relationship with a brother. Although he too was physically and sexually abusive, he was able to confirm the crazy reality that they called home, and when they managed to escape to college they would make up skits about the family — humor was one of their greatest strengths. Once, my patient submitted a play based on a family incident as her final project in a course. Her teacher commented that it was well written but was so improbable that she should learn to use more realistic scenarios. Although she and her brother at times had different memories of the same incident, or one remembered some incidents that the other forgot, the fact that so many incidents had the same qualities allowed them both to recognize how disturbed their family had been.

Often when abuse was not recalled until adulthood or until the middle of treatment, the abuse occurred at the hands of a loved parent the patient was very dependent on and may have occurred when the parent was in an altered state of consciousness due to alcohol, drugs, or dissociation. Often, while in this state, the parent behaved in a way that was completely at odds with his or her general demeanor at home and in public. Lack of recall of abuse is not limited to instances of sexual abuse.

> I recall a woman who seemed, during the initial consultation, like one of the most terrified people I had ever met. She had come into treatment because of panic attacks and multiple phobias. I asked routine questions about discipline at home, parents' drug and alcohol abuse, and so on. The patient reported that there was never any physical punishment. Her father did occasionally drink too much and could be verbally abusive but was never physical. This history didn't mesh with the terrified woman in my office. Since she had very few memories of childhood I encouraged her to speak to siblings and childhood friends to see what they recalled about her childhood. One day, soon after I made this suggestion, she arrived at my office somewhat shaken and reported that by chance she had run into her best friend from high school who started to tell her how scared she, the friend, used to be at my patient's home. "Why?" "Don't you remember, your father used to sit at the dinner table with a loaded gun on his lap. Once he made your younger brother kneel at his feet and pointed the gun to his head. Another time we came upon your father in the garage; it looked like he was planning to commit suicide." All of this had been repressed. The patient was later able to confirm her friend's recollections with her siblings.

Often in families with intense physical abuse the children are effectively psychologically isolated from each other, with the result that they cannot unite and join forces; the parents' motto could be "divide and conquer." The boy who fears his father's drunken rages feels ashamed at his relief when his brother gets in trouble and he is spared. The older sibling who has already been through a great deal of abuse may try to warn his younger siblings, but may do so in an excessively harsh, abusive manner that is itself abusive and a cause for subsequent shame, guilt, and anger from siblings. It's each child for him- or herself. To care about your siblings is to experience the unbearable helplessness of not being able to protect the people you love. In addition, the normal feelings of sibling rivalry, often exacerbated in a home with little good feeling to go around, become mixed up by the reality of abuse. Often people from these homes are so estranged from their siblings that have not talked to one another about their experiences until an outsider, a therapist, makes the suggestion. With one person I have treated, these discussions with her brother and sister have helped all three understand their histories better — together they seem able to construct or reconstruct a coherent narrative. They each remember parts of their history that make no sense without each other's parts. While all the siblings remember considerable severe physical abuse, their parents have no recall at all. In my clinical experience frequently, each individual in the family remembers better the times their siblings were abused and they were mere bystanders. This seems to be a fairly common phenomenon that I think can be explained by the tendency of people to dissociate when they themselves are in physical danger but to stay present when they witness someone else's abuse.

Often siblings' memories differ in the details but the general atmosphere is confirmed. At times there is disagreement over who was the object of some physical exchange but agreement on the details of the abuse. This is consistent with some of the cognitive literature on memory that suggests that details can be implanted and faces can be confused but the general event is retained. In most of this literature, the plasticity of memory that is found regards the details of an event, not the main action (Loftus and Ketcham 1991, 1994).

> An early treatment I conducted many years before sexual abuse was in the news was of a young woman with many somatic and psychological symptoms — severe pain in intercourse, nightmares, suicidal ideation, panic attacks, depression, and low self esteem. The patient knew at the beginning of treatment that her father had been an alcoholic and that she had been scared of him. During treatment we discovered that she had found a way to space out when he came into her room to punish her, and as we were able to track her dissociating during the sessions she began to recall previously unavailable incidents of her father's

extreme physical cruelty and sadism. After the first year and a half of treatment she awoke from a dream with an intense hypnagogic image of a white porcelain bowl of bloody corn-flakes. Several months later she remembered the day she was all alone in the house; her father was drunk, and had come up and raped her. She then had showered and watched the blood in the white porcelain tub, gone down to the kitchen, and had a bowl of cornflakes. She never remembered the event until the night she called me. This treatment was interrupted when I began an internship and so I don't know if she ever confronted her mother or sisters, but the loss of several intense symptoms following the recall of this event, convinced us of the validity of her memories.

The relationship between presenting symptoms, course of treatment, and validity of interpretations or historical reconstructions is complex and problematic. Patients can show improvement because of an ongoing relationship with a caring therapist even if the therapist's interpretations are incorrect. Certainly patients of Kleinians, Jungians, Freudians, and interpersonalists, may all improve, praise their respective therapists, and yet have been offered over the course of treatment completely different interpretations of their presenting problems. A study of schizophrenics found that patient's anxiety, as measured by corticosteroid levels, diminished when they had a psychotic insight (Sachar et al. 1972). Thus it should come as no surprise that patients' anxiety is diminished by an interpretation that offers a coherent narrative of their life, even if this interpretation is incorrect. How then can I make the statement that the severity of my patient's symptoms, and the relief of these symptoms following her "recall" of being raped by her father, convinced me that this indeed had happened? In this particular instance, I had never mentioned the possibility of incest, the patient had been quite startled and terrified by the memory, her physical pains diminished after this recollection, and her intense nightmares diminished as well. She did not want to speak further about the incest but was immediately convinced the memory was real. Other memories of her childhood, memories that were confirmed and shared by other family members, were consistent with the possibility of sexual abuse. There had been repeated instances of her father going into a rage, often when he had been drinking. The whole family had been terrified of him.

In general I find it easier to work with memories that a patient has in the course of treatment, or memories that were always present. I find that I am more uncertain about memories of patients who begin treatment with me after several prior treatments in which memories occurred and were worked on, or after membership in twelve-step programs led to the onset of memories. It is difficult for me to articulate the precise quality of evidence; nonetheless there is something about the process of remembering—a process that often involves tentative versions of events, some of which are eliminated while others become clarified and gain a sense of conviction, a process that may involve cold, detached recall of events, followed or preceded by somatic symptoms or affective storms that are not consciously attached to any images or incidents. Often it is this process that gives me a sense of conviction or continues to leave me in doubt. In the normal course of treatment there is time to wait and see, time to be tentative and inquiring. Unfortunately, this period of uncertainty is often exceedingly anxiety provoking and sometimes patients may decide to confront families before working through their own experience.

Critics of recovered memory argue that not only sexual abuse is traumatic and therefore question why patients don't remember other repressed traumatic events such as medical procedures during the course of their treatment. In fact they do. Patrick Casement (1982, 1991) vividly describes the case of a young woman who was seriously burned at an early age and had repressed the details and affect associated with this experience until a critical point in therapy. Several patients of mine have recalled intrusive or painful medical procedures that were not consciously available to them at the start of treatment. Some were able to confirm and clarify memories of such procedures with their parents. Parents are generally much more able to remember and confirm painful events that their children lived through that they were not objectively responsible for than events that involved their own violations, their own infliction of pain. One person was able with her mother's help to confirm several memories of a painful procedure that occurred when she was a year and a half old. This woman had always had pictures and sensations linked with this event but assumed she had been older when it occurred, and didn't have the name for the procedure until it was supplied by her mother.

The complexity of seeking external confirmation of recovered memories is illustrated in the following case reported by Davies and Frawley (1994). They describe a woman they call Melissa, who during treatment recovered a memory of her father's sexual abuse of her sister while she, Melissa, watched. She recalled puzzling over the incident, thinking to herself that if this were really happening, surely her mother would come. Her father threatened her at the time saying that if she talked about this, people would think she was crazy. She also recalled that several years after the abusive behavior had stopped she finally spoke to her sister about it. Her sister said that Melissa must be crazy—nothing like this had ever happened. Melissa then spoke to her mother. Her mother also called her crazy and filthy minded.

Despite an intensive treatment with much progress, Davies and Frawley report that Melissa continued to be periodically plagued by doubts—perhaps she had made this all up. Four years after terminating treatment Melissa wrote the following letter to her therapist:

> The most extraordinary thing has happened. It is not so much the event itself, which could have been anticipated . . . but the remarkable effect it has had upon me, even after all the years of analysis. My sister has remembered her abuse!! She flew in last weekend just to talk to me. She said she could not bear to talk of it on the phone. We both sat up all night long . . . I guess it had to be at night. We talked and cried all night long. Some things we remembered exactly the same . . . some things slightly differently . . . but all the essentials were close enough!
>
> But back to the effects I mentioned. Literally within seconds of realizing what it was she was about to say I experienced the most extraordinary and overwhelming sense of relief. It is truly difficult to put the sensation, the experience of mental and physical release, of tension actually flowing from my body into adequate words. My immediate impulse was to scream my sanity from the rooftops. So many of the tears were for my dead crazy self. She died so fast after all these years of vitality. My sister said it was all real; one other human voice in my midnight prison, and the uncertainty was gone. I was irrevocably sane. [pp. 104–108]

This vignette illustrates how frequently a patient's family does not recall the events that the patient has remembered. A family member or an alleged perpetrator's denial or disagreement with a memory does not confirm or disconfirm it, and yet it will often precipitate further doubting, alienation, and despair. Patients who are able to find confirmation of long held memories, or newly found ones, experience this as both good and bad news. The good news is they are not crazy and this really did happen. The bad news is they are not crazy and this really did happen. And the worst news of all is that other people must have known and did nothing.

Therapists can't simply assume that the more bizarre incidents are fabrications—often extremely bizarre incidents are confirmed by other family members.

> One severely abused patient began to remember an incident that at first neither she nor her therapist believed. She claimed that when she was about 3 some friends called her from the sandbox to tell her that her mother was screaming for her help. She recalled going back home, terrified, sensing that something was terribly wrong. Her grandmother was there and her mother was screaming that the cat was dead, it had been killed in the clothes dryer. She claimed that she recalled thinking as a child, "My mother killed the cat—this was no accident." She was most struck by her conviction at this early age that her mother had intentionally killed the cat and was acting as though a horrible accident had occurred. Many years later, while visiting her grandmother, the patient asked about this incident. The grandmother described how awful it had been that day. She and the mother were talking when the grandmother asked about the thumping sound that was coming from the dryer. The mother explained that it was probably some sneakers she had put in. The grandmother believed that the mother had put the cat in the dryer as a way of getting out of a car trip with her husband—she too felt that the mother had intentionally killed the cat. This was only one of many incidents that seemed too bizarre and were often remembered in a vague dreamlike way, that in the end were confirmed.

THE DECISION TO SEEK CONFIRMATION

Patients' decisions to seek confirmation of memories represent an important treatment issue. It is important to distinguish confirmation that can be gotten from objective documents—records from schools, hospitals, old phone books, the army, newspaper clippings, and so on—from confirmation by other family members that inevitably becomes some form of confrontation. The decision to search for external validation of personal memories is a difficult one and needs to be approached with some caution. It can prematurely foreclose the free associative search for self-understanding, it can substitute a detective search for an experiential journey, it can overwhelm patients with information they are not ready for, or it can lead to an increase in self-doubt.

The decision to seek external validation from family members is potentially explosive and needs to be fully explored; often it can have disastrous effects on both the patient and other family members. For patients it can lead to alienation from other family members if their own thoughts and memories are not shared, or if they are told they are crazy. It can also precipitate a crisis for other family members whose own memories, shame, guilt, fear, and anger are abruptly surfaced. For some family members, confrontation elicits conflicts of loyalty. At times patients are scapegoated, the target for anger at the disruption they are causing. In other confrontations, patients are relieved to finally get the support that they have always longed for. Patients should explore their fantasies and expectations, and if they have not considered the possibility that their memories will not be met with confirmation, they should be carefully questioned about this by their therapist. As we have seen in the case of Melissa and others, a family's rejection of a patient's memories is not necessarily a true indication that the events did not take place, but it can be quite devastating. Many patients prefer to think they are crazy and making it all up than to consider that their families were truly abusive. Often patients rush to confront family members as a way to deflect attention from their own internal struggles, or as a way of seeking out assurance that they still can be loved by their family even if they speak of their experiences, and they are often sorely disappointed.

At times confirmation of specific memories cannot be obtained but family members other than the perpetrator may recall the perpetrator's style of interaction that they feel would be consistent with the recalled incident, and they may find it easy to believe and support the patient. Often, whether or not the patient's recollections are accurate, the family resents having to deal with the intensity of their struggles and symptoms and the subsequent disruption of their familiar family mythology. Family members' reactions are often exceedingly informative even when they are not what the patient is desiring.

One woman consulted me with her mother after refusing to see her father who she believed had sexually abused her as a child. The content of the alleged abuse seemed to me to indicate poor judgment rather than sexual abuse. The mother's response indicated an intense need to deny the atmosphere of fear that was pervasive in the family home. This atmosphere was described by the father, a former policeman, who readily acknowledged how he had been a very scary and impulsive father and husband. Here the daughter's description of sexual abuse seemed more a way of representing an ongoing, chronic problem in the family of terror, neglect, and the absence of safety. It was easy to see how, in the context of this family, the father's use of an intrusive medical procedure that had been encouraged by the family doctor could have been experienced as a sexual violation. The mother seemed completely passive, both then and now, incapable of understanding or protecting her daughter.

Another family consulted me after one daughter told some family members that she had been sexually abused by her older brother. While the abuse was denied by the brother, other family members painted a picture of him as the family bully whose frequent tantrums were indulged by both parents. The brother had no recollection of sexually abusive behavior or of bullying behavior and resented this characterization. While sexual abuse was never confirmed, the pattern of bullying, along with the brother's denial and his parents' indulgence of his demands, was something that most family members could agree on and work with.

In yet another family, a woman confronted her mother and sister with her own long standing memories of childhood sexual abuse by the alcoholic father, whom the mother had long since divorced. The mother claimed not to know about the sexual abuse but did supply information about the father's prior history of obscene phone calls and her early concerns about how he would behave with his daughters. The nonabused sister—a much more constricted and responsible-appearing woman—was devastated by the revelation that her sister had been sexually abused and that she had no memories, and she went into treatment.

Recently a woman who has always known about a sexually abusive incident with an older brother decided to speak of it for the first time. Her brother had no recall of these incidents, but was not especially angry at the accusations and was primarily concerned that somehow they'd be able to work this through. He wouldn't apologize for events that he couldn't remember but he didn't abandon the sister who accused him. They both expressed their love for each other and their longing to be able to get past this. Their reactions were in striking contrast to the parents who instantly took the brother's side, insisting that this was all made up by their difficult daughter. The parents' reaction became a signal to me that a central issue for the woman was her parents' differential treatment of the siblings, and the woman's sense of being neglected, ignored, and pathologized.

In some families it is not only a specific incident of abuse that is denied but the idea that they were anything less than an ideal family. The patient's parents and family members are shocked at the thought of any abuse and give a description of the family that might sound to most therapists too good to be true—a sort of modern-day Ozzie and Harriet that leads one to realize that no matter what did or did not happen it would not have impact on the official family story. At times this kind of response confirms the general experience the patient had while growing up—the sense that no one would listen or care and that they would never be believed. Even when the perpetrator has acknowledged the abusive actions, other family members may refuse to explore what they knew and when, or how they didn't know and why. Often the fact of abuse, while in the foreground for much of the victim's life, remains in the foreground for only a very brief moment in the experience of the other family members. It cannot fit into the family's story of the family—the revisited pain of this neglect can be as disturbing as the specific memories of the abuse. The very silence of family members often made the patient unsure if they were remembering correctly—"How could this have happened to me if it doesn't seem part of our collective history and our family stories?"

A very painful instance of this occurs when children confront mothers with evidence of abuse by the mother's boyfriends or husbands and are met with nonchalance. At times this seems to confirm a patient's memory that her mother seemed to sacrifice her to the perpetrator to buy time for herself or to keep her husband happy. At other times the patient was conscious of deflecting the father's or boyfriend's attention to keep the mother from being beaten—a sacrifice that was never acknowledged. In such instances recall of abuse involves profound disillusionment with both parents, and an intense experience of loneliness—often this is a reexperience of a profound sense of loneliness that permeated their childhoods.

Confirmation of memories of abuse has complex consequences. At times the knowledge that parts of your history that completely affect the story you tell yourself and others about your life were lost for many years can be unnerving to patient and analyst alike. I recall my own anxiety when my first patient recalled being raped by her father—I felt as though the ground under me gave way. If this woman, about the same age as I, could have her whole sense of personal history change, literally, overnight, how could I be sure that I knew and could believe my own life story? I've seen this reaction repeatedly among my supervisees and I think it accounts for some of the deep resistance and skepticism that the subject of repressed memories engenders.

Patients who uncover repressed memories during treatment and then have these memories confirmed, have discovered the power of psychoanalysis. Psychoanalysts and therapists who witness this often feel reaffirmed in their belief in their profession—a profession that generally has few immediate rewards and relatively little direct, unambiguous feedback (Blechner, personal communication). It is easy to understand how this can become intoxicating and can lead patient and analyst to believe all new memories that occur, and to mistakenly search for memories of lost traumas as the key to a successful treatment.

But this desire is dangerous and misleading. Many people have successful therapies and analyses without uncovering repressed memories and even people who uncover real memories can have unreal memories that were never lost. The likelihood of a memory being veridical doesn't seem to be in any simple way related to the age at which it took place. Nor does the accuracy of a memory follow upon the conviction the patient has of its truth, or the sense the analyst has of its plausibility. For example, one of the people I mentioned above, whose mother filled in the memory gaps about her painful medical procedure at the age of one and a half, had another memory that she had always had of a pleasant trip to Europe. This memory included a very detailed impression of the hotel the family had stayed in. This memory turned out to be false — the image, a combination of several rooms and hotels. The person accurately remembered the trip to Europe, but the detailed impressions of the hotel in Switzerland, details which she frequently recounted, were totally inaccurate. This inaccuracy of memory has no consequences and is an inaccuracy of peripheral details. But it underscores some of the complexity and difficulty of memories. The memory of the hotel room was vivid, never questioned; as far as the woman knew she had always had this memory, yet it turned out to be false. The memory of a painful medical procedure at the age of one and a half was retrieved in the course of treatment, was questionable because it occurred at such a young age, and yet this memory was confirmed.

In conclusion, it can be said that much remains to be learned about autobiographical memory in general and our patient's memories in particular. Regardless of some theorists' claim that only a patient's experience is important, most patients and their analysts continue to think and feel very differently about events that upon recall are capable of external confirmation from those that are not (Wolff 1988). Our patients' and their significant others' responses to confirmation are complex processes that require further analytic work. To date, the people I have worked with, feel, like Melissa, greatly relieved by the presence of external validation even though what is confirmed is all too frequently the abuse and neglect by people they were completely dependent upon; at least with this confirmation they can begin to enjoy some confidence in their sense of reality.

REFERENCES

Baddeley, A. (1990). *Human Memory: Theory and Practice.* Boston: Allyn & Bacon.

Berliner, L., and Williams, L. M. (1994). Memories of child sexual abuse: a response to Lindsay and Read. In *Applied Cognitive Psychology* 8:279-388.

Brenneis, C. B. (1994). Belief and suggestion in the recovery of memories of childhood sexual abuse. *Journal of the American Psychoanalytic Association* 42:1027-1054.

Briere, J. (1989). *Therapy for Adults Molested as Children.* New York: Springer.

Briere, J., and Conte, J. (1993). Self reported amnesia for abuse in adults molested as children. *Journal of Traumatic Stress* 6:21-31.

Casement, P. (1982). Some pressures on the analyst for physical contact during the reliving of an early trauma. *International Review of Psychoanalysis* 9:279-286.

—— (1991). *Learning from the Patient.* New York: Guilford.

Crews, F. (1994a). The myth of repressed memory. *The New York Review of Books,* November 17, pp. 54-60.

—— (1994b). Victims of repressed memory. *The New York Review of Books,* December 1, pp. 49-58.

Davies, J. M., and Frawley, M. G. (1994). *Treating the Adult Survivor of Childhood Sexual Abuse.* New York: Basic Books.

Ferenczi, S. (1932). The confusion of tongues between adults and the child. *International Journal of Psycho-Analysis* 30:225.

Grossman, L. R., and Pressley, M., eds. (1994). Special issue: Recovery of memories of childhood sexual abuse. *Applied Cognitive Psychology* 8.

Herman, J. (1992). *Trauma and Recovery.* New York: Basic Books.

Lindsay, D. S., and Read, J. D. (1994). Psychotherapy and memories of childhood sexual abuse: a cognitive perspective. *Applied Cognitive Psychology* 8:281-339.

Loftus, E., and Ketcham, K. (1991). *Witness for the Defense.* New York: St. Martin's.

—— (1994). *The Myth of Repressed Memory: False Memory and Allegations of Sexual Abuse.* New York: St. Martin's.

Masson, J. (1984). *The Assault on Truth.* New York: Farrar, Straus, & Giroux.

Person, E. S., and Klar, H. (1994). Establishing trauma: the difficulty distinguishing between memories and fantasies. *Journal of the American Psychoanalytic Association* 42:1055–1083.

Robbins, L. C. (1963). The accuracy of parental recall of aspects of child development and of child rearing practices. *Journal of Abnormal and Social Psychology* 66:261–270.

Rose, S. (1992). *The Making of Memory*. New York: Anchor.

Sachar, E. J., Kanter, S., Buie, D., et al. (1972). Psychoendocrinology of ego disintegration. In *Annual Review of the Schizophrenic Syndrome 1971*, ed. R. Cancro. New York: Brunner/Mazel.

Spence, D. (1982). *Narrative Truth and Historical Truth*. New York: Norton.

Terr, L. (1990). *Too Scared To Cry*. New York: Harper & Row.

——— (1994). *Unchained Memories*. New York: Basic Books.

Wolff, P. H. (1981). The real and the reconstructed past. *Psychoanalysis and Contemporary Thought* 11:379–414.

13

The Therapy Client as Plaintiff: Clinical and Legal Issues for the Treating Therapist

LAURA S. BROWN

Until recently, the thought that one's therapy client might become the plaintiff in a lawsuit was not a common expectation for most treating therapists. Dealings with legal matters were consigned to those colleagues willing to *a priori* tolerate the demands of the justice system; court-referred clients were perceived as the most common and only barely acceptable manner in which any reasonable therapist might make contact with lawyers and courts. Most therapists were happy with this belief that they were safe from encounters with lawyers and courtrooms.

While this image of a wall between the world of psychotherapy and that of the courtroom has always contained more than a hint of denial (after all, anyone's client can be hit by a drunk driver, slip on a wet floor, or otherwise accidentally encounter the threshold conditions for becoming a plaintiff), no therapist can any longer ignore the uncomfortable reality that the person being treated in the supposedly sacrosanct space of the consulting room may now file a legal action against the perpetrator of her/his childhood sexual abuse, a decision that will commonly lead the therapist as well as the client into a lengthy period of involuntary contact with lawyers and courtrooms.

In most states (37 as of this writing), legislatures have extended the statute of limitations for the filing of civil actions against the perpetrators of childhood sexual abuse. Most of these statutes allow people to sue, with a statute of limitations starting at the point when, as adults, they recover previously unavailable memories of childhood sexual abuse. Others also allow litigation when a person has never forgotten the abuse, but has only recently come to understand that the sexual abuse, and not their intrinsic badness or unhappy fortune, was the likely cause of difficulties that they experienced in their life. Each of these are realizations that commonly emerge in therapy, often well after it has commenced. Adult survivors who were once barred by statute from bringing such lawsuits because the events in question had occurred so long ago are now increasingly choosing this as an avenue for obtaining amends, revenge, reparations, and justice. They are doing so at a point in treatment when the therapist has developed a relationship of care, trust, and loyalty with the client, and neither can nor wants to terminate his or her care of the patient in the face of this new challenge.

Almost invariably, these lawsuits seek damages for injuries to the adult survivor's mental health, since these are the most common and long-lasting damages. They are also the ones that are usually easiest to identify, since the links between childhood sexual abuse and physical injury are rarely clear by the time a survivor has reached adulthood. When such a claim of emotional distress damages is made, the plaintiff (the person bringing the lawsuit) has as a matter of law waived the confidentiality of therapy, past and ongoing, and the therapist's work with the client is likely to be placed at the center of the legal, adversarial process about to unfold. The therapy and the therapist become central players in the drama of the lawsuit against an alleged perpetrator, who is often the parent, stepparent, or other close relative of the patient.

Some therapists, uncomfortable or even frightened by the legal process, may attempt to subtly coerce clients who are considering litigation to avoid this possibility. These therapists will spend more than ample time in therapy exploring in overly graphic detail with the client the various horrors attendant on going to court, and the potential for distress that will undoubtedly be present as a result of bringing the lawsuit. Commonly this is done somewhat unconsciously by the therapist, who consciously asserts only a realistic desire to protect the patient from the potential retraumatization of the legal process.

Other therapists, who may naively underestimate what is likely to occur during a lawsuit, may do the converse, and attempt to persuade clients that a lawsuit is a useful or even necessary tool of recovery, waxing eloquent as to the healing power of confronting the perpetrator under oath and receiving the validation of a jury. This is a therapeutic strategy that Sonne and Pope (1991) have described as "intrusive advocacy" by a therapist, and is likely to reflect some of the therapist's own unexplored anger at the alleged perpetrator or even a reenactment of personal experiences of victimization, acted out via the patient.

Most prudent therapists will, of course, do neither of these things, and will cede to the patient the right to make this important decision, offering support for the ambivalence felt and the exploration that the client needs to do to take this step, and laying aside their own fears and desires in this as in other matters in the treatment. But most therapists, lay persons to the legal world, will also be concerned and uncertain regarding what they and their clients will face in the coming months, and in search of information about how to best move with their clients through the process and decipher the complexities of the legal and clinical situations that will emerge.

This chapter is written for those therapists. It draws upon my past decade of experience as a forensic psychologist, evaluating adult women and men who are bringing or contemplating civil claims based on allegations of childhood sexual abuse, and consulting to the treating therapists of adult survivors engaged in and/or contemplating litigation. It also derives from my work as a psychotherapist who treats adult survivors of sexual and other childhood abuse or adult victimization.

Some of my experiences are unique in their quality to the setting in which I practice; Washington State was the first state to pass laws extending the statute of limitations, and the legal community of the Puget Sound area is blessed with many psychologically savvy attorneys who are familiar with the complexities of working for and bringing lawsuits on behalf of adult survivors of childhood sexual abuse. Consequently, the optimism and positive attitude that

I have been able to develop about most legal practitioners and the legal process itself flies in the face of common stereotypes about attorneys. However, my work has also allowed me to cross the paths of lawyers who did not live up to the standards that my respected legal colleagues have led me to expect; consequently, the possibility that a client's lawyer will be one of the latter group is amply taken into account in my discussion here. I wish to also underscore that the information given in this chapter does not constitute legal advice, or apply in specific to all jurisdictions. Therapists are strongly advised to retain and consult an attorney knowledgable on issues of mental health practice should the need arise.

AN INTRODUCTION TO THE CULTURE OF CIVIL LITIGATION

When encountering a strange culture for the first time, it can be helpful to become conversant with its language and customs so as not to inadvertently violate taboos or fall into harm. The legal world is just such a foreign culture for most therapists, and this section contains a brief introduction to some of the important terms and guiding concepts informing that milieu. My goal here is not to create forensic practitioners, but rather to help therapists to know what to expect, and how to translate for their own illumination the jargon of litigation.

Civil litigation exists to allow private citizens to seek redress for their wrongs, particularly when no crime has been committed or when the criminal justice system cannot or will not pursue the case because of statutory or evidentiary considerations. For adult survivors of sexual abuse, the latter is normally the case; although sexual abuse of children is a crime, the statute for its prosecution may have expired, and evidence necessary for a criminal trial absent. However, the survivor has standing to sue in civil court because the alleged perpetrator had a duty of care not to harm the survivor, and is accused of breaching that civil duty.

In most states, civil litigation is conducted according to federally promulgated rules of evidence and procedure, in which the steps and standards for pursuing a lawsuit are laid out, although some details will vary with state law and local custom. Most survivor lawsuits come under the rubric of what is usually defined as "personal injury" or tort law. This means that the lawyer does not require any special sort of certification or training past the law degree to practice in this field, which is true for almost every aspect of law except tax law. Some attorneys have done hundreds of survivor lawsuits and are almost as expert in the psychological issues of survivors as are most therapists. Some attorneys are doing their first such case with no idea of what lies ahead. Personal injury suits are generally conducted on a contingency fee basis; this means that the lawyer collects payment contingent on the plaintiff winning, and receives some preagreed percentage of the damages awarded. However, this does not mean that there are no costs to the plaintiff, who must pay the fees of court reporters, messenger services, process servers, expert witnesses, and the like, the entire supporting cast of characters necessary for the conduct of a lawsuit.

In a civil suit, there is a plaintiff, the moving party who brings the case, and a defendant, the person or persons alleged to have harmed the plaintiff. The plaintiff begins her suit with a complaint, a concise statement of the harm that has been done and the sort of damages being requested. The burden is placed on the plaintiff to demonstrate liability (the defendant was legally responsible to the plaintiff) and damages (the defendant harmed the plaintiff in a demonstrable way). In some states where community property laws govern marriage, a wife is always sued along with her husband, even when she had no hand in the commission of the wrongful act (and vice versa). For survivors, this may mean that they are suing a non-offending, sometimes beloved and supportive parent or grandparent along with their perpetrator. In some states, the spouse of the perpetrator must be separately found negligent in order to obtain coverage for the lawsuit under insurance policies, which specifically exclude payments for damages from a person's intentional "torts" (bad actions); sexual abuse of a child is commonly considered an intentional tort because it constitutes criminal action. This can, again, lead to complicated family dynamics when the person being accused of negligence is placed in an adversarial position to an otherwise loved and supported younger relative. In those cases where the perpetrator commited the sexual abuse while employed in a responsible position in relationship to the child (e.g., clergy, teacher, coach), the employer may also be the target of the lawsuit under various legal theories that hold employers responsible for the acts of their employees. Concretely, this can mean that rather than simply facing one lawyer on the other side of the case, the client may be encountering a whole phalanx of attorneys representing various defendants and/or their insurance carriers. While the television courtrooms of "Perry Mason" and "L.A. Law" are always full of the drama of witnesses and evidence appearing at the last moment, in the real life of civil litigation this is an almost impossible scenario. (Although Oregon still allows "stealth" expert witnesses to be brought in, the boundaries around this practice are quite strict, and this aberration from federal standards is under review [Judy Snyder, pesonal communication, July 1993].) Instead, much of the time between filing the complaint in a lawsuit and the day of trial is taken up with a lengthy process of *discovery*. This process allows each side to find out precisely what the other side knows and is going to say.

Discovery is accomplished primarily through two means. The first is the *interrogatory*. Interrogatories are lengthy series of questions filed by each side's attorney. They ask everything from the name and address of the parties involved to explicit descriptions of acts of sexual abuse alleged to have been commited. The names of treating therapists and physicians, past and present, are another common topic of inquiry. While the client's attorney can (and probably will) object to some questions as overly intrusive or irrelevant, this does not mean that they will not eventually be asked in further stages of the discovery process. The plaintiff will have to be intimately involved in preparing the answers to interrogatories sent by the defendant; this means that the abuse survivor will be required by the rules of civil litigation to expose information to a perpetrator that she/he may wish to have kept hidden, such as difficulties in current relationships, symptoms that she/he is experiencing, and the like. The preparation of interrogatories is thus an introduction to one of the most difficult aspects of lawsuits, the manner in which they strip away the boundaries of privacy and confidentiality from the life of the plaintiff, who will begin to feel on trial herself.

A second important component of discovery is the *deposition*. Depositions are cross-examinations under oath in front of a court reporter, conducted by the attorney for the other side. Plaintiff and defendant are almost always deposed by one another's lawyers as the central players in the court drama. However, an attorney can cast the deposition net very broadly, deposing the spouses, therapists, friends, and enemies of both parties if any of the above are named in interrogatories as having knowledge germane to the case. The treating therapist should expect to be deposed, because the client, not the therapist, holds the privilege of confidentiality, and has already waived it by claiming emotional damages.

Depositions can be brief or they can last for many hours over a period of several days. In survivor cases, the latter is closer to the norm. Because there is no judge present to rule on the objections made by the attorney not taking the deposition, very difficult and invasive questions may be asked and require answers. Allegations can be made in depositions that are untrue and humiliating to a plaintiff but must still be responded to. For example, a defendant's attorney may imply in a question that the plaintiff was sexually promiscuous as a child, enjoyed the sexual abuse, or is untrustworthy in some manner that renders the claim invalid. To some degree, opposing attorneys use the deposition process as a testing ground, having the chance to observe how well the parties on the other side of the case will stand up to difficult questions.

Because the deposition is taken under oath and constitutes sworn testimony equal to that given in court, it can later be used in the trial to "impeach" the witness by attempting to show meaningful discrepancies between sworn testimony on one occasion as compared to the next. Clients who have spotty or inconsistent memories as a result of their childhood abuse experiences may find themselves taken to task in cross-examination because they are not entirely consistent in everything they say every time. If the treating therapist is being called as a witness, she/he may *not* sit in on the client's deposition as a support person; consequently, it is not helpful for the therapist to promise the client do this, since it is not allowed. In fact, no one who is going to be called in the case may serve in this sort of support role, although the plaintiff's attorney will be present at every deposition. However, that attorney represents only the plaintiff; if the treating therapist wishes representation at the deposition, he or she will have to engage an attorney for that purpose.

Under most circumstances, the treating therapist is *not* the official expert witness (more later about why the treating therapist *should not* fulfill this role). Instead, the therapist is relegated, along with everyone else in the case, to the category of "fact witness," someone with knowledge of facts germane to the case. This means that when the therapist is called for deposition (which happens almost invariably), the opposing attorney in some states may be under no legal obligation to pay the therapist anything except a standard witness fee, which will probably be less than one hundred dollars. This does not mean that the therapist cannot make an attempt to bill for the time spent in preparing for and attending a deposition; but there is no legal guarantee of payment unless the state (such as California) protects the therapist's status as a kind of expert by statute.

Not all lawsuits end up in a courtroom, nor do all of those in a courtroom end up in front of a jury. Some attorneys favor the use of mediation or private arbitration to adjudicate cases. In these settings, an attorney volunteer serves in the judicial role; the setting is more informal (usually the arbitrator's office), and there is commonly a cap set on the level of damages that can be awarded. Sometimes, cases settle out of court after negotiations between the attorneys for all parties. Sometimes when cases go to trial, there is a "bench trial" in which only a judge is present, instead of a jury trial; various factors motivate the decision to go with bench versus jury, usually the attorney's beliefs about which will lead to the best outcome for her/his client. In some jurisdictions, the jury for a civil case will be smaller than that for a criminal trial. The standard of proof in a civil case is lesser; "a preponderance of evidence" is required rather than "beyond a reasonable doubt." A unanimous vote of the jury is not required in civil cases, with various jurisdications accepting 10–2 or 9–3 votes as binding. In many jurisdictions, civil cases carry notions of *contributory negligence;* this concept means that the jury can decide that a plaintiff was harmed, but place a certain percentage of responsibility for the harm on the plaintiff. For the survivor of childhood sexual abuse, who has been struggling to escape self-blame, being told by a jury that she/he is 10 percent liable for the harm can be a devastating message indeed. (Pope [1994] cites a case in which a child who was younger than 10 at the time of the sexual abuse was assigned 10 percent contributory negligence in a survivor lawsuit, so this cannot be dismissed as a possibility, even though it may seem absurd to a therapist).

Defendants can also countersue the plaintiff, claiming that the survivor's lawsuit is malicious, unwarranted, and a cause of emotional damages to the accused perpetrator. While this may seem outrageous, it is perfectly legal, and to some degree may advantage the survivor plaintiff because it renders the accused perpetrator vulnerable to an imposed mental health examination, which can be a source of a good deal of information for the survivor and her/his attorney. However, such a countersuit often recapitulates dynamics in which the child victim was blamed by the perpetrator for "causing" him/her to commit violations on the child, and this can have profound emotional consequences for a survivor that need to be anticipated and taken into account by a treating therapist. More recently, alleged perpetrators have also sued the therapist, a topic to be discussed at greater length later in this chapter.

There are things that civil litigation can and cannot accomplish. It can lead to an award of damages to a plaintiff. But normally, via civil litigation, an accused perpetrator cannot be forced to go into treatment, required to apologize, or sent to jail. In other words, civil litigation does not stop a perpetrator unless that person is deterred by the vision of future risks to the pocketbook. If stopping the perpetrator is the client's most important goal in pursuing the case, there will inevitably be disappointment regardless of the outcome. In some situations the accused perpetrator's costs of defending a lawsuit and paying a judgment will be handled by an insurance company; this means that in some instances, the defendant will not even experience financial consequences. When awards are made by the court, they can still be difficult to collect; one attorney of my acquaintance who frequently works with survivors told me that she had become an expert on the garnishment of wages since that was often the only way to collect, in dribs and drabs, the judgments awarded to her clients. And if the survivor plaintiff loses, she/he may be liable to pay the court costs and attorney fees of the defendant; this is a common request made by each side in a civil case and is entirely legal.

The world of American civil jurisprudence is an adversarial one. Lawyers are trained to fight for their client, to do everything and anything legally possible to win. This may include treating the client, the plaintiff, in a nasty and humiliating manner in an attempt to simply scare her/him out of the case, setting investigators on the client to talk to everyone in her/his life in an attempt to dig up "dirt," and in general making life more difficult for the client. *All* of this is fair game in the legal system. It is important that the client and the therapist both know about these possibilities when entering the decision-making process about whether or not to pursue litigation. While plaintiffs' lawyers will honestly tell a prospective plaintiff that they will make every attempt to minimize the distress and to settle without a trial, ultimately they do not control the outcome perfectly enough to guarantee this protection.

It should be becoming apparent in reading these facts, which create the frame for a survivor's lawsuit, that this process will of necessity become important to and interactive with psychotherapy. As client, therapist, and the therapy process itself are examined in interrogatory and deposition, as the sometimes retraumatizing and revictimizing encounters with the perpetrator and his/her attorney occur, the therapy will be transformed, and both therapist and client will take on new and sometime unwished-for symbolic meanings to one another. Thus a number of questions emerge that warrant careful attention when embarking on this apparently perilous journey outside the safety of the psychotherapy office.

WHEN SHOULD A CLIENT LITIGATE

While it is never the place of a psychotherapist to directly advise a client for or against bringing a lawsuit, there are a number of factors that a therapist can and should raise for the client's careful consideration so that such a step is taken with the maximum of information and care. The therapist must resist any time-oriented pressures from either the survivor client or the lawyer; while it is true that a decision to file a lawsuit must be made timely to conform to statutory limitations, it is even more important that the therapist take this very first opportunity to not transform the therapy into a handmaiden of the lawsuit. Instead, the therapist can refocus the decision-making process on questions that are germane to the treatment: what is the meaning and purpose of this decision for the client, and what is her/his capacity to handle what lies ahead.

It is important to remember that no decision to litigate is cast in concrete; up until the very moment at which trial starts, a plaintiff can make the decision to stop the process. While such a course of action can be costly financially, and has other risks in the form of inviting countersuits, this point is made to illustrate how necessary it is that the client see her- or himself as the moving party in charge of whether this action will go forward. The plaintiff, not the attorney, is the ultimate decision maker. However, once a decision is made to sue, a plaintiff will encounter a series of typical and predictable stressors. The client's assessment of her/his capacity to cope with these stressors is a central function of the therapy process at this stage in the client's decision-making process, because it is useful to have at least considered these matters before filing the complaint and opening the door to the legal process.

What are these predictable stressors? First, telling the story, perhaps more than once, to a stranger, her own lawyer, and possibly to the lawyer's paralegal assistant. While at times this may be therapeutic and empowering, some attorneys seem to feel that it is necessary at this first encounter to test the clients' toughness by subjecting them to the sort of difficult cross-examination–like questions of the sort that the client will always have to deal with later on in the case. Some attorneys are exquisitely sensitive to the nuances of obtaining a survivor's story and the time and care necessary for this process; others, for reasons of their own personality styles or ignorance about the most emotionally effective ways to proceed, will respond obtusely or disbelievingly.

Once a decision has been made by the attorney to take the case on and the lawsuit has been filed, other predictable stressors will occur. The plaintiff will be faced with the necessity of answering many questions put to her/him by the defense attorney in the discovery process. Such questions are likely to feel profoundly invasive and intrusive. The plaintiff's attorney will often require the client to obtain an evaluation from a mental health expert; the defense attorney can make a similar demand on the plaintiff. Having a therapist is not a protection against this, since a treating therapist is not an expert witness and cannot fulfill this role. This means telling the story to yet more people, and having more judgments made about mental health. The fact that the plaintiff has been in therapy, indeed, the plaintiff's entire life history, including prior bad acts and expressions of poor judgment, will be exposed and placed into evidence, while that of the accused perpetrator will remain private, unless the defendant has filed a counterclaim alleging emotional distress caused by the client's lawsuit. The client is likely to feel violated and humiliated at times, betrayed by the legal system, the attorney, and others. These are predictable stressors for any plaintiff in any sort of lawsuit, rendered in sharper contrast by the underlying issue of childhood sexual abuse.

It is imperative for the therapist of any client contemplating such litigation to explore with the client her readiness for this undertaking, and to support the client in making her own decision about capacity to take on a lawsuit. Factors to suggest that a client take into account include the quality of the client's social support network, her capacity to contain affect, the degree of resilience she has developed, and her ego strength. If the lawsuit will require that a nonoffending family member also be sued because of the legal theories governing the case, the survivor must address how this will feel for her, and whether she will be able to cope with some of the inevitable wounds to what might otherwise have been a loving relationship. In several cases where I served as expert, the necessity of suing a mother or grandmother, reluctantly taken on by the survivor, became the emotional breaking point for the plaintiff as the case progressed and the schism between the survivor and a beloved female family member grew greater and greater.

The survivor who is isolated, emotionally overwhelmed, or exceptionally brittle is at increased risk for exacerbation of these difficulties in the context of litigation. A client who is counting on the lawsuit for validation, or for some kind of public statement that what was done to her as a child was wrong, may be in for terrible disappointment when discovering that the most that a lawsuit can offer can be payments for therapy and a chance to finally look the perpetrator in the eye and tell him/her about the effects of the violation. Risks for suicidality and self-harm should be honestly assessed by both therapist and client, since it is not unheard of for the survivor/plaintiff to be sufficiently triggered by factors during litigation to become suicidal and sometimes require inpatient treatment. Resources for such treatment should thus be identified prior to commencing the litigation. The client also needs support from the treating therapist to carefully examine who is being taken care of by a lawsuit; is this genuinely self-motivated self-care, or is this a step taken to please a partner, friend, or even the therapist?

In one case where I recently consulted with a defendant's attorney, an extremely fragile young woman survivor who was currently in an abusive relationship with a drug-using man was coerced by him to bring a lawsuit against her childhood perpetrator as a strategy for increasing drug-buying capital. The treating therapist, although clearly aware (from the content of session notes) of the dynamics of the woman's relationship, was invested in her going through with the litigation as well because of his assessment that it would be the best way to empower herself, and because of his hope, covertly expressed in various reports in the file, that the money from a win might enable her to leave her current abuser. Her attorney had never before taken a case for a survivor, and was unsophisticated as to the potential for difficulties that such a plaintiff might enounter in simply participating in her own lawsuit.

This woman could barely tolerate the stresses of the evaluation procedures, finding herself suicidal and in need of inpatient treatment. Had the case not settled out of court relatively quickly and easily, and without need for her further exposure to question and scrutiny; it is unclear whether or in what emotional condition she would have survived the litigation process. In this case, the plaintiff was taking care of everyone but herself, and it is doubtful that she achieved much by way of emotional resolution. Rather, she was revictimized and reconfirmed in the notion that she existed to serve the emotional needs of others.

In similar cases, when I have been engaged as plaintiff's expert and thus have a direct line of communication with the plaintiff's attorney, I have intervened with the lawyer to share my concerns about the risks to the client of continued participation in this venture, no matter how much this heightened vulnerability appeared to be evidence of greater damages that would be ultimately useful in the litigation. However, the treating therapist is most commonly the first person who is in a position to examine this question of whether the survivor will be exploited in some manner by bringing a lawsuit; not all forensic evaluators see it as within their purview to make comments such as these to attorneys. While litigation *can* be empowering to some survivors in some circumstances, and can be the experience that transforms their life in a positive way, for others it is equally likely to be profoundly disorganizing and distressing. Helping the client to assess which of these possibilities is most likely to be the case for her/him is a direction that allows treatment to stay focused on the client's therapy needs and goals, rather than becoming primarily adjunctive to the litigation process.

NEEDS AND CONCERNS OF THE THERAPIST

The treating therapists often have little or no say as to whether they will be thrust into the middle of the client's lawsuit. Although, as mentioned earlier, it is not unheard of for therapists to subtly (or not-so-subtly) suggest to clients that a lawsuit would be a counter-therapeutic choice, most therapists attempt to restrain their own anxieties and support the client, as an autonomous adult, in making this choice. However, such support does not come without costs. My observation has been that most therapists are frightened of the court system. It feels wrong to therapists, who are after all people trained to privilege subjectivities and phenomenological realities, to have "truth" exposed in an adversarial process in which the merits of a case are sometimes secondary to the skills of the attorneys in determining an outcome. The factors upon which therapists and attorneys construct reality are often so different as to make communication very difficult. Both professions are, additionally, often quite naive as to the norms and assumptions of the other, and may rely upon ·inaccurate popular stereotypes.

Because it can be quite stressful for a therapist to have a client pursuing a lawsuit, it is important for the therapist to identify those elements of self-care necessary for maintaining the frame of therapy in the face of this intrusion. Additionally, the therapist needs to identify and respond to her/his own resentments toward the client that almost inevitably will be evoked as the lawsuit progresses and the life of the therapist is made consequently more difficult.

It is as helpful for the therapist to assess readiness and strengths and weaknesses in the face of the lawsuit as it is for the prospective survivor plaintiff to do so. This assessment is not to determine whether or not a client should sue, since that decision ought not to take the therapist's needs into account. However, it is important so that the therapist can plan what will be needed in terms of one's own consultation, personal therapy, and legal support in order to guarantee continued emotional availability to clients when they undertake to sue perpetrators.

There are some common risks for the therapist of the plaintiff. These include the development of resentment, involuntary exposure and disclosure of information about the therapist to clients via the legal discovery process, and becoming the target of lawsuits from perpetrators who blame the presence of memories on therapist misconduct. As therapists, we must ask ourselves whether and to what degree we may come to resent our client for exposing us to a legal process, and then to carefully, and in an ongoing manner, examine how such resentments may be entering and affecting the dynamics of therapy. It is not unreasonable to feel this resentment, as therapists often do at various points in any therapy process. However, resenting a client for forcing our participation in a lawsuit is a special situation. Legal cases are lengthy; the opportunities to be reminded of this resentment are many and recur intrusively. The costs to the therapist in professional consultation, personal therapy, legal fees, and time lost from work for testifying may far outweigh the fees collected from the client.

Consequently it can become very important for the therapist in this situation to discover the value obtained from participation in this process as well as the real or feared losses and costs. By treating a client who is going through litigation, therapists are given a wealth of new information that constitutes the equivalent of an intensive course in mental health and the law, a learning experience that, while unsought and often unwished for, empowers therapists to become more skillful and savvy practitioners in the future. The lawsuit can also be a source of clinically rich material; if therapists avoid resisting and blaming its presence for difficulties in the treatment, and instead treat it as they would any other external phenomenon with important meaning in the client's life, they may find that the layers of meaning arising from this new and different encounter between survivor and perpetrator opens up lines of exploration in treatment that might have been otherwise invisible or ignored.

The therapist must explore what her/his fears are as well, particularly fears of exposure. When the therapist is deposed, the opposing attorney may ask questions that will reveal information not previously known to the client; if the maintenance of a nondisclosing stance has been important to a therapist's theoretical model, she or he will be faced with this involuntary self-disclosure and need to find strategies to fold this reality into how further treatment will be. The client may learn via deposition in the course of a lawsuit that the therapist is, for example, a survivor, or that the therapist has had complaints filed against him or her in the past; the client may hear the therapist's professional orientation critiqued, sometimes with disdain, by the expert witness for the other side. Clients may become angry or confused by new information about the therapist, who must in turn not only cope with her own feelings about this involuntary exposure, but also deal with this as new grist for the therapeutic mill.

If the client recovered memories of abuse during the course of therapy, there is some likelihood, given the current zeitgeist, that the therapist will be accused by the opposing attorney of having implanted those memories by the knowing or careless use of suggestive or intrusive techniques, issues addressed elsewhere in this volume. The therapist's strategy for working with the client may become the unwanted focus of attention in the lawsuit, with the question of the guilt of the perpetrator lost in the defendant's attorney's strategy of blaming the therapist. While there is currently little empirical data to suggest that most therapists either use such treatment strategies on a *regular* basis (although many therapists agree that they will use techniques such as hypnosis or visualization under *some* circumstances [Poole et al. 19954]), or that most therapists act in ways that might hypothetically create confabulated memories, the current social climate created by the False Memory Syndrome Foundation (FMSF) cannot help but inform what will occur in a lawsuit brought by a survivor with recovered memories. Since the Gary Ramona case, in which the father of a survivor successfully sued her treating therapist for damages due to the memories recovered by his daughter (who, it should be noted, did not bring a lawsuit against her father until after he had sued her therapists), many therapists have become extraordinarily fearful that should their client sue a perpetrator, the perpetrator will in turn sue the therapist. This is not an entirely unreasonable fear, especially if a client's alleged perpetrator is a member of FMSF, an organization that appears to have as one of its icons the "Bad Therapist," a stance that may implictly encourage accused perpetrators to attempt legal action against the person treating their accuser.

FALSE-MEMORY LAWSUITS AGAINST THERAPISTS

Today, in the light of the Ramona verdict, many therapists working with adult survivors are extremely fearful of being sued by an alleged perpetrator, even when their clients have not brought a lawsuit or done anything concretely threatening to the person who they believe sexually abused them. It is helpful to understand why and how the Ramona case happened, and what it actually means for treating therapists, because this information can reduce anxieties. Therapists can also increase their self-care as regards this matter by considering certain reasonable preventative steps that cannot themselves stop their client's perpetrator from suing them, but can increase their chances of winning or of having the lawsuit thrown out of court because of lack of legal merit.

Normally, people toward whom a therapist has no formal legal responsibility cannot sue the therapist because they do not have standing to do so; there is no fiduciary relationship to create liability. There are some exceptions to this in the normal course of practice, mostly arising from the legal duty to warn or duty to protect. However, Gary Ramona was given standing to sue by the California courts because his daughter's therapist had brought him into some of her sessions for the purposes of confrontation. By so doing, and by not explicitly informing him that he was *not* the client, the therapist created a legal duty of care to Gary Ramona that gave him standing equal to anyone else treated by the therapist. Additionally, this case was informed by a decision that is present in California case law, but not elsewhere in the United States, that defines health professionals as having a duty of care to nonpatients who they might reasonably foresee could be harmed by their inactions. This combination of circumstances is by and of itself an unusual situation.

It was largely this set of facts combined with the prior California court decision that led to the verdict in Mr. Ramona's favor; the jury, when queried after the verdict, were clear that they were not making a statement about his innocence of his daughter's charges, nor trying to imply that false memories had been created. They simply felt that he had been badly served by a therapist on whom he had placed some reliance. The relatively small size of the verdict in contrast to typical California personal injury verdicts in cases against malpracticing therapists was indicative of the weight given to his harm.

Thus, while the verdict in Ramona is frightening to any therapist because it implies that working with a client who is recovering abuse memories may lead to being the target of litigation, it is not necessarily a portent of things to come because the circumstances that allowed this case to come to court were sufficiently unusual and almost entirely preventable. Therapists working with survivors who are in a memory recovery process would be well served by avoiding invitations to the alleged perpetrator to participate in a therapy session unless there is explicit written informed consent indicating that this person is not the client. Therapists should consult with their own attorneys for advice in developing wording that will withstand challenge under their particular state statutes governing health and mental health care providers. The use of clearly intrusive methods for the supposed recovery of memories, such as hypnosis or sodium amytal interviews, the latter of which also figured prominently in the Ramona case, is another avoidable risk factor. Since the clinical usefulness of such techniques is questionable, given current knowledge regarding the increased suggestibility of hypnotized persons, and because the validity of material obtained in this manner is weaker than that naturally accessed by a client in her own time and at her own pace, a prudent therapist wishing to reduce risk of suits from perpetrators would probably not include such strategies in a treatment plan. The use of hypnosis for such goals as relaxation, pain control, and other non–memory-related issues in therapy should not be seen as potentially problematic, however.

Other approaches to self-care revolve around obtaining support and education that simultaneously enrich the therapist's capacity to practice in this difficult area and serve as protective measures, should a Ramona-style lawsuit appear on the horizon. Evidence of having obtained expert consultation on a case, continuing professional education on the topic of treatment of adult survivors, and knowledge of the research literature on trauma and memory can also be helpful for increasing therapists' confidence that their work falls well within the standard of care and is thus resistant to being challenged legally.

Whether or not the therapist fears a lawsuit from the perpetrator, these approaches to self-care are valuable components of surviving and thriving when one's own client is engaged in litigation. These methods create the clear emotional space necessary for the therapist to be able to listen to the clients' own fears, pain, and ambivalence about the lawsuit, the attorney, and their own decisions, which are the almost inevitable concomitant of being a plaintiff. It permits the therapist to accommodate the presence of this ghostly third party, the lawsuit itself, in the therapy arena during and after the litigation, and to·attend to it as one might any other third party — not fearfully, not in an adversarial manner, but as an important "person" in the life of the client, a "person" of sorts to whom the client has chosen to relate but about whom conflict is felt, and about whom feelings must be explored and meanings analyzed so that the client can make use and sense of his or her relationship to this powerful third party.

DIFFERENTIATING THERAPIST AND EXPERT WITNESS ROLES

Another important element of self-care for the therapist whose client is suing is to make a clear separation between the treatment role and that of the expert witness. Under all but the most unusual of circumstances, a treating therapist should not serve in the expert witness role, and should make this clear to the client and the client's attorney (Golding 1994). Often, the plaintiff's attorney who has little experience with the use of expert witnesses assumes that the treating therapist will serve in this role. Consequently, the burden is on the therapist to define the boundaries of the roles. It is thus useful to clearly assert that you are not the expert witness early in the proceedings, and to persist in this assertion.

There are several reasons why this is an important distinction, some clinical and some legal. The treating therapist commonly does a brief and somewhat informal assessment to determine a working diagnosis and treatment plan, sometimes, but not always, does psychological testing, and rarely expects to carefully read all of the relevant documents in a case. The therapist certainly does not expect to be found in the position of having to examine the client's credibility, or the validity of the client's perceptions; rather, most commonly a therapist joins with the phenomenological reality of the client and apart from clear departures from reality testing is unlikely to challenge the veracity of a client's self-reports. The therapist also has a relationship with the client; over time, when treating someone, the therapist comes to like, respect, value, and perhaps love that person, admire his or her struggles, and wish the best for the client. Consequently, the treatment professional develops a positive bias that is very useful for therapy, but not in the expert witness role.

The expert witness, on the other hand, has a very particular and circumscribed relationship to the plaintiff. Whether the expert for the plaintiff or the defense, the role of the expert is to provide information that will help inform the triers of fact, the judge and jury, to understand issues that are beyond the knowledge base of the average lay juror. To fulfill this role in a survivor lawsuit, an expert witness will take a very thorough and complete psychosocial history, looking for all possible risk factors, not only sexual abuse, and, if a psychologist, will utilize appropriate psychometric instruments as another source of data. The expert will carefully read all of the documents in the case; medical and mental health records, depositions and interrogatories, witness statements, school, military, and work records will all be scrutinized for evidence of convergent validity or meaningful discrepancies. The expert may interview collateral contacts. She or he should possess a depth and breadth of knowledge about the topics at hand, including trauma and traumatic stress responses, childhood sexual abuse and its sequelae, memory, and standard of care in therapy. Additionally, the expert will be knowledgeable about and attentive for signs of malingering or deception in the plaintiff. The expert witness must approach the plaintiff with a skeptical eye and ear, even (or perhaps especially) when retained by the plaintiff's attorney (Brown 1992, 1994). There will be no ongoing relationship between evaluator and plaintiff, other than for the former to appear at deposition and in court at the appointed times. Finally, the expert witness is familiar with and comfortable in the legal system, and knows the norms and expectations for his or her work, a level of specialized knowledge that most treating therapists neither need nor want.

The matter of skepticism and the reduced personal bias toward or against the plaintiff that reside with the expert witness both operate to give greater weight to that person's testimony than is given to the statements of the treating therapist. The expert witness is seen by the court as having less investment in the outcome of the case than does a treating therapist, who cares enough about the client to very much want her to win her lawsuit. From a legal standpoint, it is thus preferable that there be a plaintiff's expert witness who can serve in the role of fair and impartial observer. Attorneys who attempt to save money by using a therapist as the expert witness are more likely to be jeopardizing the strength of the plaintiff's case; the treating therapist should thus resist attempts by an attorney to be convinced into taking on the expert witness role based on appeals to the wish to save money for the client.

There are further reasons from a clinical standpoint for the therapist to forgo the expert witness role. Clinically, serving as both therapist and expert creates a dual and conflicted relationship, in which the therapist becomes enmeshed in the advocacy process to an undue degree, and identified with it either consciously or otherwise in the mind of the client. This can reduce the client's sense of safety in therapy to discuss ambivalence about the case, anger at the attorney, or improvement in symptoms, since all of these factors will enter into the formation of an expert opinion. Additionally, the closeness of the working relationship between attorney and expert witness can become a situation if the therapist tries to be an expert, in which intrafamilial dynamics can be played out in destructive ways among therapist, client, and attorney, and problematic triangulations are experienced among the three. Loyalties to the client versus to the lawsuit or the attorney can assert themselves in ways that disturb the psychotherapeutic frame (Brown 1991).

When the therapist is the only "expert," the negative effects of testifying in court about the client and breaking the containment and privacy of treatment are exacerbated. Although it is very likely that the therapist will be called to testify in some manner, the presence and testimony of an expert witness often, although not always, deflects attention away from the treating therapist, and allows the expert with whom the client has had minimal contact and relationship to be the one to disclose painful and difficult material about the client and address questions of credibility. Clients whose therapists have offered the primary professional testimony in their cases often describe feeling less safe in therapy, and at times have difficulty returning for treatment after a case has taken place.

Treating therapists can be of help to the legal process without being the expert witness, however. They can, first and foremost, take good notes, meaning notes that are concise, behaviorally descriptive, note symptoms, document techniques and procedures used in the therapy session and refrain from speculations and documentation of a therapist's subjective musings and impressions about a client (Brown 1994, Pope 1994, Summers 1994, Walker 1994). While many therapists find it helpful to take extensive process notes, such materials can be extremely damaging to the client in the litigation process, as the opposing attorney can and usually will take materials out of context in an attempt to damage the plaintiff's credibility. Additionally, these notes should be ones that the therapist is comfortable having the client read, since it is very likely that they will become part of the materials attached to the therapist's deposition, or the lawyer's files.

Second, treating therapists can be knowledgeable about the realities of childhood sexual abuse sequelae. A familiarity with scholarly literature (see other chapters in this volume for resources and reviews of relevant materials), a working competence regarding innovations in treatment techniques, and a willingness to define the parameters of knowledge and say what is not known are invaluable assets for treating therapists to bring to the lawsuit. Humility is also a virtue; the burden on treating therapists to be extremely knowledgeable is much less than that placed on the expert witness. It is perfectly acceptable for treating therapists to define the limitations of their knowledge base, and assert that their role here is simply and only the treatment of the plaintiff. Finally, treating therapists can keep open the lines of communication with the attorney. It can be quite helpful to obtain a mutual release of information from the client early on so that the therapists can talk to the attorney, clarify their role from the start, and state whatever concerns they might have. This also allows them to ask the attorney to take treatment needs into account; for example, to request that a deposition not be scheduled just before their vacation, or to suggest that certain activities in the case be postponed if possible in deference to a difficult passage during therapy. Most attorneys will be glad to have this cooperative working relationship with the treating therapist.

CONCLUSION

It is possible and probably desirable that a therapist whose client becomes a plaintiff in a survivor lawsuit develops an attitude of positive expectancy and openness toward the legal process. While it is true that the legal realm is an adversarial one in which truth is often sacrificed to procedure, and while the justice that one can obtain through winning a lawsuit against a sexual abuse perpetrator falls far from genuine and emotionally satisfying amends, my experience has been that my encounters with the legal system have made me a better, more careful, and more empowering therapist when I am serving in that role. By becoming familiar with the norms and customs of the legal world, and by clarifying the role of therapist and protecting the frame of psychotherapy, the therapist whose client is a plaintiff benefits from this collision of worldviews.

ACKNOWLEDGMENTS

I would like to thank the attorneys whose work with me has given me a vision of how survivor-supportive law can be practiced. In particular, Seattle-area attorneys JoHanna Read, David A. Summers, and Mark Leemon deserve particular acknowledgement. I also want to thank my colleague in feminist forensic psychology, Shirley Feldman-Summers, who has been such a vital source of consultation and comradeship in working as an expert witness with adult survivors. Ken Pope has been an extraordinary resource on the ethical challenges arising from forensic practice.

REFERENCES

Brown, L. S. (1991). *Impact of the reporting process on psychotherapy with survivors of abusive therapists.* Paper presented at the 99th Annual Convention of the American Psychological Association, San Francisco, August.

_____ (1992). Psychological evaluations of victims of sexual harassment. In *Sex and Power Issues in the Workplace: Proceedings,* pp. 75–80. Seattle: Northwest Women's Law Center.

_____ (1994). When your patient is a plaintiff: staying sane as the psychotherapist. Paper presented at "When your Patient is a Plaintiff: A New Look," symposium at the 102nd Annual Convention of the American Psychological Association, Los Angeles, August.

Golding, S. (1994). Expert opinion. *American Psychology-Law Society Newsletter* 14:5.

Poole, D. A., Lindsay, D. S., Memon, A., and Bull, R. (1995). Psychotherapy and the recovery of memories of childhood sexual abuse: U.S. and British practitioners' opinions, practices, and experiences. *Journal of Consulting and Clinical Psychology* 63:426–437.

Pope, K. S. (1994). *Sexual Involvement with Therapists: Patient Assessment, Subsequent Therapy, Forensics.* Washington, DC: American Psychological Association.

Sonne, J. L., and Pope, K. S. (1991). Treating victims of therapist-patient sexual involvement. *Psychotherapy: Theory, Research, Practice, Training* 28:174–187.

Summers, D. A. (1994). *When your patient is a plaintiff: What the attorney wants from the treating therapist.* Paper presented at "When Your Patient is a Plaintiff: A New Look," symposium at the 102nd Annual Convention of the American Psychological Association, Los Angeles, August.

Walker, L. E. A. (1994). *The Abused Woman and Survivor Therapy.* Washington, DC: American Psychological Association.

PART V

Conclusions

14

Criteria: Signposts toward the Sexual Abuse Hypothesis[1]

JUDITH L. ALPERT

It is denial to say that incest is rare. Incest is not rare. Patients, in general, do not make up abuse stories. In fact, they do the opposite. They try to hide them. Sometimes people enter treatment without any memories of abuse but, nevertheless, know that they have been abused. They may hear footsteps coming into their room at night, which terrifies them. While in the bathroom, their own size five pink bedslippers may suddenly change form and look like size eleven, black, men's tie shoes. Flashbacks emerge and reemerge. In some cases the abuse memories explicitly return.

Often analysts and patients wonder whether there has been abuse. At such times they must work slowly, scrupulously, and methodically. They must continue to enlarge, expand, and deepen the work. Over a long period of time, the truth may be known. More likely, it may never be known. Regardless, there can be working through of deep pain and true feelings. The "talking cure" is not the

---

[1]Case material is presented throughout this chapter. In order to protect the identity of my patients and the patients of my supervisees, names and some facts have been changed and some parallel phenomena have been created. In some places, material from several cases has been combined. These alterations should not diminish the understanding that should result.

"labeling cure." Over time a patient may be able to let go and progress even when uncertainty remains regarding abuse status.

Sometimes the hypothesis may be seized and accepted as valid before the work so justifies. Indeed, the working truth may be obscured if grabbed prematurely. With the present long-overdue and substantial focus on sexual abuse, the abuse hypothesis may come to mind too quickly. I have had several patients who were not victims of sexual abuse but who have wondered whether they were. Some were mental health professionals who had treated survivors of molestation and had first-hand knowledge of the power of forgetting. They remained in doubt as they did not have the symptomatology, body sensations, intrusive images, dreams, transferences, or rudimentary memories that are consistent with an abuse picture. In treatment, nevertheless, we took their suspicion of violation very seriously. We explored why they thought they had been exploited and what meaning this held for them. There was considerable examination. The abuse hypothesis did not explain more phenomena than other hypotheses and did not allow us to predict. We mutually agreed that they were not victims of sexual abuse. They were able to renounce the sexual abuse hypothesis.

One could make a case for their being survivors. One could say that they relearned to "forget," based on my skepticism. This is possible, but unlikely. The exploration was deep. The decision (of no abuse) was mutual.

CASE EXAMPLE: ALL ABUSES ARE NOT THE SAME

A patient, who is himself a therapist, suspects he was sexually abused. His speculation is based on his professional interest in sexual abuse. I point out that frequent attendance at conferences on this topic and interest in working with sexually abused patients direct us to such exploration rather than a quick assumption of sexual abuse. Nevertheless, he attempts to convince me of his abuse. Additional "evidence" offered is that he *feels* abused and identifies with abuse victims.

Over time we come to understand his identification. He is the victim of maternal neglect and emotional abuse. Up to that point in the treatment, the focus had been on mourning the loss of father. Focus shifted to his emotionally disturbed mother: We considered the instances of his mother's verbal whipping and ruthless condemnation and his undeviating pain from both not being of account to her and not experiencing her empathy. The puzzle pieces fit together. Over time it became clear that the neglect and emotional misuse supposition was the better, more credible hypothesis.

CASE EXAMPLE: MORE NEEDS TO BE KNOWN

Early in her treatment, Pam announced that she or one of her sisters was sexually abused by her father. Her sister independently wondered the same. Pam hesitantly disclosed a number of reasons for this speculation while, at the same time, consoling herself that she had no abuse memory or documentation, that abuse knowledge would destroy the family, and that she would crumble if an abuse determination were made. Her grounds for suggesting sexual abuse: her father had extramarital relationships, remarried a much younger woman who is about Pam's age, secretly drank, and was impulsive and a risk taker. Also, she knew something had happened when she was 9 that resulted in her suicide attempts at that time as well as her sudden moving from sleeping in bed to sleeping on the floor between wall and bed. She immediately declared that the move afforded her protection.

She even had information that confirmed that her mother's response was to overlook. For instance, her mother disregarded her suicide attempts. After she swallowed a bottle of magnesium supplements, the only pills in the medicine cabinet, and vomiting profusely, her nonempathic mother did not ask questions or offer help. Rather, she told her daughter never to do that again. When Pam was a college student in a foreign country and requested money for an unidentified emergency, her mother ignored her request then as well. She did not even ask about the nature of the crisis.

The first reported dream in treatment was one she had many years earlier. The dream was of her mother and father sticking fingers inside her vagina. From this, Pam wondered if perhaps her mother had aided her father in the abuse. Was she sexually abused?

Much can be explained on the basis of fantasy. Pam grew up in a repressive, religious, Catholic home. Oedipal themes were swarming, with ten swooning daughters and a handsome, privileged, king-father. Children's fantasy lives can be thrilling and terrifying. They can be based on many factors, including wishes and aspects of actual observations. The dream can be understood as primal scene material: she may have walked in on mother and father. Her suddenly sleeping on the floor can be explained as well. While it does not rule out that father came to her at night, it can be explained by a little girl's need to hide from monsters and ghosts. Her suicide attempts and despair could be due to many different factors, only one of which is father–daughter incest.

A good deal more needs to be known: what took place in the family, the mores of her culture, her symptomatology, behavior, memories, defenses, and so on. At this point, we don't know if Pam was sexually abused as a child. We may never know for sure. Over time solid evidence for the abuse determination may emerge from such material as the criss-crossing of validation from numerous sources, the content and manner of her defenses, full memories and additional fragments of memory, transference, fantasies, and the rest. It is the strength and totality of the picture that leads to a conviction of childhood sexual abuse.

CAUTIONS AROUND CRITERIA

In this chapter I present some preliminary criteria that should assist in determining whether a patient has been sexually abused and in understanding the genuine experience of the patient and what aspects of the experience have been damaging. While the chapter does not focus on psychological science, it is informed by such understanding. The sexual abuse conviction is not made alone. The assurance must be shared by both analysand and analyst as they uncover the related material.

The criteria are developed from repeated themes by my patients. In addition, our existing literatures from traumatology, child sexual abuse, and psychoanalysis as well as informal dialogue among colleagues already point to consensus on many criteria. The criteria include (1) different types of validation; (2) establishment of the perpetrator's perverse character and opportunity; (3) recall of details of abuse; (4) initial sense of strong conviction; (5) different ways of shutting out, down, and off; (6) inappropriate behavior; (7) issues around reality testing, especially in regard to disturbed relationship to body; and (8) evidence of phobias, ceremony, and prohibitions. We obtain further validation from the good fit with respect to abuse stories being consistent with symptoms and analytic material.

While the criteria indicate the informed judgment, insight, and earnestness with which one approaches the input, they will not eliminate ambiguity in the clinical, theoretical, and professional issues of great consequence to us. They will not be effortlessly used in practice. No one standard will prove abuse. The weight of evidence, embedded in the character, personality, symptoms, and memory, will lead us to the sexual abuse hypothesis. Meeting the criteria prolongs the process of abuse determination but it leads us and the patient to greater confidence in our observation and a sense of secure purpose.

The conviction of the therapist should come slowly. On day one, the doctor suspects it's measles by the fever, red eyes, and dry cough. The doctor holds more conviction on day three, with the falling temperature and the appearance of tiny white spots on the lining of the mouth. On day five, when the spots raise, turn red, and spread, he is more assured. In a differential diagnosis of measles, the doctor looks for particular signs at distinct times and for the convergence of these signs toward one conclusion. It is the totality of the picture that convinces the doctor. If, on day three, something occurs that contradicts the measles hypothesis, that hypothesis is in question and competing hypotheses come to the fore. Similarly, confidence in the sexual abuse determination develops slowly and judiciously. On the way, other hypotheses are considered and ruled out. Finally the unfolding of observed material is given coherence by, is harmonious with, and converges in the sexual abuse determination.

This analogy has its limitations. While it is helpful in pointing to the cautious, extensive, and delicate process of determination, it obscures the role of the patient in that process. The sexual abuse determination is not made alone, by the analyst, and based on the patient simply showing her measles-like symptoms. The therapist does not assign a diagnosis. Rather, the sexual abuse determination results from mutual activity in which the therapist may silently consider possibilities while actively helping the patient to explore the full, deep terrain. This exploration may involve the patient's reenactment of abuse within the analytic dyad.

VALIDATION

One criterion is validation. Sometimes we luck out and secure external validation. While there are other ways of attaining the necessary validation of the patient's traumatic experience, this external substantiation can be cleansing for a patient. It can be confirming for the analyst as well. However, cautions are indicated in attempting to secure external validation. Confirming recollections can be overwhelming to patient and to family, and can have negative effects on treatment, as Sue Shapiro indicates in Chapter 12 of this volume. It can be upsetting to know that the abuse occurred and, further, that others knew and did little or nothing to stop it. Inability to secure validation can be upsetting as well, and obviously does not certify that abuse did not take place.

To begin with the most common: eyewitness validation is illustrated by another having observed the sexual abuse, as exemplified by one patient's case. Here we are talking about certifying that the abuse occurred. My patient told her sister when memories of childhood sexual abuse returned. Her sister confessed that she knew about it, had only pretended to be asleep when Grandpa came into their bedroom and molested my patient at night, and later, her as well.

Another type of validation, which rarely occurs, is when the molester admits the abuse. For example, after a patient remembered the sexual abuse that occurred 20 years earlier, she called her abuser and confronted him. He immediately acknowledged the abuse, apologized for it, swore she was his only victim, and offered to do anything he could to help her. He even agreed to meet her, with her therapist.

CASE EXAMPLE. SHE NEEDED HIS ACKNOWLEDGMENT

In many cases in which the victim finally confronts the abuser, the abuse is denied. Consider Molly, a psychiatrist. When her father asked about her patients, she mentioned that she treated a woman who was sexually abused in childhood. She reminded him that his friend said he had been "tantalized by my daughter" and that recently the adult daughter declared she was a victim of father–daughter incest. In this discussion with her father, Molly mentioned various sexual acts that constitute sexual abuse. Also, she told her father that *he* was a child sexual abuse victim and referred to his frequent exposure to parental lovemaking, nudity, and touching of his genitals throughout his childhood and early teen years. The exchange continued. He wondered if abused daughters hated their fathers. She said that often they did not and that frequently father-love was the only love incest victims received. He wanted to know if daughters could ever forgive their abusing fathers. She told him they could, that talking about it was cathartic to the victim and that validation was healing and could be good for the father-daughter relationship. She even told him what she thought she would never acknowledge out loud — that she was abused.

Despite her probing, her father offered no information about her abuse. Molly was stunned. She thought he knew what she had never forgotten, that she was fondled by her father throughout her preteen years. As Molly always remembered the abuse, she did not need his external validation in order to verify that the abuse occurred. Nor did she want his apology. She knew she could not forgive him. He had not spilled milk or broken a pot. His heinous act did not allow for the acceptance of an apology. Rather, she needed his acknowledgment and good parenting in the present. Why was the acknowledgment of abuse not forthcoming? It may be that he had disowned and was totally split from his abusing self. Or it may be that he did not want to let Molly be sure of what he knew so well due to fear of rejection. It was at this point that Molly entered treatment for sexual abuse.

CASE EXAMPLE: THE UNVEILING OF THE FAMILY MYTH

No doubt about it, Tina's sexual abuse was first-degree of external origin. Hers is a chilling and wrenching story in which there was raging violence, coercion, disorganization, ego deficit, and deadened state. Like Molly's, her case does not provide straightforward validation. In Tina's case, the disclosure of sexual abuse added important validation to other pieces of material and they, in turn, validated the disclosure.

As an adult Tina began to remember childhood sexual abuse by her brother who was ten years older and had a history of emotional disturbance and addiction. While Tina could not remember other molesters or their diabolical acts, she knew that there were additional molesters. Tina wanted to tell her mother about the remembered abuse and to have it validated. While she had substantiation in the form of strong body sensations, she wanted authentication of a different order. Her hope was that mother would understand her, parent her in the present, allow her to know what she knew, and offer comfort and accept responsibility for providing inadequate protection from her profoundly troubled brother. Tina knew that if she did not tell her mother, there would be an unbreachable distance between them. Our decision was to have this confrontation with me present during one of our sessions. We had done a considerable amount of work in preparation for the encounter. Prior to the meeting a major concern was that Tina would forgive her mother too quickly, before she let out her extensive fury. I was not prepared for what happened.

Her "validation session" was less and more than that. It was less in that mother did not acknowledge brother's diabolical activity and her own inadequate protection. It was more in that the conniving family myth was unveiled and the truth displayed. During the session, we heard mother's story. Mother seemingly couldn't wait for Tina and me to be the audience. We learned that the father was an exhibitionist and that both mother and father had been sexually abused as children. As mother saw it, although Tina was only an infant and her brother was ten years older, the sexual activity between them was Tina's fault. The reason for such blame: infant Tina was oversexed and had a large clitoris. She elaborated that even in the womb, Tina was a masturbator.

This reasoning made no sense. However, it was instructive. Up to this point, the story we had constructed was that Tina was a victim of inadequate parental protection and of incest by her older, troubled brother. The meeting served an important function. Tina's history clearly needed rewriting. How did we come to have such a distorted story prior to the meeting with mother?

This patient's ego deficit had affected the work of the analysis and the patient's adaptation and integration of the truth. The question had to be asked: What was the mother up to consciously or unconsciously? Tina's ego had been impaired. Her reality testing was damaged. She could not tell the story of how she was treated. The story that we slowly reconstructed was built around material that flowed from the session with Mother and Tina and from Tina's memories following the session. Her mother was intent on protecting the brother, blaming Tina, and exonerating herself. Mother said some curious things such as, "The only people who had access to Tina were her brother and daddy, unless you think I was involved." Other material from this meeting made it clear that Tina's parents were voyeuristic and projected exhibitionism onto her as a secondary gain. They could enjoy righteous wrath with poor little Tina.

After the meeting, Tina was flooded with fresh and vivid memories that involved her being observed and played with as a sexual object by her parents and being made to play with their genitals as well. She recalled many such instances of abuse. It did not take long for us to determine that Tina was fair game, the appointed victim, the burnt offering. She had been scapegoated by the family members for their own crimes and used in a pornographic film, as an object for exhibitionist sexual thrills. This is the narrative that emerged.

SUMMARY AND CONCLUSION

Analysis emphasizes psychic reality and interpretation and focuses on the conscious and unconscious personal meanings analysands assign to past and present events. Sometimes, however, in the course of reality testing we figuratively leave the office and work outside the boundaries of the patient's psychic reality. A patient's abuse disclosure to the abuser, to the eyewitness to abuse, or to additional significant others can assist greatly in finding and assigning truth-value to a narrative. There are many forms of validation. Eyewitness validation certifies that the abuse occurred. Another validating source is the molester himself. Although he seldom confesses, his rationalizations afford admissions. An example: "I have never done it since." Objective corroboration of abuse disclosures should be sought after and is helpful. However, it is difficult to obtain (Briere 1990, Briere and Zaidi 1989, Rich 1990) More frequently when there is a strong suspicion of abuse, analyst and analysand plod along in the work of recovering, reconstructing, and reintegrating any existing traumatic memories and their associated affects.

ESTABLISHMENT OF PERPETRATOR'S PERVERSE CHARACTER AND OPPORTUNITY

If we were to encounter an adolescent patient who has dreams of having intercourse with her father, we might think of her as epitomizing the workings of psychoses or of wishes turned into fantasies or dreams. Nevertheless, some dreams are unveilings of actual experiences. Establishing the perversity of character of the declared violator and that he had opportunity to violate her is an important contribution to acceptance of the molestation as real. When these exist, there is support for abuse. Confirmation of them alone is necessary but not sufficient to establish abuse. My intention here is to use vignettes to convey the utility of considering the establishment of perverse character and opportunity. While none of the vignettes used here lacks scandal or shock, I have avoided the outermost illustrations that sensationalize and require weighty detail to fit usefully into this discussion. The rather appalling, although relatively humdrum and commonplace examples used here, give clarity to the technical and conceptual issues.

CASE EXAMPLE: WORKING OUTSIDE PSYCHIC REALITY CAN BE USEFUL

Kim, a college student, entered treatment with no memories of abuse. Her mother and aunt had been abused by Kim's grandfather and had only recently, in their adulthood, remembered the brutal offenses. They were in treatment and encouraged her to enter therapy, too. Given her symptoms of lack of interest in sex, sleep difficulties, the nature of her nightmares, and her experience of not feeling, they believed she too was a victim of sexual abuse by her grandfather. Kim had spent a lot of time with her grandfather from the time she was born until his death, when she was 4. While she had an extraordinary memory, she did not remember the existence of the basement in her grandfather's house where her toys were lodged and where grandpa and she would play. Because she was unduly depressed over his death, she had therapy as a little girl. Back then her therapist informed her mother that Kim was probably sexually abused by someone close to her. The abuser was never identified and this child's treatment ended after a few months.

The vignette unquestionably establishes that Grandpa had the perverse character, time, place, and opportunity to abuse Kim. His confirmed perverse nature and the opportunity for debasement was consistent with the emerging coherent picture of abuse. Once her life history was edited to include the early trauma and its connection with later ones, the dramatic memory gaps, fragments of memory, nightmares, symptoms, and the catharsis of emotions burning underneath all made sense and facilitated our reconstructive work. Other early material emerged and gained cohesion and context as well. Further, over time, the symptoms disappeared. We could finally understand why, as a child, she overreacted with a guilty depression to her grandfather's death. Coercive sexual abuse had made her angry, and at the enemy's death she believed that her anger had killed him. Establishing the perversity of character of other family members and that they had opportunity to know about the abuse and did not assist can be elucidating as well.

CASE EXAMPLE: SHE DID NOT ASSIST

Polly would spend two weeks at her grandparent's house each year. Only granddaughters were allowed to visit, and only one could visit at a time. As grandpa refused to turn the heat on downstairs, there was no choice but to sleep upstairs, adjacent to the grandparents' room. Inconsistencies, denials, and special arrangements are an important part of the indictment. Without question, Grandpa had the time, opportunity, and place to abuse. However, Grandma and Grandpa slept in the same room. How could she allow the unbearable breach?

What is clear is that the drawing of the house floor-plan was useful in determining that Polly's grandmother had the place, time, and opportunity to know. When the grandmother was told that Polly was abused by grandfather during these childhood visits, she said that Polly would get over it. This made Polly wonder whether grandmother knew about the abuse while it was ongoing. Grandma would wake when little Polly went downstairs and opened the refrigerator in the middle of the night. If Grandma was such a delicate sleeper, why hadn't she awakened when Grandpa entered Polly's bedroom at night? Her grandmother had the motive to be oblivious to the abuse. She had a history of complex and deep-seated degenerate behavior, which is irrelevant to elaborate on here.

There are many such instances that don't make sense and that support abuse. Take the case of father and daughter sharing the same double bed while mother sleeps in the living room "because Mom is a finicky sleeper." Or the case of an 8-year-old girl being given a double bed. Or the case of a key to the bathroom kept above the door ledge on the outside of the bathroom door. Or the case in which only Grandpa was allowed to adjust the shower. Or the case in which all the internal doors within a house have been removed. Such inconsistencies from normal and expected behavior have distinct explanations.

RECALL OF DETAILS OF ABUSE

When one patient was a 7-year-old child, he witnessed the rape and murder of his mother. He related the details of his mother's decapitation. He later learned from his father and older sister that his mother did not bleed from the killing. Nor was there decapitation. It appears that the observed blood was his blood, which gushed from his head onto his eyes when the intruder threw him against the corner of a table. In this context, his inaccurate report is understandable. Research that focuses on the accuracy of memory and emotional arousal is considered in Chapters 1 (Alpert) and 3 (Brown). This research finds that emotions may promote memory. The point here is that we cannot assume that the description of abuse details indicates the event of abuse exactly as it is reported. A memory of a childhood experience will be told from a child's perspective and may contain confusions and contradictions. It is very complicated, as the above example indicates. However, remembering details of an abuse event may provide further substantiation for a strong case of abuse. Similarly an individual may have no memories and, still, may have been abused.

Nor can we assume that the reporting of abuse details indicates the creation of an abuse fantasy as a compromise between wish and defense. Similarly, it doesn't follow that not remembering abuse details means that there was no abuse. It is the totality of the picture that leads us to sexual abuse. Contributing to that totality is the content and magnitude of abuse detail.

CASE EXAMPLE: "MY HAIR WAS CAUGHT ON HIS SHIRT BUTTON"

For this patient, the content and magnitude of detail as well as the manner in which these memories returned and were reported, together with other genuinely sturdy material, led to the sexual abuse hypothesis. She remembered the event and related minutiae: the smells on the country walk, his words, the wetness, his heavy weight, the feeling that she would be crushed, the feel of the pulling of her long hair caught on his shirt button, the explicit sexual acts, the sick feeling, the shape of the cloud she attended to as a means of escaping the seedy moment, and the instant when she saw her mother after the abuse event. Sometimes her memories returned in a flash. It was as if she were watching a movie and was reporting what she saw. Sometimes the memories returned slowly, one particular at a time, much emotion, and then no memories for a long period. It would be too terrifying to remember any more. Sometimes when the details returned late at night, she would fear the dusk and would stuff her evenings with the clutter of clubs, people, and noise in order to attempt to escape her inner world. The content, the magnitude of detail, and the manner in which the memories returned and were reported, together with other material, were consistent with sexual abuse.

INITIAL SENSE OF STRONG CONVICTION

Often sexually abused victims have a strong *initial* conviction that they were abused. However, over time defenses may rise and the conviction is minimized or denied. There is some laboratory research support for this statement as well (Guenther and Frey 1990). Details such as what they were wearing or where they were may be remembered with equally strong initial conviction. One woman said that she was sexually abused as a child. She said this without emotion. She was sure she was not a victim of physical abuse. She mentioned a number of other heinous nonsexual acts that she was sure had not happened to her. She simply *knew* that she had been sexually abused as a child. This initial conviction existed without concrete sexual abuse memories. Here, too, while it does not follow that such initial conviction means there was sexual abuse, it is one of many signposts.

SHUTTING OUT, DOWN, AND OFF

Many abuse victims shut themselves out, shut themselves down, and shut themselves off. The shutting down is believed to be an attempt to compensate for chronic hyperarousal as van der Kolk indicates in Chapter 2 in this volume. They shut down on a behavioral level by avoiding stimuli suggesting the trauma, while they shut down on a psychobiological level by emotional numbing for everyday as well as trauma-related experience.

When they were overwhelmed as little children, parts of them stopped growing. Later, as adults, development continues to be slowed. They shut themselves out, shut themselves down, and shut themselves off. They shut themselves out by disregarding opportunity that they believe they are unworthy of and by isolating themselves from others whom they perceive as honorable, unlike them. They shut themselves down by not taking in. Learning is affected. They utilize energy keeping information out. They cannot know what they do indeed know. It is too heinous. Since it is difficult to select what comes in and what doesn't, they may reject everything rather than risk allowing in the abuse material. In this way schooling, careers, and life shoulder the consequence. There is a physiological explanation as well. It has been advanced that excessive stimulation of the central nervous system at the time of the trauma may result in permanent neuronal changes that have a negative effect on learning, habituation, and stimulus discrimination (Kolb 1987). Van der Kolk, in Chapter 2 has furthered this thinking.

Finally, many abuse victims have developed a defensive structure that keeps them shut off. Research indicates that many child incest victims have chronic problems with affect modulation ranging from extremes in hyperactivity to psychic numbing (Cicchetti 1985, Lewis 1992). Often, as adults, they do not know what they feel. Sometimes they do not feel. Sometimes abuse victims think they have multiple personalities. Sometimes they actually do. Abuse victims frequently separate themselves from the full impact of the trauma while it is occurring by means of dissociation. Dissociative defenses allow individuals to compartmentalize perceptions and memories. However, dissociation may also delay the necessary working through and putting into perspective of these traumatic experiences after they have occurred (Spiegel 1992).

One victim described how she would leave her body during the violation by "watching" munchkins spinning in the dryer. This calming fantasy enabled her to leave her body and offered an explanation for the spinning, confusing, disorienting world she experienced during the sexual acts. As a child, she saved herself by leaving her body. As an adult, dissociation had become a way of life. She continued to look at the world as if she were outside, a nonparticipant. Her experience is that of not being present. When engaging in sex, for example, she compiles a grocery list in her head. Her body participates in the sexual act while her mind is elsewhere. She wonders if everyone does the same. She described the two people she believed lived inside her: the one who knew she was abused and the one who said she was not abused. The knowing part had split off from the unknowing.

The experience of not being present is expressed in a number of ways. Another patient orders an omelette at a restaurant. It comes. She does not see it. She orders it again.

Some abuse victims attempt to make life more tolerable by not allowing themselves to feel. The anguish is too raw. The barrier that they created as a child, and that protected them at the time, hurts them as adults. This defensive style may result in the sensation that they feel nothing. A sense of depersonalization may be reported in which their personal history is recalled as if it happened to another. One sexual abuse survivor pronounced that she is not a real person with feelings. Having labored hard to turn off feelings, she no longer could feel the seething passions churning underneath. Desperately wanting to be a tender, compassionate, sympathetic person, she turned to literature and film in order to learn about the emotions associated with various situations. This disunity of consciousness found in the dissociative disorders is well documented in the literature (e.g., see Spiegel 1992).

INAPPROPRIATE BEHAVIOR

One way of shutting out, down, and off involves inappropriate behavior. At the end of the first session, a patient kissed me in appreciation as she was saying good-bye. Incest victims grow up in homes in which sex and sexuality may predominate, in which there may be a family bed, in which doors may be nonexistent, and in which children's bodies may be seen as the property of adults. They have grown up in homes in which boundaries have been broken and in which intrusion is the norm. Often, these children are not simply born into sexual insanity. Usually the unbalanced behavior is featured in other arenas also. Abusing parents or their partners may wake their victim-child in the middle of the night, for instance, to show gifts bought for family members. As a consequence of this unfitting parental behavior, these children, as adults, often do not know where to hew the line themselves. Further, they know that they do not know. This awareness of ignorance steers anxiety.

Parents of these patients are often inappropriate and intrusive and may attempt written, telephone, or face-to-face contact with their adult child's analyst. Abuse victims who are themselves parents raise many questions about sexuality and parenting such as: Is it appropriate for me to let my 3-year-old son touch my breast? Should I not undress when my 9-year-old son is in the room? Is it okay to let this little girl sleep in the same room as my 5-year-old son? While other parents have questions about sexuality and parenting, they take on new meaning with a parent who was abused as a child. Abuse victims also puzzle about affairs that are not sexual. They do not want to do what was done to them and they often do not trust their own judgment. They wonder, for example, if it is inappropriate to borrow items from friends without permission or to replace such items if they break them. They wonder whether they have made something out of nothing. If, for example, the patient is very sick, she may wonder if she is making it up as she similarly wonders if she is concocting the abuse story. Often they do not trust their feelings and wonder if they have a right to feel as they feel. This doubting makes sense within the context of their defenses. For a very long time, sexual abuse victims have been telling themselves that they do not know what they do indeed know and that they do not feel what they do indeed feel. Significant others may have been giving them the same message.

With many abused patients, the issue of limits is often brought into the analytic session. Some want a clear statement of limits in the analytic room, while others seem to break boundaries regularly, moving into spaces that are not part of the office, for instance, or opening doors in the office that other patients know not to open.

By means of their behavior or questions, they bring the issues of rules, procedures, customs, and conventions into the analytic room. They are asking: What are the limits? What is yours? What is mine? Can I take what is yours? Can you provide a context of safety? They are showing that the abuse really happened by making it happen again and again within the analytic hour, as they identify with the passive victim or the bold aggressor role. They want limits in order to protect themselves. They want clarity, rules, and order. One woman, for example, was terrified that she would marry an abuser. She wanted to know the characteristics of abusers in order to avoid marrying one.

ISSUES AROUND REALITY TESTING ESPECIALLY IN CONNECTION WITH THEIR BODIES

Abuse victims often hate their bodies, believing that their bodies betrayed them and got them into terrible trouble. They are filled with self-hate. Suicide and other attempts to hurt self and body are related to this hatred. While nonabused patients may have a disturbed relationship to their bodies, the intensity of this self hatred is notable. The body ego has holes in it like Swiss cheese. It leaves holes in their vision of their body. The parts of the body that are involved in the abuse become split off, damaged, hated, and ejected from their self-image. The ultimate rejection of the body is suicide, and suicide is not infrequent in sexual abuse victims.

Victims work harshly to be rid of the damaged parts. They find novel ways to attack themselves for having participated in the abuse. They pluck pubic hair, yank out semen, extract blood from their stomachs using knife points, and attack their arms and faces with fingernails. They may vigorously assail facial blemishes, viewing these irregularities as badness coming out.

EVIDENCE OF PHOBIAS, CEREMONIES, AND PROHIBITIONS

Victims of sexual abuse suffer from inexplicable phobias, ceremony, and prohibitions that suddenly make sense and disappear when the sexual abuse determination is made. It is believed that the inability of victims to integrate these traumatic experiences and, instead, to ceaselessly relive the past is mirrored physiologically and hormonally in the misinterpretation of harmless stimuli as likely hazards, as van der Kolk indicates in Chapter 2.

We have referred to a number of these phobias, ceremonies, and prohibitions throughout this book. There is the woman who was afraid to fly in airplanes. She had no memories of sexual abuse when she entered treatment. What we learned in our work was that, as a little girl, she had stared at the model airplanes on the abuser's bookshelf during acts of sexual abuse. She dissociated from the abuse during the events and, over time, repressed them. The associated horror and dread of the abuse became attached to the airplanes. While there may be several reasons why her phobia disappeared, one highly likely possibility is that it disappeared as a result of recovery, reconstruction, and reintegration of the traumatic sexual abuse memories with their associated affects.

One patient's life was filled with ceremony. She felt compelled to spend six or eight hours within any day acting out fantasies that re-created the past. In between the helpless re-creations of her past, she would pace, sit, or lie on her couch in the position in which she used to sleep as a child. There were several major fantasies, each having multiple versions. For instance, the fantasy we named "safe on stage" involved her talking to another person (performance), while an older person with whom she was infatuated observed and admired her. The various versions of this fantasy differed with respect to the individuals involved and the content of the conversation. What was constant was her performing and her being observed and admired by an older, valued person. This ritual mirrored the paternal watch from her childhood. She was attempting to repeat the watch and to take out the sexual aspects that were part of and that followed the watch. Ritual constituted a major part of her life. Then there are the prohibitions. Some of the most common involve sexual acts or positions within the sex act. Sometimes it is sex itself that is prohibited. While ritual and prohibitions do not preoccupy all victims of sexual abuse, when they do, we find that they usually dissipate or vanish when the abuse story applies and is finally told.

GOOD FIT: ABUSE STORY CONSISTENT WITH SYMPTOMS AND ANALYTIC MATERIAL

We obtain further validation from the good fit with respect to abuse stories being consistent with symptoms and analytic material. When it comes to symptoms, we are not starting from scratch. Rather we can stand on the shoulders of colleagues with whom we consult and who have written about sexual abuse. In this way we know a great deal about the current symptoms, complex feelings, defenses, behavior, fantasies, dreams, modes of responding, repetition in life of incest-related patterns, transferences, countertransferences, and family dynamics associated with child sexual abuse. Dissociative symptoms and those symptoms associated with posttraumatic stress disorder have received much attention in the literature. While many of the chapters in this book consider such symptoms, Hegeman and Reis (Chapters 7 and 8) give significant consideration to dissocation. We can determine whether the abuse hypothesis is consistent with what we know about a patient, her family dynamics, childhood, and current symptoms, and with the analytic material that emerges.

Diagnosis, however, is complicated. Childhood sexual abuse can manifest itself in many different ways, and the nature of symptoms or syndromes varies widely, as do the factors surrounding the abuse. There is no primary characteristic pattern associated with child sexual abuse, and other coexisting risk factors may contribute. The range of symptoms is extensive and abuse determination must be multifaceted. In addition to considering initial and long-term symptoms, other evidence is needed to confirm sexual abuse. Another note of consequence: As some victims appear asymptomatic, the absence of hysterical, initial, or long-term symptoms cannot be used to eliminate the abuse hypothesis. More is needed to support or eliminate this conclusion. Phobic fear, for instance, is not "proven" by observation of behavioral avoidance of marriage or work, but when repression of assertion or erotic behavior appears as a characterological symptom, consideration of traumatic origin is much in order. Further, as I indicate in Chapter 1, most people who were sexually abused as children remember all or part of what happened to them. However, in those cases where there is no memory of sexual abuse, we never really know if there was sexual abuse. We cannot say incest occurred. At the most, we can only say that, based on what we have heard, it is likely.

Sexual abuse has impact on the sense of self, character structure, and interpersonal relationships. Some of the long-term effects of abuse are depression, self-destructive behavior including self-mutilation and suicide attempts, disturbances of self, cognitive and developmental sequelae, interpersonal isolation, relational problems, sleep disturbances, recurrent nightmares and daydreams of intrusive images, insomnia, eating disorders, somatic disturbances such as anxiety attacks, and such problems around sexuality as inability to relax and to enjoy sexual activity, avoidance or abstinence from sex, sexual guilt, and sexual promiscuity (Briere 1988, Browne and Finkelhor 1986, Kluft 1990, Kendall-Tackett et al. 1993, Price 1992). These have been referred to throughout this book. For a review of this literature see Alpert (1991), Finkelhor (1990), Herman and colleagues (1986), Kendall-Tackett and colleagues (1993), Ulman and Brothers (1988), van der Kolk (1987), and Wolf and Alpert (1991). Sexual abuse survivors are diagnosed as multiple personality disorder (Putnam et al. 1986) and as borderline personality disorder (Herman et al. 1989). Often evident are symptoms of posttraumatic stress such as hyperarousal, sleep distrubance, startle response, and numbing and detachment symptoms (Kluft 1990, Putnam et al. 1986, Shengold 1989, Spiegel 1992, 1994). Clients may present with life situations that parallel and/or reenact early abusive experiences.

As patients recount their childhoods, it is beneficial to have knowledge of the frequent behaviors and initial effects of sexual abuse. The play of sexual abuse victims is believed to be telling. Some characteristics of their play include intense sexualized play with an emphasis on castration anxiety and fear of loss of object, stereotyping of symbolic play, especially phallic and thrusting play, exaggeration of normal curiosity about sexual issues and the genital difference, confessions and retractions, and a preoccupation with fantasy and reality (Sherkow 1990). There is literature that suggests that sexual abuse in preadolescent girls is associated with cross-gender behavior and gender conflict (Cosentino et al. 1993, 1995). In an extensive review of the initial and long-term outcomes on male children and adolescents, Watkins and Bentovim (1992) indicate that sexual abuse in male children is more common than previously believed and that consequences can be exceedingly injurious.

A comprehensive recent review and synthesis of the impact of sexual abuse on children identifies such frequently noted symptoms as fears, posttraumatic stress disorder, behavior problems, sexualized behaviors, and poor self-esteem. Studies, in general, report that about one-third of abused children are asymptomatic. There are several possible explanations for this: inadequacy of current measurement techniques, the denial state of the asymptomatic children at the time of evaluation, and the relatively less-damaging type of abuse afflicted on these children (later abuse, abuse over a shorter time period, less violent abuse, abuse by a more distant relative) coupled with their greater psychological and social resources for coping (Finkelhor 1990, Herman and Schatzow 1987). Expressed in another manner, we might say that the victim conceals her true, archaic, conflictual, and anguished self so utterly beneath a compliant false self that she appears to have sustained no damage from the abuse (Grand and Alpert 1993). This compliance allows her to continue in her collusion with and attachment to her abusers. Accordingly, the therapist must raise questions when a patient who was symptom-free in later childhood shows many signs of sexual abuse as a young adult. The therapist entertains doubt of the reliability and validity of the symptom-free appearance. If, for instance, the abuse occurred in early childhood and repression and reaction formation occurred in middle childhood, a failure of an unstable defense system occurs in adolescence and early adulthood, which brings back the evidence, a "return of the repressed." We must keep in mind this communiqué of consequence: in attempting to maintain a relationship with the abusing parent while, at the same time, processing and suffering relentless trauma, the child relies on such defenses as dissociation, repression, splitting, denial, and idealization. For a discussion of how these defenses may become intertwined into one's developing character structure, see Price (1993a, b).

There is a literature as well on family dynamics in incestuous families. This literature, too, should be studied as a background for understanding patient's stories. Typical incest family systems include a rigidly patriarchal family structure, a distant and strained marital relationship between parents, and a socially isolated family (Cohler 1987, Hulsey et al. 1992, Swanson and Biaggio 1985). In the parents' background we often find abuse histories, misuse of alcohol, and disturbed parent–child relations. Also not unusual is the finding that the abuser misuses alcohol and, in the case of father–daughter incest, the mother is depressed, passive, withdrawn, and extremely dependent. When all these puzzle pieces fit together, it makes a strong case. For instance, the abuse hypothesis may explain more phenomena than other hypotheses in a patient who is having flashbacks of her father inserting his finger in her vagina and who has many of the long-term symptoms and family dynamics consistent with sexual abuse. There was a time when the patient sometimes had difficulty swallowing. The reflex fully returned when it was associated with ingesting sperm and considered within the abuse context. Suddenly, too, her desire for sex in public bathrooms such as in hospitals and elementary schools took on new meaning. It recalled the excitement of the little girl having sex with her father while listening for mother's approach. While we do not know whether she was abused, the evidence was growing.

The abuse hypothesis becomes even more plausible when we see repetition of the incest-related phenomena in life and in the analytic hour. A triangle, for instance, was created when I sent a heterosexual female patient to a male psychopharmacologist. This triangle provided the occasion for reliving aspects of the earlier secrecy and the feelings of exhilaration, confusion, agitation, and corruption involving the sexually abused girl, her mother, and her father. The transference is telling. Her feelings from the early abuse were reflected in the initial distrust and perception of me as abusive. And the evidence was augmented again.

There is a risk in presenting a laundry list of effects. Obviously not all patients who have been abused present all the effects. Some may present only a few. Furthermore, these effect-lists cannot manifest the victim's ungraspable experience. We do not have a vocabulary to apprehend every aspect of the experience. We can only be witness through the imagination. Abuse gives new meaning to the word *destructive*. If *destructive* is meant to connote the devastating effects of sexual abuse on the developing ego, then the word as it is commonly used conceals rather than expresses the extent of the damage. The word does not take into account the storm of confusion and aloneness of the person trying to sort it out. It does not take into account the helplessness of the abandoned child who does not have a court of appeal. Her state can be likened to Klein's depressive position. While the child has known since infancy that her mother is the source of both good and bad, now she may learn that her abusing kin is the source of good and *exceedingly wicked*. This recognition has vast implications. She rediscovers her helplessness and total dependence. She may love and hate the same abusive family member and this loving and hating leads to conflict. She may hate herself for loving. She may hate herself for hating. She will see herself as vile.

There is ambivalence and there is anxiety that her own destructive impulses will destroy this object that she ambivalently loves and hates and is dependent on. There may be mourning and pining for the good object felt as lost through her own badness. An example is Kim, described earlier, who blamed herself for her grandfather's abusive behavior and who overreacted with a guilty depression to his death when she was 4 years old. The coercive sexual abuse had made her angry, and at his death she believed that her anger had killed him.

Also, the word *destructive* does not take into account the alienation that comes from not being able to identify with the family group anymore. Nor can the victim identify with society. She feels shame. After abuse, she feels different. She has a feeling of not being a part of the human race. One of many reasons why the therapist is so important is that the therapist become a delegate of society. When the victim feels important enough to be listened to and accepted by this delegate, she can begin to feel akin once again with society. Then there is the defensive system. The word *destructive* does not take into account the separation anxiety, the compulsive need for retribution, the smashing to the ego's growth, and the question of withholding of love. She needs to have restitution. She has an overcompulsive need for love and a fear of love. This is what the monster does to the ego development.

There is also a risk in presenting vignettes in order to exemplify how the abuse hypothesis lends coherence to symptoms. Writing about something gives that something configuration. However, each case is obviously different and no one case can serve as an archetype or can lead to mastery in identification of all other cases. We have no choice but to concede to the paradox that we need illustrations and that they will be inadequate. Stated simply, they won't fully do it for us.

We learn about the unknown by referring it back to what we know. These brief examples as well as those throughout the book collectively provide a range of the abuse picture that will raise the consciousness of the analyst and serve as signposts toward the sexual abuse hypothesis. They also serve as signposts for caution. The analyst was not there when the abuse took place. The analyst may never know for sure if there was abuse. The analyst does not make the sexual abuse determination. Rather, the analyst silently considers possibilities while actively helping the patient to explore. While the following case depicts a damaged survivor, which resulted in limited treatment goals, it also portrays an abuse story that is consistent with the symptom picture that has emerged in the trauma and analytic literature cited above.

CASE EXAMPLE: TATTERED CONSCIOUSNESS

Almost every session that first summer Sheila wore the same outfit: cut-off and very short, tight blue jean shorts, big black leather war-boots, and skimpy, snug tank tops. Her hair was extremely short and her lipstick was extraordinarily red. She looked tough and heavy metal. She seemed much older than her 23 years.

It was stimulus-response: the stimulus was therapy and the response was the restoration of abuse memories. She wanted to know and had finally found a safe place to allow herself to know and to eventually tell. While the memories returned immediately, her telling was not forthcoming. Her lack of ability early on to communicate her suffering reflected an earlier time when there was no one to hear or to listen. The missing of sessions early on could also be tied to the many times when there was no one available to hear. Initially her feelings from the early abuse were reflected in the distrust and terror she showed me in many different ways. Belligerence, for instance, was quite apparent in the office and was expressed in myriad ways such as her not talking loudly enough to be heard. This belligerence, which early on served the purpose of warding off attack and denying the inner suffering, was the central mode of relating to me in the beginning of the treatment. The emerging transference fit in with the abuse hypothesis. (For a consideration of some transference and countertransference themes inherent in analytic work with adult survivors and consistent with what is noted here, see Davies and Frawley 1994, and Price 1994.)

Three months into treatment, she told me her abuse recollections. One memory was that her brother molested her.

At first she discounted this knowledge and rationalized that the genital touching and his positioning his penis in her vagina was "normal kid's play." At the time of the first sexual violation, she was 3 and he was 12. There were numerous other sexual abuse events that she subsequently remembered involving her with her father as well as with other relatives.

There were abundant bits that together bolstered the judgment that she was a survivor of child sexual abuse. One example: While rummaging through her attic she found a drawing she did at age 6 which showed genitalia outside clothes, her brother touching her in private parts, lips looking like a penis, passive girl victim without arms, and a big and powerful molester. In immature, undeveloped writing the heading on the drawing was "Dear Mom." Sheila had a story to tell. The drawing was a cry for maternal protection. Obviously this drawing is not verification that she was abused. It is possible, for example, that this drawing resulted from abuse in a different way, by Sheila having been a captive witness to the primal scene between others. Another chip which adds to a good fit with an abuse story: Mother descriptively reported the way Sheila played with Barbie and Ken dolls, which was a simulation of the sex act.

Sheila had many of the symptoms of a sexual abuse survivor. At age 15, when the sexual abuse stopped, her body began to scream relentless illness and divulged the physical manifestations of sexual abuse. As an adult, her body continued to scream illness as well as other cataclysmic weaknesses. Canes, medications, and medical leaves of absence are part of her life. She suffers from insomnia, depression, dissociation, self-destructive behavior, relational problems, and problems around sex. Psychosomatic reactions are indicated in the literature when there is inhibition of expression of trauma. Specifically, research indicates a causal link between the inhibition of expression of traumatic experience and an increase in symptoms of the respiratory, digestive, cardiovascular, and endocrine systems in people with posttraumatic stress disorder (Krystal et al. 1989, van der Kolk and Saporta 1991). Further, recent research supports that learning to express the memories and feelings associated with the traumatic event results in a rejuvenation of some of the psychophysiological and immunological capabilities in people with traumatic histories (Pennebaker and Susman 1988).

Her family structure is typical of incestuous families. Her mother was sexually abused as a child by an older brother as well as by other family members. Clearly her mother was not protected as a child and did not know how to protect. Sheila was the second oldest and the only girl of ten children. In this elite powerful brother group, she held second-class citizenship. Abuse sometimes begets abuse: Her brother, who was her abuser, had been abused himself. Misuse of alcohol is common in incestuous families. Her father was an alcoholic who sexually, physically, and emotionally abused her. Even in the present he still acts entitled to a free use and abuse of that which is hers. She had stored her cherished childhood table in a neighbor's dry basement. Despite her protestations, her father sold it. She continued to feel unheard from and powerless about her wishes for him not to take.

In addition to the sexual abuse, she was abused in other ways. As a child she was given too much responsibility. She was a little teenage-camel carrying unwieldy burdens. She had to care for her maternal aunt who slipped in and out of comas, as well as several younger brothers. She desperately wanted her aunt to die. While the weight of this responsibility would have been heavy for most mature people, for an 11-year-old girl it was virtual bondage.

As an adult, Sheila continued to feel tortured as she had as a youngster. As a child she had learned that she must not care for or protect herself. In her late teens and early adult years she was involved with heavy drugs. Her most dangerous exploit involved sadomasochistic bondage in which an unknown master whipped her. This event was arranged by a third party and involved payment. In Sheila's case, sexual excitement was not activated by the rotation of childhood trauma into victory (Stoller 1975). Her motivation was money and not the fire of excitement. She did not experience orgasm even when beaten. She repeated this perilous encounter a few months later. This time she was one of two women who was hit on her face with wood. She was rescued by her friend when whipping with metal studs was introduced.

Early on I placed limits on the sadomasochistic activity. I said that we could not work together unless she gave it up. I protected her. Immediately she was grateful. She felt safe.

She had used herself as if she were worthless. She did it because she didn't feel and she wanted to. She did it because, by doing so, she felt in control. She could turn this deranged master on and be awarded money. He depended on her to compensate for his impotence and she despised him for depending on her. In this bondage game, her way of winning was by losing.

She had incorporated her mother's inability to protect her. There were many instances of her not knowing how to protect herself. She had a history of behavior involving display, tempt, tantalize, allure, and entice which was followed by anger at men who pushed themselves sexually on her. Sex, when it is unwanted, is never her fault. However, Sheila seemed to be continually placing herself in situations in which she was not protected; men would pounce, and she would scream rape. As an example: She said she was raped. Without question, she had the feeling of being raped. What had happened was she met a man. He made sexual comments. She said that she was not interested but that he could be her friend. They were at a party. It was late. They both drank a lot. She said that he could stay over at her place but that there would be no sex. They slept together in her bed without clothes on, which is the way she always sleeps. She woke up and found him on top of and inside her. She did not want this, she had told him, and she knew this was rape.

Some part of her wanted to trust the daddy and to give him another chance. She had to give up the omnipotent fantasy that she was safe. His action took away the illusion of a safe princess. We talked about how this was similar to putting money on the street and trusting people not to pick it up. She had thrown away her body and someone picked it up. This is not just an example of repetition compulsion. It represents a hope that things would be different and the ending signifies an ache that the solution does not work.

Suicidal talk was a constant. Her plan was to jump out of a bathroom window at work. While she was afraid of hitting ground, she was enticed by the fall. The surrendering, the letting go and looking for the fastest solution, was similar to the losing of self in drugs and sex. Incest victims are unable to regulate emotions or to communicate their inner experience. For this reason, self-destructive behavior becomes a means of expression (Shapiro 1992).

The work was time-limited and content-focused. The name of the game with Sheila was lack of protection. She had not been protected as a child and was not protective of herself as an adult. Mother's lack of protection was evidenced in not protecting her from the numerous family sexual molesters. Mother did not adequately parent or protect in the present either. When Sheila told her mother about the brother abuse, her mother put forward the philosophy: "To know all is to forgive all." We talked about how one could say "poor hungry tiger" if one saw a tiger eat a baby lamb on the television screen. However, if the lamb were to say that, it would be psychotic. From the lamb's perspective, the tiger is bad. The mother seems to act as if the tiger is a television tiger and is not recognizing that it is her baby lamb who is before her, all hurt and bloody and chewed. In turn, Sheila gave the same privilege to her friends that her mother gave her brother. She gave herself.

This is loathsome material. Her family had many problems. They did not know how to parent. Sheila had some serious physical problems. She suffered from the shame, frustration, deprivation, and fear that go along with an unprotective, distant, preoccupied, in-and-out mother who sent her to father and other abuse. We considered her wish for a mother who was present, available, and accessible. We focused on how to meet the dangers of the world. We considered her defensive solutions and her hitting back at the universe. We did not work in the classic analytic frame. We worked practically and pragmatically to plan her future. We focused on her overwhelming body pain and, for the first time, she shared her incapacity, felt accompanied in her pain, and felt cared for. She was able to look at the role she played in feeling lonely. We focused on self-management, and on how she needed to care for herself. Although she was very clever, she had limited skills and education. We worked to plan her future. We worked in a holding, related emotional frame that would bolster both her confidence and attempts to go forward.

While I have presented only selected aspects of this case, it nevertheless illustrates some of the family dynamics and devastating effects of sexual abuse. Moreover, it offers an instructive narrative about intervention in an ongoing crisis. With acting out and repetition of learned victimization, the crisis intervention of choice is the analyst's participation and enactment in that internalized scene. Joining the patient, acknowledging its horror, and, most important, giving full empathic support moves the patient toward an integration of a reality.

CONCLUSION

It is very clear that when psychoanalysts deal with sexual abuse, we do not assume that the patient's internal struggle is primarily generated by conflict within the patient, as might be the case with other encounters between the ego and impulse. Over and over again we find the conflict is generated between the patient and the environment and it is this environmental trauma that leads the patient to defend and, in turn, sets off the inner conflict.

Traumatic neurosis can only be understood in the context of the personal history of the victim. The availability of understanding, encouragement, and integration of catharsis and reality testing of personal past and present is critical and crucial. It is important that the victim is released and can let herself know what she does indeed know and have that knowledge validated by another. The aim for inner and outer life is to be coherent to the self. She must know that there is evil, greed, and self-indulgence in the world or else she will take it on herself. Applicable externalization of cause is important in healing. If she can know herself and the inner and outer reality, she can integrate herself. The world and herself must become coherent to her. The criteria delineated here should assist the analyst and analysand in moving toward a coherent self and world.

The criteria could be conceptualized differently. Some of them are irrelevant to some sexually abused victims. Some have yet to be delineated. These are not the only criteria; however, they should assist in determining whether a patient has been sexually abused and in understanding the genuine experience of the patient and what aspects of the experience have been damaging.

One theme in this book is that, in some situations in which there are no abuse memories and no external validation, we may never know whether there was sexual abuse. Another theme is that the sexual abuse determination is not made alone by the analyst. The woman who has many of the symptoms of incest victims, who as a child slept in the master bedroom in a double bed, and who is from an abusive, primitive family filled with Peeping Toms and alcoholic adults, might be a sexual abuse victim. Over time she remembers fragments: hands and worms in her childhood bed, hands putting vaseline in her anus "because you have diarrhea" ("But I didn't have diarrhea"), and so forth. Her sister provides external validation. Over time even more is remembered. All the pieces fit together and support the abuse determination in a powerful way. The comprehensive picture is convincing. It is this extensive, thorough, incest-laden rendering that needs to emerge.

ACKNOWLEDGMENTS

The author gratefully acknowledges Drs. Ruth-Jean Eisenbud, Sue Grand, Bruce Reis, and students in her 1995 course in the New York University Postdoctoral Program in Psychotherapy and Psychoanalysis for their comments.

REFERENCES

Alpert, J. L. (1991). Retrospective treatment of incest victims: suggested analytic attitudes. *Psychoanalytic Review* 78(3):425–435.

Briere, J. (1988). The long-term clinical correlates of childhood sexual victimization. *Annals of the New York Academy of Sciences* 528:327–334.

―――― (1990). Accuracy of adults' reports of abuse in childhood: Dr. Briere replies (invited letter). *American Journal of Psychiatry* 147:1389–1390.

Briere, J., and Zaidi, L. Y. (1989). Sexual abuse histories and sequelae in female psychiatric emergency room patients. *American Journal of Psychiatry* 146:1602–1606.

Browne, A., and Finkelhor, D. (1986). Impact of child sexual abuse: a review of the research. *Psychological Bulletin* 99:66–77.

Cicchetti, D. (1985). The emergence of developmental psychopathology. *Child Development* 55:1–7.

Cohler, J. (1987). Sex, love and incest. *Contemporary Psychoanalysis* 23(4):604–620.

Cosentino, C., Meyer-Bahlburg, H. F. L., Alpert, J. L., and Gaines R. (1993). Cross-gender behavior and gender conflict in sexually abused girls. *Journal of the American Academy of Child and Adolescent Psychiatry* 32(5)940–947.

―――― (1995). Sexual behavior problems and psychopathology symptoms in sexually abused girls. *Journal of the American Academy of Child and Adolescent Psychiatry* 34(8)1033–1042.

Davies, J. M., and Frawley, M. G. (1994). *Treating the Adult Survivor of Childhood Sexual Abuse: A Psychoanalytic Perspective*. New York: Basic Books.

Finkelhor, D. (1990). Early and long-term effects of child sexual abuse: an update. *Professional Psychology: Research and Practice* 21(5):325–330.

Grand S., and Alpert, J. L. (1993). The core trauma of incest: an object relations view. *Professional Psychology: Research and Practice* 24(3):330–334.

Guenther, R. K., and Frey, C. (1990). Recollecting events associated with victimization. *Psychological Reports* 67:207–217.

Herman, J. L., Perry, J. C., and van Der Kolk, B. (1989). Childhood trauma in borderline personality disorder. *American Journal of Psychiatry* 146:490–495.

Herman, J. L., Russell, D., and Trocki, K. (1986) Long-term effects of incestuous abuse in childhood. *American Journal of Psychiatry* 143:1293–1296.

Herman, J. L., and Schatzow, E. (1987). Recovery and verification of memories of childhood sexual trauma. *Psychoanalytic Psychology* 4:1–14.

Hulsey, T., Sexton, M. C., and Nash, R. (1992). Perceptions of family functioning and the occurrence of childhood sexual abuse. *Bulletin of* the Menninger Clinic 56(4):438-450.

Kendall-Tickett, K. A., Williams, L. M., and Finkelhor, D. (1993). Impact of sexual abuse on children: a review and synthesis of recent empirical studies. Psychological Bulletin 113(1):164-180.

Kluft, R. P., ed. (1990). Incest Related Syndromes of Adult Psychopathology. Washington, DC: American Psychiatric Press.

Kolb, L. C. (1987). Neurophysiological hypothesis explaining posttraumatic stress disorder. American Journal of Psychiatry 144:989-995.

Krystal, J. H., Kosten, T. R., Southwick, S., et al. (1989). Neurobiological aspects of PTSD: review of clinical and preclinical studies. Behavior Therapy 20:177-198.

Lewis, D. O. (1992). From abuse to violence: psychophysiological consequences of maltreatment. Journal of the American Academy of Adolescent Psychiatry 31:383-391.

Pennebaker, J. W., and Susman, J. R. (1988). Disclosure of traumas and psychosomatic processes. Social Science Medicine 26:327-332.

Price, M. (1992). The psychoanalysis of an incest survivor: a case study. American Journal of Psychoanalysis 52(2):119-136.

_____ (1993a). The impact of incest on identity formation in women. Journal of the American Academy of Psychoanalysis 21(2):213-228.

_____ (1993b). Incest and the idealized self: adaptations to childhood sexual abuse. The American Journal of Psychoanalysis 21(2):213-228.

_____ (1994). Incest: transference and countertransference implications. Journal of the American Academy of Psychoanalysis 22(2):211-229.

Putnam, F. W., Guroff, J. J., Silberman, E. K., et al. (1986). The clinical phenomenology of multiple personality disorder: review of 100 recent cases. Journal of Clinical Psychiatry 47:285-293.

Rich, C. L. (1990). Accuracy of adults' reports of abuse in childhood (letter). American Journal of Psychiatry 147:1389.

Shapiro, S. (1992). Suicidality and the sequelae of childhood victimization. In Sexual Trauma and Psychopathology, ed. S. Shapiro, and G. M. Dominiak. New York: Lexington.

Shengold, L. (1989). Soul Murder: The Effects of Childhood Abuse and Deprivation. New Haven, CT: Yale University Press.

Sherkow, S. P. (1990). Consequences of childhood sexual abuse on the development of ego structure: a comparison of child and adult cases. In Adult Analysis and Child Sexual Abuse, ed. H. B. Levine. Hillsdale, NJ: Analytic Press.

Spiegel, D., ed. (1992). Dissociative Disorders: A Clinical Review. Lutherville, MD: Sidran.

_____ (1994). Dissociation: Culture, Mind, and Body. Washington, DC: American Psychiatric Press.

Stoller, R. J. (1975). Perversion. New York: Pantheon.

Swanson, L., and Biaggio, M. K. (1985). Therapeutic perspectives on father–daughter incest. *American Journal of Psychiatry* 142(6):667–674.

Ulman, R., and Brothers, D. (1988). *The Shattered Self: A Psychoanalytic Study of Trauma*. Hillsdale, NJ: Analytic Press.

van der Kolk, B. (1987). *Psychological Trauma*. Washington, DC: American Psychiatric Press.

_____ (In press). The body keeps the score: the evolving psychobiology of post traumatic stress. *Harvard Review of Psychiatry*.

van der Kolk, B. A., and Saporta, J. (1991). The biological response to psychic trauma: mechanisms and treatment of intrusion and numbing. *Anxiety Research* 4:199–212.

Watkins, B., and Bentovim, A. (1992). The sexual abuse of male children and adolescents: a review of current research. *Journal of Child Psychology and Psychiatry and Allied Disciplines* 33:197–248.

Wolf, E., and Alpert, J. L. (1991). Psychoanalysis and child sexual abuse: a review of the post-Freudian literature. *Psychoanalytic Psychology* 8(3):305–327.

Index

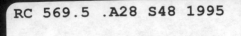